Being an Actor

Also by Simon Callow

Dickens' Christmas
Henry IV Part Two
Henry IV Part One
The Night of the Hunter
Oscar Wilde and His Circle
Love Is Where It Falls
The National
The Road to Xanadu
Acting in Restoration Comedy
Shooting the Actor
A Difficult Actor: Charles Laughton
Jacques and His Masters, translator

Simon Callow

Being an Actor

Picador
New York

For Peggy,
without whom this book would never have been written,
and my grandmother, Vera Guise, without whom there would
have been nothing to write about.

www.picadorusa.com

Picador® is a U.S. registered trademark and is used by St. Martin's Press under license from Pan Books Limited.

For information on Picador Reading Group Guides, as well as ordering, please contact the Trade Marketing department at St. Martin's Press.
Phone: 1-800-221-7945 extension 763
Fax: 212-677-7456
E-mail: trademarketing@stmartins.com

Library of Congress Cataloging-in-Publication Data

Callow, Simon, 1949–
    Being an actor / Simon Callow.—1st Picador ed.
        p.   cm.
    Includes index
    ISBN 0-312-42243-1
        1. Callow, Simon, 1949–   2. Actors—Great Britian—Biography.
I. Title.

PN2598.C17A3 2003
792'.028'092—dc21
[B]
                                                                    2003048283

First published in Great Britain by Methuen London

First Picador Edition: August 2003

10 9 8 7 6 5 4 3 2 1

Contents

List of Illustrations

Queen's University, Belfast: *Fin de Siècle*, devised and presented by the tubby aesthete on the right – me, aged eighteen

Drama Centre, London, 1973: as Kite in *The Recruiting Officer* with Allan Hendrick and Wayne Brown (Photo: Richard Addison)

Lincoln, 1973: as Peter in *A Taste of Honey*, my first named part (Photo: Gerald Murray)

Gay Sweatshop: with Michael Dickinson in *Passing By* (Photo: Barbara Birks)

Joint Stock: with Paul Kember and Bill Gaskill reviving *The Speakers* (Photo: John Haynes)

Becoming Joe Berke: me, the man himself and an aerial view of Ann Mitchell – first day of *Mary Barnes*

Devil's Island: as Krichevski with Jane Wood, Gillian Barge and Suzanne Bertish (photograph amended by David Hare to commemorate an incident on the first night)

As Verlaine in *Total Eclipse* (Photo: Donald Cooper)

Dexter spellbinding Kestelman, Callow and Marjorie Yates: *As You Like It* (Photo: Zoe Dominic)

Dressing Rooms. Mozart. Stafford T. Wilkins. Making up for Lord Foppington, Lyric Hammersmith, 1983 (Photo: Simon Annand)

National Theatre: with Scofield – the first runthrough of *Amadeus* (Photo: Nobby Clark)

Micheál MacLiammóir as Oscar Wilde. Simon Callow as Orlando (Photo: Nobby Clark)

Foreword, 2003

Not so long ago, I was having my passport checked by immigration at JFK Airport. Examining the document, the officer, an attractive young black woman, said: 'You're an actor?' 'Yes,' I replied. 'Still?' she asked, without looking up.

It's been a long time: thirty years.

Over the twenty years since it was written, through various reprintings and one new edition, this little book has been amended with the addition of previously unprinted material (too late for the first edition), a new foreword and a coda. The main text has never been rewritten. I have resisted that because my entire point in venturing on such a precocious theatrical autobiography in the first place was to express the experience of acting as I was discovering it. Hindsight has no place in such a testament: bliss was it, in that dawn, to be alive, and to be a young actor was very heaven. *Being an Actor* came into existence to express the carnal delight of a young thespian setting out on what seemed to be the boundless ocean of a life in the theatre (while noting a few inconveniences of that life along the way), and though the theatre has changed enormously in the last twenty years, the essential challenges remain the same: coming to terms with oneself and with one's craft. Whatever current theories may prevail, acting is always essentially the depiction of characters in situations, although the depiction can of course take many and various forms. The primary impulse of the actor—to stand up and say 'Look at me! Listen to this!'—is a constant, the *sine qua non* of the whole enterprise, and I see no diminution of that impulse. More people than ever are drawn to acting.

I suppose the crucial thing that has changed is the sense of what it is all for: why people become actors, and why other people want to watch them. At the end of the book I have added, in the spirit of *What Katy Did Next*, an account of my own subsequent career in the theatre since writing the book to show how that change has manifested itself in the life of one actor. If the original book set out to show what it's like to be an actor, this supplement shows what it's like to be a middle-aged actor, and aims to show a little more of the way the world works (or doesn't) for actors. But first, please read what the thirty-something Simon Callow had to say—eager, unformed, intoxicated by the possibilities.

Foreword, 1995

I wrote this book a little over ten years ago. It was my first book and I committed it to the page in a blaze of enthusiasm. It took three breathless weeks to write; the publisher set up each chapter as it arrived. The subject was one about which I had been thinking for ten years, and I felt urgently driven to deliver myself of my thoughts. The book was meant as a celebration – a love letter to my profession, in fact – but also as a warning. Something, it seemed to me, was amiss with the theatre in general and the art of acting in particular. I said what it was I thought was wrong in terms as vivid as I could muster.

Who was I, a relatively unknown thirty-year-old, to sound off so intemperately? Someone had to, I nobly felt, so it might as well be me. Just before publication, I was seized with sudden fear, convinced of two mutually contradictory things: first, that nobody would read the book, and second that it would bring my career as an actor to an end. I had said that I was gay (the only actor, as far as I was aware, to have freely done so in public), and I had attacked the people who handed out the work. The prospect of a life without acting – my oxygen, my food, my drink – was a terrifying one, so publishing *Being an Actor* was an act either of supreme courage, or foolhardiness, or suicide, depending on how you saw it. Hello writing, I thought, good-bye acting.

Reading the book today, I can scarcely remember the person who wrote it. It is his book, that crusader, that optimist, and I have changed not a word of what he wrote (apart from adding a few paragraphs that failed to make the printer's deadline the first time round). Much water has passed under the bridge, however, since it was published. At the end of the book I have brought the story up to date – not my story, but that of the British theatre.

Preface

Leonard Hill of Goldsmith's College asked me to give a talk about acting. Somewhat to my own surprise, I wrote ten thousand words with the title 'The Actor as a paradigm of the human condition'. The title was a joke, but I was nevertheless trying to give an account of the whole experience of an actor – not merely the career, but the psychological and emotional circumstances in which we find ourselves: what it's *like* to be an actor, externally and internally. When Nick Hern of Methuen asked me to expand it into a book, I was delighted at the opportunity to elaborate my subject. In the event, I have contracted it. The book, though longer, is much more modest in its scope than the talk. In the first section, I've described the career of one young actor of the seventies and eighties: me. I don't know of any other attempt by an actor of my generation to describe the theatre in which we work, so I hope it may at least have some documentary value. The second section grew out of a letter I wrote to Edward Bond in which I tried to explain to him what acting entails – what actors go through. Not much has been written on this subject, either. Finally, the last section nails my colours to the mast. It's a manifesto, in which, having criticized various aspects of the present theatre, I propose an alternative approach.

I should feel that the book had served a purpose if having read it, non-actors (I include people who work in other capacities in the theatre) were to say: 'Oh, *that's* what it's like' and actors were to say: 'Yes, that's what it's like.'

PART ONE

One

When I was eighteen, I wrote Laurence Olivier a letter. He replied, by return of post, inviting me to join the National Theatre company – in the box office. I accepted immediately, and as I crossed the foyer to be interviewed by the box office manager, I thought, crystal clear and without any sense of destiny about it: 'One day I shall run this place.'

Which was rather strange. I was a hopelessly lost adolescent working in a library wholesaler's, sending crateloads of Mills and Boon romances to the corners of the British Isles, sure of only one thing: that I didn't want to go to university. I'd had enough of education. I wanted to *live*, I said. The inadequacy of my grammar school had turned me into an auto-didact. There was nothing, I insisted, that an arts course, the only one for which I was at all eligible, could teach me that I couldn't find out for myself.

What to do instead, though?

Not many alternatives presented themselves to a mind stuffed with *fin de siècle* notions of burning always with a hard, gem-like flame. Most careers seemed either insufferably bourgeois or unattainably remote.

Into the second category came the theatre. There it was, vivid and real, but quite other. I loved going to the theatre, though there was no special family tradition of doing so. True, my grandmother had run away to go on stage before the First World War; my greatgrandfather had been a clown at the Tivoli in Copenhagen, then a ringmaster, then an impresario for Sir Oswald Stoll; another greatgrandfather had coached Sarah Bernhardt in the role of Hamlet. This was all legend to me. Like most people, I saw the acting profession as an exotic tribe with its own customs and rules, into which one was born. The idea of *becoming* an actor was as unlikely as becoming Prime Minister or Pope. Somebody had to; but how?

I had, it is true, been overwhelmed at an early age by two acting performances, both in films: Olivier's Richard and Laughton's Hunchback; and I was liable at any moment to become possessed by one or the other. I was a monstrous show-off and infant transvestite, mostly with and for my flamboyant grandmother; and for many years I topped the bill in the school playground, regaling astounded twelve-year-olds with my jelly dance and cod Shakespearian recitations. All this was in the past though (I had also won first prize in a fancy dress competition as a Can-Can dancer, but I kept fairly quiet about that). As the shutters of adolescence closed on these youthful excesses, there was no legitimate outlet for all the energy. At none of my schools was there drama of any kind. So when I thought of careers, it never occurred to me to go on the stage. Behind everything that I did think of, however, was the idea of acting. It was the *acting* in being a barrister that made me think of that; it was the *acting* in being an ambassador that appealed. I just didn't see it.

So I left school baffled and badly adrift. I started to visit the theatre more and more frequently, being almost morbidly drawn by the colour and intensity otherwise absent from my emotional and social life. Olivier's National Theatre, then at its zenith, was the great magnet. Six bob seats in the gallery to see *The Royal Hunt of the Sun*, *Much Ado About Nothing*, *Juno and the Paycock*. One day, at a performance of *The Three Sisters*, a thought crept into my brain: 'I would be part of this.' My heart beat wildly, I kept turning the thought over and over until I was almost too excited to move. It wasn't simply the performance, moving and remarkable though that was. It was the whole enterprise: the ushers, the atmosphere, the graphic layout of the programme: the result of a number of people drawn together, working at full stretch to produce a unique experience. *People* had done this. Perhaps I could be one of them. What had I to lose?

And so I wrote three foolscap pages to Laurence Olivier, telling him all this, adding at the last moment a PS in which I made it clear that I was willing to serve him and his theatre 'in however humble a capacity'. His reply was gracious and swift; and here I was, crossing the foyer, succumbing to mild megalomaniac delusions. I suppose I thought that if I'd come this far, anything was possible.

The interview with the box office manager quickly knocked such nonsense out of my head. A grim, lizard-like man, Pat Layton, who prided himself on never having seen a single show at the National (he once blushingly admitted he'd seen 'half' of Othello), indicated that my duties would be largely confined to the mailing room. With time, I might eventually be allowed to man 'the window' – the advance window, that is: the 'this evening's performance' window was his special preserve, and he used to sit at it like an iguana on a rock, eyes darting

4

to left and right, doing what he liked best: refusing people tickets. He was at that time one of the most courted men in London, and it cannot be said that he wore his power lightly. Occasionally, one of the recipients of his favour would appear at the window, and would receive his smile: a terrifying sight, the glint on the blade of the guillotine.

Pat ran a tight ship. He was the number one; there was a number two; and two number threes. Beneath them, us, the juniors, and a huge army of casual staff needed for the booking periods, during which the mail was delivered in fifteen or twenty sacks a day. The juniors sat and answered the telephones and dispatched tickets in a tiny office which had been Lilian Baylis's. That gave a frisson (the only frisson). Otherwise it was relentless slog in that tiny space. The work itself was like oakum-picking. To be sure, we laughed a lot: silly side-splitting jokes about people asking for two tickets for *Three Sisters* ('Won't it be a bit of a squeeze, madam?'), and the lady who couldn't get her tongue round the title, and who, after being helped by the box office assistant – '*Rosencrantz and Guildenstern are Dead*, madam' – replied: 'Oh dear, I shan't be able to come then, will I?', and the legendary woman who'd demanded tickets for Louis Armstrong's farewell concert, apparently misled by the title *Armstrong's Last Goodnight*. When Peter Brook's *Oedipus* created a scandal we thought of answering the phones: 'Dirty Old Vic'.

Best for me was the constant infusion of gossip from the theatre itself: rumours of scandals both personal and artistic. I learned to call all the actors by their first names, even though I'd hardly met one. Jeremy this, Charlie that, and I hear Frank's leaving after *Much Ado*. Sometimes one would find an excuse to take something down to the box office itself, and one of them would be there, bantering with Pat. His repartee was on a fairly unsophisticated level, being largely concerned with physical functions. I felt I'd made a major breakthrough the day he greeted me with 'What you want, cunt?' I was wrong. You never knew where you were from day to day with Pat. I felt certain that I was in favour the day he went to the safe, pulled out a battered old book and said 'Want to borrow this?' It was *Last Exit to Brooklyn*, then a banned book. 'Read the bit where the queers go round the park picking up the used Johnny bags and sucking them,' he said affectionately. 'That'll make you throw up.' Even this outburst of camaraderie proved delusory, however, and it was weeks before he spoke to me again.

No, the box office as such was not fun. But I was happy. It was exhilarating to be part of something which was at the front of the national consciousness. The theatre's affairs – I felt they were ours – were reported in the newspapers. There was an unbroken stream of extraordinary people crossing the foyer. We were definitely something big. Above all, it was wonderful to know that 'Sir', as Olivier was universally called, was on the premises every day, and often on the stage. I could sneak in and see him any time I wanted.

The canteen, too, was a great revelation. In those days there was a chef who in his tiny kitchen managed to make ravishing things at deliberately low prices; the combination of quality and cheapness persuaded most of the actors to eat there, which maintained the sense of company: everyone who worked in the building was deemed to be part of The Company. Sir always ate there, and generally chose to eat with the ushers or the box office staff. I can't say that I ever actually spoke to him; or indeed to any of the actors much, beyond a smile or business exchange – 'Tickets for tonight?' – and so on. But here they were, in quantity – the mysterious endangered species, rarely glimpsed, and never by the light of day – actors! I liked them; and what's more, they seemed, if not exactly ordinary, human. I saw what they did on stage, exotic peacocks, and I saw *them*; and I could see that the journey from the one to the other was possible.

The way to the canteen lay through the pass door in the auditorium. One would sneak through, trying to catch sight of John Gielgud or Maggie Smith, straining to hear what Peter Brook or Tyrone Guthrie were saying. So this was actors' work. In the canteen, one would hear bitter recriminations, or wild laughter over someone's retort, or again deep anxiety over this problem or that. It all seemed highly charged, but possible. The magic that had so dazzled me had been worked on. In other words it was, after all, a job, and not some divine succession. Actors were made, not born.

On Monday nights, the theatre was dark. The box office staff were the last to leave the theatre, through the stage door. On those nights, passing through the empty auditorium made my heart stop. It seemed to me a sacred space, Stonehenge. It was throbbing with energies and a curious power – an altar without a tabernacle. One night I lingered, and, certain that I was the last, instead of walking across the wings through to the stage door, I stepped on to the stage. Feeling that at any moment I might be struck dead by God or Laurence Olivier, I

6

said 'To be or not to be' – just those words – and bolted. It was a shock, hearing my own voice so loud and resonant; but just as shocking was the physical, or even the psychical, power momentarily released, a small earthquake. Had I found the famous Spot in the centre of the stage? Or was I just overwrought?

Whichever, there was now no longer any question of what I wanted to be. I was impatient to do something about it. Pat Layton's bleak regime was no longer to be endured; but I was in any case obliged to make a decision about my immediate future. Back in the almost unrememberable past before I'd joined 'The Theatre', I had in desperation applied to a university. I couldn't now see any future without a degree. I was sure that Oxford or Cambridge would be out of the question, so I inclined towards Trinity College, Dublin, not only for its romantic aura but for being *out of the country*. Then I discovered that the British government won't give you a grant to study there, so I decided, in my comic ignorance, to apply for the next best thing: Queen's University, Belfast. They accepted me.

The academic life was still anathema to me, but I saw that I could use it to further my violent ambition: to get on stage at all costs. The only alternatives, as I thought, were amateur dramatics or some kind of highly unlikely sideways leap from the box office. It's a measure of the lopsided view of theatrical realities gained from working at the Old Vic that I never thought of drama school at all. I could at least see that a university drama society was far more feasible than the other alternatives, so I set off for Belfast, cynically determined to act my little heart out.

On my first day, I made straight for the Dramsoc's little wooden hut, and was received with open arms, undoubtedly because of my glamorous connection with the Old Vic box office. For the first production, alas, I was *hors concours*, because the director had elected to set the seventeenth-century Norwegian comedy in Belfast, and my lips and tongue were not yet round that perverse patois. I was allowed to play the small part of an English-accented barrister: my first appearance on any stage. This I did with, if anything, rather too much feeling. Next term, however, glory. Or potential glory. I was cast as Trigorin in *The Seagull*. We were to tour the campuses of the North and be entered in the Irish University Drama Festival, which no less a legend than Micheál MacLiammóir was to adjudicate. It was a crucial experience. The production was monstrous. The director had made the discovery, as all directors do, that Chekhov describes three out of four of his great plays as 'comedies'. So, we would play it for laughs. This approach led the production to be known as *The Seagoon*. As for me, I was appalling. The earth opened up under my feet every time I stepped on stage. It was a shallow, nasty piece of work. I didn't know what I was doing, while at the same time knowing all too well. By now, I had become an avid theatregoer, and I knew what was good. This was not.

'My very dear friend Mr Simon Callow,' said MacLiammóir, adjudicating. 'Not, I fear, a born actor. A born writer, perhaps [this was on the strength of an article I'd written about him] but not a born actor.'

'Micheál,' I said to him afterwards, 'you said I was not a born actor.' 'Ah, but you could *become* one,' he replied.

I was 'his very dear friend' because, after the article for which I'd interviewed him at his home in Dublin some months before, I'd been seconded to him as his dresser and general factotum for the duration of the Festival. He gave two performances of *The Importance of Being Oscar* as part of his adjudicator's fee; during them, transcribing his notes, or accompanying him to lunch, or sitting over a bottle of Bushmills in the Grand Hotel in Belfast, him remembering Orson Welles or talking about the latest film he'd seen – from the front row because he was now so blind – we had become quite close. He was the first actor that I'd really known, spent any time with. Bedizened, berouged and blasphemous, he spoke of Yeats and Ireland and Beauty and Art and Illusion, all in capital letters. His incomparably rich and mellifluous voice was as capable of the most scandalous scurrility ('I feel fucked – but not in the way I like to be') as of haunting evocations of the great dead and ruminations of a philosophical character ('I've always felt that Beethoven, like the Christian view of heaven, was not for the likes of me'). At the interview he'd seemed to give his whole personality to this rather unprepossessing adolescent; when the tape-recorder was switched off, he proceeded to give the unofficial version, which was even more glorious, though certainly less printable.

He was a real Man of the Theatre: actor, designer, director, playwright. He'd given his life to it, and what's more *in Ireland*. When he might have made a mainland, or indeed an international, career, he had learnt Gaelic, returned to Dublin, and with Hilton Edwards created a glittering showcase of the most modern European plays (English language premières of Cocteau, Giraudoux, Anouilh), Eng-

8

lish classics and his own and others' Gaelic plays; what's more, in so doing, he never for a moment stopped being scandalous, provocative and downright naughty. I loved him and now I love his memory.

Simply being in Micheál's company was delightful in itself – having lunch with him, sitting next to him for the shows he was to adjudicate, writing down and then transcribing his comments, basking in the great warmth of his large self. Being his dresser, however, was quite something else, an experience compounded equally of pity and terror, and my first encounter with the reality of performance.

I would arrive at the theatre somewhat before he did, to iron and arrange his clothes. I was a stranger to these arts, and he showed them to me, as well as the arts of packing a suitcase and preparing his interval drink of gin-and-tea. He always arrived in the highest good humour, full of jest and profanity. He divested himself of his clothes to the accompaniment of a seamless patter of erotic speculation, literary quotation, character assassination ('of course when poor dear Cyril Cusack played Hamlet in a selection of costumes purloined from sundry shows of the previous season, he became the Prince of Great Denmark Street') and self-revelation. As he stood in his underpants he gazed in a melancholy manner at his groin. 'My testicles,' he said, moodily, 'have become *distended*' – the bulge did seem unusually substantial – 'as a result of a virus contracted, I fear, from a seaman. Are you a virgin?' The unexpectedness of the question made me blush. 'No,' I lied. 'Good, good. And to which are you more inclined, men or women?' 'Both,' I lied again. '*Very* good,' he said, 'although I must confess that the older I get, the less I am able to enjoy the company of women – except of course our own dear Enid who is so notorious a Sapphic as to be virtually *hors concours*. And now, my dear boy, the time of the performance must surely be approaching?' I was keeping a close watch on the clock. I had been firmly instructed that I was to announce when there was half an hour before the curtain rose, when there was a quarter of an hour, when five minutes, and finally, when it was time for us to go to the stage.

As the time approached, a change came over Micheál. The patter became a trickle and finally dried up. His make-up – which in fact only amounted to touching up his street make-up – was quickly effected; his costume consisted of nothing more than evening dress, and of course a green carnation. He sat in front of his mirror staring, haunted, at his face. He seemed barely to hear the calls. As the curtain got closer and closer, he started to tremble. Sweat trickled through his rouge. He grasped on to the table in front of him till his knuckles were white. The stage manager arrived to give him his call. He reached out for my hand. 'Lead me,' he said. 'I can't see, d'you see.' Down the pitch dark corridor we went, his fingernails digging ruts into my palms, while with his free hand he crossed himself again and again. 'Jesus Mary and Joseph. Jesus protect me. Jesus.' We reached the stage. I said: 'There are three stairs now.' 'Where? *Where?*' I helped him up, one, two, three. He fumbled with the black cotton drape, pushed it aside, and was on stage. In the pitch black, the light dazzled, but I heard big, solid, welcoming applause, and then Micheál's voice, rock-steady, as if he'd been on for hours: 'To drift with every passion till my soul . . .' I slipped round to the front and watched the ebullient unrecognizable figure juggle words and emotions, drawing his audience of largely middle-aged, middle-class Belfast burghers and their wives into his charmed circle, luring them into a world of sophistication and wit that they would under any other circumstances abhor, somehow making them feel that he and they shared a secret and a wisdom. He used to claim that he was really a *seánachai*, a storyteller, and here was the spell in action.

I fell under it so completely myself that I forgot that he was so nearly blind that, whenever he performed the show, he brought with him his own carpet with a bright bold pattern that he might follow, and so not fall off the edge of the stage. Such was his command and apparent inexhaustibility that I almost forgot the interval too. In the nick of time I flew to the dressing room, scooped up his gin-and-tea, and met him at the edge of the stage. He quaffed the proffered cup in a gulp, and faltered down the steps, drained, old, and silent. I bubbled about his performance, about the piece, about Wilde; he grunted almost inaudibly. In the dressing room, he found an armchair and slumped in it, loosening his tie and his cummerbund. Suddenly, for a minute, he slept, then woke and stared ahead of him. 'This is the last, the *very* last.' A bucolic figure appeared at the door. 'Mr Mac, I've come to pay my compliments.' 'Who is it? Who is it?' he said panickily. The man moved closer. I didn't know whether to stop him or not; didn't know the form. 'You stayed with me and the wife in what was it, '51 or '2, I should think, in Dundrum.' 'Of course, of course, my dear fellow, of course, how sweet of you to come to see me.' He grasped the man's hand: 'Wonderfully kind. Now you must excuse me, I have one or two small preparations to make. Please remember me to your dear wife.' The man left in a glow. Micheál groaned. 'Who on earth was that? Twenty years ago. I can barely remember my own name. A good man, though, kind of him to come.'

He turned to his mirror and reassembled the genial aesthete of the performance. A little make-up; a change of shirt; a sharp breath to allow the cummerbund to be re-fastened; and we made our now less nerve-racking journey down the black corridor. He ascended the steps almost jauntily, and stepped into the light twenty years younger, as before.

At the end of the show he was tired, but triumphantly so, like a boxer who's won. After a crumpled minute or two, the earlier Micheál, so different from either the urbane charmer of the stage or the desperate fearful man of the corridor, re-appeared – most welcome, he was, too, this larky, naughty boyish Micheál. 'We chorus girls,' he'd say, grinding his hips. Again he regarded his inflated groin, covered in red pants. 'Fish-net, they call them,' he said, his eyes wide with amazement. 'Some catch,' I ventured. He laughed generously, and then said: 'So you were in Morocco,' referring to something I'd mentioned in passing two months before when I interviewed him. 'My god, when Hilton and I were in Morocco, in the thirties, it was like the *Arabian Nights*. It was at a dinner party in Tangiers that I received one of those shafts of inspiration that come rarely, too rarely: an ineffably tedious woman approached me and said: "I've heard you prefer men to women. Is that true?" With barely a flicker I replied: "Of course. Don't you?" And it has been my singular fate to have heard my happiest inspiration attributed on innumerable occasions to Noël. Dear Noël – we were together as child actors, of course, and to this day, whenever we meet, all too rarely nowadays, he says: "I'm *still* one month younger than you."'

The one week that I spent at MacLiammóir's side had an over-whelming impact on me. It was a headlong plunge into a bubble-bath spiked with cinnamon: froth, gaiety, relish, discrimination all pouring out of a personality that I now knew to be human to his fingertips: vain, generous, frightened, brave. It seemed to me that he offered a vision not only of what the theatre and acting might be, but a vision of life's possibilities, too.

The only other actor I knew at all was Victor Henry. Between them, they covered a lot of ground. Victor was the caricature of the self-destructive, demon-driven artist. He chewed whisky glasses till the blood ran down his cheeks. He picked fights, five foot four and weedy, as he was, with truck drivers. ('D'yer want me to take me glasses off? Is that what's holding yer back? OK, they're off. Now whatcha gonna do?') He thrust his hand up waitresses' skirts. Filth poured in torrents from his mouth. He destroyed other actors' performances if he didn't think they were good enough. He himself would appear on stage smashed out of his skull, giggling and making other actors laugh – and then suddenly he'd do something so extraordinarily pure and intense that your heart would stop beating. He was the most absolute actor I've ever seen. He alarmed me to the point of terror, but when he spoke about acting and the theatre, raging against the pusillanimity (he was playing Jimmy Porter at the time) of the entire theatre, except for himself and some – *some* – people at the Royal Court, insisting that the theatre's only job was to wage war on bourgeois mediocrity, I agreed with him, and wanted to be up there with him: me, as I felt, the embodiment of bourgeois mediocrity.

Between them, these two impossibly different men fuelled my vision: the one celebrating in the most sophisticated and self-aware way civilized values, the other leading the attack on complacency, screaming 'Wake Up and Be Alive'; one seducing and alluring, the other exhorting and electrifying. To combine the challenge of the one with the invitation of the other!

I met them both while I was at Queen's, and they both gave an extra shove to my determination to leave the place. Within four months I had confirmed my dislike of the academic life ('You mean, Mr Callow,' said Dr Purcell, my brilliant English tutor, 'you want less analysis and more synthesis?' 'Yes, sir.') and discovered acting. Why wait around when I knew exactly what I wanted to do? 'Safety net! Safety net!' they all shrieked. 'No!' I cried back, 'I think I'm on to something. I must test it. Am I an actor, or am I not?' Through it all, I was sustained by an enormous strength: I knew how bad I was. Had I thought that I was any good, I would have been lost. 'If I have a safety net to fall back on,' I said, 'I'll never do anything. If I don't have a safety net, I'll have to make a go of it. There'll be nothing else.' There was an element of bravado in this, and also a deep resistance to continuing work on my paper on 'The Ulster Linen Industry in the Sixteenth Century' now I'd discovered something real: real work on something really useful to real people.

There were other reasons, though.

More tempting was the notion that I would stay and devote myself to the Dramsoc – not from the point of view of acting, because I knew that more experience would only teach me how to paper over the cracks in my performances more efficiently – but the managerial side. I had become intoxicated with the possibilities of theatre: had begun to discover the Aladdin's cave of dramatic literature, had started to read the theorists, Craig, Appia, Artaud, Stanislavsky and had become immersed in actors' biographies. I was terribly seduced by the idea of turning Belfast's Dramsoc into a campus version of Orson Welles's Mercury Theatre. The resources were there; financial resources, up to a point; physical resources, our own theatre and unlimited human resources. I'd already staged a slightly bizarre but effective 'entertainment' called *Fin de Siècle*, a celebration in verse, prose and epigram of the 1890s in English literature, and not actually been booed off the stage; I had vast plans for a trilogy based on Orestes (Euripides, Sartre and Eliot), each part of which would exemplify the dramatic theories of Craig, Stanislavsky or Artaud; and I had written to Peter Barnes for permission to stage *The Ruling Class*, which, though it was still running in London, he very kindly gave. I had a nuclear explosion of projects. But in sober moments, I knew they were doomed.

For one thing, the first ominous rumblings of the Ulster holocaust could be quite distinctly heard. I, like most students, was a member of the People's Democracy, pledged to exact equal rights for the Catholic population. We marched, we debated, we distributed leaflets, we sang *We Shall Overcome*. Paisley counter-marched. The B-Specials, sinister in long black raincoats, struck us with their batons, as we trudged through the rain, kicking the autumn leaves under our feet. At one heady moment, we almost brought the government down. We summoned the Minister of Education, Captain Long (everyone was a captain in those days), to give an account of himself. Into the crowded MacMordie Hall he came, surrounded by his henchmen, on to the platform, to cries from the mob of 'Sieg Heil! Sieg Heil!' He was about to speak when someone cried out, 'Would Captain Long, as a gesture of good faith, ask all the special branch men in the hall to withdraw?' The little man with his steel-rimmed spectacles and foxy little moustache looked frightened. He bent down to consult his gang. He straightened up, went to the microphone, cleared his throat and said, 'Gentlemen, if you wouldn't mind,' and a third of the hall emptied. We were as amazed as exhilarated. Nothing in the meeting seemed real after that. The extraction of promises, the passing of motions, the election of officers, everything seemed possible; somehow we all knew it was phoney. It was theatre. Our orators – Mike Farrell, six foot two, heroic, rhetorical; Cyril Toman, tiny, bearded, analytical (Tomanchu, to some of us) – were straw men, something out of a movie, or some dimly remembered tale of the Easter Rising, or the October Revolution, or even the Storming of the Bastille or the Peasants' Revolt.

All the while, in the wings of our little pageant, the real men were waiting to take over.

So I had to go. Not from fear of bombs or bullets – there were none, yet – but because as an Englishman, I had no place in this primitive blood-feud. I was told so, again and again. Standing on a street corner, mildly expounding the PD line, or handing out a leaflet, my accent would be detected and 'Go home. It's nothin' to do with you,' would come back from Protestant and Catholic lips alike.

And of course – I blush to admit it in face of the appalling gravity of what was growing daily before our eyes – it was not a place to make theatre. Suddenly, and rightly, any project had to be conceived in terms of 'the situation'. Why don't you do *Oedipus* with Paisley as Creon? Or Tiresias? He's a priest, isn't he? He's certainly blind.

And then – the final and perhaps most pressing reason for leaving – there was the problem of me. Who was I? It was a question I often asked myself. I had devised a quite new personality for Belfast. I'd grown a beard, my first, which in time became quite copious; I wore a brown suede coat with an astrakhan collar and a large brown fedora; I *always* wore a tie and a waistcoat. Small children, not surprisingly, used to throw things at me in the street, as I strode along grandly, imagining myself, I guess, a kind of cross between James Robertson Justice and Wyatt Earp. My social behaviour was of a piece with this bizarre appearance. I held court permanently. In the canteen, in tutorials, in my little flat at Magdala Street, I opined. Yes that's exactly what I did, *opined*, day in and day out, on every subject. It came as quite a surprise to me. Not that I'd been reticent up till now, but I suppose nobody had listened, particularly. My strangely commanding presence (where had *that* come from?), the Old Vic, the English accent, all compelled attention. I'm glad to say I was not taken in by it. This stranger called Simon Callow was getting daily more remote from what was going on inside. He had a career of his own. 'Blah blah blah,' he'd go, and people would laugh or agree or hate (quite a lot of that); but no one would ever have believed that behind all that was a cowering, desperate, sobbing creature, beating with tiny fists on the door of life and feeling doomed to perpetual exclusion from the human race.

I was, in fact, in a state of continuous torment. I hated myself for my cowardice, for not having lived. I was still a virgin, and couldn't see how one ever made contact with another human being in that way. I read steamy books about decadence, listened to tortured and transfigured music. I had long and terrifying periods of utter blankness, feeling nothing. I tried to write, to paint. No go. I couldn't find a crack in the wall of my personality through which to escape. I used to get drunk rather a lot, and conceived passionate devotions for deeply unsuitable people, all the while locked under the lid of 'Simon Callow', whose name, significantly, I found it so hard to say. I think if I hadn't found acting, I might have gone mad, or else died inside. The relationship between Inner Man and Outer Man was strained to breaking point. It was war, and one of them had to win.

So I determined to leave. That April I went into hospital with peritonitis; I came out with a clear plan of action. I'd read all the drama school prospectuses. RADA seemed to be a holiday camp; the Drama Centre a concentration camp. I knew which was the one for me; I knew how bad I was.

I returned jauntily to Queen's, took a most agreeable leave of my tutors, all of whom were deeply charming and sympathetic – in fact I thought that one of them was going to leave with me – sat my end-of-year exams in a very devil-may-care way, allowing myself the luxury of writing a searing polemic against the teaching of English literature instead of answering the questions, and popped down to the jolly old metrop to become an actor laddie.

Down I went, clutching my vision and my problem very tight to my chest, staking my all on the Drama Centre, believing that it would kill my two troublesome birds with one stone. In fact, I determined that if the Drama Centre didn't accept me, I was destined not to be an actor (they would know at a glance, I felt sure), and I would join the Merchant Navy. So much for safety nets.

My last gesture as a student of Queen's University was to purchase with the remaining pounds of my grant a one-way air ticket to

Amsterdam. This was, so to speak, Plan B. I had a friend there who worked for the International Courts. I would sleep on her floor for the first night, and then become a sort of strolling player, learning my craft on the road, at the same time plunging headlong into teeming humanity. I had already had one stab at this, after I left the Old Vic and just before Belfast, when with two schoolfriends I went to Morocco. The only result had been even deeper emotional confusion and a torrent of purple prose in my diary. So it proved with Holland. The only gain of what turned out to be a six-day sojourn (visiting the Maritshuis and reading *An Actor Prepares* from cover to cover) was an understanding that one doesn't find oneself by going away. There was no evading an eyeball-to-eyeball confrontation.

So I returned to London disappointed but wiser.

I had now to earn a living. I thought cleaning might be a good idea. This was something I was rather good at. I might get to meet 'real people' – the ignis fatuus of my late adolescence. Roger Lobb, how-ever, a chum from the Old Vic box office and now the National Theatre's box office manager, was appalled. He didn't approve of my leaving university in the first place, but becoming a cleaner seemed to him pure masochism, some curious *goût de la boue*. He took me along to the Mermaid box office, where the incomparable Joannie Robinson took me on without so much as a glimmer of a realization that I was about to make her life very burdensome for the next six months.

Joan was of an altogether different breed to Pat Layton. She *liked* the job, for a start. And the Mermaid was unimaginably different from the Vic. It, too, had its great man at the centre of things. Bernard Miles, however, was a satyr to Sir Laurence's Hyperion. At the Vic iron discipline and stern formality prevailed. There, Olivier had ensured that everything ran like clockwork; here the altogether more antic spirit of Bernard Miles, who had not only raised the money for the theatre, but personally laid a large number of its bricks, was in charge. The Mermaid was teeming with life from ten in the morning when its doors opened to closing time at midnight, as people popped in for morning coffee, lunch, tea, supper, or just to look at the exhibitions. Sometimes they even came to see a play. Genial chaos prevailed at Puddle Dock. The theatre's uncommonly spacious foyer, rigged like a ship, consisted of a series of booths providing various services. The atmosphere seemed to have more to do with a circus or a funfair than a theatre, the staff seemingly chosen as much for their eccentricity as for any special qualification for the job. The snack bar, for instance, was run by Jose and Caroline Moreno. He had been a brilliant high-wire novelty juggler, she his spangled assistant, triumphantly pointing as he performed his death-defying feats. They had in no way adapted their personalities to their new profession: Caroline maintained the superb flare of her nostrils and the commanding erectness of her spine as she made sandwiches and dispensed coffee; Jose, bringing over a pile of plates, found it impossible not to juggle with them. The customers took it all very calmly. Over at the Whitbread Bar, Connie, its bewigged mistress, trilled appoggiaturas of silvery laughter and gurgled wickedly as she presided over her regulars. These were mostly defectors from El Vino's, not one of whom would have been seen dead actually watching a play. As the evening wore on, her precariously poised wig would creep forward. She would yank it back. Again it would creep forward; again she yanked it back. By the end of the evening, unnoticed either by Connie or the clientele, it was often back to front. Next to the bar was the bookstall, presided over by Charlene Agnew, a stooped and scholarly American lady of uncertain age, who lamented the theatre's slide towards musical comedy.

When it was time for the show to start, the house manager, Sama Swaminathan, would emerge from his little cupboard under the stairs and weave his way through the throng to ring the ship's bell that hung prominently in the foyer, adding to the Mermaid's somehow nautical flavour. Sama had been the very first person to stand on the stage of the theatre on its opening night, as a tiny twelve-year-old clad in the turban and flowing silk garments of a maharajah. Now, ten years later, and not very much bigger, he passed smoothly through the crowds, impeccable in dinner-jacket, seeming a little incongruous in the medieval fair that swirled around him, though in any other theatre he would have been the only person correctly attired. The general manager, John Collins, was also in a dinner-jacket, but it cannot be said that he seemed entirely comfortable in it. One of Bernard's discoveries, he had started at the Mermaid as a carpenter, then within a couple of weeks become technical manager of the theatre only to be suddenly promoted a few brief months later to supreme command. His thin features and pencil moustache, added to his obvious sartorial discomfort, lent him a shifty air, as if he were expecting a raid from the police at any moment. And who knows . . . ? Round the back of the theatre was the restaurant, under whose windows the river still lapped, swans gliding by from time to time. Here the Countess Wanda Krasinska was in command, elegant, precise and exotic – when, that is, she was allowed to be by her immediate superior, Bernard's brother-in-law, a retired gentleman-farmer by the name of George Hinchcliffe. George, rubicund, bucolic and generally bellicose, seemed to have been installed simply to make a nuisance of himself, at which he succeeded triumphantly. Bernard set great store by the irritation factor, practising it himself with some skill.

In the box office, calm of a sort reigned. Joan Robinson, surely the most gracious box office manager who ever lived, instead of growling at her customers like most of her West End colleagues, would happily engage in conversation with them about the state of the roses in her Sanderstead garden or the merits of the present production. Her only vexation was the constant stream of innovations – special reductions, combined theatre-and-dinner tickets, three-seats-for-the-price-of-two, and so on – which would flow from Upstairs, an institution she heartily loathed and whose name she would pronounce with tight lips and a roll of the eyes heavenwards, in its general direction. Otherwise, the box office was beautifully if somewhat idiosyncratically organized around the making of tea, an art of which Joannie was mistress. The air was full of the aroma of her home-grown roses. Arfs and I, her trusty assistants, would converse in muffled shrieks at the back as we discussed his colourful love-life, struggling the while with the baffling arithmetic of ticket agents' percentages – $7\frac{3}{8}$ per cent of £97/13s/6d., that sort of thing.

The most dramatic event of the day was Bernard's visit. He'd just been knighted, but a memo had come from Upstairs indicating that anyone who addressed him by his title could expect instant dismissal, so Bernard it was. Fresh from a chat with his parrot and having perhaps just terrorized an innocent stockbroker in the restaurant ('Don't tell me,' he'd say, 'don't tell me – Ben Gunn in Crewe? No? Blind Pew, Cardiff? No, no, I've got it: Squire Trelawny at the Bristol Old Vic.'), he liked to pop in and check the till and the booking sheets. If business wasn't up to much, he'd immediately get the House Full signs and put them on the pavement, a surprisingly effective ploy. He also liked to answer the telephone. Members of the public innocently trying to get a couple of seats for Friday night would be treated to a lecture on Minor Elizabethan dramatists, invited to have a drink with him and persuaded to hold their office party in the restaurant. Tiring of this, he would launch into a substantial portion of his music-hall routine, the scholar of a few minutes earlier transforming – Before Our Very Eyes – into the Uncrowned King of the Cotswolds, a genuinely hilarious performance. The work would grind to a halt, until Joannie would tell him to stop it and get out. Laying a rather active hand on her bottom – 'Stop that, Bernard!' – he'd take his leave, to be followed by a distraught Josephine, Lady Miles. 'Have you seen Bernard? He's threatening to repaint the set. The designer'll walk out if he does.' And her sad, noble face would suddenly crack up in giggles as she set off to restrain him, a hopeless and never-ending task.

When we had a successful show, there would appear at the box office window a stream of Bernard's friends, an astonishing array of legendary personages – one night it would be Elisabeth Bergner, the next Eva Turner, all speaking most warmly of Bernard, another proof of the strange breadth of his charm. Arfs and I would peer round the ticket books to goggle at them. On other occasions, someone Bernard had met on the top of a bus would turn up and politely ask for the ten free tickets he'd been promised – this on a night when there was a forty-strong waiting list for returns. Joannie would sigh, and by some peculiar magic get everybody in. If – and this was very rare – she didn't manage to squeeze someone in, she'd as likely as not make them a cup of tea.

I'm not entirely sure that Bernard knew who I was. He invariably addressed me as Stephen. Eight years later, though, when I was back at the Mermaid, acting in *The Doctor's Dilemma*, he came up to me in the foyer as I was on my way to my dressing room, and asked me to show some people to the restaurant. I think he'd finally recognized me as a member of the box office staff. A couple of years later I went to see him and Josephine to talk to them about Charles Laughton, whom they had both known, and I realized that he knew perfectly well, and in some detail, who I was. He'd been teasing me all along, like those hapless stockbrokers.

I was a bit of a handful in the box office, trying to revise the system that Joannie had so ingeniously evolved. I kept on producing new forms which she couldn't make head or tail of. One day, she sent me to John Collins, suggesting that he might like to use me in some other department. I thought this might be a golden opportunity to segue onto the stage – Box Office Clerk Superstar – and more or less said

19

so. 'No, no,' said John, 'That's not what you want to do. Mark my words, in ten years' time the theatre will just be a branch of the catering industry. You should go and work in the restaurant. First, though, we'll put you in accounts to get the financial background.' So I started work for Shastri Alladi, the theatre's melancholy accountant. He had good reason to be melancholy, the Mermaid's income being what it was, but there was something quite independently depressed about him. When I would come across a set of figures that didn't seem to tally, he'd shuffle over in a snowstorm of dandruff and cigarette ash, produce an eraser and, with infinite sadness, make it right. 'You done a poop,' he would sigh, 'you done a poop.' After a couple of weeks, we parted company – too many poops, I suppose – and I returned to the roses and the tea.

During the long hot summer when I was at the Mermaid, I'd spend the slacker hours reading old programmes which Joannie, as a sort of unofficial archivist, had kept throughout the theatre's ten year history. It was a staggering record, a repertory of which a National Theatre would have been proud: Dekker, Marston, Ibsen, Shaw, Henry James, Henri Becque, Brecht, Hauptmann, Goncharov. And new writers, Bill Naughton, Fred Hoyle, Antrobus, Milligan. Radical productions, like *Henry V in Battledress*. And the Molecule Club, dramatizing science. I'd no idea whether the productions were any good. I was sure there was little or no money, and everything I knew about Bernard suggested that smooth surfaces would not be among his priorities. But the fact is that they were done, and done with spirit. As I read the programmes, the thud thud thud of the builders' pistons came relentlessly through the walls. This was the beginning of the reconstruction of Puddle Dock: the new embankment road was being laid, separating the theatre from the river. The streets beyond the foyer, too, were being remade. Bernard's theatre was lifted up above a motorway. Of course there were good productions after that – it was the same theatre, after all, and the same Bernard. But the world of theatre had changed. Rough Theatre was out. The Big Two started doing Bernard's repertory in big lavish productions and he found himself in vague competition with the West End. Well, ten years is a pretty good run of creativity and flair, and Bernard's theatre, like Bernard, was one of a kind: popular, personal, putting plays and actors before productions.

Joan, meanwhile, tiring of my revolutionary activities in the box office, decided it was time for me to move on, so she made a discreet call to John Ball, at the Aldwych Theatre, recommending 'this lively and intelligent young man'. So I became the RSC's box-office assistant, having at least learned some of the financial realities of the theatre (the box office is precisely at the interface between the product and the public) and gleaned something of Joan's great and important art of 'dressing the house' – disposing the available patrons around the auditorium in such a way as to make both actors and audience feel that they were part of a flourishing concern. Not that the RSC, during that glorious summer when they were offering *Twelfth Night* and *The Winter's Tale* with Judi Dench in Christopher Morley's miraculous designs had many empty spaces on the seating plans. The World Theatre Season, Peter Daubeny's gallant challenge to theatrical Little Englanders, was another matter: crammed for the French, the Russians and the Germans, when the Czechs and the Argentinians played, sales were so wretched that I was sent out with sacks of complimentary tickets to inflict on unsuspecting nurses, then as now reliable renta-audiences.

One of the most striking moments, however, of my time there was the day after the first night of Peter Brook's production of *A Midsummer Night's Dream*. The entire directorate of the RSC had gone to Stratford to see it; returning the following day for a meeting in London, they filed past the box office on their way upstairs, silent and ashen-faced, aware, perhaps that they had seen something so radical and yet so complete that they would have to reconsider everything in their approach to their own work. This world in which one's work could matter so much seemed more than ever one of which I must become a part.

Two

It was from the Aldwych that I sallied forth one afternoon, officially to a dental appointment, but in fact to meet my destiny. Down to Chalk Farm I went, through the Methodist portals of the Drama Centre, into the waiting room, where I was immediately mistaken, by two different people, for a teacher ('Boom-boom, blah-blah,' though I was shrieking inside). From the audition room came curious yowls, sobs and shouts. Fear really seized me then. 'I'll never be able to do *that*.' A door burst open. A short dark man with streaming hair, his eyes ablaze and wild, giggling the while, strode into the waiting room (he'd left the audition room by the wrong door) followed by a pre-Raphaelite girl, a student, who was sobbing and saying, 'He's *incredible*, he's *incredible*.' Then it was me.

I tottered into the room, to face the panel of four sombre judges sitting at a trestle table, looking towards the altar of the ex-church, which was, I supposed, the stage. The student on the panel (everyone had a student: did that make it worse or better? I couldn't make my mind up) beamed at me, encouragingly.

'I'm going to do Wendoll from *A Woman Killed With Kindness*,' I gasped. I had a very firm rein on myself. My bowels were pulled up to my thorax, my diaphragm was hugging my spine, and my finger nails drove deep gullets into my hands. I walked like the condemned man I surely was on to the stage, expecting at every moment to fall down. I made it to the middle, and started shouting the speech. After a line or two, I realized that my right leg was shaking uncontrollably. I suppose it wouldn't have mattered so much if I hadn't been wearing metal quarter heels, and if the altar hadn't been made of concrete. An insistent tattoo was threatening to drown the speech, so I summoned up every ounce of willpower, bound every muscle in my body, and finally got the leg to be still. This muscular tightening, though, had a rather bad effect on the rest of my body, in particular my jaw, through which I was now tersely spitting the speech. I knew that must be wrong, and a furious debate ensued, the result of which was that for the last four lines, I released all muscles, my voice was restored to full scream, my leg thumped away like a pneumatic drill, and a noise like the clacking of a thousand castanets echoed round the room. 'I need to sit down for the next speech,' I lied.

This was a scene from *The Government Inspector*, the drunk scene. Relieved of the burden of having to stand up, or rather not fall down, I laughed and burbled my way through the speech, and leaped out of the chair at the end of it down to the trestle table to hear the verdict: was I an actor or wasn't I?

They thanked me; then someone said 'A great deal of what you did was very interesting indeed. But do you think that a person of your age (I was twenty!) and experience (*The Seagoon?*) would feel at home with people much younger and much less mature than yourself?' Yes, I thought I could cope with that. 'What is it exactly that you want from a drama school?' 'Technique,' I said, without hesitation, like every drama student, past, present, and to come. 'TECHNIQUE?' he withered. 'What do you think you mean by TECHNIQUE?' It suddenly did seem an awfully stupid word. 'Well, um, I'm specially interested in comic acting, and –' 'COMIC ACTING?' 'I mean, I, um, admire Maggie Smith a lot.' 'I see.' I don't remember what I said after that, or anything much at all, till I was out in the corridor with my student. 'They liked you a lot,' he said. 'Thank you,' I said hollowly, knowing that a life on the ocean wave was more or less inevitable now. 'Yes,' he said, 'he only ever speaks to people like that when he really likes them.' Two days later, a letter arrived offering me a place.

The relief was enormous. So I *might* be an actor. The next test would come in three years' time, when I left drama school. Then we'd see whether I could make a living at it. If not, then – well, I supposed I'd be too old for the Merchant Navy by then, but I was determined that if I hadn't made it within a year, I'd clear out.

Meanwhile, I worked all the overtime I could to save money for being a student again. I'd been living quite comfortably on my Aldwych wages. Now I starved. Just as well, because my anti-safety-net stand now began to get me into trouble. I applied for a grant to go to Drama School and was turned down out of hand, because of course I'd not only had one grant, I'd left before the end of the course *and* I'd failed my last exams. There was no appeal. I determined to go it alone: that is, pay my fees, and my keep. I had the sum required for the fees already saved, which I duly delivered in pound notes to the Drama Centre. For the rest, I would work. I would do box office work at home at the weekend, and nights I could spend ushering at the Old Vic. I didn't care. This was to be the great life-changing experience, and I didn't mind what the cost was, financial, physical, mental or moral. I arrived at the Drama Centre in a mood of boundless expectation and absolute commitment.

And fear.

On Sunday 27 September 1970, I sat down in my room on Primrose

Hill – £5/12/6d. per week: how would I pay for *that*? – and wrote myself a letter. It begins:

Tomorrow I start at the Drama Centre. I am terrified. I dread the total exposure: it seems to me that one will be obliged to make a full and immediate declaration of personality, lay all one's cards on the table ... however this might terrify me now, it is in fact my whole reason for engaging in the enterprise: through my crucifixion, I expect my redemption. To bring me at last face to face with myself, warts and all, beauty spots and all, is the object of the exercise. I say this with some shame. The object of the Drama Centre is to produce actors. Well. I may become an actor. Indeed at the moment, I can't think of anything else that I *could* be. But my main purpose in pursuing this course is therapeutic. Perhaps that's what acting is to *all* actors; and perhaps all acting is almost accidental, a sort of symptom, or cure, of an illness – produced, like the pearl, by grit.

This could be the beginning – not of a New Life – but of Life Itself. Shall I really begin to Live? At no time have I truly felt myself *in* Life; always in the wings, watching closely sometimes, often bored, finding ways of amusing myself but never for long, because the real world was always *out there* – but now, suddenly I'm on!

I ended by wishing myself luck.

The next night, I wrote:

It is not too late to leave.

Everyone is better than I am. They look better, read better, mix, talk, *act* better. I must be mad to have come here at all. I am so nervous that when I try to reply to my wisecracking neighbour, my mouth works, but no words come ... at first it was difficult to believe that one had really made it here at last. It seemed unreal, and one was basking in glory of this achievement, when one was suddenly rolled over into the deep end. Then it was hard to connect what was being said with what had brought one here. The tone is practical, undeceived and undeceiving.

In fact, it was incredibly hard going to begin with. I didn't seriously for a moment doubt that I'd come to the right place. It was so *bracing*, like Gordonstoun. I joked (to myself, it was some while before I could actually talk to other people) that perhaps one should collect a Duke of Edinburgh Award with one's diploma. I was terribly impressed by the triumvirs who ran the school: Yat Malmgren, Christopher Fettes and John Blatchley. Searching, visionary and practical respectively, I thought them on that first day. Later I felt that they had taught me in turn the what, the why and the how of acting. One worked terribly hard, starting with a movement class at nine; through classes in Yat's bewildering work; Christopher's blazing account of world drama as a single arc from its ritual origins through to the present day; a rigorous account of the Stanislavsky work; John Blatchley's (he was always *Mr* Blatchley) mask work; voice work; and ending with work on a play. We finally fell out at seven, running home to prepare for the next day. I, of course, then went off to slave over box office accounts from half of London's theatres, and at the weekend to tear tickets for the National Theatre's audience. Thank god for that job! Not only did it pay me a few bob, but the friendly bar manager, Max Maxwell, knowing my straits, used to fill a great brown paper sack every Saturday night with whatever was left over from the buffet. I would stand on Waterloo Station staggering under this huge Red Cross parcel full of salmon sandwiches, shrimp canapés, lumps of cheese, tomatoes, bottles of milk and loaves of French bread. For three days I ate like Onassis – then back to my short commons of two eggs a day, packet soups and various cans furnished by my mother. (She had a peculiar weakness for giant gherkins which I could never share.) In general, the diet was beneficial: I lost weight and looked better, though I was of course very tired.

It was quite obvious that another term of this kind of regimen was out of the question. One day Christopher Fettes told me that he'd managed to pull a string, and that my application for a grant would be reconsidered by ILEA. This time, instead of power-crazed house-wives and superannuated Drama Advisers, the committee consisted of officials, and an actor, Paul Daneman, whom I'd so loved as Richard III ten years before. I think my panegyric to Wolfit, his performances during the Blitz, and the heroic touring work, rang some kind of bell; at any rate, I was awarded a full grant, and life seemed full to over-flowing. I was commended at the end-of-term interview for industry, and for, as Christopher Fettes put it, 'unsuspected reserves of kind-ness' (I brought him a cup of coffee very late one night when he was struggling with some impossible lighting plot). Little did I suspect, flushed with my grant, intellectually stimulated as I'd never been at university, and plain punch-drunk from exhaustion, that my position in the school hung by a thread.

The fact is that I wasn't doing very well at all.

The school's work, in almost every department, demanded funda-mental adjustments of thought. It's not that the work is *difficult*. It's certainly hard: it requires application and discipline and concentration. But you don't need a PhD to understand it. The Stanislavsky system, for example, which the Drama Centre teaches with absolute fidelity to his texts (*not* Lee Strasberg's), is essentially very simple, some would say too simple. What's hard is getting it into one's bones. Similarly Yat's work, though resting on a very complicated and rather beautiful theoretic structure, is at heart a work of identifying and utilizing sensations. I was avid for ideas, eagerly debating with the teachers the validity of this or that proposition, extrapolating philosophical truths from theoretic crumbs. I was very high. All my dreams, ravings, visions and aspirations were at last feeding into something practical and *important*. The Drama Centre buzzed with the sense that we were engaged in work which was essential to the well-being of society, the survival of the race, and the affirmation of art. It was like being in Intelligence during the war. Deadly serious, semi-secret, requiring 100 per cent commitment and – there's a war on. I couldn't have been happier, *being* a Drama Centre student. The only snag was, I couldn't do the work. Exercise after exercise failed, but not usefully or instructively; it failed because I wasn't really doing the exercise.

The problem, of course, was SIMON CALLOW. That skilfully fashioned and perfectly credible suit of armour remained obstinately in place. I had assumed, like all virgins, that the loss of my virginity would transform my life, that problems would vanish, and one would take one's place with swarming humanity. Well, I lost it, good and proper, in the first week of term, and spent some time in an undignified attempt to make up for wasted time. But it was SIMON CALLOW who'd lost his virginity, not ME. 'Blah blah blah,' I went, in bed and out. 'Blah blah blah,' in exercises. 'Blah blah blah,' or its physical equivalent, in movement classes: kinetic codswallop. My aim in all these areas was to entertain, to impress, to amuse. It all happened a millimetre beneath my scalp. I can quite distinctly remember going home, sitting at the table in my little flat and thinking of droller and droller quips for use in improvisations. It was no wonder that the staff became impatient with me. They must have felt that there was something there, but that I was deliberately refusing to let it out. They were right. The ingenuity I expended on justifying what I was trying to do was of a high creative order. My devotion to Outer Man – putting him through his paces, making him do this funny voice or that, indicate this emotion or that – was total.

It's not as if they were asking for anything earth-shattering (I of course thought I was *giving* them something earth-shattering). The early work, in every class, was simplicity itself. Stanislavsky is based squarely on the concept of Action: that everything in a play is done *in order* to achieve a want of some kind. This resolves into the formula: OBJECTIVE (What do I want?); ACTION (What do I do to get it?); OBSTACLE (What stands in my way?). The ACTION subdivides into ACTIVITIES, the separate means that I use to get what I want. There are INNER ACTIONS (which I use on myself) and OUTER ACTIONS (on other people), INNER OBSTACLES (my problems) and OUTER OBSTA- CLES (the problem of other people). The whole sequence of actions in a play adds up the character's SUPER OBJECTIVE (their whole thrust in the world of the play). I don't think I've over-simplified. There's more to it than that, but the theory of ACTIONS is the core of the whole work, and it couldn't be simpler. At first I resisted it intellectu- ally – 'No one ever wrote a play to this formula,' I said and it's true, no one ever did. But Stanislavsky wasn't writing inductively, he was writing from observation of actors whom we wouldn't call Method actors at all – particularly the great Italian actor Salvini. No, I submitted to the theory soon enough; but doing the really childishly simple exercises (I want the money. X has it. What do I do to get it?) proved impossible. We all had the most enormous difficulty in think- ing in terms of actions; just to formulate them in terms of transitive verbs, as they obviously must be, seemed brain-bustingly difficult. Wild-eyed students would roam the purlieus of the college, feverishly ransacking Roget's *Thesaurus*, only to have their favoured verb shot down in flames by the teacher. 'In order to WHAT?' they'd demand. 'What MEANS are you using?' God, it was tough – like training for the SAS.

For me, the biggest problem was to show myself wanting something. To want anything is to put oneself into a position of frightening vulnerability and then to pursue a course of action to achieve that want is to show oneself at one's most naked. It can be very ugly. Under no circumstances was I prepared to do that. I quipped, I pos- tured, I clowned, I devised quite complicated scenarios, not lacking in literary worth. What I would *not* do was show anything of myself. Without my doing that, I was wasting my time and everyone else's.

'Fun and games,' Doreen Cannon would say, laconically. 'I *don't believe* it,' Fettes would roar. The whole question of emotional truth was one on which we all got desperately stuck. The early exercises encourage the hang-up – but they're indispensable. To give in to one's emotions in the company of one's peers, to be able to taste them, in order to use them eventually, is essential; and without emotional freedom, nothing will happen, because the expression of wants will be forever inhibited. 'Follow your impulses,' Mrs Cannon would drawl, through gum, 'you may never have another.' Doreen was the principal teacher of Stanislavsky, a pupil herself of Uta Hagen, and through her, in the direct line of succession from Strasberg. Not that Doreen was a slavish adherent of Strasberg's. But emotional truth, she demanded. Oh, did she ever.

When I had tackled my emotional inhibitions head on, in the notorious Emotion Memory Exercise, nothing had happened. The form of the exercise is that the student lies on a couch while his fellow students sit around him in a circle. In an atmosphere of intense concentration, the teacher leads him to reconstruct an event of great emotional intensity: extreme tears, extreme panic, extreme laughter. Detail by detail, the teacher leads him: 'And what colour was the wallpaper? Describe the furniture. What were you wearing? Was it hot?' and so on, until the subject enters completely into the past, leaving the present behind. 'I'm trying to write but the pen is broken, so I put it down and open a drawer, which is empty, so I try another and then the door opens, and my uncle walks into the room. "What do you want, uncle? Why are you looking at me like that? No, I don't want to, I'm frightened. No, please . . ."' The results are often extraordinary: girls with tiny Minnie Mouse voices suddenly bellow like oxen; stoics weep hysterically; po-faced people laugh till the tears run down their faces. My own flat-mate reconstructed his expulsion from monastery school. As the memory took hold, he fell out of his chair on to the floor, dragging himself along the ground with his bare hands, his fingernails digging into the floorboards, emitting a terrifying growl from the pit of his stomach. He crawled behind the piano, panting, eyes flashing. The teacher was visibly rattled, and so were we all. It was hot stuff, but we all felt that if acting wasn't about confronting oneself in the darkest alleys of one's life, what was it? Giving vent to the creatures in one's own black lagoon, in the presence and with the support of one's closest colleagues, might enable one to give them to the audience too.

It just didn't work for me, that's all. How disappointed I was in myself. I had dredged up a memory which had certainly been traumatic at the time. I'd been in hospital, having my tonsils out. I was due to leave, my mother arrived to fetch me, I got dressed and packed, when the doctor said: 'Better just have one last check-up, just for safety's sake.' He did, and I had a slight temperature, so I had to stay for another day. That's all – but the effect on a seven-year-old was understandably devastating. I howled and howled till dawn; and after a tonsillectomy, that's no joke. I thought it was the end of the world.

Step by step the teacher took me through the details. 'Which bed were you in? What colour were your pyjamas?' etcetera. Slowly I felt myself falling like Alice through the hole. Emotions began to well but then, at the crucial moment, some inner clamp sat on them, and though I whimpered somewhat, it remained a trickle, not a torrent.

It was Doreen Cannon who opened the floodgates. Scene: the classroom at the Drama Centre called the Church, the room in which my right leg had hammered its quarter-metal tattoo. Up there, on that same concrete stage, I was about to perform a 'Life-and-Death' exercise: an extreme situation calling for desperate measures. My scenario was to return home from work early and find my girl in bed with another man. I entered, surveyed the scene coldly, uttered withering phrases, shamed them by my sang-froid, and sulked after the man left. Altogether, I behaved much as people do in West End dramas about infidelity, or indeed, for all I know, in life. The script, was, though I say it myself, rather fine, polished and accurate and economical. Mrs C thought otherwise. 'Don't believe it,' she almost yawned. 'Is that *really* what you'd do if you found your girl in bed with another man? Oh dear. I *am* sorry for you both.' Not *me*, lady, I nearly said, the CHARACTER. You know, *him* (except that in the Method, one never says *him*, only *me*). I bit my tongue, and thought: 'Pearls before swine, too bad you can't see it.' But then I thought, 'I'm *sick* of this, day in, day out, whine, whine, it's never good enough for you, I'm always made to feel emotionally impotent, well I'm *not*.' Through these fumings I heard the New York accent wearily say, 'OK, let's try it again. Only this time, try to give yourself a chance.' Without replying, I turned on my heels, walked out of the room, and paced up and down outside waiting for the cue to begin the scene, gorging like a hungry dog on my hatred of the woman. 'OK, let's go,' the drawl drawled. I opened the door. I spied the adulterous couple. A noise like a lion's roar came from my throat. I seized the man, plucked him out of the bed and hurled him across the room. The girl came to me pleading and sobbing. I flung her back on to the bed. I rent her clothes into tiny shreds. The man, genuinely frightened, said, 'Simon . . .' Another roar, and I picked up a three-seat settee and smashed it on the ground. It broke in half. Ann, the girl, by now really, as herself, terrified, started to cry. 'I've never seen you like this before, stop it, stop it.' 'GREAT!' came a cry from the room. 'Great. That's what it's all about! Do you see that, do you understand that?' she said to the class. 'That is a breakthrough.' A newly, unfamiliarly animated Doreen came up to me: 'Great, well done, you should be very pleased.' I was still a bit shaken by the mighty emotions which had been passing through me, and had not altogether forgiven Doreen for provoking them, so I just nodded. Later, people who'd been there repeated her praise and said 'Wow!' and suchlike. It took me a day to work out what had happened.

Nobody, certainly not Doreen, and not even I, thought it was good acting. What it was was a powerful emotion carried through to its conclusion. The remarkable thing was not the emotion, but that I had allowed myself to show it: to show myself. On reflection I realized that for as long as I could remember, I had *never* shown myself to be angry. I regarded it as undignified, and bad policy. I believed that the moment one lost one's temper one became weak. I certainly never used physical violence, even as a child. I probably thought, tiny as I then was, that I was bound to lose any physical contest. And here I was, hurling people across the stage, and roaring like a wild animal. It was obviously all there inside me, and when I gave in to it, my voice, my body and my whole stance changed. I felt enormous power and freedom. I did, in fact, feel alive. My dream was being fulfilled.

It seemed that my breakthroughs must always come obliquely. The great one, the one that transformed all my attitudes, came neither in the Stanislavsky work, or Yat's work, but in Christopher Fettes's class, 'Analysis'. This class, dealing with the origins and growth of the drama, was always my favourite, because to me it was everything university should have been and never was. Christopher has a spontaneous intellectual expressionism, seeing history and art in starkly vivid terms, plugging all human experience into a vision of the human condition part Freudian, part Nietzschean: theatre embodying the struggle against oblivion, the celebration of desire, a licensed revolt against society, and at the same time civilization's opposition to anarchy. His eclecticism was radical: Euripides' *Orestes* would be illuminated by Lou Reed, Wedekind's *Spring Awakening* made sense of in terms of German Romantic excess, Richard Strauss, *Liebestod*.

A feature of his class was that we did it ourselves. A chronological sequence of topics central to dramatic history (Dionysos, the Greek

City State, Spanish Comedia, Molière, and so on) was doled out. Each acting student, with a partner – usually a student director – was then required to present it to the class, in whatever form he chose. One could lecture, or write a play, or make a documentary, whichever was most vivid; the form was free. My first subject was 'Perikles and the Greek City State'. With Penny Cherns I co-wrote it, and co-directed it, and I'd written myself a leading role as Testikles, a kind of Athenian Alf Garnett.

In all the anxiety over the show, worrying whether it was clear, whether everybody knew where to come on or go off, I had no time to think about my performance, no time to wonder about its effect on the group, or on Christopher, or to ask, 'Was I funny?' or 'Was it clever?' I just did it. Suddenly, for the first time, I was acting. Not performing, or posturing, or puppeteering. I was *being in another way*. At a stroke the mask that I had screwed on to my face fell away. I was free, easy, effortless. For the first time since I'd arrived at the Drama Centre I understood what playing a character was. It was giving in to another way of thinking. *Giving in* was the essential experience. 'Leave yourself alone,' they'd been saying to us since the day we arrived. Now suddenly I was. To my surprise I found that it was not an entirely unfamiliar sensation. Even at his uptight, armoured worst, SIMON CALLOW had always been able to forget himself in the temporary assumption of another identity – for a line in a funny story, or for the devastating impersonation of a tutor. It was here, if anywhere, that any talent for acting that I might possess had resided: the knack of throwing off self-consciousness and finding, however briefly, a pool of liberated energy which was nothing to do with how I presented myself in life. My overawe at the intellectual framework of the Drama Centre and my emotional constipation had snuffed the little flame out, and with it, my spontaneity. It had seemed unworthy. When I saw that it was the same thing, that that was *it* – the direct flow of energy transforming the brain, the heart and the body – I was as one re-born. It was then, in that moment, that acting became second nature to me. I was unstoppable. I had the taste of the thing in my mouth. From being a spectator, dragging myself up to do exercises that I felt doomed to fail in, I suddenly couldn't perform enough. I volunteered to be in everyone else's improvisations and exercises as well as my own. It wasn't to be seen. It wasn't to impress. It was to *do* it, to revel in this newly discovered joy, to romp around in the adventure playground that I myself had become. This epiphany fell almost exactly half way through the training. Before and after were as day from night. I wonder what the staff made of this sudden transformation? It coincided with a second year production of a Feydeau farce in which I played with great freedom and flair, so they probably attributed it to that. But it was *post hoc*, not *propter hoc*. Of course the fact that admirable Greville Hallam had come as it were from the world outside to do the production and approached it much as he might have approached a professional production, assuming that all the usual work of the school had been done but never using it himself, was an enormous advantage. I was able to consolidate my breakthrough.

The point was that through the happy accident of hitting my own centre, everything I'd been taught in the past eighteen months made sense because now I had felt it for myself. The circle was now complete. The intellectual understanding fused with the sensation. Not only was I doing the right thing, I knew what it was, so I could do it again. And again. It was mine.

The ludicrous thing was that the whole eighteen months had been spent in trying to get me to do precisely what had just happened. I felt like saying, 'Oh *that's* what you meant! Why didn't you say so?' They had, day in and day out. The problem was that I thought the suit of armour, the mask, SIMON CALLOW, *were* my centre. I had sung songs, impersonated animals, donned garments, adopted accents; but it was always something that I imposed on top of what I was, always something I was DOING TO MYSELF, instead of letting it do me.

Every aspect of the training was transformed by this discovery. Stanislavsky classes immediately made sense. If one simply put the character into the situation, brought him to the stage – that is, wanting what he wanted, encountering what he encountered – he *always* played an action, with a hundred varied activities, because he would, quite spontaneously, in life.

Movement and voice classes similarly opened their secrets to me. I at last left behind the puffy creature who had stood blushing in his bulging leotard on the first day, desperately trying to think himself not there. I fell and I stumbled, like a tipsy centipede. I couldn't convert words into movements: which was left or right? Leg or arm, did he say? The pianist might as well not have been there for all I marked the rhythm. The pain, actual physical pain, was constant.

Now, eighteen months later, I was not more beautiful, not more graceful, but I was MOVING WITH MY OWN BODY; and in voice classes, I was speaking with my own voice. It had dropped an octave. Warmth was entering into it; the staccato nasal noise that I had arrived with was no more to be heard.

If I begin to sound like a model student, nothing could be further from the truth. It's simply that things were happening at such a pace, the sensation of barriers crumbling and vistas opening up was so intense, that I had the feeling that everything was momentous, epoch-making. For me it was, but I had such a long, long way to go.

Yat's work was still puzzlingly difficult. Nevertheless I had no doubt, and have none now, that what he was saying expressed the profoundest truths about acting. His work addresses itself directly to the very nature of acting: not 'What is it for?' or 'What are the conditions which give rise to it?' It attempts to say what it *is*.

The work itself is a synthesis of Laban's analysis of movement (splitting it into its component units in terms of their direction of energy) with Jung's theory of psychological types (sensing, thinking, intuiting, feeling). What it amounts to – the theory known as Movement Psychology – is a praxis of character in action, an account of the physical embodiment of character and impulse. The intellectual framework is complex and all-embracing; but its difficulty stems from its grounding in sensations. How can one talk about sensations? Feeling them, being aware of them, learning to identify and separate them, to crystallize and concretize them, to be able to summon them and use them: that's Yat's work, and the whole work of the school was dominated and unified by it. It was the river into which all the other streams flowed.

But it was difficult; for us and for him. It can't be demonstrated and imitated, like dancing, because its essence is experience. One learns what a sensation is, not what it looks like; and sensation is at the heart of acting. Emotional, intuitive, physical, and intellectual sensation; quick sensations and sustained ones; direct and flexible, bound and free, strong and light.

Then, too, there was John Blatchley's mask class. It was a wonderful class, and I was a total failure in it, in all its phases: the early work, in which one mimed little scenes in a leotard; later, animal observation classes, in which the animal of your choice transmogrified into a comparable human; then the half-masks; and finally the full masks.

All totally eluded me. I could see my fellow-students doing wonderful things, but the moment I got behind a mask, my invention dried up, my body seized up, and my nose blocked up. I told myself that a mask wasn't necessarily a physical thing, that the new understanding of character which I had arrived at was exactly equivalent to wearing a mask: I behaved under the influence of the image.

Despite my failure, it was valuable to watch other people soaring, and it was one of the many strands of tradition that the school incorporated. Blatchley had the mask work from Michel Saint-Denis, who in turn came from Copeau. Yat brought something of the tradition of Weimar's artistic ferment. Laban grew out of that, and Yat had been part of the group who first performed Joos's *The Green Table*. The Stanislavsky work was taught *à la lettre*. Christopher Fettes brought a wholly European breadth of philosophical challenge to every aspect of the work, as well as the altogether different vigour of Joan Littlewood for whom he'd acted.

Yat believed – he was talking about the flow of energy on a stage, the same thing that I'd suddenly violently experienced at the Old Vic when I'd blurted out Hamlet's line – that theatre was black magic. He never said what the black magic should be used for. It was typical of him. Lie was the What, never the Why. That was Fettes, who spoke of a primitive function of theatre, binding the community, affirming fertility, celebrating man's triumph over nature. Blatchley, dear, genial, indispensable Blatchley, who provided a link with the actual theatre in which he, unlike the other two, worked, spoke of presentation, of allowing the vision to find an audience. He was How.

There were no classes at the Drama Centre in fencing, dialects, or clog-dancing. They reckoned that if you needed them, you could pick them up in ten minutes. They were right.

Getting a job was another matter. Three obsessional, passionate, exultant, despairing, incestuous years were, suddenly, up. And yet one seemed to have been there all one's life. Immersion in the murky waters of one's psyche, relentless wrestling with one's own recalcitrant instrument, imaginative and emotional struggles to encompass the world views of fifteenth-century Spain and nineteenth-century Russia, all seemed oddly irrelevant. This world of ours, where teachers were gods and sages and tyrants, where our daily development was charted and examined as anxiously as any patient's in an intensive care unit, where temperaments and personal crises cast giant shadows, seemed suddenly dwarfed. The world outside was the real one, little known, feared and longed for. Those of us who had come through three years, older, wiser, battle-scarred, were children again, beginners, outsiders.

The last term was spent preoccupied with more important things than the end-of-term showings, which had once seemed bigger than any Broadway opening. Where did one want to work? Who would *have* one? How did one get a provisional union card? For the first time, the prospect of not actually working for some while, if ever, became real. Could all this have been for nothing?

I had some quirky ideas. Deep in my heart reigned a Buddhist calm. When I'd auditioned for the Drama Centre, I'd thought if they didn't take me, I'd join the navy. When they did, I thought, 'Wonderful. But if, after three years' training I don't work soon, and if, at the end of a year, I haven't made a go of it, I'll jack it in.' That was the innocence of inexperience. I'd never really done it, so how was I to know how addictive, how indispensable to one's system it would prove? Moreover, although by now I was doing very well at the school, had played very good parts in the end-of-term showings and had been praised for my performances, I wasn't convinced that I was anything but a lightweight as an actor. I was living with a man who, although his performances at the school hadn't been nearly as accomplished as mine, was possessed of a personal intensity and certain physical endowments – a voice, a face, a body – that I felt qualified him to be a much more remarkable actor than I would ever be. I viewed with equanimity the possibility that *he* would be the actor, and I would support him in whatever way I could. It wasn't till many years later that I understood the wisdom of Ruth Gordon's remark that it's not enough to have talent – one has to have a talent for having talent. As it turned out, I had it; John didn't. After a short time, he gave up acting altogether, not from lack of primary talent, but from lack of secondary talent.

That state of mind, however, that kind of openness to the possibility of failure, must have stood me in good stead. Instead of writing to all the repertory companies for auditions, I wrote only to people whom I admired, asking them to come to see the plays. I wrote to Charles Marowitz, to Peter Ustinov, to David Jones at the RSC (hoping he would remember me from box office days), and finally, to Micheál MacLiammóir. I had a dream that my first job would be for him. Did he remember me, I wrote. I'd love to work for him in however humble a capacity, and so on; I enclosed a photograph and a stamped addressed envelope. 'No,' he replied, 'I can't say I do remember you, but I *greatly* admire your photograph' (which I knew he could hardly see), 'Why don't you get in touch with my partner Hilton Edwards?' I did, and after many changed appointments – telegrams flying back and forth across the Irish Sea – I found myself standing on the curious stage of the Gate Theatre, Dublin, addressing a charming man with an enormous nose and a very English English accent, who sat in the stalls, laughing a great deal at my little speeches. Micheál was ill, unfortunately, the worst was over but he was still very weak, he sent his warmest greetings, and fond memories – he now remembered me very well indeed. Hilton was sure that something could be found for me in the upcoming season; the address was correct? and the phone number?

Of course, I never heard from them again. Of the others, Peter Ustinov never got my letter – it came back to me a month later, unopened – David Jones was busy, Charles Marowitz *nearly* made it but at the last moment . . . None of it seemed in the least bit real. The idea of these famous people tottering down to the old Methodist Hall in Chalk Farm, the idea of working in various theatres up and down the country, indeed, the very idea of myself as an actor, all seemed in the realms of fantasy. As a result, it seemed neither surprising nor particularly thrilling when a phone call came from Peter Farago, then at the Young Lyceum in Edinburgh, asking me to join his company for the Edinburgh Festival. I'd met him at the Drama Centre, he'd seen a second-year showing, and now he was asking me to work with him. So that's how it happened.

The job started two days before the last day of the last term, and I was released early to take it up. On my last night, having given my last performance at the Drama Centre, and in a kind of charmed trance, I was invited by Christopher and Yat into the office for a private diploma-giving. Somehow an Iranian student with rather poor English got caught up in the little group, and what was to have been an intimate leavetaking took on a note of farce. None of us really said anything much. The diploma was handed over. I made for the door. 'Oh,' said Christopher, 'we'd like you to have this to drink on the train.' A bottle of red wine. Three months later I drank it with the director of my first rep. I offered a toast to them.

Three

I was twenty-four when I left the Drama Centre. I was stuffed full of visions and hopes – but I wasn't exactly wet behind the ears. I had been around a bit, had worked in theatres, knew something of the conditions of the theatre. I expected no triumphal progress, and I was fully aware of the value of the equity probation ticket to which my first job entitled me. Even so: I was a little surprised to find myself, four weeks later, sprawled on the steps of the Assembly Rooms in Edinburgh shouting 'Noo!' and 'Aye!' in company with a dozen or so highly talented young actors plus a handful of amateurs, providing a human soundtrack to the cream of the Scottish theatre, banging away in Lallands in the Festival production of *The Thrie Estates*. It wasn't so much disillusioning as odd: the last thing one could possibly have expected. If it had been a commercial, or spear-carrying at Stratford . . . but just lying around, listening to this incomprehensible pageant? Some members of the soundtrack team on the steps found it deeply insulting to their professional dignity, and a mood of bitterness, not assuaged by slugs of alcohol and the occasional infusion of marijuana, swept through the little group. Unscripted, undirected mutterings were heard at unsuitable moments: the occasional oath, or contemptuous laugh. It was as if a small group of medieval Scots folk had decided to do a production of the *Marat-Sade* at the Winter Fair.

We were, too, most of us, involved in a production of *Woyzeck* staged by a gentle Roumanian, Radu Penciulescu, whose limited English vocabulary was mostly translated directly and wrongly from the French. 'Be more disponible,' he would cry, agitatedly. 'Disponible?' people would mutter. 'What the fuck's disponible?' and then do what they thought it might be. He was generally quite pleased. But then he would scream, 'Don't pose!' The guilty actor, feeling himself accused of narcissism, would become very upset, and then struggle to be spontaneous. 'Don't pose,' the cry would come again. 'I'm *not* posing.' 'Yes, yes, between this word and that one, you are *posing*. You shall not.' Enlightenment. *Pausing* was the offence. Much less shaming. A great deal of rehearsal was taken up with such linguistic diversions. A couple of us spoke French, and helped out where we could ('He says, more feeling'). The production was definitely avant-

37

garde (the first time I'd encountered that) and so were Radu's working methods. We did a lot of touching of each other's bodies, and sensing the energy in the room, and we spent a *long* time compiling lists of our favourite words in the text. We began to wonder exactly what would appear on the stage in, what was it? ten days? We had been cast, yes, that was a good start, but beyond that ... I suppose the mood of restlessness penetrated even the language barrier because one morning Radu came in with a production. He blocked the play in detail, introduced us to certain scenic effects (the lake in which Marie and Woyzeck drown, for example, was to be represented by a huge white floorcloth, which Woyzeck would slowly shear down the middle till he drowned – a brilliant effect) and then ran the play with great discipline. During this phase of the work, I, who had been cast as among other things the Old Jew who sells Woyzeck the murder knife, frankly rather bored and also keen to make a mark, said to Radu: 'Look, I think I should play this character in a very anti-Semitic way. That seems to be part of the world of the piece. I'd like to play him like Irving would have played Shylock, and what's more, I think he should be blind.' 'Show me,' said Radu. I'd never thought of any of it till the moment before, so I just plunged in and did it, lisping and Fagin-like, with a pair of sunglasses for blindness. Radu looked at me in wonder. 'But this marvellous. This fantastic. Incredible, yes, yes.' Later I discovered that he used to cite this incident to his students in Bucharest as an example of an experimental approach to acting.

It was very hard to use the work of the Drama Centre on any of my so-called parts. Such as they were, I had got them in one. It was altogether a curious baptism. Instead of the intense work and intellectual struggle to make sense of the Spanish *comedia*, or Pirandello's *grottesco* style, or whatever, one sat around most of the time, waiting to do one's bit, or participating half-heartedly in exercises the point of which was never clear. As I wandered round Edinburgh, poverty-stricken, living in a room the size of a cupboard with broken filthy windows stuffed with newspaper, sleeping on a folding bed which because of the dimensions of the room could never be fully extended so I had my feet halfway up the opposite wall, I tried to take stock. I'd had no time to assess what the Drama Centre had given me, where or who I was now, and what I wanted. Just getting a job seemed miraculous enough. It was, but in every way it was a freak experience, so what now?

It was a lonely time, because I had left a fixed universe, in which I had a distinct place. Meeting a new group on the first day of rehearsal, people who hadn't the slightest idea who I was, though they seemed to know each other, was an upsetting experience, and always would be until the time came when everyone in any group one cared to join had either seen one's work, or was one's best friend's best friend. The sense of not existing for the first few days of rehearsal persisted for many years; but was never as bad again as here, in Edinburgh. On the first day, the first day, that is, of my first job, my father died, in Africa. I barely knew him, so I was more struck by how hard it was for the director to break it to me. Finally I guessed: 'Oh, you mean my father's dead. Oh don't worry, we weren't very close at all.' That night I went to a production of *Hamlet*. Then something primitive stirred inside me.

It was none of it how I'd expected it to be. I'd thought in terms of hard-working obscurity, leading eventually to glory. I regarded myself as being in training for the 'great challenge'. I'd read that John Gielgud thought it took twenty years to make an actor. I'd try to whittle that figure down a bit, but I knew I must start serious training immediately. The present experience was obviously a sort of interlude, a brief pause between intensive bouts of preparation.

I resolved in future to play only leading roles, because I reckoned that was the only way to learn. The oddity of Edinburgh was that in a sense the glory had preceded the work. The international press was there, one was associating with artists of great renown, and one wasn't being paid badly (£30, not unhandsome for 1973). At that moment, my moment of decision, a phone call arrived from Robert Walker, whom I'd never met, saying that he'd just taken over a rep ('Um, what is it – oh yeah, Lincoln') and would I like to join him to play in *A Taste of Honey* for his opening season. Of course this was the Voice of Fate, so I went.

I recall Edith Evans having said somewhere that she had the luck, at the beginning of her career, only to work for and with good people. If she hadn't, she said, she would undoubtedly have picked up an awful lot of bad habits. I had the luck, at the beginning of my career, to go from job to job without a day out of work, always in that way to capitalize on what had gone before, and always again to do something new, something different, with different people, and so never to get into easy ways.

Lincoln under Rob was indeed the most astonishing lucky break. I don't know what the board of the theatre thought they were getting, but I'm sure it wasn't him; or us. A bouncy lot of tearaways we were, a couple of us pretty fresh out of drama school and full of all *that*; others who'd ploughed lonely furrows in the alternative theatre, had no time for mainstream theatre but were thrilled to be in a building, with a company, and the chance of a really radical policy; and a number of quirky individualists who added an original colour all of their own. The plan was to 'softly softly' the burghers of Lincoln with a conventional opening couple of plays, and then ease in the radical stuff. It's been tried before. The English repertory system is a graveyard of radical intentions, and it is always the Board who are the grim reapers. What took us somewhat by surprise was that it was *A Taste of Honey* that was regarded as radical. The following double-bill of *The Real Inspector Hound* and *Erpingham Camp* was received with slightly more favour, mainly because there's something in the heartless savagery of Joe Orton which appeals to the Lincoln temperament. The bomb dropped with Howard Brenton's *Measure for Measure*: Angelo is Enoch Powell, the Duke Harold Macmillan, and Claudio is black. Or rather, the bomb fell into a bucket of water, and fizzled out. It was ignored. Would the audience out-number the cast? was the nightly question, not too frequently answered in the affirmative. Winter brought *A Christmas Carol* and *Aladdin*, for which houses were guaranteed. For me, it was just one good meal after another: Peter, the man with an eye-patch, in *Taste of Honey*, Erpingham, Magnus Muldoon, the Duke/Macmillan, Cratchit and later Scrooge, and then, crowningly, Abanazar. It wasn't weekly rep, more like fortnightly, although we did the double-bill in ten days, but it was hard, hard work, cramming lines into one's head, making instant decisions about characters, rarely having time to think about the meaning of things, but sometimes hitting it smack on the head. It's a system which, as Edith Evans implied, can lead to nasty habits, facility, generalization, cheap effects, and above all, in the sheer practical urgency of getting the thing on, losing touch with why one puts on plays at all. On the other hand, it sharpens memory, demands discipline, encourages decisions, and makes for boldness – half-heartedness is impossible. I learnt almost as much again on my feet, in six months there in Lincoln, as I had in three years at the Drama Centre. I *couldn't* have learnt what I learnt there at drama school. It's only *doing* it that teaches.

Also, it was fun; perhaps more so in retrospect than at the time. Perhaps it *wasn't* such marvellous fun rehearsing the pantomime on Christmas Day and painting the set that evening because the designer had decamped; perhaps walking into the theatre at 9 a.m. to be told that you were taking over the part of Scrooge, having never been anything but Bob Cratchit, wasn't quite such a laugh; maybe falling six foot through the trapdoor wasn't the funniest thing that had ever happened to me in my life; and maybe playing biting political satire to an audience of ten on Guy Fawkes' night wasn't a riot. But we were all in it together. There was never any sense of Rob being the boss, or any possibility of one just getting on with one's job: everything that went on in the theatre concerned us all equally, and we were all free to be involved in decisions. So for me there was a dual responsibility: being a member of this group, and playing leading parts in the plays. Above all in this kind of situation, so much depends on the actor's taking the thing in both hands and making a go of it. The rehearsals are too brief for any time to be spent on building up the actor's self-confidence; one's mind is focused on The Show. And that's very healthy. Because of this atmosphere, one's last inhibitions disappeared. Emotion was still the big shyness for me, so I was amazed to hear myself say to Rob one day when we were rehearsing *Measure for Measure*, 'How do you want this speech, Rob? Melancholy? Hysterical? Bitter? Tearful?' 'I dunno,' he said, 'show me.' So I did, one after another, as if I were a kind of emotion machine, ending with convulsive and deeply felt tears. 'Oh, tears, definitely tears,' said Rob, as they coursed warmly down my cheeks. And so I did, at every performance, without huff or puff.

It's a question of direct contact between your brain and your nervous system, and 'we open on Tuesday' has a wonderful way of concentrating the mind. What was also indispensable was Rob's capacity to create the amniotic fluid in which creativity can flourish. He would, I imagine, be the last person in the world to cite concentration as his outstanding gift, but in the moment of creativity, in the rehearsal itself and maybe only for as long as the actor is actually acting, his concentration is absolute, almost childlike. It's wonderful to act for him, aware of his eyes open wide, hypnotized by what the actors are doing. (It's like a sunray lamp, or one of those time-lapse films where the lifespan of a flower is speeded up. The growth is palpable.) I never for a moment doubted that Rob loved my work, even when he criticized it fundamentally. Often since, I've felt that directors approached me with a net and trident as if I were a wild animal who might suddenly produce a lethal burst of over-acting; but then those directors approach *all* actors that way: it's acting that worries them, not me.

It was a wonderful start: playing a succession of huge roles for a director who relished my work in a wholly democratic environment with actors whom I loved and admired, all of whom had more experience than I, and all of whom were exceptionally generous to me, on stage and off, this actor pointing out my inability to sustain the vocal energy till the end of the speech, that one the strange restlessness which afflicted my feet whenever I stepped on stage. It's a tricky business, helping one's fellow actors; these people did it with tact and charm. In fact, come to think of it, I've *never* been treated destructively by a fellow actor. I've known nothing but kindness and generosity from them. So much for legend.

After a performance of *A Taste of Honey*, Ann Mitchell, at that time married to Rob Walker, and a member of the company, said to me: 'It's *very* good, doll. Lovely, accurate work.' She was a highly experienced, very talented actress, and it meant a lot to me, but I deflected the compliment: 'Isn't X wonderful, though?' I said, of another member of the cast. 'Not bad, not bad at all,' she said, 'but he doesn't *love* it the way you do.'

As people do from time to time in one's life, she had defined something for me that I could never have put my own finger on. It was love, consuming, obsessive, love. I dreamed only of new and better roles. Lincoln was like the first affair where one never wants to leave the bedroom. One can't get enough of it. My personal life proper had withered away. In the sexual round dance that is so characteristic of a young rep ('And who has been having whom?' an old-time actor-manager is alleged to have murmured on Monday mornings, before rehearsals), I was left without a partner. It didn't matter. I had my art to keep me warm.

Lincoln had given me an easy familiarity with my art which was a gift impossible to purchase. The roles, and their more or less success-ful realization, had given me confidence; the directness of my dealings with Rob and the other actors had instilled fundamentally democratic ideas into my heart: I was taught never to expect anything less than equal treatment, and for the most part I got it – and gave it; and the sense of responsibility for the running of the whole theatre took the pressure off My Career, My Performance, and so on. 'How was the theatre doing? What more could one do to help it?' My years in box office had given me a healthy interest in the nightly returns, and at Lincoln the interest was satisfied. Not all managers are so free with The Figures, their sacred domain. They believe that the actors should be *protected*, as if the actors weren't the first to know the size of the house, and sense exactly what percentage were on complimentary tickets.

Winter of '72 was a grim, dark time. The three-day week was upon us, the television blacked out at ten o'clock, and the fairy lights strung along Lincoln High Street were never allowed to be lit. Crisis followed crisis in the theatre, the artistic director was in a state of open war with the administrator, the stage, the green room and the auditorium were equally cold (thank god for the lights on stage!), disease was rife throughout the company, actors survived from day to day on a diet of port and antibiotics, and the audience for the pantomime proved strangely aggressive – seven- and eight-year-olds greeted Abanazar's appearance, divested of his evil, tripping on lightly holding a daffodil, with cries of 'Fook off, yer fooking puff.' I had played Bob Cratchit with a temperature in the hundreds, and had nearly died when a mouthful of polystyrene snow, inadvertently gulped while singing a merry Christmas song, went down the wrong way. I'd lost a stone taking over from Scrooge, and my evil chuckle as Abanazar left my throat bleeding and raw. Talk other than a whisper was impossible, and anyway, one's throat-spray was rarely out of one's mouth.

Then, the call from Edinburgh came. Edinburgh! Serene, grey, formal, organized. It was Peter Farago again (my first ever employer) wanting me to play Bāsho in *Narrow Road to the Deep North* and tour the east of Scotland in *The Fantasticks*. Robert said, 'You must go,' recast the part I was rehearsing in the next play, kissed my brow and sent me on my way with many blessings. Within two months, the whole brave little experiment at Lincoln was over. Now there's no theatre there at all. I don't think they want one.

Edinburgh, of course, does. I don't think they specially wanted *Narrow Road to the Deep North*, but that's what they got, along with my worst performance to date. There was the usual problem of the new group, but that wasn't it. There was the problem of the play, one of my favourites, which I had loved so much in London at the Royal

Court. It has an austere surrealism, along with a kind of running alienation: 'My name is Bāsho. I am, as you know, the famous seventeenth-century Japanese poet, who brought the haiku verse form to perfection, giving it greater range and depth.' I couldn't decide whether it was really Japanese, or Lewis Carroll (which it almost is), or Brecht. I couldn't see the character, and I didn't understand his development in the play. I had a hunch that I should play him like W. H. Auden, chain-smoking and drawling his verse absently. The director, Peter Farago, was committed to a certain style, or rather, stylization, and resisted my idea with many very persuasive reasons. I became convinced of his approach – intellectually. My body, my heart and my inner brain, I'm afraid, held out. In retrospect, I'm sure he was right, and I was wrong. But that's not the point. I was in that most uncomfortable position for an actor: having given up *my* instinct, but not being able to follow the director's. I vowed that I'd never do that again: that I'd always fight it out until I had something in which, for preference, we both believed in, or at least, *I* did. It was I, after all, who would be standing on the stage. An actor who performs in a certain way because the director told him to, is not really there at all. He's in the past, his mind always harking back to the rehearsal room, thinking desperately: '*What* did he tell me to do now? Oh, god, I'm sure that's wrong,' and so on. The performance will never grow, the actor's tension will block off any real expressive vibration because another, irrelevant person has clambered on to the stage between the actor and the audience: the director. The actor must *own* his performance, and the director must make sure that he does.

All this came to me in a rush as I brooded on the failure. It was nobody's failure but mine. Out of it, however, had come something really valuable. Without these kind of failures, I decided, one would never grow, because the pain connected with them – the unimaginable embarrassment of standing in front of paying customers ashamed of what one is doing – would burn the lesson indelibly on one's brain. Alas, it seems every lesson has to be learned afresh every time. At the beginning of every job, Cyril Cusack is alleged to have said, one feels as if one had never had one before, and at the end of every job, one feels as if one will never have one again. One thing I *do* know, though, is that it's essential to live through one's failures, not dismiss them, or blame them on others. Every failure is *your* failure; and every failure, as Christopher Fettes used to say, destroys the power of the theatre, kills to however small a degree its capacity to pierce the audience to the heart. Enough dreary performances, and people will stop looking to the theatre for revivification. As, to a large extent, they have.

The tour of *The Fantasticks* was a gas, one of the perks of the profession. One can have enough of such perks, but it was my first tour, my first real experience of fit-ups and get-ins, of playing a different theatre every night, of bed and breakfast, of late-night meals in dubious Chinese restaurants, of sharing digs with people whose various secrets were remorselessly revealed: smelly feet, snoring and strange nocturnal emissions – verbal and otherwise. One also quickly learns who can be relied upon to quibble over the bill, who is vile-tempered at breakfast, who tells the best stories, and who not to lend a couple of quid to.

The whole experience was odd in this way: it was as if we were treading in the footsteps of whole vanished generations of actors whose world of digs and landladies and number one tours had really vanished, too; as if, spookily, we were on a sort of Cooks' tour of what it was once like. I'm afraid they would not have recognized the hearty, well-fed, pot-smoking crowd that we were, having a three-week spree down the coast. But oh, it was fun, I think.

My career continued miraculously seamless. Mike Ockrent had come to see the dress rehearsal of *The Fantasticks*, and asked me to join his new company at the Traverse, Edinburgh, his first permanent group. We would do new plays and classics, everybody, cleaners, actors, bar staff, director, would earn the same money (£30, a little less handsome than it had been a year before), all would be involved in all decisions, and so on. There would be seven of us, and we started on Monday.

That was a time of real ferment. The seven of us and Mike struck sparks from the beginning. Our opening production was of the English première of Ingmar Bergman's version of Strindberg's *Dream Play*. Together we evolved a remarkable idiom in which to play it, doubling, trebling, quadrupling parts. The little Traverse was all but turned upside down to find the most flexible playing space. The important thing was that we were all involved in suggesting exercises, elucidating mysteries in the text and commenting on the progress of the work. The result was an unusually unified production.

Next we did C. P. Taylor's version of Sternheim's *Burger Schippel*: the first time I had worked with a living author – Cecil Taylor, that is, not Sternheim. It was, in fact, Cecil's play, suggested by the German original. He'd made it entirely his own, eschewing the expressionist jaggedness and laconicism of Sternheim in favour of his own warmth and passion and class comedy. I was amazed to meet the dear man, his head always slightly to one side in the attitude of a puzzled pup, gently questioning in his Glasgow Jewish manner, and wearing a pair of CND sandals. It was hard to connect him with the violently farcical text, even if the upper-middle-class characters' syntax gang sometimes agley. Listening closer to him, however, one distinctly caught the origin of his dialogue's propensity for long flexible, oddly unfinished sentences, and parallel monologues, punctuated with phrases both elegant and earthy. This was the Cecilian style, hard at first to master, but then a joy in proof.

A string of crises, however, commenced on the first day. The democratic method of casting had produced a cast that, as not rarely, ultimately satisfied no one. We were all slightly moody at the readthrough, but no one, I think, doubted that the Schippel was the right person. Our horror and embarrassment were the stronger therefore when we discovered, as the readthrough proceeded, that he had rewritten all his lines, and was duly speaking them, without request or apology, in the presence of the author. That most tolerant of men went over and conferred amiably with him, taking his points, and to some extent agreeing with him. The next day, Cecil appeared with a new text for Schippel. We started rehearsing, to discover that the actor had rewritten them *again*. What's more, the rewriting was to no one's liking. It made Schippel into a fearless working-class hero with an Anglo-Saxon, not to say coprophiliac turn of phrase (instead of 'Well, gentlemen, I have one thing to say: sod off' the new line was 'I have one thing to say: why don't you all take a good stiff shit to yourselves'). It was impossible, untrue to Cecil or Sternheim and inconceivable that the German high bourgeoisie who were the subjects of the play could have anything further to do with the man. This was *the first scene*. We confronted the offender *en bloc*. Cornered, he became abusive: 'All right you can keep your fucking bourgeois little play. I'm off. You've turned it into a fucking West End vehicle, that's what you've done.' It was a harsh phrase to use to the little band of idealists. A year later, when the play indeed *did* end up in the West End, with Harry Secombe playing Schippel, some of us examined our consciences. But our abusive friend was wrong, then and later. He'd wanted to turn it into a strip cartoon of class confrontation. Cecil, no boulevardier, was after something much more complex. It wasn't Sternheim but a curious mix of German and English genres, Wilhelmine satire tempered by English domestic farce. Against every odd, it worked.

The casting now had to be stood on its head. A sort of musical chairs ensued, in which every member of the company ended up with a new role, except for me. I was still playing Wolke, the civil servant worried that 'it' might not quite be big enough, the second baritone of the male voice quartet at the centre of the play. Now, I love music, especially classical music, but my ear is woefully unreliable. There seems not to be too much wrong with my voice, but the ear – crippled. Even those who are well disposed to me can't forbear from some such phrase as 'I didn't know you couldn't sing' or 'God, you really *can't* sing, can you?', piercing me to the depths, because, oh, I should so like to be able to. On the few occasions I've found myself inadvertently forced to, I'm always surrounded by well-wishers saying 'There's no such thing as tone-deafness, you know' and 'It's just a matter of confidence.' This brings me to screaming pitch. Even the well-wishers hearing me struggle to find a note which is perfectly simple to them, are baffled. 'Lalalala,' they trill, a look of eager encouragement on their faces, as if that might do the trick. I become hysterical and behave really badly. Tears are never far away.

Schippel was the worst. I was supposed to sing *harmonies*. The very word sends a shiver down my spine. The second baritone line isn't easy for singers, but for me . . . I strained till I was red in the face to disentangle my note from the cluster of sounds hovering in the air. A droning noise would emerge from my mouth, very quietly. The Music Director would stop, patiently. 'What was that note, Simon?' And I would have to sing it alone. The others were aghast at the remoteness of this utterance from the required note. 'Just relax, it'll come.' At this, I broke completely. 'It *won't!*' I shrieked. 'You might as well tell a multiple sclerotic that he's going to run in the next Olympic Games.' I said I behaved badly. At this point, James Snell stepped forward and earned himself an unconditional place in heaven. 'We can swap parts, if you like. I'm sick of playing juves, I'd love to play a character part for once in a while.' He was playing the young handsome prince who falls in love with the daughter of the household. 'Oh Jimmy, would you? Oh how wonderful.' I got a bit maudlin. It'd never occurred to me in a million years that I might play the prince. Not my line at all; but instead of *singing* . . . So we swapped.

To be precise, the prince wasn't exactly a juve. In Sternheim a Byronic figure, musing over fresh white linen underwear and ironically deflating himself with Shakespearian quotes, in Cecil he'd become a more headlong person, a kind of desperate romantic, going to extraordinary lengths to achieve his conquest. I didn't believe the audience could take me seriously in such a role – too short, too fat. I couldn't take *myself* seriously as a prince. So I turned him into a frog. I edged him towards comedy, tentatively at first, then more boldly. I imagined a semi-crazed Hapsburg, or even the Kaiser himself, posturing, grasping, absent-minded, utterly in love with music. As he began to grow, Cecil, who never stopped rewriting for a moment, saw where I was going and came along with me, in fact outstripped me, to the point at which I was saying (there's nothing quite so prudish as a heavy drinker who meets an alcoholic): 'Oh come now, Cecil, I can't say that, it's ridiculous.' 'Uh huh. And what's that business you're doing in the second act? That's supposed to be classical acting, is it?' And of course, I would say it, because it was wonderful stuff, but old Sternheim was left afar off, by both of us. It was wonderful to be written *for*. It was like Hollywood: today's rewrites would be filed at ten in the morning, learned by the afternoon, and played in the evening. This must have been the way Molière's plays were written, I thought, or Shakespeare's. Maybe what seemed cryptic in their plays had come about in exactly this way, in response to a particular actor's performance. I imagined future performers cursing me for incomprehensible idiosyncrasies in the role.

Rehearsals proceeded in a mood of hysterical abandon. I don't recall playing any scene from beginning to end without the entire company, the stage manager and the director collapsing, tears rolling down our cheeks, emitting curious barking noises, like seals at feeding time. The more precise and grounded in reality the work became, the less control we were able to exercise over ourselves. This is normally ominous for a comedy ('The less funny the actors find it, the more the audience will,' runs the old adage), but once installed in Poppy Mitchell's costumes, and on her set, the anarchy was contained, and transferred to the auditorium, where it belonged.

Schippel was a *succès fou*, the first I'd ever known. It was a hot ticket. Again, it was fascinating to observe that before the notices appeared (this was really the first time I'd had *notices*, as opposed to comatose accounts of the performance by a reluctant gardening correspondent) the audiences had slowly warmed up by the first act, were chuckling in the second, and bellowing in the third. After the notices, which essentially said THIS PLAY IS FUNNY, they were chuckling in the foyer, roaring at the first couple of lines, and paralytic thereafter. The whole nature of the performance was transformed.

For me it was the thing every actor hopes for, a part you can play better than anyone else. The combination of temperament, physical endowments and personal readiness for the part is elusive. It comes maybe four or five times in a career. It's generally an ending, rather than a beginning, too, a sort of summary of what you can do up to that point. It is, therefore, very dangerous. People will want you to do it again; and again; and then suddenly, it seems they won't ever want to see you do it, or anything else, for the rest of their lives. Then they forget it, and you can start all over again. I bumped into David Burke. He'd seen the show, liked me, and said so. 'A word of advice,' he added. 'Take care. Having seen this, people will always think of you when they're casting an underwritten part. Don't do it. It's a mug's game.' I didn't.

The Traverse season ended with a new play of no great worth, during which I had my first row with a director. He'd directed it with obsessive attention to inflection and gesture, both of which he demonstrated. For the most part, we obeyed. Some of the cast had been rehearsing with him in London, and I hadn't seen a script until the morning of my first rehearsal, so I didn't have any clear image of the part or play. From our first seconds together he was imposing the tightest of straitjackets, and one was powerless to move. This went on for a couple of weeks, actors being adjusted like dolls in a shopwindow. We submitted, awed by his fanaticism and creatively castrated by the insistent drone of instructions. The dress rehearsal arrived. We performed the play, and sat waiting for notes. His face of thunder was oppressive. 'I have told you everything, everything. What is wrong? Where is the LIFE!' We took it on the jaw. Then he said, 'OK, we do it again. This time with LIFE.' It was midnight. 'No,' I said. 'No?' He gaped. 'No?' 'No,' I said. 'At least, I'm not. There would be *no point whatever*.' 'No point?' 'No. Look, the reason the play has no life is because we're imitating you.' I spoke slowly and loud, the way one does to small children and foreigners, which he was. 'It's not ours, we're puppets.' 'Everybody feel this?' Nobody denied it.

'What you say we do?' to me. 'I should do a very fast burlesque run, playing it for laughs. Tomorrow.' Eyes opened wide. 'FOR LAUGHS?' He was an Israeli. This was not part of his world-view. 'Everybody feel this?' They nodded. The bit they liked was 'tomorrow'. 'OK, we do it.' It was a great adventure to him. We did it, and it was an improvement but of course you can't undo three weeks' work in a romp. It was never right. On the first night, however, for some reason it worked. The audience roared with laughter (it *was* a comedy). At the interval, the director came backstage and screamed 'What are you doing to my play? You are *destroying* it!' The leading actress who at that time rejoiced in the name of Gracie Luck (she has since, sadly, changed it) said, quite calmly, 'Get out of my dressing room, you creep, and never let me see you again.' We didn't.

None the less, the play was revived, along with everything else, for the Edinburgh Festival. We played three different shows a day for three weeks. By the midnight show, it was very hard to know which play you were in. The audience seemed pretty confused too, as they tottered out at 2 a.m. One night I was mugged. I didn't care. I barely noticed. We sleepwalked through the last week.

Schippel was the uncontested hit of the season. We detached it from the repertory and started on our travels. First we went to Belfast, and then London. Belfast was a terrible shock. It was never a beautiful city, but this was a vision of hell. Every one of the wonderful bars we used to drink in had been blown up. The streets were lined with barbed wire. Every alleyway was chicken-netted and guarded by soldiers. You were frisked from head to foot in every shop. Armoured cars would suddenly pull up, soldiers would leap out scattering to every doorway, their guns cocked. A small group of them would surround a car, drill a hole in the window, fill it with foam, and then detonate it. A muffled boom, and it was dragged away. Throughout the performances, at regular intervals, one could hear the sound of explosions or gunfire. The audience remained imperturbable, while we quaked. We were the first mainland group to play in Belfast since the fighting began. I have never before or since experienced anything like their appetite for theatre, and especially for comedy. They ate us up passionately. It was so moving, their need, and the thought that our work, which can so easily seem like icing sugar, a flourish, an embellishment, could be so deeply, desperately, desired, was deeply moving.

After our last performance, the whole company was invited to the house of a friend of mine, a buddy from the old days, now an interviewer, and the subject of daily threats to his life. I sat with him and other friends, as they calmly described their ordinary lives. One told me without any emotion of how her uncle, a judge, whose offence had been to belong to a Catholic-Protestant Friendship League, was gunned down at breakfast, watched by his three-year-old daughter. As she spoke, a record of Schumann's *Fantasy in C* played in the background. Tears streamed uncontrollably down my face. 'Why don't you *leave*?' I said. 'Oh,' she shrugged, 'you know.'

We left for London the next day. This sobering reunion with Belfast, seven years after I'd first left it, seemed the completion of some kind of a cycle. I didn't return to Edinburgh. It was the last time I would live for any length of time out of London; the last time I would know a city in every detail and yet never feel a part of it. I had come to hate Edinburgh's noble, symmetrical greyness. Unfairly, I projected an inner emotional greyness of my own on to it; I bitterly resented its hypocritical trick of donning a party hat for the three gaudy weeks of the Festival, only to tear it off the morning after and be the stern dominie again. These feelings were little to do with Edinburgh, much to do with exhaustion. I had finally tired of acting, day in and day out. The first flush was over. My love of the theatre wasn't in the least diminished. In fact, Roy Marsden, Janet Amsden and I had maintained a seven-month symposium every lunchtime in Henderson's Salad Bar, adumbrating visions of a future theatre. We drank in each other's ideas and experience. I discovered Marx and Trotsky and the principles of hydraulics and the nature of folk-dancing; and everything seemed relevant to our dream of a theatre which would be celebratory and expressive and intellectually challenging. These were the dark days of Heath. The whole fabric of life seemed to be collapsing. I lay awake at night trying to resolve my feeling that theatre was a childish pursuit, of minority appeal, and a tinsel stepsister of the greater arts. One day, in the middle of the night, I sat bolt upright. 'I shall join the Workers' Revolutionary Party, and bring theatre to the factories.' Then I slept easily, the first time for many weeks. My resolve didn't survive the dawn. I was confused and emotionally drained. Acting had been feeding off my inner resources for two years without interruption. I had barely allowed myself to touch another human being in that time. Nun-like, I had kept myself pure for art. My purity was now turning sour.

After Belfast but before London, I blew the last of my patrimony on a trip to Rome. There, I rediscovered all my appetites, and returned sane and healthy.

Four

On the morning of the first day's rehearsal for *Schippel* in London, I went to consult a palmist. So sure was I that a cycle had come to an end, so flushed with new hope and health, that I wanted a pointer to the way ahead.

He examined the impression of my hand. 'You are about to embark on a new job which will bring you fame, fortune, new avenues of employment. It will start very soon . . . perhaps even . . . today.' He was absolutely right. We repeated the Edinburgh success in London. It was the same company, more or less the same space (the old Open Space Theatre in the Tottenham Court Road). Nothing was lost. On the first night, five minutes before the show was due to start, I discovered that the cleaners had mistakenly thrown away my monocle. I duly played the part without it, feeling quite naked. Then, in the middle of the love scene, my false moustache began to come adrift. As the audience began to notice, and before it fell off of its own accord, I took it between my thumb and my forefinger, tore it off, and in a heroic gesture, flung it into the wings. Round of applause. The next morning's notices were enthusiastic – not least for my moustache. In his review, Irving Wardle described me as one of the finest young character actors on the British stage. A few days later, the one agent that I'd set my heart on, Marina Martin, who'd turned me down when I first applied to her, phoned me and said, 'I was wrong. Please join us.' Up till now, I'd felt no need for an agent, but when I did, some intuition took me to her, where I've stayed ever since; which was more to my advantage than hers for many years. It would be some years yet before I earned a salary in the theatre which equalled what I'd earned in the Aldwych box office in 1968; except for the curious interlude of the transfer of *Schippel* into the West End as *The Plumber's Progress* under the substantial umbrella of Harry Secombe. Harry had come to the Open Space one night, filling it with himself and his laugh. Within days he'd bought the play and given us to understand that many of the original cast would be kept on; among them, me.

So Mir Bashir, the cheiromant, had not spoken with forked tongue after all. Just as he had said, from being a hardworking, unknown actor, I now had acclaim, an agent, work, and the prospect of a certain amount of money. It wasn't exactly a Cinderella story but it was a Great Leap Forward, a change of gear. It certainly proved the axiom that luck = opportunity + readiness; there was, too, a combination of adaptability and stubbornness that seemed effective. In the same way that I'd decided that the Drama Centre was the *only* school worth contemplating, I'd fixed on Marina Martin as the only agent I wanted. I refused to consider anyone else. But what luck to have been in Edinburgh at exactly the moment that Mike Ockrent was forming that particular remarkable group of people. If Roger Kemp, for example, hadn't given his extraordinary performance as Hicketier in *Schippel*, nothing more would have been heard of it. Again, what luck that the original Schippel proved to be so recalcitrant. What luck that Charles Marowitz should have come to the Traverse and booked the show for the Open Space.

This, and not that: the essence of luck. I had been its great beneficiary since the beginning, since, I suppose, writing to Laurence Olivier. I had somehow hit on *my* vein of luck with that impulsive gesture. I might otherwise still have been sending romances to Glamorgan public libraries, not doing it badly, perhaps, but getting nothing for nothing. So much in the theatre had come to me effortlessly. The needle was in the right groove.

Between the Open Space performances of *Schippel* and its subsequent apotheosis at the Prince of Wales Theatre, I played small theatres and small parts. The latter was not a good idea. I was peripheral to an all-star production of *The Doctor's Dilemma* at the Mermaid, my old stamping ground. The engagement was chiefly memorable for Bernard Miles thinking I was still in the box office and asking me to take some people round to the restaurant just before the curtain went up. And for my being off; that is, missing an entrance. It was a matinée, my dressing room was full of delightful people talking vivaciously and I didn't hear my cue. Eventually an increasingly insistent voice could be heard over the tannoy: 'Mr Callow, you are *off*!' I suddenly felt very ill indeed, rushed out of the dressing room, to run slap into Frank Thornton: 'Too late, old boy, too late.' And then James Villiers: 'Haha, haha, haha.' I stood foolishly in the wings, willing the play ten minutes back in time, then crawled away, a hollow feeling in my stomach, shame burning bright red on my brow. At the interval, I went to every member of the cast in turn. They were all very decent. 'Never mind, could happen to anyone, done it myself,' etcetera. Derek Godfrey was particularly magnanimous in view of the fact that Redpenny's non-appearance at a crucial moment had transformed him into the most heartless character on the English stage. Finally I came to an actress of a certain age 'who had not, in fact, been on stage at the time, and was not personally affected by my absence. She received my apologies generously. 'Not at all, darling,' she said, in the cut-glass accent that was always a surprise after the charladies she was usually called upon to play, 'It must be so much worse for you than it is for us. Because, after all' – a pitying little smile – 'when you come down to it, there can't be *any* excuse, *ever*, can there?'

She was absolutely right. The very least of one's professional obligations is to be on stage when one is supposed to be; and it is made quite clear that the stage-manager's calls are a courtesy: it is up to the actor to be following the show relay over the tannoy. The incident, and the grande dame's *ex cathedra* utterance, made me realize what a very different world of theatre I had strayed into. For me, it was the first time I hadn't been part of a group of equal responsibility and equal financial status. Redpenny is a small, purely functional role, and I had, sometimes subtly, sometimes explicitly, been made to feel it. What there was in the part, I had found in the week before rehearsals began. As for the company, it was divided between the known and the unknown. Fraternization was superficial. We, the unknown, somehow felt like juniors, like children. This feeling was enhanced by our having to understudy 'the principals'. Understudying is a soul-destroyer, unless, perhaps, you're covering a role, Othello, say, or Macbeth, that you want to play one day. The frustration stems from the fact that one understudies a performance, not a role. If the actor one is covering falls ill, and one has to go on for him, there is naturally and rightly no question of one giving one's own interpretation: it would throw all the other actors, who are quite nervous enough as it is. But what if one disagrees with Mr X's performance? The result is a horrible double-bind. One longs to play the part one has learned with such effort, and rehearsed once a week for the length of the run; on the other hand one has no chance of doing the part the way one really sees it. So one longs not to go on.

To the problem of understudying, there is no ready answer. It's essential that every actor be covered against illness. The moral pressure inside all of us against missing a performance is huge; to force actors to risk their health simply because if they don't play, the show can't go on, is monstrous. John Dexter has an admirable practice of rehearsing the main cast and the understudy casts alongside, sometimes getting the understudy cast to perform the play for 'the principals'. It's the upstairs-downstairs feeling that is so hateful. Understudies are indeed doing the principals a great service; taking a great weight off their minds. But they have a creative contribution to make which is on the whole subordinated to their cloning function.

So for small parts. These are always crucial in any play. They have a vital function in the narrative, they establish the social milieu in a way that nothing else does, they underpin the play with their own resonances. They are also much harder to play than large parts. Very often they have huge gaps, in which the concentration has to be sustained – two hours in the dressing room between appearances is deeply enervating; there's very little time in which to establish three-dimensional character; and if you blow your one speech, you have no opportunity to make up for it later. Above all, you have to come to the stage warmed up. Leading characters have a comfortable stretch in which to get the engine ticking over; the small-part player must be glowing from the first moment.

At Lincoln and Edinburgh, there really *had* been no small parts, because we mostly all played several; so the hierarchy of roles came as a novelty to me. That hierarchy, I saw, rested on an army of drones, who called themselves 'professionals'. To a certain actor, of a certain generation, Professionalism with a capital P was the ultimate criterion, as if it were the crowning achievement, instead of the bare minimum.

55

It was a stick with which to beat the young, the rowdy, and the trendy. The Method, Brecht, the RSC and the National with all their 'unnecessary' and 'wasteful' rehearsal time, were all clobbered.

The Professional learnt his lines, jotted down his moves in the margin and remembered them the next morning, knew the *trick* of this author or that, and had a store of business, inherited or observed from other actors, which would serve for any occasion. He liked to share a little joke with the director, then withdraw to the other side of the room and study his script, because he knew his place. He detested actors who monopolized the director's attention (unless they were the star, to whom different rules applied). He complained bitterly about actors who didn't know their lines and who changed their moves. His question was: 'Are you going to do that, love? Because, you see, it makes it awfully difficult for me to play my line if you're going to do yours that way.' He'd make this little speech within earshot of the director, to whom he'd appeal with his eyes, while favouring the offending actor with a slack and humourless smile. He wore a tweed jacket and grey flannels and a polo-neck jumper. Sometimes, exotically, this would be varied with a safari suit, khaki from head to toe, except of course, for his hush puppies, which were invariable.

Conversation is of other Pros, and especially, of their japes: X's outrageous behaviour in Barrow-in-Furness, the gag Y perpetrated at the Palace, Attercliff in '42. Never, ever, is there any mention of inspiration, audacity, originality, intensity of feeling. These are not thought to be the ingredients of theatre. What one goes to see are accomplishment, adroitness, cleverness. The satisfaction is in seeing the time-honoured craft put through its paces by well-known faces. It's comforting.

This is in no way to gainsay the skill, charm and warmth of so many Pros. But behind the voluntary servitude lies a resentment. Part of it is disappointment at not having become a star. The system is two-tiered, every star sitting atop a thousand Pros, all of whom without question came into 'the business' out of love and raving ambition. Then they were streamed, and found themselves in the Pro division. Besides the disappointment, there is about many Pros an unattractive combination of timidity and cynicism which points to a sense of having been cheated.

It was my first encounter with all of this. Immediately afterwards, waiting for *The Plumber's Progress* to start, I was back in my more natural hunting ground, the fringe, running up an overdraft. I worked at Verity Bargate's wonderful Soho Poly Theatre and Thelma Holt's Open Space in its last days in Tottenham Court Road. Timothy West, Martin Coveney and I, playing respectively a diner, his stomach, and a waiter, were on a cut of the box office, which, though sold out from beginning to end, made us nine pounds each. I also got Tim's cream jacket thrown in, as a kind of tip.

Then a friend suggested me for the lead in Gay Sweatshop's third production. I was deeply sceptical about the whole enterprise. Ghetto theatre, I said. What next? Plays by chartered accountants, about chartered accountants, for chartered accountants? I regarded gay liberation as shrill, exhibitionist and counter-productive. 'I don't see myself as A Homosexual,' I said to my boyfriend. 'I'm a human being first – one who just happens to prefer sleeping with men.' He was kind enough not to point out my self-oppression, and for that matter my self-delusion. He could have asked me if I was able to put my arm round him in public, whether my family knew this central fact of my life, whether I didn't feel that public acknowledgement of my proclivity would damage my chances of employment. He didn't; so I started to read the play in a hostile mood.

I knew at once that I must be in it. It was *Passing By* by Martin Sherman, a very simple story, funny and romantic, about two young men going to bed together, catching each other's hepatitis, recuperating together, and finally falling in love. At the end, they part. It's beautifully written. The character I was being asked to play is quirky, funny, emotional. But it wasn't that. It was that at no point did either of them say: 'Isn't it terrible being gay?' or 'I have this very intense relationship with my mother.' Mothers weren't mentioned – but nor was being gay, and that struck me as revolutionary. When had I ever seen any film or play about gay people, in which *homosexuality* was not the subject or the problem, as opposed to simply the condition of the protagonists? What images did we have of self-accepting, un-agonized, uncaricatured gay people? I remember – after a childhood spent combing world literature for examples with whom I could identify, paddling around in the murky waters of Tchaikovsky and Gide and Oscar Wilde (the gay saints: depressives, suicides, and jailbirds all), recoiling from the drag queens and psychotics of *Last Exit to Brooklyn*, thinking 'Is my life going to be like *that*?' – finally coming upon Christopher Hampton's *Total Eclipse*, how grateful I was that, desperate and unlovely people though Rimbaud and Verlaine sometimes were, they never spoke of their 'condition', never tried to analyse why they were as they were, but simply loved each other urgently, with every appearance of sexual and emotional satisfaction. But for every one of those, there were ten *Boys in the Band*, and a hundred Larry Graysons. At every possible opportunity one was reminded that one was a problem, or a freak, or doomed to a tragic end. Even in this oppressing society, that wasn't true – as I knew from my own life. The 20 per cent of gays, who in revolt against the oppression, had adopted defiant and outrageous lifestyles and gained a kind of acceptance – offering no ambiguity, they posed no threat – had monopolized the media.

Now here was Martin Sherman's quiet and funny play, telling it like it is. It overturned my life after a reading. Perhaps it would do the same for others. Playing it was, indeed, extraordinary. The tiny Almost Free, smallest of all the fringe theatres, was packed every day with men who had never seen anything like it before. They were deeply moved. It was a touching story; but it wasn't that. It was as if a secret that had been kept for too long were finally being told to people who knew it individually but had never seen it acknowledged. The quality of attention was transformed. It was their lives they were watching. For the first time since Belfast, I felt the energy coming *the other way*. Their appetite for the play was insatiable. Now surely here, I thought, is an essence of theatre and it's a political essence: the actors were acting, as it were, on behalf of the community; or a section of it, in this case. Us, not glittering away behind the footlights, but making common cause with the audience – showing them something of urgent interest. All theatre, in any case, I suddenly realized, is inevitably political. It *always* makes a statement, even if that statement is only: 'Isn't bourgeois life wonderful?'

From this time on, I knew that it would be impossible not to ask myself 'What is this play saying?' If I agreed to do the play, it would always be *I* who was saying: 'Listen to this play's statement.' How could I do that if I didn't believe it? This is surely the great difference between modern actors and their predecessors. They were prepared to be hired, for their skills to be put to whatever use the hirer required. They were *tabulae rasae*, 'artists', who were unconcerned with politics. But ours is a time for taking sides before it's too late.

For me, it was the closest I had come to playing myself. It was the first upset to my 'glory' theory of acting. That theory postulated that the actor's job was to go on making more and more extraordinary shapes, using a more and more varied palette: the actor as juggler, as magician, but also as weaver of spells and raiser of spirits; the actor as druid, dealing in images and archetypes; the actor as imitator, stealer of faces. What I had ignored, or avoided, was the actor as *himself*, member of the human race, fellow-sufferer, man in the street. Simple-mindedly, I had seen all the variations and colours as impersonal, external. I hadn't seen, or hadn't wanted to see, that an inner journey would produce another range of colours and resonances. I was playing only the right hand of the keyboard. Now I found the courage to open up the closely guarded secret places of myself. I had, as it were, found the left hand. Later (slow developer!) I discovered that you could play both hands simultaneously; and that was by far the best.

From Gay Sweatshop to *The Plumber's Progress*, there was a certain amount of culture shock to be endured. The production was by no means lavish, but by comparison with the budgets at the Almost Free (£3 a week; set £50) the enterprise seemed Babylonian. The lordly, giggling presence of Harry Secombe added a touch of unreality. As one walked down the street with him, he was stopped every five yards for an autograph or a giggle, both of which he dispensed unstintingly. He bought us meals, and cakes. He photographed us. He was a dear. Moreover, he was determined to play the part as it was written. He had the greatest respect for the play and wasn't interested in 'gooning' it. Several of us, at his insistence, remained from the original production. It was wonderful, a chance to improve what had already been good, with the stimulus of new people. But it didn't work out like that. If a thing is good in one medium, leave it there. If we'd just transferred the first production to a small theatre like the Duchess or the Mayfair, it would be running today. As it was, we were struggling to forget what had worked beautifully in a shoebox up the Tottenham Court Road, and find new solutions suitable to an ex-revue theatre in Coventry Street. In my innocence, I behaved appallingly to the actress playing opposite me. I kept telling her, helpfully, what her predecessor in the role had done. Finally, in the nicest possible way, she lost her temper. I saw her point immediately – but I was still in no man's land. Cecil seized the chance to improve the script. As so

59

often, however, the improvements were no improvement at all. The designer, Poppy Mitchell from the Traverse, had no budget to speak of. The central item of her Traverse design – a huge table which completely filled the playing area – looked like a coffee table on the vast width of the Prince of Wales stage.

Off we went for the tour: to the vast and now defunct Opera House, Manchester. Trying to get through to the gallery was like standing at the bottom of a mountain and trying to reach someone at the top. At the beginning of each performance you opened your ribs and didn't let them down till the end. By the time we got back to London, both of my sides were covered in bruises. The reception in Manchester was baffled, centring on the 'language' in the play: 'not words I expected to hear coming from Harry (Family Man) Secombe's lips', etc. Spirits were not high as we started previewing in London. A gala performance for the Variety Club of Great Britain was a mistake. Comedians are not generous laughers. Some of them came back stage and told Harry to stop all this acting nonsense and be himself. He stuck valiantly to his colours. The first night was of a piece with the run-up, with friends and loved ones laughing too much, and everybody else laughing too little. The reviews were unable to categorize the piece, admired individual performers, but wouldn't have sold a ticket to anyone but an avid connoisseur of Goons in German Expressionist masterpieces.

And so the run began. It lasted four and a half months, immeasurably longer than I'd ever played anything before. The first couple of weeks were an adventure, learning how to play the theatre, devising new business, joking with Harry. Then one began to notice that the audiences were really very poor indeed, and very odd. Mainly they consisted of Harry's fans. The actors who started the play off had the displeasing experience of acting through chatter and noisy consultation of programme notes ('Where is he?' you could clearly hear.) My lot was different. I came on after Harry's first exit, so they were already getting ready for the interval. Moreover, his exit line was a piece of 'language' which they weren't sure they'd heard correctly, so they would pass it among themselves for a few minutes ('Did he say "sod off"?'). Programme notes were again consulted, but no, they'd never heard of me, and as it became apparent that I was initiating another plot development, extreme restlessness set in. The second act was livelier, because I was on with Harry. Cries of advice would come from the stalls: 'Put one on 'im, Harry.' 'Knock 'is monocle out.'

When Priscilla Morgan descended daintily down a ladder into my arms, the cry was: 'Get 'em off, girl.' The advice always seemed to come from women in the front row, of indeterminate age or size, always wearing pebble glasses. When they laughed, it was a wonderful rich, dirty belly laugh. The audience would be at the stage door waiting for their boy at the end of the show to tell him they hadn't enjoyed it as much as the last thing he did – he was theirs, and they weren't going to stand by and watch him make a fool of himself in public. Sometimes they'd say something to me. Once someone said: 'See you at the Palladium next year, boyo.' I'm still hoping.

After the first couple of weeks, the novelty of all this wore off too. It became demoralizing. The show had, after all, in its former lives, been something of a hit. Now guaranteed laughs failed to materialize, and the more one tried, the more laughs one lost. At the time I was baffled. We all felt the same. One day I realized that what I was missing was the adrenalin, and trying to engender it by will. Once I realized that, I relaxed and some of the pleasure came back. One stopped trying to thrill the audience and just gave a good performance, as an end in itself. It worked and the last few weeks were really very enjoyable. It took another long West End run – twice as long, nine months in *The Beastly Beatitudes of Balthazar B.* – to go through all the same things, but this time to learn by them, and to observe exactly what the mechanism was. It wasn't, in fact, until the next show, that I knew I'd learned anything at all.

Harry became terribly ill – double pneumonia and bronchitis. On Wednesday night, his understudy went on; on Friday, *he* succumbed to influenza; and on Monday we arrived at the theatre to find that the show had closed on Saturday. That was the West End, that was.

That day I'd started rehearsing what was to have been a lunchtime play to keep me off the streets during the day. It now became my full-time employment. £10 a week, now, very generous for the fringe, but a nasty slump after £85 at the Prince of Wales. The play was Snoo Wilson's expressionist masterpiece *The Soul of the White Ant*. It's set in South Africa, and I played the small-time slob, Pieter de Groot. What amazed me was how much better I was acting than I had done before *The Plumber's Progress*, how much better than I had done in *The Plumber's Progress* only a week before. Growth occurs by stealth. I found that my use of the text was much more assured, more direct, and more varied. Instead of spreading one emotional or intellectual contact over a whole speech, I was differentiating line by line. How or when this development had occurred I didn't know, but I was sure that it had something to do with the length of the run, and the loss of adrenalin, which had forced me on to my real resources, which I was now able to use. John Gielgud said that had it not been for his work in Peter Brook's *Oedipus*, which he regarded as a failure, he would never have been able to play the headmaster in *Forty Years On*. Now I knew what he meant.

The Soul of the White Ant, enlarged, transferred to the Bush Theatre, for whom I then played, *inter alia*, Princess Anne, Geoff Capes and a fascist cricketer, in David Edgar's *Bloodsports*, and the Roman satirist Juvenal in his one-man show *Juvenalia*. I say 'his' one-man show because from the beginning, when Richard Quick had shown me the *Sixteen Satires* as we whizzed down the east coast of Scotland, touring *The Fantasticks*, we had seen the show as an act of justice for the embittered satirist. On his behalf, as it were, we hired the Bush Theatre so that he could at last get it off his chest: *it* being almost everything, a comprehensive denunciation of his Rome, and, if you chose, our England. There was no messing around with togas. He'd stepped straight out of his time capsule into Moss Bros – he was a gentleman, he knew how things were done – and down to the Bush, barely able to refrain from pouring it all out before he ever hit the stage. I was fascinated by the figure of the conservative romantic. We searched around in *The Satires* for something that he *liked*, for the man in repose. Finally we found it: an idyllic account of his country villa (which he'd bought after finally receiving a government stipend, and after which all the sting goes out of the satires) in which he describes one of his servant boys a little over-lingeringly, with a semi-erotic paternalism which is at the heart of his kind of conservatism: the overgrown schoolboy who idealizes innocence above all, because he himself could never really cope with adulthood. The misogyny which stems from this state of mind is more searingly represented in Juvenal than anywhere in world literature. Playing him, I took Evelyn Waugh for my model, but listened to records of Lenny Bruce. Juvenal's satiric technique is very like Bruce's, the evocation of surreal visions, the sudden summary with a trenchant phrase, the underlying sense of injustice. The mix of first-century Rome, thirties England and sixties USA was stimulating. It was of course deeply offensive, but democratically so. No one escapes Juvenal's lash: blacks, queers, women, toffs, navvies, *women*, Greeks (special hatred reserved for these), emperors, WOMEN, eunuchs. It's somewhat the world of *Private Eye*. I found it curiously touching. As I sat in my dressing room, during the longest five minutes in the world, the five minutes before a one-man show hits the stage (you think: 'Please let there be a bomb scare. Please nobody have bought tickets'), I used to stare at a photograph of a 1914–18 Tommy which I'd found in some junk shop, imagining him to have been killed at the Somme, and lament the useless betrayal of innocent youth. I'd got the left-hand, right-hand principle licked now. The soldier gave me my chord.

I've done three one-man performances now. It's wonderful and terrible for the same reason: everything depends on you. What's no fun at all, though, is that in rehearsal, all the notes are for you, too. After a runthrough, one listens resentfully to the never-ending stream of criticisms thinking, absurdly, what about the others? Don't they get any notes? Oh well, if I'm as bad as all that, perhaps we'd better cancel the show – and so on. Directing a one-man show, contrary to popular imaginings, is not easy: a severe test of tact, humour and pacing. On the other hand, it's very cheap if you take the company out to lunch. Simon Stokes passed all tests – tact, pacing, and lunch – with flying colours.

The project was deeply personal for me and the adaptor, Richard Quick. We'd nursed it for three years, hawking it round every unlikely place, until finally the Bush agreed to do it as part of a package including the David Edgar play. They never expected to break even, though in view of the smallish cast, they didn't expect to lose, either. In fact, they made a few bob, and at the end of the run, they not only replaced my electric razor which had been stolen, they gave me a small bonus, which was unheard of. It's things like *that* that move one deeply, not the *Evening Standard* Award. (I imagine. I'll know for sure when I get one.) The first night was an emotional occasion. I'm afraid Richard Quick and I got startlingly drunk in my flat on Black Russians. The party only broke up when I started to sing Russian songs at three o'clock in the morning. The neighbours – music lovers – complained bitterly, and we subsided into alcoholic stupor. The next morning (two hours later) Richard was up getting the newspapers. Bingo! The review that meant the most to me was the one which said: 'The best one-man show since MacLiammóir's *Importance of Being Oscar*.'

Five

While I was at the Bush, my agent phoned, breathless with the news that a certain well-known director wanted me to play the lead in a 'Play for Today' on the television. This was *it*: the breakthrough we'd all been waiting for. I went down to Thames Television's London office, where I was greeted with unusual warmth. 'I'm *so* glad to meet you. I saw your performance in *The Soul of the White Ant*. I thought it was quite remarkable, marvellous. I think you're a wonderful actor, a *great* actor. Has Lindsay Anderson seen your work? No? I'll phone him, god, you are good. I'm not just saying it because you're here – I've been saying it all morning. Haven't I?' He turned to the casting directors, who nodded gravely. 'I know you're going to be excited by this play, it's a marvellous play, by simply the best writer on television. Your part – it's fantastic, and I couldn't for the life of me think who could play it, and then, coming down the motorway, I suddenly realized that *you* were the only person who could really pull it off. It's not the lead – in fact in terms of lines it's really quite small – in fact, um, he doesn't actually *have* any lines – but oh, it's a marvellous scene – just the one scene, in fact, but what a scene! Let me tell you about it. You're sitting watching the television – in longshot, there's somebody else talking in the foreground – and you're a policeman and – this is wonderful, you'll love this – you're watching *Police Five*! What d'you think? Isn't that *sensational*?' I quickly adjusted my horizons, and agreed that it was, indeed, remarkable. After all, I thought, it'll be a few bob which I could well use.

I never heard from him again. Not, that is, until eight weeks later, when he phoned to tell me not to worry that he hadn't been in touch, he'd given the part of the policeman to someone else, but he was now thinking of me for another part, not quite so juicy, but *very* interesting. I said, 'I'm awfully sorry, I've accepted another job.' A terrible silence on the other end. 'Who with?' 'Joint Stock.' 'Well sod you,' he said, and rang off.

It was David Hare who had asked me to join the company. He too had seen *The Soul of the White Ant* (which he'd just taken on a hilarious tour of Holland, where the audiences invariably gave us standing ovations. As they generally consisted of no more than six or seven people, this somehow felt more like a reproach than an accolade) but instead of the TV man's hyperbole, Hare had outlined an approach to work that interested me strangely.

Joint Stock had been founded by Bill Gaskill, Max Stafford-Clark and Hare to try to break the mould of the relationship between the writer and the theatre group. There would be improvisations, explorations and exercises with the group and the writer, who would, after the workshop period, go away and write the play. It would then be rehearsed in the usual manner. *The Speakers*, from Heathcote Williams's book, had been the first fruit of the work; a great success. It was followed by *Yesterday's Men*, in which the group, after an inconclusive attempt during the workshop to make a piece about the life of a particular community, turned its attention to mercenaries, expanding the working method to include interviews with people involved with every aspect of the question. Next had come *Fanshen*, the company's greatest achievement, written, of course, by Hare.

What he said next fascinated me most. 'We're trying to break away from the dishonesty of rehearsals where the actors go to the pub and slag the director off behind his back, while he and the writer sit and bitch about the actors. This is both dishonest and counterproductive. What we want is openness and maturity from everyone.' I signed up on the spot.

The project was a kind of history play which Tony Bicât was going to write. The same group of characters would be shown over the three acts evolving historically. Act One: the thirties; Act Two: the seventies; Act Three: the nineties. It wasn't the same person, merely the character type. What would X, a thirties poet blinded in the Civil War, be in the seventies, and the nineties? My character, for example, Stalin's emissary in the first act, became a Lord Goodman figure in the second. We used the Joint Stock apparatus. We interviewed city editors, we researched thirties poets, we improvised, we invented. The first act characters had been established by Bicât, the rest was open. Hare guided and elucidated up to a point; but one of the features of this method is that one simply never knows what it'll throw up. It moved into strange areas. We were never quite sure what the work was about, though there was no lack of invention.

Hare had got together a feisty group, including a number of romantic individualists, a Marxist, an anarchist and an EST Graduate. When we came to projecting the future, our differences became a problem, because we simply couldn't agree. One day, Hare made us all sit down and say in turn what we thought we would be doing in 1990. The responses varied from living on a boat, to getting married again, to forming a revolutionary party. I just said: 'Acting,' because I couldn't foresee any future which wouldn't require actors, and in which people would not be impelled to become actors. Hare's vision was concretely apocalyptic: 'There will be some form of violent revolution, because it is inconceivable that the majority of people will continue to live in the misery in which they find themselves.' Eventually we hammered something out. Bicât was present at all the rehearsals, suggesting exercises and writing down whatever we produced. He then went away, as we all did. Some of us languished unemployed (a snag of the Joint Stock method). Others went on a European tour of the revived *Speakers*. It was quite something. *The Speakers* is a free-form piece, moving from public scenes in Hyde Park, to private scenes in the speakers' homes, or Rowton House, or wherever. The audience perambulates, being invited to heckle the speakers. It was a huge success wherever we went in Europe: Belgrade, Zagreb (where a Yugoslav policeman interrupted a character who was about to light up a cigarette, to be told, in character of course, to fuck off, at which the audience applauded) and Hamburg (where the ending, in which two London bobbies clear the audience out of the hall, was fiercely resented). It all held together, however, until – Dublin. In Dublin, everything changed.

We were booked for a midnight spot at the Abbey, as part of the Dublin Festival. That means that most of the audience had been drinking since 11 a.m., just for a start. We, however, were caught up in the cross-currents of something much bigger. We had decided to do the show with the iron safety curtain down and the audience on stage with us, our great scaffolding lighting tower slap in the centre. So at ten past twelve, we started. Immediately we were heckled as we had never been heckled before: filibustering was more like it. Eventually, when it was impossible to continue or engage the hecklers in any kind of dialogue, I said to one of them, as my lower-middle-class Socialist Party of Great Britain speaker, 'OK, mate, you seem to have a lot to say for yourself, why don't you come up 'ere and tell us all about it.' He clambered up on to the box, opened his mouth, was unable to orate, so said, 'Oh fuck off the lot of youse, you're all a loud of cunts.' Ironic applause, and I was able to continue. The speaker to my left had hit on the same ploy. His heckler, however, similarly silenced by standing on the box, unzipped his fly and started to urinate on the stage. Mild cries of 'shame' and much mirth. Suddenly, there was an irruption on the other side of the audience. 'That's the bastard that killed Frank Stagg!' A tiny white-haired gentleman was suddenly surrounded by a posse of tough-looking men, all from the audience. It was Mr O'Dalaigh, the President of the Republic, on an incognito visit, and the posse were his bodyguard. Swiftly, he was removed from the theatre. His accusers, who seemed to be connected with our filibusterers, were jostled by remnants of the bodyguard, to cries of 'Shame, let them alone, you pigs,' and so on.

Theatre in Dublin has to put up with a lot of stiff competition from life.

We speakers were valiantly droning on through all this. At last the moment came for the switch from public to private scenes. The lights change, and the focus is on Van Dijn, the tattooed speaker and his thirteen-year-old helpmate. These scenes, which had commanded rapt attention all over Europe, the audience climbing over each other to be closer to the actors, peering over our shoulders and looking into our nostrils, were actually *heckled* by the Dublin audience, or that element of it clearly bent on disrupting the performance. We ploughed on. Then they hit on a new ploy. In the dark portion of the stage, three men climbed up on to the lighting tower and started swaying it back and forward. If it collapsed, which it was in grave danger of doing, it could easily kill people, not to mention the conflagration that would immediately ensue. The theatre manager was popping about, looking desperately anxious. He beckoned to me. I was the Equity deputy. 'What do you think we should do?' I wasn't sure. I thought that if we could contain the situation we should continue. I hadn't been able to speak to all the actors. I knew that some of them, like me, were frightened by the ugliness of the mood in the audience, but others were angry and defiant. The men had been dragged off the tower, which was now stable, but the uproar, which showed no signs of abating, was impossible to act through. One could hear bottles being broken, and the snarls of angry men. I leapt on to a box and screamed for silence which, unaccountably, fell. 'We are workers,' I said, improbably. 'Like any other workers –' I suppose I thought the disrupters were the Red Brigade or some Irish equivalent – 'we must have proper working conditions. We're not getting them. If you want

67

us to continue, you must give us a fair hearing. It's up to you.' Total silence. I stepped down. The moment my shoe touched the ground, all hell broke loose. We left the stage. The manager came to see us in the dressing room. 'Of course, there's no question of the show carrying on. But some of the audience are asking if you'll talk to them, and explain your decision.' We did, and there followed a most extraordinary discussion. On the way to the stage, I said to the Abbey's Artistic Director, the enchanting Tomás McAnna, 'Sorry about all this.' 'Oh don't worry,' he exclaimed, 'this is the Abbey. We're used to riots here.'

The audience, now sitting in the stalls, were certainly in combative mood. There was no hint of an apology, nor much sympathy. Clearly the stage was regarded as a gladiatorial arena. If you didn't like the heat, you should stay out of the kitchen. Their underlying assumption about the relationship of the audience to the actors seemed to be that a state of suspended hostility was the norm, and that by varying the rules and inviting participation we must expect aggression. They were particularly adamant that you couldn't only vary *some* of the rules: one couldn't say 'Participate in some scenes, but not in others.' I could see the force of that, though it had never bothered anyone else in any other part of the world. They had seemed to regard theatre as a game, and what fun it was to be allowed to join in, from time to time. But Dublin clearly regarded theatre as a form of unarmed combat, in which only the fittest survived.

There's no getting away from the fact that theatre contains an element of hostility. Every actor knows that. Standing on the stage is an aggressive act. It says: Look at *me*. Listen to *me*. It says: I'm interesting, I'm talented, I'm remarkable. Oh yeah? says the audience. You'd better prove it – why should you be up there instead of me? Is it mere thespian paranoia to feel that everybody in the world wants to be an actor and secretly resents the lucky few who make it? Certainly, the audience in the theatre is not far from the audience in the Big Top watching the funambulist, thrilled by the risk he's taking, but unconsciously longing for him to fall. At the very least, the fact that he *might* fall is a large part of their enjoyment.

The story made the Dublin front pages the next day. From then on, the audiences were unnaturally well behaved, lobotomized. We were lucky to get a heckle at all. The element of danger essential to *any* performance was no longer there. So I suppose it is a matter of degree. We do want to have our cake and eat it. We were saying: So much danger, no more. And *we* say how much.

There were no riots when we played in London. I however received a great lesson from Bill Gaskill who directed the revival. Rehearsals before the tour had proceeded very smoothly. Most of the answers to most of the questions were already known. I was playing seven characters, and the essential requirement was to differentiate them, which is most easily done with accents, which are specific both geographically and in terms of class. Where would the English actor be without his repertory of accents? They can convey an enormous amount of information in the minimum of time, and they immediately give you a shape and an energy. Three-line parts become someone, from somewhere, with a history and expectations. There are dangers, of course: some accents are inherently funny to a metropolitan audience, while others make 'A Point'. I was never allowed to use the Belfast accent of which I was so proud because it immediately became a political statement. The rule, apart from these exceptions, is always to be specific and accurate. Anyway, for me *The Speakers* was almost an accents audition. One of my characters was an old wino called Bolling who queues for admission to Rowton House, but is denied it because of his bed-wetting record. The situation and even the man's name are inherently comic, so I produced a curious adenoidal old gargoyle for the occasion. This turn became something of a rehearsal favourite, and on tour grew more curlicues. When we were about to open in London, we did a light run through, to find new positions and so on. We came to Bolling, whom I touched in lightly but probably quite broadly, too. 'For Christ's sake,' said Gaskill, really angry, 'how much longer are you going to patronize that man?' 'I, um, um.' 'He's going to have to sleep in the streets. Do you realize what that means? He may die.' 'Right,' I said, suddenly blushing.

It seems strange, but I'd never really thought about my duty to the character. It's an ugly sight to see an actor use the character (who after all, represents someone, something, from life) to entertain or to divert the audience. I'd been doing it all my acting life.

We went straight from the tour to *Devil's Island*. One member of the original workshop objected to the way the play had turned out, as he was perfectly entitled to do, so with one new actor we went into rehearsal. Hare's rehearsal technique is very swift and to the point. Unlike the two other founder-directors of Joint Stock, he doesn't

69

favour exercises or long discussions. When a crisis arose, he'd hold a quick pow-wow, the aim of which was action. Once this was decided on, it was put into effect, pronto. He was ruthless with us as actors, deploying his satiric tongue to erase the enemy, generalization. Overacting, whether actual or incipient, he regarded with dread. He liked to see results. Having no theory of acting, he dealt directly with what he saw before him, and was tireless in fine adjustments. Up a point this, down a point that. He was equally painstaking and ruthless with writer and designer. The script was rewritten daily, he couldn't have demanded more of the designer if we'd been doing it for the Metropolitan Opera House, instead of a tour of small regional art centres.

At the end of the whole Joint Stock episode, I came to the conclusion that what it had been all about was standards. If any one person embodied that ideal, it was Hare.

In many ways, though, this rehearsal period was uncharacteristic of the work. The preceding workshop had been more typical. The research and interviews with 'real people', which was so characteristic a part of the process, was gone into in some depth, and the political perspective was the authentic Joint Stock one. The material, however, was so idiosyncratic, so much part of Tony Bicât's fish-eye view of the world, that many of the procedures simply didn't apply.

The national tour was a triumphal progress, delighting students on campuses everywhere. At Nottingham we performed at midnight in the Playhouse to a largely Equity audience, and had our awakening. Metropolitan audiences were clearly not going to like it. They didn't. And that was that.

I was (nevertheless!) asked to stay with Joint Stock as part of the new permanent ensemble. The company was at a crossroads. *Fanshen* had changed everybody's lives in almost every way. The experience of making the play had forced all the participants to question every aspect of their lives, and above all their theatre practice. It was impossible, the group had felt, to make a play about a fundamental revolution in day-to-day living without applying those ideas to the work itself. What were the economic relations within the group? Who, in the chain of command, needed whom? What was the purpose of theatre? How should the nature of the work be affected by the political perspective of the performers? William Hinton's account of the effect of the revolution on one village had been a revelation of how change could and should penetrate the daily life of every section of society. Maoism seemed a radical alternative to the centralist Bolshevik tradition which most left-wing theory embraced. Above all, the *form* of the Chinese revolution had seemed of direct relevance; the constant questioning and above all self-questioning seemed directly applicable to the rehearsal process. Moreover, a praxis had evolved during the rehearsal period which seemed to point to an approach to all plays: namely, the articulation of the political point of every scene into a slogan which the scene then exemplified. The work on *Fanshen* demanded a reformulation of the aims and structure of the group.

In a word, the group regarded itself as *Fanshened* – turned around, its whole way of thinking transformed.

Arising from this intellectual and, so to speak, spiritual, confidence, there was a feeling that the work should be established on a permanent, year-round basis. Hitherto each project had been convened separately, generally originating with its designated director. Economically speaking, it was highly inconvenient; and artistically, there was no continuity. Despite the organizational and administrative burden which would obviously multiply, a permanent group seemed an inevitable development.

Bill Gaskill and Max Stafford-Clark then, by an unavoidably painful process, gathered together a group, drawn from all the previous companies. Euphoria reigned at first. We would form ourselves into a collective: of course. What decision could be taken that didn't affect us all? Fine: we would take all decisions. The old board voluntarily disbanded, offering itself in an advisory capacity should the need arise. Budgets would be submitted to the whole group for approval. Minutes would be kept by members of the group in rotation, and the chair would rotate too. 'The group' consisted of everyone who worked for it, stage managers, lighting, designers, actors, administrator, directors. After heated discussion, it was agreed to appoint Max as Artistic Director, though on the strict understanding, we solemnly insisted, that the job simply meant executor of the will of the group. We paid ourselves (the phrase 'paid ourselves' had a fine ring to it, at first) equal salaries, and those who were employed part-time, i.e. directors and designers, were paid on a rate computed from multiples of that (two weeks' preparation, four weeks' work, two weeks' maintaining the show equalled eight times the company wage). In reality, however, there was no equality, because the 'collective' were contracted 52 weeks a year and could earn nothing to supplement our quite meagre earnings, whereas these designers could and did go where they liked and earn vast fortunes. Moreover, in the nature of the thing, there was no equality of authority in the group. Bill and the designer Hayden Griffin, for example, were internationally famous in their spheres. The grant we had from the Arts Council to a large extent depended on their continued participation. If they disagreed with a decision they could say, 'Well that's it, I'm leaving.' We needed them more than they needed us (who depends on whom? as *Fanshen* said), and that's almost a definition of inequality.

There was, too, the question of personal authority. None of us could hope to stand up to Bill Gaskill on this level. At once oracular and mischievous, dictatorial and dialectical, he would alternate delphic pronouncements with professions of child-like ignorance: 'I don't understand.' A slightly frosty Socrates, he would relentlessly ask 'Why?' When challenged himself in the same way, he would lapse into silence, of which he is the master. Minutes would elapse as he sat there, his head tilted slightly skywards, eyes glazed dreamily, tiny popping sounds emanating from his closed lips. Sometimes it seemed as if he would never speak again. Then a brief dogmatic phrase, the burden of which was: 'Because I say so.' Alarming as these silences were, the warmth of his occasional bursts of approval was overwhelming. Whether he was present or not, Bill loomed over the whole life of the collective.

We were, after all, beginners. We struggled to master the difficult art of meetings. Never could it be said of us, as it was of another theatre collective: 'Wonderful meetings, terrible shows.' It soon transpired that there were those who could take minutes and there were those who decidedly could not; similarly, chairing the meeting proved to be an elusive talent. It got better, but by that time it was clear that the power didn't reside in the meetings at all. Of course, there was much more to it than that. There was publicity and bookstalls and flags and decisions about touring dates and so on, all of which were pursued enthusiastically by those to whom such things are interesting – me, for one. But in the crucial sphere, the artistic, the meetings barely impinged at all. *Fanshening* had not occurred. The work was uniquely interesting and rewarding; but we had not found a praxis – and the position of the director remained the traditional one.

Our first project, initiated by Gaskill, was *A Mad World My Masters*. He had always been interested in Jacobean City Comedy, and wondered if a modern equivalent could be found which would be interspersed with scenes from Middleton. Barrie Keeffe was invited to write the modern version with us. We had a hilarious and fascinating workshop period. Gaskill is a master of improvisational work, and has a special interest in masks and *commedia* techniques. He brought all his wisdom to bear on the exercises which covered an enormous range: exercises of character, of conning, of costume, of home-made masks (I *still* couldn't work with the damn things). We ransacked local newpapers for accounts of confidence tricks. We brought impersonations of people we knew. (Bill had the idea that basing characters on actual people was very rich. I couldn't agree with him more: I'd been doing it all my acting life.) Friends of friends would come and show us conjuring tricks, or Find The Lady routines.

At one point we read the Middleton original. Bill was disgusted by our lack of feeling for the text, and the idea of paralleling the modern with the Jacobean was abandoned. Instead he proposed a kind of modern *Canterbury Tales*, with a group of characters who were of our times, and could only be of our time. Our list included trade unionist, gossip columnist, hippy, and so on. Barrie fixed most of the interviews. One simply met one's victim, plied him with questions, and then reported back to the group in character, as the victim. They would then quiz one. It was, like the rest of the work, richly entertaining. Barrie sat quietly watching, taking notes.

Six weeks later he'd produced the funniest new play I've ever read, which somehow miraculously combined all our work – everything that we'd done. I doubt if an exercise hadn't somehow found its way into the play – with a plot of his own invention, in a whole which was distinctly Jacobean *and* a gallery of modern rogues right across the class board. He'd written a character for each of us which was based on something we'd improvised. My old Latin teacher had somehow become a multi-phobic, royalist, Angela Rippon-obsessed insurance magnate. It was the Joint Stock method in all its aspects at its best. But it wasn't *Fanshen*.

We started trying to rehearse it as if it was. We tried to find a political slogan for every scene. THE WORKING CLASS IS FORCED BY CAPITALISM TO TURN TO CRIME was a caption suggested for a scene in which a gang of inveterate East End con men met to discuss their plans. Even punctuating every line with the slogan made little odds. It was impossible. Who-depends-on-whom? questions were of little avail. Status games had more value, but everybody's status in the play was so clear that they were really unnecessary. It became increasingly obvious that it was a play of broad comic gestures and above all of bravura stylized language.

Bill became restless. Finally we had a meeting at which he confessed that it seemed to require a kind of production which he was not willing and perhaps not able to do, a 'Tyrone Guthrie or Franco Zeffirelli sort of thing'. He also had doubts about the play: was it a Joint Stock play? Were we approaching it as a Joint Stock company, or just as an *ad hoc* group might? He'd lain awake for nights worrying about these things; now, in the *Fanshen* spirit, he was bringing it to us. We sympathized, and said that he should have told us earlier. After all, the whole point of the group was that problems were everybody's problems. I admired Bill for his frankness. He's absolute in his approach to things: it's his glory. He asks questions relentlessly and won't be fobbed off. If he's dissatisfied with something, he withdraws from it, however grand, important or lucrative it might be. Now he was refusing to pretend that he was satisfied with this play, or with the rehearsals.

I, on the other hand, was deeply satisfied with it, and longing to play Claughton, *my* part, the part of a lifetime. This was profoundly *un*fanshened of me. Well, I *hadn't* been fanshened, that was all there was to it. I also felt that the appetite of the actors for their roles was of paramount importance. Whatever our political objectives, we couldn't possibly think it more radical to produce boring theatre than lively theatre. Could we? I didn't say any of these things, which was again very unfanshened of me. I felt that the mood of the meeting was against it, so I shut up. Later I became much more vocal in our counsels; now I submitted to the plan, which was to tell Barrie to re-write the play, sharpening the political content. Several actors seized the opportunity of putting in for this or that. Gillian Barge was bored to death with playing another middle-class misery, so the character was dropped. Many suggestions were made, some of them improvements. Barrie duly wrote it all down, and went off again. We filled in the gap with working on Shakespeare texts and having theoretical arguments; Bill and I mostly. We argued especially about character. It was my deep conviction that all acting is rooted in character. It was a semi-Stanislavskian point of view, but mainly derived from the misery that I experienced as an actor until I had a firm grip on who I was in the play. Bill countered by saying that character was a bourgeois concept based on identification. He said that for him who a character was was of no interest, only what he did. These discussions drove me back to the *Messingkauf Dialogues* of Brecht, which I now began to understand for the first time. If a play, says Brecht, is a report on an event, the audience only needs to know as much about the characters of the play as makes the event clear. I could see the force of that but I knew in my heart exactly what kind of performances I liked to see. I had been moved when Bill had talked to me months before, in a hotel room in Zagreb as we swigged whisky halfway through the *Speakers* tour, about working with Edith Evans: 'It was like being in the presence of a force of nature. Waves and waves of warmth came from her as she rehearsed, a sea of warmth.' '*That's* what I want to see!' I cried, 'that's what we should be striving for as actors.' 'No,' Bill said, 'it's not possible any more.' 'Why?' 'The conditions for what we call great acting no longer exist.' I didn't say anything, but I couldn't accept it. If it was good, we must try to do it. I resisted his historical fatalism. Behind it I detected an almost romantic despair at the prospect of ever seeing extraordinary acting again. Politically speaking, of course, the sort of rampant individualism that great acting represents was anathema to him, and his great effort then was – and has been for the last many years – to attempt to discover a truly collective style of performance. I was never wholly convinced, however, that his heart was in it. Predictably, of course, when I spoke of my admiration for Laughton's work, he roared with laughter till the tears ran into his beard. 'Laughton!!' he hollered. If only I had read Brecht's panegyric of him at that time! It wouldn't have made any difference as far as Bill was concerned, from now on I was Ben Greet re-incarnated.

These discussions were exhilarating – the first time I'd encountered a rival theory of acting to the one that I'd been brought up on. The Drama Centre stood at the opposite pole to Brecht. I wasn't sure at all that I was a 100 per cent Stanislavsky man but I began to realize that for me a character must be a living thing, with its roots deep in me, or it was nothing.

In due course, the play arrived and the discussions stopped. We had three weeks left out of the original eight, so we had to get straight to work. Not before Bill delivered a bombshell, however. 'I think it's too boring for everyone to play the characters they've improvised. I think we should cast votes to determine who's to play what, with only one rule: no one can play the character they were going to in the first place.' I felt like crying. I saw the role of my life vanish before my eyes. 'If Joint Stock means anything, it must mean constant challenge. It's all too predictable what everyone will do with the cast as it stands. And besides, I can't bear the idea of directing Will Knightley as *another* Cockney wide-boy.' What he could or could not bear the thought of at that moment was not of surpassing interest to me, but I saw the force of his argument about challenge. Eventually, after a number of re-counts, I was elected to play Sayers, the monomaniacal copper who devotes his life to protecting Claughton. The part had been David Rintoul's. I'd never contemplated playing him for a moment. I wasn't bitter – it was a wonderful part – and I enjoyed playing him as much as anything I've ever done. But marrying a wonderful girl is not the same as first love.

Rehearsals were excruciating. Bill moved into top gear. His overriding concern was language – rightly, it was difficult, *wonderful*, difficult stuff, calling for classical breathing and phrasing and attack. But the meditative experimenter of the workshop became a Toscanini-like martinet the moment we got on the floor. 'Again. Again. Can't you *hear* it? No, not *that* operative word.' For me, he reserved his most withering sarcasm. 'Is it your intention to play *every* scene like PC Plod?' Once he lost his temper: 'Oh I'm so sick to death of your pathetic fart-arsed excuses for your own pathetic inadequacy.' After that we didn't speak to each other for a week. Then one day he said: 'Pick up those chickens when you leave the stage.' 'Why,' I asked tersely. The character had no possible reason for doing so, indeed every reason for not doing so. 'Poetic image,' he said gnomically. Snatching up the poultry, I thought to myself: 'And what, had you asked me the question, and I'd replied "Poetic Image", would your response have been?' The injustice of it all.

It *was* unjust. His whole manner during these three weeks was to me indefensible. The kind of tension that charged the rehearsal period destroys any creativity, whatever its gains in proficiency. Now, I would walk out. Then, I stewed in misery and self-doubt. No other worker in any other sphere would put up with it. They'd strike. Happily, all this is becoming a thing of the past. The Josef von Sternberg approach is on its last legs, not voluntarily, of course, but because of the increased rights of the actor. The final argument against it – never mind human dignity – is that the work is not better for it. Unless the actors are freely, creatively engaged in the work, it will be a dead thing. An efficient machine, perhaps, but never a living work of art.

It seemed to me that if anything were against the spirit of Joint Stock it was this old-fashioned assertion of direct supremacy. I raised the matter, no doubt somewhat over-emotionally, at meetings. My objections were minuted and circulated and presumably read by Bill, but nothing was ever done about it. The play was a hit, what was I complaining about? There were no doubt faults on both sides, the reasoning went, but what rehearsal period would ever be free of that? I wasn't claiming faultlessness; what I was attacking was the director's right to call the shots, to impose *his* mood, to exploit his crucial position in the process to behave badly. As our year and a half wore on, I returned to the fray again and again. Joint Stock, contrary to its aims and structure, was a directocracy. Again and again I asked the question: What is Joint Stock? What does it stand for? The most common reply – a way of working with writers – didn't seem to me an adequate basis for a permanent group. We had practice, I claimed, but no theory, and therefore nothing central to which to relate the work, and no higher appeal against the will of any particular individual. On what were we united? Not politics, for sure. We were all of a leftward inclination, but the range embraced by that was a source of division rather than unity: libertarian, anarchist, Marxist, Maoist, parliamentary democratic, I R A. We even had a full-blown anarcho-syndicalist. The fact was, there was no reason for us to have anything in common. We'd been chosen on the basis of the appeal our work had to Bill and Max. How else would they choose? But then to say, now run your own lives, was extraordinary. None of us thought so at the time, me least of all, but as the year rolled on, this paradox became more and more obtrusive.

The answer to the conundrum was, in fact, simple: Joint Stock stood for the taste of its directors. The Joint Stock style was the Bill Gaskill style, the Max Stafford-Clark style. This style didn't stem from a political position or even an aesthetic theory: it was just their taste, what they liked to see. Well, that's fine, that is in fact the only way to make theatre of any value. Noël Coward, wonderfully terse, said: 'Do what pleases you, and if it doesn't please the public, get out of show business.' But what was all this nonsense about a collective? By far the largest group within the collective were actors, but did they have any say in the style of the productions? Just let them try. And the style of the productions *was* the productions. So once again, just as in any other, non-collective, unfanshened company, those who stood on the stage were fulfilling the will of someone else, for reasons of which they were not altogether sure. To be fair, many of the group shared the theatrical taste of Bill and Max. I happened not to. But was it right that the first question one had to ask anyone who was going to join Joint Stock was: Do you share Max and Bill's taste? Of course no one did ask but they should have. It would have been more honest.

On and on I raved in this vein. Most of the group found the whole issue irrelevant. They were grateful to be associated with work of such quality. And indeed, the work was of a very high standard – technically, in terms of design, in the polish of the company work – and that was due entirely to the directors, who were not in the business of slumming. That, as I said of David Hare, was finally the great distinguishing feature of the work. We never really had the great aesthetic political debate about whether 'polish' in that sense wasn't bourgeois, making the play into an *objet d'art* instead of a vital communication. We couldn't have that discussion, because we had no framework of ideas. When push really came to shove, the directors' final recourse to any challenge was: 'Because I say so.' Not good enough, I maintained.

Through all this debate (I exaggerate its importance in other people's lives – it was only in mine that it had assumed such monumental proportions) the work continued. It was a tough and demanding life at all times. Not only were we playing every night and doing the workshop of the next play – Brenton's *Epsom Downs* – by day, we were also planning our approach to a larger audience, and hence a larger building. We hit on the Round House, that irresistible engine-cleaning shed in Chalk Farm which had, siren-like, drawn a procession of intrepid theatre workers, from Arnold Wesker on, to its bosom, only for them to be lost in its treacherous depths. There's something rough about it, balanced by the wonderful symmetry of its shape, not to mention its proletarian origins, which is deeply attractive. We were fully apprised of the problems, and thought we had an answer to them. Thelma Holt had just taken over the building and welcomed us eagerly. Our plans were extensive, centring on a seating structure in the round: obvious, inevitable, expensive. Fund-raising was the next step. I spent hours with that champion fund-raiser, Ms Holt, who gave me her private list. I wrote forty letters. Five replied: 'Our fund is not large and by this time of the year is very nearly exhausted.' I knew how the fund felt. Somehow we juggled our budgets – spent half our grant, that is to say – to be able to build our seats. We also spent a lot of time talking to the Board of Management of the Round House, who were understandably anxious about the future of their building. Talking to these impresarios and financiers was instructive. Our trump card was always Bill Gaskill. Not only was his reputation deeply reassuring, his skill in these situations – acquired over years of running theatres and mollifying boards – was impressive, striking a balance between the visionary and the commercial which is exactly what boards want to hear. Everything connected with the move to the Round House was deeply instructive. It failed, one has to admit, certainly in terms of box office, but for me it was the great achievement of our time together. Everybody was directly engaged in something other than their main job – I organized a photographic exhibition and pursued a scheme to get a flag on to the roof of the building – and at that moment, the group really did seem to have an identity of its own. We all felt responsible, personally involved, in the move. It had been our decision, influenced by Brenton's craving for a larger auditorium, crystallized by our sense of moving towards a radical, populist kind of play, and not deterred by Max's grave reservations about the effect the huge space would have on the work.

To the Round House with *Epsom Downs*! The play, as we performed it, was a delightful, Frithian genre piece, stuffed full of theatre devices of great charm. Prior to that, however, it had been Howard Brenton's best play. The transformation was one of the hazards of the Joint Stock method.

Instead of starting from scratch, this time we were presented with a completed first act, which we would work on with Howard, who would then alter it as required. He was very keen on this collective process, saying he needed it to develop the play further. The single act was an extraordinary account of a modern feminist haunted by the ghost of Emily Davidson and driven by her to follow her example and shoot the monarch's horse on Derby Day. It had a *Rashomon*-like time structure, whereby the opening gunshot was followed by three scenes the central event of which was the gunshot. The scenes between the two Emilys (the modern feminist was Emily Davidson too) were immensely powerful. It was tight, compelling. Then we exposed it to the Joint Stock method. First we went to the Derby, and several other race-tracks. That was great, very valuable. Then we talked to someone from Gamblers Anonymous (very informative), someone from the Gypsy Council, a horsebreeder, and Lord Wigg. All very rewarding. Then we'd asked two feminists to tell us about Emily Davidson. They did, very censoriously – she was something of a feminist black sheep, had defied the Pankhursts and done no good to the movement with her romantic gesture. They then asked if they could say something about the play, which they'd been given to read. Of course, feel free. They tore it to shreds – on feminist grounds. What was a feminist doing at the races anyway? What was a feminist doing with a gun? Why were we portraying a feminist as crazy and obsessive?

Every comment hit Brenton in the gut. His conscience throbbed. He blushed deeply. 'We suggest,' the woman said, 'that you rewrite completely.' Which is what, tail between his legs, he did. Politically they were right. Artistically, they were wrong. To put it another way, the artistic effect of the play as it stood was politically correct. As a poetic leap, it expressed passionately a deep truth about the position of women. It was not a documentary. It was a work of art. Art may be too important, as Plato felt, to be left to the artists; but those who presume to comment must learn to think like artists, not journalists, or politicians.

In the end the play was entertaining, and celebratory, but it was de-gutted. Reviews were OK. To fill the Round House we needed ecstasy, what we got was mild enthusiasm. People marvelled at what we'd done with the building, but it still wasn't enough. The acoustics remained dreadful, though the sight-lines were splendid. We played to 30 per cent. Then we transferred *A Mad World My Masters* for which you could hardly get a ticket at the Young Vic, and that bombed too. We started to revive *Fanshen*, which, ironically, had been the lure for tour-bookers to take *A Mad World*. The rehearsals for this were among the most exciting I've been involved in. This was Gaskill at his magisterial best combining his pedagogic and directorial gifts. His understanding of the style of the play was absolute. Here the elucidation of the political point of the scene was indispensable, and radically altered one's playing of it. Here, indeed, character is of no interest at all. Serving the argument of the play is everything, and the excitement which it creates in the audience is the excitement of thought: palpable, visible, thought-processes at work. One day, Gaskill said: 'This is a play about learning. In every scene you must ask, what is being learned?' This articulation of the play's super-objective (which for me is the basic function of a director) had a transforming effect on the whole production. It's a very hard play to perform, because it demands pure intellectual concentration. To *act* thinking is hard; impossible, in fact. You must *think* – that's all there is to it. In this sense, all *acting* is wrong: acting feeling, acting sensing, acting intuition, are all bad, if not impossible. Thinking, feeling, sensing, intuiting: they must be present, not the imitation of them.

And so off we went on our travels, to relive the delights of bed and breakfast, late night poppadoms, and for me, provincial public librar-ies, where I was trying to write my doomed Wilhelm Reich play. Sometimes, the touring allowance we had decided TO PAY OURSELVES being somewhat better than usual, we would dine out at the innumer-able *haute cuisine* establishments which litter the countryside. This was agreeable, but as the tour wound on into the bleak winter, it became apparent that we'd all had enough – of the whole damn thing.

Back in London we held a meeting at which I reiterated my tired old points about the lack of a policy and the directocratic structure. Abuse was hurled around the room, but essentially it was clear that the permanent company's days were numbered, and that a return to the former very fruitful one-off production system was wise. The collective was disbanded, or rather expanded to include everyone who ever worked for the company, as a kind of parliament which would advise and vote.

From my selfish point of view, I had learned more than at the time I realized. Even then, I felt much wiser about the process of making a company. The question of style had been put in the forefront of my brain, where it has remained. The question of the director's role has similarly obsessed me ever since. The practical questions of funding, publicity and budget now made sense where before they'd been mysteries.

For almost the whole period, I had felt on a leash as an actor. From *Fanshen* I had learnt something quite new but from the other productions, I had always felt myself to be kicking against the traces. Once again, I had the feeling that I was being regarded as Donald Wolfit on speed, to be cornered and tamed. This was frustrating and angering. I vowed to work no more for people who didn't like my work, and whose work I didn't like. I made a resolution: Never to appear in work which I would not want to see myself.

I went into hospital to have a tonsillar remnant out. It was the day before Christmas Eve, and, I had no doubt, the end of an era.

Six

When I came out of hospital (how could I have put up with tonsillitis for seven years without doing something about it?), I was raring to go, to discover the brave new world that must be awaiting me. It waited a bit longer. I had the first unemployment I'd known. It lasted three weeks, but to me it was three years. I had been so defined by my work for so long that when I was denied it, I collapsed completely. I had a succession of colds – colds on top of colds – and walked around in a trance. I couldn't seem to understand anything. This god-given pause for reflection and stocktaking was spent fretting as I became more and more convinced that my career had flickered out. Everyone, I thought, imagines that I'm in Joint Stock for the rest of my life. I haven't had a London opening for six months, I've been on tour for three, and they've simply forgotten who I am. I'll have to start all over again. I did have a project in hand, but I couldn't concentrate on it at all. It was the Reich play; or rather the Reich non-play. All I had was a body of research, and a skeleton structure of the play. To tell the truth, all I really had were a couple of vivid images for scenes, which was, strictly speaking, more of a directorial than an authorial achievement. I'd bumped into Ken Campbell at a party a few weeks before, and we'd discovered a mutual interest in Reich; I shyly boasted of the play, and he said, 'Come down to Liverpool and do it for the Science Fiction Theatre.' 'When?' I gasped. 'April 4th,' he said, plucking a date out of the air. 'There's only one snag,' he went on, 'we don't have any money.' 'How shall I live?' 'Oh, we don't let our people starve. It's one of our rules.' I blinked at this genius with Ilford vowels. 'Look,' I said, 'I haven't really written the play yet. I'm finding it rather hard.' 'You don't want to worry about that. I always think it's very stimulating for the actors if they haven't got a script on the first day. Something always happens.' On this basis – that I wouldn't be allowed to starve, and that I didn't really have to write the play at all – I sort of agreed. I even went over to Liverpool from somewhere nearby on the tour to check the space out. It seemed rather small. 'We'll knock the walls down,' said one of Ken's lieutenants. Catching on to the spirit of the place I said, 'We could turn the whole building into a huge orgone box.' 'Yeah, yeah, we could try and get UFOs to land here.' I couldn't top that, so I left. Ten yards down the road, it seemed less feasible. Back in London, it was clearly totally impossible. I phoned Ken and told him. He seemed neither disappointed nor surprised. 'OK,' he said breezily, and rang off. My day as the Orson Welles of the fringe had not yet come.

Then my agent phoned to say that they were doing *Schippel* on the television and wanted *me*. Wanted me? Someone knows who I am? Some people really have long memories. The reappearance of *Schippel* was a confirmation of the end of an era for me, because it had been the beginning of it. It was fun to do it again with greathearts like Dan Massey and Felicity Kendal. Cecil was there too, bemused as ever, wearing the same sandals. It was all very gentle and nice. But what next?

I was asked by Max Stafford-Clark to play Ritsart in Snoo Wilson's mad and mysterious new play, *The Glad Hand*. We were just talking it over, when Gillian Barge, another Joint Stock veteran, came to breakfast. She was rehearsing a Tennessee Williams play at the Bristol Old Vic. 'They're starting rehearsals for *Titus Andronicus* in ten days, and they haven't got a Titus.' 'Look no further,' I said. 'I can mention it, if you like,' she said, and a day later I had a call from Adrian Noble. We'd been at Drama Centre together, so it was all very friendly. I explained that I was really committed to Snoo's play. He understood, and that was that. I didn't sleep too well that night, imaginary iambic pentameters pounding away in my skull. A friend phoned next morning. 'This is one of the great days of my life,' I said. 'This is the day I turned down Titus Andronicus.' 'What?' he screamed. '*The Glad Hand*'s an awfully good play,' I said, weakly. 'It may be,' he snapped, 'but you're not telling me that it's a better play than *Titus Andronicus*.' I wasn't. I got hold of Adrian that minute and said, 'I'll do it.' 'Great,' he said, 'see you on Monday.'

He didn't seem in the least daunted by his inexperience. I was. Years of working with modern prose texts had not prepared me in the least for *Titus*. Nor, it must be admitted, had the Drama Centre. So concerned were they to establish the ABC of acting, that they never had time to proceed to the A-level work which verse requires. I wrote to a friend at the time that I'd started work by giving a bad imitation of bad Shakespearian acting, moved on to imitating bad Shakespearian acting well, was finally on the brink of a passable imitation of a good Shakespearian performance, and wondered whether I'd ever simply give a good performance. There were certain odds against it.

At the end of the first week, the Marcus Andronicus succumbed to mumps. As well as the tedious spectacle of actors wandering around anxiously feeling their glands (for 'actors' read 'me'), there was a new Marcus to be found, and the whole work of the first week to be repeated – Marcus, not the most rewarding role in the canon, is nevertheless rarely offstage. For me, the titanic emotions of the role were cruelly difficult to attain. I always felt false. The series of blows that befall Titus is very nearly comic in its relentlessness – daughter raped and de-tongued, hands cut off at the wrists, sons decapitated, and then, notoriously, his own hand cut off by himself on stage, followed, understandably, by rage against the gods and madness. It's a tall order. I felt myself too small, my voice too weak, my means too limited – and I was right. Only experience and the gradual expansion of one's instrument – oneself – can enable one to play such scenes. In fact, just playing them goes a long way towards it. As for the rest of the play, I was quite good in the opening triumphal return – much aided by a massive drawbridge and medieval march music, supplemented by expressionist lighting effects. The very end of the play, the final slaughter, and the eating of the people pie is a bravura coda which went well. But it was in madness that I was best. These are the most remarkable scenes in the play, and the grotesque irony and crazy leaps of thought made a direct appeal to me. I was able to be light, too, which was a huge relief. The strain of being heroic in the earlier scenes was desperate. Heroism is outside my range. I cannot find the heroic state of mind within myself. It may be too simple. Time and again when I've failed with characters it's because they're simple people, and I can't reach them.

These things, and others, came out in the run. My chief preoccupation, as the first night approached, was my voice. We'd run the first act on one day, the second on the next, and after both I'd been a little raw. Behind schedule because of the mumps, we never ran the whole play until after an entire day of technical rehearsals that is, at eleven o'clock at night. The next day there was a dress rehearsal at three, and then at 7.15, the first public performance. Halfway through this my voice began to falter. By the end of the play, I had NO VOICE AT ALL. The following night, it was barely recovered, and had gone by halfway through. Next day I went to London to see the throat specialist, who with one puff of his famous spray totally restored it, gave me a little spray of my own and sent me back to Bristol with the stern injunction not to utter a word off-stage for the rest of the run, which, give or take a murmured meal after the show one night, or an occasional beer, I obeyed. This monastic regime probably had a very good effect on my karma, and hence the performance, which, as my voice gradually edged back to its former sturdiness, began to improve. I discovered a rule: it is only necessary to establish the essential nature of a character once, very clearly, at the beginning of the play, and then you can play every variation you like. With Titus, I learned that *if* I established the warrior very strongly during that massive first scene – 'Hail Rome, victorious in thy mourning weeds!' I could play the rest very lightly, and in so doing actually enhance his strength. Tricks, some would say. I'd say art. Of course, the first thing that goes when one's voice is under strain is lightness, so I didn't discover this principle until late in the run. The loss of one's voice is upsetting and disorientating. One's inner ear is outraged by the failure of the voice to produce the sounds it has just ordered. One compensates with one's body and one's face, and the result is less and less expressivity. Only when the voice returns does one realize quite how much extra, ugly work the body has been doing. It's like talking to foreigners, knowing the words mean nothing, and trying, ridiculously, to signal the meaning by emphatic diction, smiles and grimaces.

The return of the voice also enabled me to begin really to taste the verse. I discovered that it was like surfing. Unlike most modern writing, the words, the metre and the rhythm contain their own energy. Once you've liberated it, it carries you forward effortlessly.

It's a question of putting one's brain into the words and one's emotions into the rhythm. The metaphors have such a vigorous life of their own, that they sweep through one unaided; that is to say, if the rhythmic conduit has been firmly established. I have to confess that in these matters, as with Shakespeare in general, I have found the Stanislavsky system of no use. Metaphor is the problem. It cannot be coerced into the activity-towards-an-action straitjacket.

I returned to London with the smell of red meat in my nostrils. I did a good play at the Royal Court in which I was exceptionally bad. I played a man in a tight corner and, as ever, it eluded me totally. He was in fact based on someone from 'Real Life'. Had I met the man, or if he'd been described to me in detail, I might have been better. As it was, one night, he stumbled into my dressing room, blind drunk. 'I am you,' he said. 'Or rather, you are me. You were good. I thought it was good when they killed me in the play. I cried, but I thought it was good.'

It's a little spooky, playing people from life. Playing dead people can be spooky, too, but of course, it's worse when they're alive. I sometimes wish I had the courage of Laurette Taylor who said to Tennessee Williams's mother on the first night of *The Glass Menagerie*, 'Well, dear, how do you like yourself?' When we were doing *The Speakers* in London, one of the speakers I played, the extraordinary dancing orator, Norman, came to see the show. When I started to play him, he joined in. Afterwards, I said, 'Norman, I'm afraid I've never seen what you do, so I made it up.' 'That's . . . all right,' he said, in his curious, laboured utterance, 'it's probably . . . better . . . because . . . it's . . . yours.' In fact, a peculiar thing about impersonating the living is that, however you play them, they love it, it's just such a thrill seeing themselves up there.

Many of us in *Mary Barnes*, my next play, had this experience. David Edgar had fashioned a remarkable play out of the book of the same name by Mary herself and Joseph Berke. He'd put it into the context of sixties England and the contemporary interpenetration of political and psychiatric developments. His version was many times more sophisticated than the 'terrifying tale of madness and redemption from R. D. Laing's Kingsley Hall' promised by the American paperback edition of the original. Not that it was short of either pity or terror.

Peter Farago, my first boss from Edinburgh, was directing it at

Birmingham. He sent me a script, asking me to read the part of one of the therapists. I sent it back by return of post, demanding instead the role of Eddie, as a nervous Joe Berke had asked to be re-named in the play. My chutzpah was astonishingly rewarded. I got the part.

I immediately went to meet Joe. He proved quite different to the narrator of the book as I'd imagined him. I'd expected a dynamic thrusting Californian figure in jeans. What I saw before me was much more interesting, an extremely unconventional looking man, large, bald, bearded, olive-skinned, wearing glasses through which he looked at me with disconcerting steadiness as if I were a television set. He didn't speak till I was finished, then there was a little pause, and he'd start: long, complex sentences, formidably intelligent, laced with indiscretions and the kind of jokes I discovered psychiatrists like to make about each other and their patients: 'she's raving mad, he should be locked up,' and so on. At first, I wasn't sure I liked him. Was it the psychiatrist's manner, aloof and all-knowing? I suspect I was disappointed that instead of the guerrilla of the psyche I thought I'd discovered in the book, this man was a professional; not an inspired hippy, but a rigorously analytical, highly organized intellectual. In time, I saw that this man was infinitely more interesting to play than the man I'd sloppily imagined. My visit to him had been a one-man Joint Stock workshop; thank god I'd done it.

I saw at this first meeting that he was very warm – not in his manner, but physically. Warm as an animal is warm. I could understand Mary feeling that she could throw herself against him without destroying either of them. Then Joe's wife Roberta came in, and gave some idea of her side of the story: what it was like to be married to someone so deeply involved in the fate of another person; one, moreover, who would stop at nothing to assert her primacy in his affections.

All this I was able to bring with me to Birmingham. Peter had assembled a wonderful, intelligent, searching cast. Patti Love had already deeply immersed herself in Mary Barnes. On the first day, Mary herself came to Birmingham. She burst into the room in her flowing clothes, sought out Patti and cried: 'Mary!' The two women fell into each other's arms and spent the day together, painting great murals. Back in the rehearsal room, we were discussing with David Edgar what it all meant, the contending psychiatric theories, the attitude of East Enders to having a centre for schizophrenics on their back doorstep, how exactly the liberations of the sixties had come about. We talked through the play for four days, till everything was understood by everyone. In this way, we were all focused on the whole play all the time, and never on 'my part'. It required some delicacy. The subject of schizophrenia and its handling is harrowing, and Patti was already daring to go further into the experience of it than I've seen an actor go. In a sense, mine was an easy performance to give: it was just a question of reacting to Patti. It was important, however, to be scrupulous about the professional means of these people; they were doctors and not amateurs. The relationship between Patti and me continued, *mutatis mutandis*, offstage as well as on. *Mary Barnes* is the only production I've been involved in which really followed the Strasberg path in its quest for total emotional reality, and Patti's performance is the only 'Method' performance I've acted with. It was exactly what was needed. Any kind of technical reproduction would have been offensive. For my part, I was concerned to make Eddie as Joe-like as possible. He should be difficult, demanding, and ruthless in his fight for Mary's interests. Joe had already told me that his relationship with Mary had been successful because they were so alike. I wanted that to be clear. I also wanted to show the mechanism of the liberation of Mary, how it worked. I wanted to take away the miraculous dimension. I called it de-Kellerization. David Edgar concurred and rewrote. There was, for instance, a very brief but crucial scene in which Eddie gave Mary crayons for the first time and told her to draw, which she did, and which was the beginning of the beginning for her. We fleshed it out, so that it became both more tentative and more premeditated. When I told Joe about this I said, 'The previous version was so godlike.' 'But,' he said, 'that's how it *was*.' I was worried that he might not like the unglamorous self that I'd created. On the first night, however, he threw his arms around me. 'I wish I hadn't changed the name to Eddie,' he said. I realized that I was now much fatter than he. Unconsciously, I'd been gorging myself. Moreover, I had decided that the character was a heavy eater, so I'd contrived to be eating something in every scene, as well as the two complete meals that the play demanded. I'd grown a beard, and had my hair cut very short. We stood side by side. Maybe I had gone too far. My gut was pendulous. I taxed him with losing weight, and asked him how. 'Cancer,' he said, then roared with laughter. That was a side of him we never quite got into the play.

While I was in Birmingham, I spent the days learning Arturo Ui. Rob Walker had phoned one morning at breakfast – the way these things always happen -- and said, no commitment, but would I fancy playing Arturo at the Half Moon. And then, a couple of months later, he phoned me again with dates which meant commuting from Birmingham for a couple of weeks, but what the hell. This time I knew I must be word-perfect before rehearsals started and so, in the kitchenette of my digs, I dinned the parodistic pentameters into my skull. In doing so, I discovered much, and was forced into taking many decisions. It is, in my experience, impossible to learn *words*: you learn the thought patterns of the character, of which the words are the inevitable expression. If you learn the *words*, you lay down rail tracks which you must follow, and any sense of the thoughts and impulses which gave rise to the words is very hard won. The only way for me to learn, at any rate, having nothing remotely resembling a photographic memory, is to ask of each fresh line, how did this line give rise to that? and try to reconstruct the mental journey. Hence, very logical characters are very easy to learn, those with eccentric thought-patterns, like Lord Are in Bond's *Restoration*, extremely hard.

My hours in the Birmingham kitchenette made me strongly aware of the artificiality of Brecht's conceit, a play about Hitler where the dictator and his henchmen are Al Capone and his gang, written in blank verse, and containing many close allusions to, and parodies of, *Richard III* and *Faust*, amongst other things. It's a very sophisticated work, and one which hardly does justice to the magnitude of Hitler's evil. That's, I assume, why Brecht left it in his bottom drawer, unperformed in his lifetime. His declared intention was to show that 'there are no great criminals, only great crimes'. He wanted to belittle Hitler. Unfortunately (but surely inevitably) he wrote, in Arturo himself, one of the great virtuoso roles of the modern stage – so the audience will invariably love him, and want to see more of him, and at the end, cheer him – whether it's the actor or the character will be a point of confusion. In a sense, this is exactly the Hitler-effect, but it's a paradox I'm sure the Augsburger didn't intend. It is the perennial problem of all political drama, which left-wing dramatists constantly encounter: the depiction of villainy is always attractive (a) because villainy is energy, and energy is irresistible; and (b) actors enjoy playing villains, and actors' enjoyment is infectious.

Certainly Arturo demands a brilliant display of acting skills – and it got it: from Ekkehard Schall, the first actor to play it, and Leonard Rossiter, whose performance was so worryingly branded on my memory. Olivier says that much of his Richard III stemmed from his determination to make it as different as possible from Wolfit's, highly acclaimed a few months before. I was equally determined to erase Rossiter's image from my brain. He had played Arturo as a kind of psychopathic robot-moron, a brilliantly defined cartoon, all of a piece. Looking closely at the text, I saw another possibility. The layers of reference (Hitler-Capone-Richard III) and the deliberate stylization of the Shakespearian doggerel mingled with gangster jargon suggested to me that it might be very much to the point to emphasize the miscegenation, instead of trying to unify the strands, as Rossiter had so brilliantly done. Moreover, it seemed to me to make a valuable point about Hitler: that he had been constructed by other people's needs, by their plans for him (the bankers, Roehm, and so on); that he had, in effect, been put together from spare parts. Learning the part, I discovered (it's like that: one doesn't find oneself planning a voice, it simply pops out) two quite distinct voices, which seemed to belong to two different people: an aspirated Italian-American slur (on the same principle as Brando's 'Godfather' voice, that he'd been shot through the gullet, and lost his larynx) and Hitler's own strangulated shriek.

I had uncertain plans for the physical appearance, but I knew it should also be made up from spare parts. I knew that he should be sub-human, a Frankenstein's monster, with a curious capacity for galvanizing people with sudden maniacal tirades which would be gone as soon as they came. I had read the Hitler literature (if you can call it that) and seen the Riefenstahl movies. The question always arose: How did he do it? One sees an insignificant blinking little man with the moustache of a clerk wearing a crumpled mac scampering about in a distinctly unheroic way. Why didn't people laugh? – Nobody laughed. Fleetingly, one sees why. At Nuremberg he inspects the Hitler Jugend. One by one, he meets the flagbearers. He takes the flag, places the bearer's hand on it, and, with his eyes, he asks a question. The boy is visibly shocked. Silently, he replies in the affirmative. Hitler moves on. Some psychic energy at work there; or if it's just a trick, it's a good one. From time to time in the production I would turn such a look on to one of the gang and, like in a cartoon, he would sway backwards. Hitler's tirades are also curiously hypnotic.

They start by being quiet and dull, then he seems to be getting angry. Certain words erupt contemptuously from his mouth. The words seem now to be shaken from his gut. He seems possessed, diabolically possessed, tormented by rage and resentment. The voice is hoarse (he must have been riddled with nodules) but cutting, climbing into higher and higher octaves. The barbed German consonants wrench themselves from his lips, like nails out of a bomb, devastating and lacerating the enemy. Then it stops. Goebbels' canned applause breaks out, and the Führer stands there, blinking, spent. Even that's oddly compelling. I don't speak German, so the emotional effect of the words (which I believe is quite considerable) is lost on me but I know that if I had seen it in the flesh, I couldn't have walked away. The same thing is true of Ian Paisley, whom I *have* seen. In fact, the technique is remarkably similar, with the difference that Paisley is a massively built man who suggests that he would gladly smash any opponent with his fists, whereas there's a physical lightness about Hitler, an almost feminine quality which adds to the oddity of his manifestation. The Hitler salute, as given by him, is almost camp, a little throwaway wave from a broken wrist. Paisley is real, a farmer, or a pugilist. Hitler is – invented, improbable. My spare-part theory seemed on the right track. One thing I was absolutely certain of was that there should be no vestige of psychological truth in the performance. It was to be a series of disconnected impulses, as if his nervous system and his brain had likewise been made up of scraps from the laboratory dustbin. I remembered Wilhelm Reich's description of a cancer tumour – the capacity of the cells to sustain their structure has collapsed, and the components of the cell float around aimlessly but fatally. *That* was Arturo's inner life, as far as I was concerned.

I came to the first readthrough with all this fully fledged. In a way, that's a lousy thing to do to a group of actors, because it almost forces them to approach the piece the same way. Robert was taken by surprise too. He'd conceived the play as a Fritz Lang *film noir*, and the set had accordingly been designed as a metal jungle, the world of underground garages and disused boiler rooms. My kabuki-like performance seemed at war with this, but Rob saw that the two approaches could be combined to striking effect. Eventually, between us, rehearsing in a filthy basement in Bethnal Green, we hammered out a style which owed something to almost everyone. I called it the *grottesco* style, which sounded right. I haven't the slightest idea what the *real grottesco* style (there is one) might be. We'd borrowed everything else, what's a label between friends?

I had to finish rehearsing every day at four, to catch the train to Birmingham. After the show, I caught the last train out, or the first one the following morning. *Mary Barnes* closed on Saturday night, *Arturo* opened the following Thursday. We were desperately behind. The highly ambitious set wasn't usable yet (Iona MacLeish had already begun to convert the Old Half Moon, that much-loved rat-infested ex-synagogue, into a gleaming jungle of fire-escapes, sliding doors and metal gates, but at the dress rehearsal, we couldn't walk on it); there was no lighting plot as yet; certain scenes had simply not been staged. Right up to the last moment, I was still trying to insert a scene instead of the one in which Arturo is haunted by his victims. (Hitler wasn't haunted: the scene's only there because of the parallel scene in *Richard III*.) In my scene, Arturo came on with a birdcage, inside which was a canary, sweetly singing. Arturo whistles to the bird, the bird whistles back, he opens the cage and plays with the bird, clucking and gurgling. Then he eats it. Feathers sticking out of his mouth, he slyly leaves the stage with the empty cage. Partly on grounds of taste, largely because of the difficulty of making an edible canary, the scene was never included. Meanwhile, I'd caught a violent cold and deep depression set in. We were going out on as long a limb as we could. The first preview was played without a lighting plot, in full glare of the working lights, with me emerging from a dustbin to play the last scene because we'd never had time to stage it on the set, the whole performance accompanied by a fine shower of mucus from two holes in the side of my false nose.

I phoned all my friends and told them not to come. It was going to be a disaster. And then the First Night came, and it wasn't. Every seat was sold for every performance, extra performances were put in, extra *seats* were put in. A man was overheard in the street outside the theatre offering £20 for a ticket (face value 80p). We were a hit.

Not that it made the slightest difference to us. We were still struggling along – Maggie Steed, Janet Amsden, David Fielder and the rest of us – on £75 a week, making the interminable journey to Aldgate East in the moody November chill, wondering by Wednesday whether we could run to an extra cup of tea at Sidoli's round the corner – never mind a pint in the pub after the show. Working conditions in the theatre were not of the most glamorous, either.

Across the balcony, groaning under lights and audience overflow, we walked to the laughingly named 'dressing room', in fact a corridor which also did duty as a wardrobe and electrical store, at the other end of which was the lighting board. Here the ten of us sat, shivering and damp, our make-up spread haphazardly in front of us, as we took turns at the jagged lump of mirror into which we darkly peered. Fortunately, we had collectively decided on Standard Expressionist, so broad outlines were all that was called for. At the end of the show, like a thirties miner's family, we gathered round a bucket of warmish soapy water to swab the stuff off. The beginning of the show was marked by the arrival of the rather thrilling Tom Donellan, buccaneer stage manager and lighting operator, who would kick the door open with his heavy boots, crying, 'Right, you bastards, you're on.' And we were, seconds later. In such circumstances it was hard to feel like the toast of the town.

Immediately after *Arturo* opened we withdrew to an even dirtier rehearsal room, this time in a condemned building, where, wearing overcoats and burning old sets to keep ourselves from dying of exposure, we rehearsed Toller's expressionist masterpiece, *The Machine Wreckers*. I played Ure, the evil industrialist, and Old Reaper. While the play was in rehearsal, the huge Neue Sachlichkeit exhibition opened at the Hayward Gallery, and proved a major source of inspiration. Toller was no neo-realist, but this was his world, his Germany, and the faces alone were extremely suggestive. I also felt that in the circumstances of our performance – that is, in a small space, with a company of ten or so, instead of the vast stadia and massed trade union forces of the original production – it was necessary to counterbalance the wild and sweeping visionary simplifications of the play; the grainy precision of Neue Sachlichkeit painters like Otto Dix seemed to offer exactly that, as well as an acting challenge of some interest. To achieve the focus and clarity of the painting by Christian Schad that I'd decided to take as my model for Ure required the inner state of a Victorian notable having his photograph taken: absolute stillness, iron concentration and a deep sense of seriousness. I wore the evening jacket and bow tie of the man in the portrait, and sat in a swivel chair atop a high platform surmounting my machine. Oh, the artistic licence of the Old Half Moon! The reckless mixture of style! For my performance as the Old Reaper, the influence was Blake and distant memories of a picture of John Gielgud as Lear designed by Noguchi, white-face with straw hair shooting unrealistically off his brow. The costume designer and I conspired to integrate these two models, but it wasn't till the last moment experimenting with make-up that I suddenly realized what it needed: a mask. Someone was sent off to Theatre Zoo, and back came an old man mask, which, denuded of its spectacles and moustache had exactly the right effect. Behind it, I crooned the semi-biblical speeches of Old Reaper in a Wick accent, which is oddly Scandinavian. The result was that most people in the audience didn't realize that I was playing both Ure and the old man, and all my hysterical strugglings in and out of full evening-dress, sometimes actually on the move from one side of the set to the other, went unappreciated. It was nice, however, to meet people afterwards and hear them say, 'You were good, but the guy playing the old man was *fantastic*.' Ironically, my performance of Old Reaper was Quite Wrong, according to no less an authority than John Willett. I had predicated an entire life on the name, assuming that he had lost his time-honoured profession of reaping with the advent of the Industrial Revolution, and that he was now adrift and alienated in a world of machines. Hence the smock and clogs that Tony Macdonald, the designer, had provided for me, and the strange rustic burr from Wick. Not at all, said Willett. He's not The Old Reaper as in a symbolist play by Maeterlinck, but Old Reaper. Reaper's just his name. Had he been called Old Smith would I have grieved for my anvil? Privately, I think that what I misunderstood was richer than what Toller intended, and I was disappointed to think that the bucolic patriarch I had imagined was simply another, ten-a-penny, raving visionary. I could hardly expect a scholar to agree, however.

To everyone's mild surprise, *Machine Wreckers* was a great hit, too. The company then moved happily on to *Guys and Dolls*, while I went back to *Mary Barnes*, which now came to the Royal Court. As usual, the gap proved immensely beneficial. The ten days' re-rehearsal were concentrated, economical and highly productive. Coming back to a play in this way is exhilarating. One can clear up things that had been troublesome and irritating, and enrich what is already good. There is a danger too of tampering with excellence, which has to be strongly resisted. It's very easy to conclude that one's performance was radically unsound, and to determine to alter it totally. Acting promotes such insecurity and uncertainty that one can easily lose one's bearings altogether. It's so hard to be sure because one is inside oneself. One is one's own instrument, and inside the complex maze of one's own personality, one can go sadly astray.

It was good to be with the *Mary Barnes* group again. Doing the play had been a very intense experience – audiences in Birmingham had been numbed by the journey through which they were taken. Applause seemed somewhat out of place, especially in that Birmingham studio, the set at the end of the room in which the audience sat, and no sense of separation between stage and auditorium. Friends came to the dressing room ashen. They'd light up a cigarette with shaking hands and as often as not burst into tears. Frankly, it was not quite what one wanted. Having gone through all that emotion on stage, what one now wanted was a little camp banter, champagne out of a lady's slipper, and so on. Wearing dirty clothes, squatting on splintery floorboards, having a pint of milk spat into one's face, or in Patti's case, being covered from head to foot in pseudo-shit, one wanted glamour, bright lights and amusing conversation. It was necessary to protect oneself against what one went through with complete commitment every night. The more experience one has, the more one learns to husband energy, to use exactly as much as is needed and no more and above all, to use it on the stage, and nowhere else. At the beginning you spend hours working up to the state required of you for a part. Eventually you discover that that is neither necessary nor valuable. It leads, in fact, to bad acting, because the 'state' up to which you work yourself then permeates every scene you play, leading to generalization. The important point is not to feel a lot, but to feel accurately.

The more serious we were about the play and the more intensely we played it, the more jokes we made about it. An outsider could easily misunderstand the nature of these jokes. There *are* jokes made by actors which betray contempt for the work, and indeed for their work in general. Our jokes were trench-jokes. Some of them were rather good. The favourite genre was subtitling the play. Two examples (both referring to the celebrated – and deeply moving – scene in which Mary appears to Eddie covered in her own excrement): *Diarrhoea of a Mad Woman* (mine) and *Close Encounters of the Turd Kind* (David Edgar's).

Much changed in London as a result of the play being confined behind a proscenium arch. It became 'A Play'. The metropolitan audience also seemed to want to be entertained. It was a kind of evening out. One had to govern them very firmly. They were always on the verge of laughing at the funny mad people. John Gielgud remarks somewhere that the problem in playing *The Importance of Being Earnest* is to stop the audience from laughing at every line, so as to enable them to laugh much more every four lines. An element of control is always involved in the actor's relationship with the audience. They will sometimes try to make it a different kind of play to the one you're trying to give them, and in general it will be a less rich one. I think we succeeded in getting the audience to surrender their armour and open themselves to their deepest anxieties. The play became a tearaway success. Queues wound their way round the building every night, during the vile winter of '78, snow on the ground, garbage from the dustmen's strike piled up the side of the theatre, tube stations overflowing from the busmen's go-slow. Nothing stopped them from coming. It was not so in the West End, which was deserted. There were plans to transfer the play, but they foundered. On the whole, I think we were all quite glad. It was gruelling (how did Patti play a matinée on Saturdays?), and, willy-nilly, it was becoming more extrovert, more of 'A Show'. The original production had an ineffable sense of being overheard, a piece of life bundled on to the back end of that big room in Birmingham. Such things are fragile, and it was now becoming sturdy and serviceable. It was good to end it before worse happened. What is incomprehensible, however, is that it was never filmed. It was a unique combination of people, and the interaction with the audience had produced an extraordinary intensity. It should have been recorded *then*. It's all gone now. It'll never be like that again. One feels a little sad about the evaporation of all one's work. More often than not, however, theatre work resists translation to another medium without radical alteration. This, however, was screaming out for celluloid. Ah well.

I've never appeared in a play which created such personal responses in an audience. There appear on stage a number of characters towards whom different members of the audience would polarize. The four most obvious were Mary, whose voluntary descent into herself in order to undo the false life that she had lived touched something very deep in many people; Eddie, the 'good father', who permitted Mary to make her journey and provided her with an indestructible bulwark against which she could hurl herself with impunity; Brenda (Ann Mitchell), the 'sufficient mother'; and Hugo, based on Ronnie Laing, the guru, God-figure. Almost everyone one spoke to had found themselves drawn to one or other of the therapists, as they identified with Mary. It was as if everybody found a need inside them to do what Mary had done, and a craving for someone to take them through it. Women, especially, spoke to me in terms of *longing* for an Eddie-figure; men kept telling Ann Mitchell how deeply her performance had affected them. I was amazed at how people I'd known for years would start the conversation by discussing their own psychoanalysis – which I'd known nothing about before – as if I were an analyst myself. The confusion between actor and role had been a problem before. The first night was almost eerie in that way. It was a real shrink's night out: Joe Berke had invited, it seemed to me, the entire Pelican psychiatry list – David Cooper, Morton Schatzman, even, until the interval, Laing himself. He introduced me to them as 'Joe Berke'. 'Who are you then?' I asked. 'I sometimes wonder,' he replied.

Though *Mary Barnes* was extremely well reviewed, none of us, actors, designers or director, got specially good notices. They were of the order of 'Peter Farago's clear production', 'Simon Callow played Eddie sympathetically' and so on. Which is probably as it should be, but it's a clear example of the difficulty for critics of assessing the actor's actual achievement. I have no doubt that Eddie is one of the best performances I've given, a real naturalistic performance, exact, exposed, honest and alive. But because it seemed effortless, and because the character was essentially in support of another character, it escaped attention. Even Patti, who certainly gave, as I've indicated, the most emotionally generous performance I've ever seen, but also performed miracles from the technical point of view, achieving vir-tuoso variations of mood and colour, didn't get anything like her due as an actor, because she was so convincing. This despite the fact that the critics had all seen her giving many other performances, all quite different from this one. Pianists always pour scorn on the idea that Rachmaninov is harder to play than Mozart because it looks like it. Similarly, real virtuosity in acting is passed over in favour of mere flashiness. I know, because I've done both.

A year after my first hiatus, I had another. Again, it was unendur-able, especially as in the past year I'd given three performances which had had as much critical acclaim as anything I'd ever done; *The Times* had nominated Arturo the Best Performance of the Year. And here I was, sitting in my bed-sitting room, impoverished and forgotten. That's the hardest: acclaim being followed by unemployment. One feels like a puppy, picked up and fussed over until a new diversion occurs, at which one is summarily dropped back on to the floor. I suppose it's a reasonable price to pay for a profession which is free of nine-to-five monotony; but I'm afraid it has a horrible effect on one's psyche.

Before too dreadfully long, I got a small part in a television play (virtually an extra, swelling a progress, starting a scene or two) and then a huge one, which is again slightly unsettling. One moment a nobody, the next a star (hollow laughter). In a sense, it was like starting all over again. The kind of decent reputation that I'd been building up in the theatre held little water with the seasoned veterans of the canteen at the Acton Hilton, as the BBC rehearsal rooms are affectionately known. I earned more, however, from the bit part in *The Dybbuk* than from the entire rehearsal period and run in both London and Birmingham of *Mary Barnes*.

Television is a halfway-house between theatre and films: a TV play is rehearsed in exactly the same way as a theatre play, though in less time, a long way away from the studios. Most of the roles I've played on television have, moreover, been very theatrical. *Instant Enlightenment Including VAT*, in which I played the chief trainer of an EST-style weekend course, was in some ways the most theatrical of all. Most of it consisted of me standing in front of rows and rows of aspirants, running verbal rings round them until they finally gave up their resistances and received 'enlightenment': the realization that their lives were in their own hands.

It was a virtuoso role and a half. I'd read a number of accounts of EST and 'Max' was clearly based on the charismatic, wisecracking Werner Erhard, inventor of the training. I bumped into the director a few days before rehearsals started and told him that I'd been working on the elusive Californian accent. 'Californian?' he said. 'He's not American, you know. Max is English.' 'But it's *written* American,' I said. 'Transatlantic, if anything,' the director replied, 'but I assure you, he's English.'

At the readthrough I accordingly played him English. It worked, after a fashion. Over the next couple of weeks of rehearsal, it began to work better and better, as I discovered English charisma, English wisecracking. We did a runthrough which was fairly satisfactory, and then we broke for lunch.

While I was eating, in the canteen, the Production Assistant came up to me and discreetly murmured into my ear that when I'd finished eating – 'don't rush, take your time' – the producer would like a word with me. Chilling words. I ostentatiously dallied over the last mouth-fuls of BBC salad, and then walked slowly to the rehearsal room, prepared for a trouncing, if not the big E. Mingling in my breast with fear was a feeling of injustice: the work was going well. It may not be very *exciting*, but it was accurate, efficient. On what grounds could they sack me?

At the end of the room were the producer, the director, and the writer, looking grave. After a couple of pleasantries, we all fell silent. Then the director spoke. 'Simon, we all think you're very talented' – oh God, I hadn't realized things were as bad as *that* – 'and you're doing some marvellous things with the part, but . . .' 'Yes?' I said. 'Well, it's difficult to put one's finger on . . . there's a lack of . . . it's not very . . . charismatic.' The other two looked ill, but clearly agreed. My first instinct was to say: 'Oh yes it is.' Instead I spoke slowly and carefully. 'I think I'm doing justice to the text as it's written' – cries of 'Oh yes, goodness, marvellous, marvellous' – 'so I imagine I haven't got the character right. Perhaps that's because I've never seen the actual man on whom it's based. Could you tell me how you see him?' 'Well,' said the director, 'he's very charismatic, and . . .' 'No, I mean what does he look like, how does he behave?' The director appealed to the writer. 'Andrew?' 'Well,' he said, 'he's a bit like Richard III, plus Elmer Gantry, oh, and a lot like your Arturo Ui. Does that help at all?' 'No,' I replied. 'But I tell you what I could do. I could play him American. Would that help?' 'Oh *could* you? Oh would you? That'd be marvellous.' The director asked me if I'd like a day off to work on it. No, I said, let's run it now, straight away.

And suddenly there was charisma.

This all occurred a few days before we went into the studio; in a sense, it was still being worked on as the cameras shot the perform-ance. The finished recording as a result has a freshness which is not always so in studio work.

Not that I saw it till about a year later. The day it was scheduled to be transmitted, I arranged to watch it at a friend's house. On the tube

I glanced at the *Evening Standard* to see how they'd introduced it. 9 p.m., BBC 1. It wasn't there. It had been replaced in favour of an urgent football match. It was later slipped discreetly into the schedules and passed more or less without comment.

The two jobs lasted a total of about eight weeks. Having paid off my considerable debts, I languished in poverty. I now had a total of forty pounds in my bank account. Defiantly, I spent it all on hiring tails from Moss Bros to go to a friend's birthday party that weekend. On Monday, my fate was transformed.

Seven

It started with an obscene phone call, the burden of which was, would I like to play Mozart in Peter Shaffer's new play? The heavy breather was John Dexter, and like most communications with him, the conversation was conducted largely in Anglo-Saxon. His main concern was whether I could play the piano. My negative reply led him to question my legitimacy, and to compare me to the genitalia of both sexes. He intimated forcefully that it might be in my interests to learn, and then invited me to lunch with him and the author at the Savoy. 'He's only a writer,' he said. 'Don't worry about him – but you'd better shave and wear a tie, we don't want him to have to use his imagination too much, do we?'

My only previous encounter with Dexter had also been at the Savoy. I'd been summoned from Bristol, where I was rehearsing Titus, 'to have a kipper with him'. He promised I wouldn't be wasting my time. I took the overnight train and found myself crossing the foyer of the Savoy next morning. I feared the worst. The man's reputation as an actor-eater was formidable. Grown men crying, that kind of thing. Well, *I* was not going to be intimidated. I didn't need him – *I* was playing Titus Andronicus, after all, at the Bristol Old Vic. Let him just so much as hint at rudeness, and I'd leave.

There followed one of the most agreeable forty-five minutes of my life. He thanked me warmly for making the journey, insisted that I eat before we said a word about business, plied me with the best kippers I'd had in my life, regaled me with anecdotes about Olivier (which go down even better with me than kippers) and finally informed me that he was about to do a production of J. P. Donleavy's *The Beastly Beatitudes of Balthazar B.* Peter Firth would play the eponymous role, and though he was ashamed to say he'd never seen my work, everyone (and he meant *everyone*) agreed that I was the right person to play Balthazar's chum Beefy, and so he was offering me the part, now he'd met me and heard for himself that I could 'speak'. I was to read the novel – the play wasn't 'right' yet – and Sheridan's plays. Rehearsals would start in six weeks. On my way out, he reassured me about *Titus*, and gave me a parting Ethel Merman story. On the first night of *Gypsy* she'd been asked whether she was nervous. 'Noivous?' she asked. 'Why should I be noivous? If dey could do it as good as me, dey'd be up here.' And finally, he said, 'Remember: take to the stage as a bird takes to the air. It's your medium.'

I never heard another word from him.

Until, about eight weeks later, a letter came, which said that he'd abandoned the project because he couldn't get the script changes he wanted. I was to keep in touch and let him know what I was doing – whatever and whenever. During *Mary Barnes* I had sent him a parcel of all the reviews of the previous year, but he didn't acknowledge it.

Now here I was sitting at lunch with him and Peter Shaffer. He was ebullient and sweeping. The design would be thus, and thus. X would play Salieri, and if he didn't, then it'd be Y, 'if I can curb his mannerisms'. Tomorrow he would 'audition managements' to see who offered the best deal. And so on. It was very exciting. Then I went away, to return at four to collect the script and meet Shaffer for tea. 'You'd better get to know each other without me cramping your style.' Cramping wasn't quite the word. I returned, and Peter and I had a very peaceful tea. He's a quicksilver conversationalist and I was soon as exhilarated by his company as by Dexter's. We parted in the Strand, still talking. He said, 'I think you'll be marvellous in the part.' All this confidence from people who'd never seen me act – Dexter still hadn't. I felt very happy, and in the grip of Great Events (Dexter always makes you feel that). I read the script, all five and a half hours of it as it then was, and knew that if it was the last part I ever played, I must play Mozart. One scene above all convinced me that the play was going to be the most enormous success: it's also the

scene in which Peter Shaffer's theatre brilliance is seen at its purest –
and this was *writing*, not production. It's the scene in which Mozart
takes Salieri's footling little march and turns it into 'Non più andrai'.
The entire relationship of the two men is contained in a gesture of
such economy that it almost makes the play redundant. Any actor
reading the scene would salivate. I drooled. I had some reservations:
but in fact the play changed so much by the first readthrough that it
was scarcely the same play. It was to change again almost completely
by the time we opened. It is still changing. Peter is the opposite of a
lapidary writer. The form of his work is open to constant improvement. Its theatrical essence remains unaltered.

I phoned Dexter to communicate some of this. 'Good,' he said
briskly. 'We start in April, in which case, it *will* be the cruellest
month, *won't it?*' I began to see that the stories might not be totally
unfounded. We rang off on a cordial note.

I never heard another word from him.

Until one day, my agent phoned. 'John Dexter wants you to play
Orlando for him in *As You Like It* at the National Theatre.' My
numbed silence was followed by a yelp of disbelief. 'This is folly,' I
said. 'Kamikaze casting. On the other hand, if John Dexter thinks I
can play Orlando, I can. Besides, it's obviously going to be the kind of
production in which someone like me would play Orlando. He's on.'
Was I to play Mozart as well? Nobody knew; but when the contract
arrived, it said: Orlando and Mozart. I went into training. I lost
weight. I stopped smoking. I thought young, romantic and handsome.
I tried not to think of the boredom I'd felt reading Orlando, or that I
thought I really was grievously miscast.

I met Sara Kestelman – Rosalind. I liked her immediately. What I
didn't realize was that as actors we'd have the instant rapport that is
such a god-sent bonus. The moment we started working together, we
became an ensemble of two, the Kestelman–Callow company. It's a
matter of unquestioning trust and immediate sub-textual communication. We knew each other intimately as actors long before we knew
each other as friends; when this is the case, acting becomes jazz. The
extraordinary thing is that this can exist between actors who don't
like each other very much at all, and not exist between the closest of
friends. When the two come together, chemistry and camaraderie, it's
the best thing in the world.

While I was backstage at the National, going to meet Sara, I bumped into Dexter who had, as usual, just stepped off Concorde. 'Have you worked out why I cast you yet?' 'It certainly wasn't my face,' I said. He growled. 'It's because of the first speech – or rather, because of what happens before the first speech.' 'But John,' I said, 'nothing happens *before* the first speech. That's why it is the first speech.' 'That's how much you know,' he said, and strode off to frighten someone else.

One's first day at the National is like one's first day everywhere else, rolled into one. Having walked round the underground corridors several times I finally arrived at Rehearsal Room One, an enormous room about twice the size of most theatres I'd worked in. It was full of people, some of whom were actors, but who were the rest? They seemed to be having a good time, anyway. There was a mood of reckless gaiety in the air, a cocktail party in full swing, but which also suggested that it might turn into a lynching mob at a moment's notice. One or two people came up to me. I drivelled. The casting director (the one who'd said to me on the phone 'We're so glad you're joining us, Simon. When we heard you were playing Orlando, we *did* laugh.') asked me how I was feeling. I said, 'Extremely ill.' 'Quite right,' she replied. Some actors introduced themselves, and murmured appreciation of things of mine they'd seen, which was a huge relief. There's nothing more completely insecuring for an actor than to meet colleagues who haven't seen him act, though they may have heard of him. If neither, of course, it's worse. Feeding my anxiety with a pitchfork was the fact that Dexter himself, though by now he may have heard all too much about me, had still not seen me act. If only we could *start* for God's sake. It felt like a reception to which the honoured guest had not yet turned up. And yet I longed for it never to start, for the play somehow to be in the repertoire without anything happening. Finally, just like the Special Branch men in Belfast, half the room withdrew, and it was the beginning. I walked towards the semicircle of chairs like Gary Gilmore out of the condemned cell: half in love with easeful death, sure that after the readthrough there would be a discreet little conference, Dexter would put an arm round my shoulder and explain that it was all his fault, but . . . it wasn't that I was a bad actor, it was just that I was wrong for the part. Such fantasies pass through an actor's brain with amazing speed and frightful vividness. They stem from your need to prepare yourself for disappointment which in a profession based on hopes and aspirations is endemic. You dare not want anything too much.

There was no readthrough, so my fate remained undecided for the moment. Dexter dismissed first readthroughs and director's first day statements of intent. He then made a very lucid statement of intent, decrying all previous productions of the play as lyrical and mellow, whereas it was, initially at least, harsh and tragic. The mellowness and lyricism are hard-earned, a journey through winter to spring and summer in the forest. It was, he warned us, going to be hard work. There would be a movement and voice class at the start of each day which would NOT be voluntary. While he was working on the private scenes the rest of the company would be working in another room, having read *The Golden Bough* from cover to cover, discovering the ritual background to the play. He would be blocking the play the following morning, and running it on Saturday. Now everyone had to go, because *Undiscovered Country* was opening tonight, so would they go as QUICKLY and QUIETLY as possible EXCEPT for Mr Lomax and young Mr Callow.

And then without pause he started as he meant to go on. 'This speech is said to be unplayable. Well, it's NOT, as you are just about to prove to us. Mr Lomax here has seen Orlandos come and go, haven't you Harry, dear, so you'd better be good.' He looked at me over his half-lens glasses. 'It is in fact a fine example of Elizabethan prose, as good as anything by Philip Sidney or any of the others but I don't have to tell you about THAT, do I, because you've been well brung up. Young Mr Callow is one of these newfangled University Actors, Harry, and we all know about THEM, don't we?' I tried to protest, delighted that things were taking such a convivial turn, and especially delighted that I wasn't having to act. Perhaps I never would. We could just banter away like this for hours. Banter is a characteristic Dexter technique. The mixture of erudition and bully-ing is characteristic too. I imagined that conversation with an eighteenth-century sea captain might have been much like this. Now, however, one of his other manifestations was imminent; in fact, the essential manifestation: the trainer. For rehearsals, he generally wears a tracksuit and plimsolls, circling the acting area, shouting out com-ments, criticism or advice. His conception of acting is at heart athletic: it's a skill, requiring physical address and mental stamina. The intui-tive aspect of the art is something you do at home -- in front of the mirror, he'd say, or in the bath. He's not interested in the process, merely the results. It was a bad day for the rest of us when he met

Laurence Olivier, who is that sort of actor supreme. What marvels he conjured up on the train to Brighton! In general, I find this impossible. My idea of rehearsing is messing around, trying things out, following strange impulses, and seeing what happens – for me a rehearsal room is a kitchen, where you combine ingredients as they come to hand, testing, tasting. Finally, you apply flame, and the thing grows; exactly how, one never knows. You put the dough into the tin, but what shape will the loaf be? It's out of your hands.

For John, the rehearsal room is a garage, and he's the mechanic. Sweating and with oil on his hands, he assembles the components. The trick is to get the right components, and put them together in the right way. It's almost like a jigsaw puzzle. For some cars, there exist plans which are known to be reliable; for others, you have to work it out all on your own. As cars, so plays, for John. He's the best play-mechanic in the world. Not that he isn't eager for the actor's contribution. Nothing pleases him more in the world than an unsolicited piece of business. But – 'Don't describe it, DO it.' I never satisfied him more than the day we were rehearsing the dreaded Sonnet that Orlando pins to the tree for Rosalind. I said, 'It seems to call for a physical expression of his love, John.' 'Don't talk about it –' 'Do it, I know. OK.' 'O Rosalind,' I cried, and did a cartwheel. 'MARVELLOUS,' he shouted, and *ran* on to the stage to edit it. 'At last,' he said, 'you're inventing.' I was actually copying. I'd been at his behest to the Chinese Acrobats, and this was my (rather modest) tribute to their work. The scene had been a stumbling block for me ever since the first day we'd rehearsed it, when John – this is very typical – had said 'I got hold of a copy of the film of *As You* that Larry made with Elisabeth Bergner. He did something absolutely extraordinary with this speech.' 'What?' 'I'm not going to tell you. Just do something equally extraordinary, that's all.' I don't know whether the cartwheel was that, but it pleased John no end.

On this first day, with no one in the vast expanses of the rehearsal room but Harry Lomax (Adam), Ken Mackintosh (the assistant director), John and me, he said: 'I want you to hit a precise note on the word "As" every time you do it. It's a speech direct to the audience – yes, I KNOW he says "Adam", we'll come to that in a minute – you're VERY ANGRY, you've got to tell someone about it. By the time Orlando walks on to the stage, you've got to be homicidal. Right? OK, let's see it.'

This was it, the high-diving board. All alone in the middle of that vast space, with dear Harry a few yards off, I spoke my first words as a National Theatre artist. Or, rather, word, because after my first 'As', John shouted 'No, no, no, no. "As!"' He imitated the correct note. After three or four more stabs, I got that right. The next phrase then came under scrutiny. 'I don't think it can be as boring as that, you know, you've got to *grab* them.' Then it was my breathing. Then it was phrasing. Next came articulation: 'Consonants, consonants, consonants. The Olivier is a bastard acoustically, but I'm going to crack it if it kills you. On!' There was relish in all this. I thought at the time, this is his revenge on his RSM – except it was me that was getting it in the neck. I began to feel incapable of speaking or moving. I blushed violently. I wasn't going to give in. Then the carefully memorized speech began, under dint of so much repetition, to sound meaningless. I dried up once or twice. I was on the verge of tears. Dexter roared with laughter. 'Don't get angry with yourself,' he said sweetly, and came on to the stage. 'It's good, you're going to be marvellous, but *watch your articulation*. It's not as good as you think it is. Honestly, university actors, Harry. Think they know it all, don't they.' And that was that for the day.

I staggered away, not knowing whether I could take a whole rehearsal period like this. It wasn't the barrage of insults – they seemed quite friendly – it was the approach. I had never ever been able to tap any kind of creativity under these conditions. To John, all problems are technical problems. To me, a technical problem is always the symptom of another deeper one. When the inner questions are solved, the others disappear. The brilliant director for me had always been the one who spotted the inner problem, or, more commonly, who created a rehearsal atmosphere where those problems came easily and naturally to the surface.

There was no question of that here. The rehearsal atmosphere was gladiatorial. Step on the stage, and you were in the Circus Maximus, with the lion – Dexter – stalking you relentlessly. The desire *not to displease* took precedence over the desire to do the part well, or even the desire to please, which would at least have been positive. I took a decision. I would surrender myself to him totally. Not for five years had I done that with a director, but this was different. Right or wrong, he was clearly A Considerable Person, and I would be bound to learn something. I told myself that it was like being an apprentice at the Comédie-Française, or a kabuki trainee. In that spirit, the thing was possible. I never really solved the inner problems (maybe they were insoluble) and for that reason, in my opinion it was not a good performance. I did learn a great deal – about articulation, about simplicity, which was John's unvarying note: 'Simpler, SIMPLER,' about simply standing on that Olivier stage – but I never engaged with Orlando creatively. I gave John's performance, not my own, and I never ceased to feel his glowering presence from the first day to the last. In fact, when he came to see the production some months into the run, I was so aware of his actual presence that, striding down to the foot of the stage to hurl the opening speech at the audience, I thought, God, is this what John said, is this where he wanted me to stand, which note was I supposed to hit? And I immediately dried. 'As I remember, Adam –' (what? as I remember what? *what* do I remember?) 'Line!' Within the first two seconds of the play, I had disgraced myself professionally in front of 1,200 people. That's what happens when the work's not yours.

Work on the so-called wooing scenes was altogether different. John pointed out that these scenes, far from being love scenes, as they're so often spoken of, are teaching scenes. Orlando is systematically disabused of whatever fancies he may entertain on the subject of married love. He's being prepared by Rosalind for the conclusion to which the whole play drives: marriage. The sexual confusion which makes the scenes so juicy and 'modern' was plotted by John with infinitesimal care; the master mechanic at work. He seemed to know in advance the exact physical realization of each twist of the scene. Sometimes he'd come and say, of his own work, 'That was all wrong, I've cracked it now.' Sometimes Sara or I would be moved to invent a gesture or an inflection which he'd immediately incorporate. These sessions were intimate and intense, normally just the three of us and a stage manager, often just the three of us. If Rosalind was teaching Orlando, John was teaching us. I still wonder (as I wondered with Bill Gaskill) whether teaching is the proper activity of the rehearsal, but I'm very happy to have spent these hours working on that incomparable text and in the closest communion with a brilliant actress and an exceptional man of the theatre. Nothing quite resembles the creative closeness of this kind of rehearsal. The telepathy that develops enables the work to flourish tropically. Sometimes the emotional warmth is deceptive; maybe it's not as marvellous as you think it is. Late-night rehearsals have to be watched especially closely. Many a breakthrough proves to have been chimerical in the cold light of the next morning.

The bubble burst after the first night. We had all been spellbound by the dynamic little figure, organizing, controlling, abusing, enthusing, rushing on stage to physically drag an actor from one side of it to the other, demanding one day that we all listen to Dowland for twenty minutes, the next howling at some unfortunate lad who had deviated from the movements decreed him. There was a treacherous double-bind that he sometimes resorted to: 'Can't you invent *anything*? Haven't any of you got the slightest drop of imagination?' followed by 'Who told you to do that? Did I tell you to do that? Do as you're told.' Despite the hectic pace of life, we all felt in possession of something extraordinary. We swaggered around the building, Dexter's team, the breath of fresh air after the doldrums at the National (the strike, and so on).

I spent the day of the first night in a state of extreme exhilaration. My trust in John was absolute. All that remained was the actual performance. In this innocent mood, I strolled into my dressing room to read the *Evening Standard*. There on the make-up table was an old tobacco tin. Inside were smears of ancient greasesticks, and a fragment of a cigarette packet which said: 'Noël Coward's make-up tin.' Now I noticed a note which said: 'My father always swore this was genuine, now I'm giving it to you. You're a marvellous Orlando. Good luck. Dan.'

I was terribly touched by the present itself, of course, but almost more so that Dan Massey, whom I'd known slightly since we did the television *Schippel* together, should have remembered my first night. He was doing his last performances in *The Philanderer* in the Lyttleton. I rushed down to his dressing room. He wasn't in it, so I slipped a note under his door: 'I am moved beyond words. Thank you, thank you, thank you. Simon.' On the way back to my dressing room, I bumped into him. 'Dan, I've just slipped a note under your door. I can't thank you enough.' He smiled sweetly, but looked baffled. Typical modesty, I thought. By the time I reached my dressing room, however, I had doubts. Somehow he hadn't seemed like a man who has given another a priceless gift. How curious. I looked at the tin again. I looked at the note. Dan ... Dan ... oh my God! I rushed round the corridor to the other communal dressing room opposite, until finally I located Daniel Thorndike. 'Dan,' I said, breathlessly,

'Dan, did you . . .?' 'Yes,' he said, smiling. 'Oh, thank you, thank you, it's wonderful.' Of course, he had told me that his father Russell had done a tour with Coward. 'Thank you,' I continued to burble. By now, I was almost late, so I rushed back to make myself up into some credible impression of a young romantic hero. The farce of the make-up tin had taken away any remaining vestige of nerves, and I made the short journey from the dressing room to the stage without trembling.

At a signal from the stage manager, I walked out to join the actors playing harvesters. This was John's 'what happens before the first speech': bundling up the straw, in which Orlando, the younger son, is humiliated by being made to work in the fields with the labourers. After desultorily bundling up a little straw, I strode angrily to the foot of the stage: 'As I remember' – straight to the audience – 'Adam!' – the old fool isn't listening – 'it was upon this fashion' – direct to the audience again. It was an arresting beginning, and a solution to the problem of 'that first speech!', as everyone who's ever played Orlando refers to it. The problem was that the speech, discursive, flexible and narrative, isn't written that way. I realized this for the first time on that night; and from then on, nothing else that we'd so carefully wrought in rehearsal seemed right.

The auditorium itself, the dreaded Olivier, held no terrors for me. As you stride on to that stage, it's as if you could embrace the entire audience in your outstretched arms. Denys Lasdun's Attic inspiration pays off, certainly for the performers. No, it was the *production* that was so awkward.

The first night gave us the lie. It *was* extraordinary; but it didn't work. Not only did it not work for the first-night audience – it simply didn't work. Wonderful insights had been bought at the price of bendings and twistings of the text; and above all, there was no release of joy, no sense of the culminating harmony which is the destination of every Shakespearian comedy. John had brilliantly pinpointed the discord, he had opened up a legitimate vein of tragedy underlying the play. But he'd not been able to resolve it; which is exactly what Shakespeare so fundamentally does.

Clearly, a director's present preoccupations have a great influence on the way in which he reads the play. John was, for one reason and another, obsessed with the idea of ingratitude, so *As You Like It* became a play about ingratitude, which requires a considerable stretch of the imagination – or rather, it leaves out the crucial element of ingratitude *pardoned*. In this he was unShakespearian. The wooing scenes, moreover, are indeed teaching scenes – that was a wonderful insight – but they're also scenes of wit and games-playing, and that we never found. He had, moreover, grafted on to the play a whole apparatus of frankly passé anthropology, in the form of fertility rituals and harvest ceremonies. That seemed to me to be his defiance of the 'university brigade' – learneder than thou.

All of which seems to be severe criticism of the man. It's not intended as such; he made wrong choices; he went up blind alleys. That's everyone's privilege, and he was to succeed as brilliantly with *Galileo* the following year as he failed with this – more so, because the Brecht was an unqualified success, and *As You Like It* was only a qualified failure. What it seems to put in question is the propriety of so much standing or falling on one man's personal vision. Never at any point were any of us consulted on the meaning of the play or the gesture of the production. Forty intelligent and gifted people were committed without choice to embodying John Dexter's view of the play. Other directors are less fanatic than John, but it's always essentially the same: the design decisions have been made long before any actor is hired, the music commissioned, and most elements of the production finalized before the first readthrough. No actor ever asks a director: 'And what is your view of the play?' (Although when Bill Gaskill asked Edith Evans to play Queen Margaret for him, she sat down with him and they went through her text line by line. When she was convinced that they agreed on an approach, she accepted the part. Not before. This seems to me not only decent but sensible.) Few directors ever say to an actor: 'This is my angle on the play. Do you share it?' No, it's just understood that it's going to be John Dexter's *As You Like It*. An actor can always leave if he doesn't approve. But that's nonsense, of course, economically and artistically.

What then is the function of the director? It's not a question of skill. The director's skill is a distinct commodity, like the designer's and the actor's. It should be at the service of the company, realizing the group's understanding of the play and its needs. This should be the case above all in an ensemble such as the National Theatre purports to be. Otherwise, they're simply a pool of actor-drones, called upon as if they were faceless functionaries with no brain or understanding of their own, glorified galley-slaves. These people are artists at the pinnacle of their profession. Until actors are accorded equal responsibility with the director, the theatre will always be the fitful expression of one man's understanding. But theatre is not that kind of an undertaking. A play is not a score, with specific notes which have to be played as they're written, needing one man to co-ordinate and discipline a group of players. A play needs to be discovered, *un*covered one might almost say, liberated. Every single actor has a personal responsibility in this matter; every scene, every part needs to be implied from the bare text. This is an active undertaking, not a passive one. Much of the circumscribed creative excitement of the present theatre stems from this passivity.

I felt this acutely when I played in John's production of *Galileo*, which was the best the directocratic system can offer: a highly polished, crystal clear, gleaming great machine of a production. I was miserably unhappy in it. I would probably have been uncomfortable in *any* production playing the little monk, Fulganzio. But with John standing in front of me making 'get on with it' gestures on some lines, and 'slow down' gestures on others, I nearly had a nervous breakdown. Playing a small part for John is very different to playing a large one. Time is limited, there is a scheme to be fitted into: get on with it! Discussion is out: 'Don't talk about it! Do it.' And if something hasn't worked: 'Never apologize, never explain.' In jest, John had written to me when he offered me the part, 'You can play the scene two ways: sitting down or standing up. Never let it be said that I'm not a flexible director.' It wasn't a joke at all – except that by the time he came to rehearse the scene, he'd decided on sitting down, so that was that. I couldn't ever get any sense that I was doing other than utter the words with externally applied emotion. One day I arrived late for a rehearsal. John snarled at me when I came in, I ran to my place, slipped off the edge of the stage, and twisted my ankle – not badly, but it swelled up spectacularly. John laughed. I'd been punished, and was now forgiven. I went into the scene, trying not to hobble. Incredibly, the scene was much better. Concentrating on the ankle not only took the heat off that damn text – it no longer seemed like a speech, but words said by someone – it also gave me a physical life. Something began to stir. It seemed to me hugely to the advantage of the play that the little monk should have a social and physical reality. I communicated my insight to John. 'Could I not,' I asked, 'have some physical disability as a result of malnutrition?' 'And where,' he asked, 'will you have the parrot, on the left shoulder or the right?'

At the first rehearsal John had declared that we were going to get rid of all the Marxist rubbish in the play; moreover, he said, this wasn't a play about the church or even science, but about Brecht himself, who knew he'd sold out. John may have been right or wrong, but how could we not discuss such a fundamental proposition?

In all this, John Dexter is cited merely as an extreme instance of the standard structure of theatre practice.

Amadeus, which, as I discovered through that indispensable adjunct to the National Theatre's somewhat faulty internal communications network, the *Evening Standard*, was to be directed by Peter Hall, was a strikingly different experience. In many ways we approached the play almost experimentally. We had to. We were travelling through completely unknown country.

Before rehearsals started, I had been as pleased as Punch. When I was first asked to play Mozart, I was almost overwhelmed with self-congratulation. This was the Big Break. Also clearly a very flashy role. Peter Shaffer had selected – I don't say invented – a brilliantly vivid Mozart: vulgar, childlike ('infantine', the text said), hyperactive, ultimately touching, but in many ways unendurable: a show-off, touchy, and ungenerous to fellow-artists. It was shocking even if you knew enough about Mozart – if, for example, you'd read the letters – to know it was a part of the truth. The play isn't a biography of Mozart, and Shaffer was under no obligation to present a full-blown portrait; but what was there, was true. Mozart, if you like, glimpsed by lightning. The role itself, moreover, made a journey from outrage to dejection and finally suffering that was uniquely satisfying.

There was, too, the prospect of being re-united with Felicity Kendal, with whom I'd already had Instant Rapport when we worked together on the television *Schippel*, and close contact with Paul Scofield, giant.

I thought that I had a very clear idea of what I was going to do. I had a giggle, as prescribed by the text (borrowed from David Frost and tuned up two octaves), I had a voice, I had some idea of the physical life of the part. All this I produced at the readthrough.

It was clearly impossible.

It was impossible to believe that the little beast I'd produced (in direct response to the text) had written a note of the music around which the whole play revolved. It was equally clear that it would be impossible for an audience to sit and watch this all-farting, all-shrieking monstrosity for more than a few seconds at a time.

At the end of the readthrough, Peter Hall thanked me for having given such a brave performance – and we all know what *that* means. I tottered off to that evening's performance of *As You Like It* distinctly baffled. It seemed so simple on the page, so eminently playable. Why didn't it work? Crisis. It was quite clear that the shapes and the situations of Peter's play were right; it was also clear that Mozart's function in the play was to provoke and disturb all around him. There could be no soft-pedalling; but one had somehow to find a way of combining his dramatic function with a real man. Struggling with the part was agonizing – embarrassing, painful. I felt forced and heavy-handed, a cackling, prancing robot.

I was not the only one with problems. The play was far, far too long. Paul's part was dauntingly long, but which of the many delect-able speeches should go? Cutting and rewriting didn't make learning it any easier, either. But rewrite he must. Peter Shaffer is, in his relation to actors, almost an experimental writer, a spontaneous Joint Stock man. His response to what the actors do, to what the scenes require and what they can do without, is lightning. At an early stage, Peter Hall had drawn attention to Shaffer's speech patterns in everyday conversation, above all to the cascade of words, and said we should learn from them in our handling of the text: not milking any particular word or phrase, but with a sense of the whole arc of a sentence or a speech – an excellent observation.

Hall has great sensitivity to text, and fine taste in terms of acting. He was wonderfully helpful in judging between one invention and another. He creates, too, a relaxed and genial atmosphere which is very productive. We laughed a great deal. It was delightful.

But I had by no means resolved my crisis. Felicity and I flung ourselves into the hurly-burly of the Mozarts' domestic life with great abandon, sometimes even getting Shaffer's words right. Paul and I, very different acting animals, had found each other's wavelengths. I'd overcome my awe and was feasting hungrily off the extraordinary riches he was sending my way. One day, we were rehearsing the scene round the piano. Over our heads, there was a tiny flicker from a lighting fitting. We carried on acting. The flicker persisted, and so did we. A flame leapt out, and shot along the cable above us. We continued with the scene. By now, the whole ceiling was ablaze. The stage management were dragging tables and sound equipment to the other side of the room. We kept on acting. Finally, the scene came to an end. Without moving, as bits of the ceiling fell about our ears, Paul turned to me and said: 'Are you really going to do it like that?' We bolted for the door. Somehow then I realized that we were a team. (As we got into the corridor and firemen rushed into the room from which smoke was now billowing, Michael Rudman sauntered past. 'Simon Callow overacting again, I suppose,' he said.)

Such diversions notwithstanding, I was still at sea with Mozart. I understood the play very well by now. Picking up on Peter Hall's remark about Shaffer's quicksilver speech patterns, I had observed that the play was a spinning top: until we had it up to speed, the pattern would never emerge, it would never hum. Very astute, very clever. Yes, but what about my performance? Physician heal thyself. No amount of speed would make up for my inability to find a credible human being. One day, in great depression, I had sat with the Peters on the edge of the Olivier stage, where we'd just had a runthrough very nicely up to speed. 'I still haven't got it, have I?' I said. 'It's coming,' they both said. 'If only we can believe that he wrote the music,' Hall added. 'I know, I know,' I said, 'of course that's true, but my problem is more fundamental. There's no one *there*.' I asked them who, in an ideal world, living or dead, they'd like to see play the role, so that I could get a sense of its parameters. Wisely, they refrained from naming anyone. 'Anyone in *life*?' I pleaded. 'Or literature?' I was desperate for a point of reference. Tentatively, Hall suggested the young O'Toole – 'before he had his nose fixed'. I hadn't known him, so it was no help. I trailed away sadly.

Then quite by chance I picked up Otto Deutsch's hefty *Mozart: A Documentary Biography*. I'd read everything I could get my hands on, but had been daunted by the bulk and dryness of the title of this. Within minutes of flicking through its pages, I knew I'd struck gold. There he was, the little bugger: a speaking likeness. Mozart portrayed in letters, memoirs and laundry bills by his contemporaries. Most of the biographies start from the standpoint of his music; here was the way people really saw him – partisan, sometimes one-sided, but immediately vivid – a picture of a light, tiny, mercurial, volatile, immature, prodigiously energetic, bird-like creature. There were stories of him leaping from the piano-stool to run under the table like a pussy-cat; tapping his fingers incessantly in complex rhythms; making

Queen's University, Belfast: *Fin de Siècle*, devised and presented by the tubby aesthete on the right – me, aged 18

Drama Centre, London, 1973: as Kite in *The Recruiting Officer* with Allan Hendrick and Wayne Browne

Joint Stock: with Paul Kember and Bill Gaskill reviving *The Speakers*

Above:
Dexter spellbinding
Kestelman, Callow
and Marjorie Yates:
As You Like It

Right: As Verlaine in
Total Eclipse

National Theatre: with Scofield – the first runthrough of *Amadeus*

Lincoln, 1973: as Peter in *A Taste of Honey*, my first named part

Gay Sweatshop: with Michael Dickinson in *Passing By*

Devil's Island: as Krichevski with Jane Wood, Gillian Barge, David Rintoul and Suzanne Bertish (photograph amended by David Hare to commemorate an incident on the first night)

Becoming Joe Berke: me, the man himself and an aerial view of Ann Mitchell – first day of *Mary Barnes*

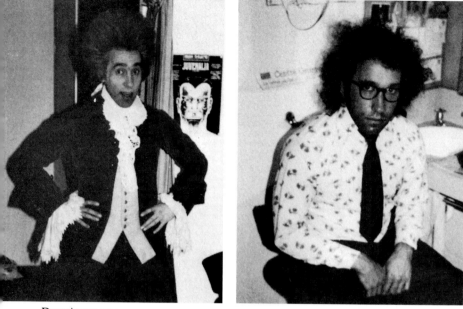

Dressing rooms
Above left: Mozart
Above right: Stafford T. Wilkins

Making up for Lord Foppington, Lyric Hammersmith, 1983

Micheál MacLiammóir
as Oscar Wilde

Simon Callow as Orlando

absurd and childish jokes. Much of this is in Peter's play. The beauty of Deutsch's book is that it puts these details in the context of a whole life. One entry, an excerpt from the memoirs of his brother-in-law, Josef Lange, provided the best key of all: 'Never was Mozart less recognizably a great man in his conversation and actions than when he was busied with a great work. At such times he spoke confusedly and disconnectedly . . . he did not appear to be brooding and thinking about anything . . . either he intentionally concealed his inner tension behind superficial frivolity, for reasons which could not be fathomed, or he took delight in throwing into sharp contrast the divine ideas of his music and these sudden outbursts of vulgar platitudes, and in giving himself pleasure by seeming to make fun of himself. I can understand that so exalted an artist can, out of a deep veneration for his Art, belittle and as it were expose to ridicule his own personality.'

The moment I saw this Mozart, Shaffer's text fell into place. Every word, every gesture that he had written was consonant with the man. They simply needed a framework of character to unify them. Once I had found that, the playing style of the piece came easily. Psychological realism was out of the question in view of the kaleidoscopic sequence of scenes. Something akin to revue technique was called for, the capacity to start a scene bang in the middle of it, and to wipe it away as soon as it was finished in order to make room for the quite different emotions of the next. Shaffer's is a theatre of gesture. The whole body, the mask of the face, ways of speaking, external details are all of the essence of Peter's work. The wig, the giggle, the little hop, and so on. The definitive Shaffer performance was Robert Stephens's Atahualpa in *The Royal Hunt of the Sun*, pure gesture, voice, movement. It's a linear technique, not in depth – legerdemain the indispensable quality. The glory of Shaffer's work, and one of the reasons for its great popularity, is the opportunities it affords directors, designers, and perhaps above all actors.

From now on, for me, the tracks were down and I simply had to travel along them as fast as I could. The outstanding remaining problem, which I never ceased to work on till the last performance, was to somehow make it credible that the man had written the music. It was essential to believe that inside the giggling, shit-shanking, hyperactive little man was *The Marriage of Figaro*. I listened to the overture to that work morning noon and night.

With all our problems, we never paused to think that we were doing a major new work by the most successful dramatist in the world. We even stopped thinking that the play might in any way be controversial. We just wanted to get it right.

Finally we tumbled on to the stage. From the first preview there was never any question that, whatever the critics might say, the effect of the play on the public was going to be enormous. Playing it I had again the experience I've only had on two or three previous occasions: a hunger from the audience, a feeling that they were getting something they'd done without for too long. Everyone who appears in the play feels the same thing: there's a magnetic pull coming from the auditorium. The combination of words and Mozart's music in the play had an extraordinary impact. At any rate, not one performance of the two hundred or so that we did failed to ignite an electric charge in the audience; nor was there one which wasn't better than the one before. The play and the production were both flexible in a way that enabled one to work on one's performance incessantly.

After six months of playing, a breakthrough occurred: I attained real grace and lightness, instead of striving for it (paradox!), and it became credible that I'd written the music. It was the result of my falling in love.

At last I found the courage to be charming. I realized that up till now, not only as Mozart but in every part I had ever played, because I was certain that no audience (and of course, no man) could ever accept me as attractive or charming, I determined to make it clear that I wasn't trying, that what I was was ridiculous, ugly, overpowering, and chose instead to command admiration for my honesty and self-exposure. In fact, the greater honesty, the greater self-exposure, was to offer myself as I was, just as attractive and charming as I actually was, not trying to be more or less. It had taken eight years to learn this simple thing.

Strange how your life feeds straight into your work, but never in the way you expect it to. Falling in love dissolved some inner knot which had been inhibiting the ease which must have been at the heart of Mozart as it is of his work. Had I fallen out of love, however, I would have been able to retain the development because I now had the taste of it. As it was, the inner stream grew and grew until it became a river.

For some months, life and art had been engaged in a torrid dance in which it was hard to say which was following, which leading. It seemed to start with my work on Shakespeare's Sonnets. I was drawn to them so violently because of an aching frustration in my heart strangely at odds with my outward appearance. In the world's eyes, I must have seemed strikingly successful. I was playing leading roles at the National Theatre, in a bright blaze of publicity, and sometimes to actual acclaim. The roles themselves were challenging and rewarding. One of the roles was that of the greatest musical genius who has ever lived, in a play by Peter Shaffer. In it, I was playing opposite Paul Scofield and Felicity Kendal. In *As You Like It*, I was acting with Sara Kestelman. I had made many new friends. I was financially solvent for the first time in my working life. I had been promoted from the communal dressing room where I started my life at the National to sharing one with the enchanting Mark Dignam. I spent delightful hours with other actors in Joe Allen, a sort of after hours extension of the National Theatre's Green Room, which I now discovered – could now *afford* – for the first time. No one could ask for more. Except that I was deeply unhappy.

The performances were my only satisfaction, but they were somehow sterile. The gulf between me and the characters I played was widening. At the end of each show, I felt a fraud. Though I had lost weight and was in peak condition physically, as for love and sex I felt *hors concours*. I had somehow slipped back years to an earlier me. I was a vat of stagnant emotion.

Then I read the Sonnets.

Eight

Michael Kustow phoned me one spring day. He'd just come across a new order for Shakespeare's Sonnets. Would I like to read some of them with another actor as a Platform Performance? Sure, I said, and put the phone down. A couple of minutes later, I phoned back and said surely just one actor would be better, as they're all in Shakespeare's voice. He agreed. Two minutes later, I was on the line again. 'If we're to test the order,' I said, 'we have to do them *all*, don't we?'

Again he agreed, and we were on. I'd had far too little contact with Shakespeare, and even less with poetry. Time to take the bull by the horns.

To be candid, I barely knew the Sonnets: only the two most famous – 'Shall I compare thee to a summer's day?' and 'Let me not to the marriage of true minds admit impediments' – and the first lines of a few others. I had no idea of the riches buried in that little volume, because, like most people who try to read them, I'd been daunted by the sheer number of poems in one form, and by the cryptic nature of many lines. It was this that John Padel's new sequence rectified. His theory was complex, almost fantastic, yet oddly credible; but the new sequence was nothing short of a revelation, an emotional journey of the most harrowing kind, touching in its course the boundaries of madness. It seemed to me the most graphic account of *amour fou* I'd ever read, an account, not of sexual passion or deep symbiotic intimacy, but of idolizing, self-denigrating enslavement to one who embodies everything one feels oneself not to be; Aschenbach's emotion for Tadziu, mine for Jonathan A., and countless others. Not only had I been there before, I was there at that moment. Poor Shakespeare! Poor me!

For the first time, I began to have a sense of who Shakespeare might actually *be*. Read in Padel's order, the Sonnets are the unmistakable record of lived experience. Even when one struggles through the Quarto edition, the sense of overwhelming passion leaps out from the page, and there is a curious impression of a submerged drama, with three distinct characters: the writer, his mistress and a young man (W.H.). Padel's theory brings the drama to the front of the stage. In doing so, he throws a bright light on Shakespeare's personality and his nature as an artist.

There are two strands to the theory. One is numerological, dividing the sequence into groups of four or three, which then form larger groups within the whole collection. It seems highly feasible that Shakespeare, with his sense of harmony and balance, might be drawn towards such structures; numerological considerations were in any case a common Elizabethan preoccupation. Padel's order has its own mathematical beauty – seventeen sonnets for W.H.'s seventeenth birthday; eighteen groups of four for the eighteenth, and so on – but the real excitement is the inner emotional sequence that it reveals. It was now possible to read at least one hundred and twenty of the sonnets consecutively and with cumulative effect; especially in the light of part two of Padel's work, the background.

This was his story: Shakespeare had been commissioned by Mary Herbert, Countess of Pembroke, to write seventeen sonnets for the seventeenth birthday of her son William. The boy was of an ascetic disposition, showing no interest in love, sex, or, above all, marriage. His father the Earl was chronically ill. If he died before William attained his majority unmarried, the Queen would appoint a guardian, who could prove unscrupulous. It was a matter of some urgency, therefore, that he marry. Hence the Sonnets, whose theme was to be the importance of marriage. After inviting him to her country estate, Wilton House, and encouraging him to improvise some sonnets as a kind of audition, Mary Herbert duly commissioned Shakespeare, handing him a miniature of the lad to work from. The first seventeen sonnets are on the appropriate themes of procreation, preservation of the line and renewal. A surprising warmth enters into the urgings – at one point the poet urges the young man to marry 'for love of me': an unknown writer, executing a commission. Apparently the sonnets worked the trick, because William agreed to come to London to meet a prospective bride. While there he met Shakespeare for the first time. Together they went to the studio of a painter (Hilliard?). Four sonnets, teasing and slightly bawdy –

> But since she pricked thee out for women's pleasure,
> Mine be thy love and thy love's use their treasure

– but also surprisingly personal –

> But when in thee time's furrows I behold,
> Then look I death my days should expiate

– celebrate the visit, all centred on painterly images. Some kind of arrangement was reached *vis-à-vis* the potential fiancée, but then W.H. asserted his independence and broke it off. Mary Herbert was back to square one. Now she decided that before she could even think about marriage, she needed to get the boy interested in sex. To that end, she promised him that he could live, on his own, in the Pembrokes' London home, Baynard's Castle, hoping that in the big city his fancies would surely turn to love. To expedite the process, she turned again to Shakespeare. As a member of a notoriously immoral profession, he would undoubtedly know a thousand means of initiation. Her request found Shakespeare in a curious emotional state. He had become increasingly preoccupied with thoughts of the boy – the boy he'd only met once. His beauty, his remoteness, his nobility began to coalesce into an image of perfection. Shakespeare was thirty-three, prematurely balding, a member of a despised profession, and a bereaved father – his son Hamnet had died two years before. His sense of mortality was acute; also his sense of social unworthiness. The young aristocrat seemed in possession of everything that Shakespeare wanted and would never have. His feelings for the boy – that is to say, the boy that he was now inventing, because he knew nothing of him beyond report, a miniature, and a brief meeting – included paternal ones, wishing to protect the golden youth from the ravages of time and society, and a kind of transference, loving in the boy the him that never was, loving W.H. perhaps as he himself longed to have been loved.

So Mary Herbert's new approach to Shakespeare – asking him in effect to arrange for the boy's sexual initiation – was peculiarly distressing. Torn in many directions, his response was oblique. A ploy of the Elizabethan theatre may have come to mind whereby actors would nudge the boy players into heterosexuality by sending them on errands to their mistresses, who would introduce them to sexual delight. Shakespeare's variation on this was to write a series of poems to his mistress – the famous 'dark lady' – celebrating the ecstatic delights of their shared bed. These sonnets W.H. would deliver to her. Conscious no doubt of what he might be doing to his own emotions, he withdrew to Stratford, sending the mistress-sonnets in groups of three, each covered, as it were, by another group, related in imagery, to W.H. himself. These 'covering' sonnets form a great arc of 72 (18 x 4) which is the very heart of the whole collection – a delineation of the terrible progress of Eros, from confidence and exultation, through melancholy, doubt, betrayal, forgiveness, awareness of rejection, desperation, self-annihilation, to final withdrawal. The rejection was both personal and professional, because now W.H., gaining confidence and suddenly aware of his power as a patron, began to surround himself with a coterie of rival poets, who, at his regular salons, flattered him with sycophantic verses. Shakespeare sat mutely through these sessions until at the end he produced twelve sparring sonnets, a proud statement of integrity. But he refused to compete with the florid effusions of Chapman and the rest of the group, and finally, riven with pain, he severed the connection which had brought him ever-increasing anguish. The *envoi*, a kind of ghostly epilogue to the whole sequence, comes from the pen of a man who has passed through the extremes of feeling and has been drained to the dregs of his being.

Every April for eight years afterwards, Shakespeare sent William Herbert four sonnets. The depth of his feelings made it impossible for him simply to walk away. But these sonnets are of an entirely different character to the cauterizing set of seventy-two. These are poems from one equal to another – not social equals to be sure, but equal in love. The disparity between W.S.'s feelings for W.H. and those he got in return has disappeared, a firm, if sometimes threatened, friendship taking its place. The poems come out of the full life of a leading dramatist and actor, while the earlier sonnets inhabit a hysterical world of their own. In these poems, too, the great theme of the whole collection becomes more and more clearly voiced. No longer is it Shakespeare and William Herbert who stand at the centre of the stage, but The Poet and Time, engaged in desperate war. The last sonnet of all hurls defiance –

No! Time, thou shalt not boast that I do change
and ends –
This do I vow, and this shall ever be –
I will be true despite thy scythe and thee.

Neither Kustow nor I were in any position to assess the academic soundness of Padel's work. We were agreed, however, that the reordering made a radical difference poetically and emotionally, and that the story Padel told was fascinating. As we worked on it, we became more and more convinced of its truth. My identification with Shakespeare's emotional experience was total. It seemed to be my life he was writing down. The psychological realism was shocking and sometimes overwhelming. Time and again, I wept as I read, and so did Kustow. The combination in Shakespeare of the singer and the sufferer, the word-man of genius plus the unerring follower-through of emotional truth, is to be found at its most intense in the Sonnets. Sometimes it seemed to us that the man himself was present. Certainly, I felt that I knew him; and I knew what he was, in the root of his being: he was an actor. A dramatist, too, of course; but what is a dramatist but someone who plays all the parts, makes up all the words, and writes them down? The first Greek dramatists were actors; or, if you prefer, the first Greek actors were dramatists. The most immediately striking thing when one plays in a Shakespeare play is the independent life of the characters. They seem to be writing themselves. There is no sense in the plays of Shakespeare's personality. Of course, the inner organization, the hidden structure – these point to a consummate artist. And the language is ineffably rich and apt and expressive – but it is always the language of the character who utters it. Somehow Shakespeare became each character, and then just let him rip. He must have observed everything, absorbed everything – and it must have translated straight away into art. The mental ferment must have been unendurable; and emotionally exhausting. Any emotion, once born in him, had to be followed through. Where the rest of us scent the approach of dangerous and painful emotions and take care to kill them before they get hold of us, he was helpless. John Padel's sonnet theory, and the clear evidence of the poems themselves, shows the process at work. From the giving of the commission, his insatiable emotional appetite was at work. Once embarked on the idea of procreation, and once in receipt of the miniature, he was doomed to live through what he did. From the very beginning, his dramatist nature was at work, inventing the character, first of all of W.H. then of himself, and finally of his mistress, compelled to work the plot, in which he was the leading participant, to its bitter end.

Suddenly the Droeshut portrait of Shakespeare made sense. That neurasthenic washed-out creature with his all-seeing eyes was merely a channel in which the world around was converted into metaphor, action and character. I imagine him barely having a life, as such. He was never off-duty. Speaking to people, he must have struggled not to start imitating their accent, twisting his features into their face.

And *that's* what it's like to be an actor.

He must have wondered who he was, must have been in a state of continuous ontological flux. He must have sometimes needed to hold on to the table to avoid falling down. Hence his quest for aristocratic patronage, for property, for a coat of arms; in a word, for stability. And hence the underlying structure of so many of the plays – the disruption of order followed by the struggle for its re-establishment, whether in government or marriage. His world-view is essentially that of a structure in imminent danger of breakdown, just as his personality must have been. The vividness of his account of breakdown, whether in *King Lear* or the Sonnets, suggests close personal acquaintance with it.

Our excitement during this period was breathless. Every day we seemed to come closer to the greatest dramatist in the world, who was also one of its greatest enigmas. We felt as if we were going where no one had ever gone before; not to mention the exhilaration of daily contact with these beautiful painful poems. I had meanwhile replaced my W.H. with the real thing. The poems themselves had somehow opened my heart, I was brimming over with loving emotions, and perhaps inevitably, I found a repository for them. The two-way exchange that ensued fed straight back into the poems (and into my other work: *As You Like It* became a great love-song too). It was a second adolescence, almost – love everywhere.

We started the public performances slowly, feeling our way. I introduced the theory, too, speaking directly to the audience, then retired behind the podium, dressed from head to foot in black, save for a single medallion, which sometimes shot beams of reflected light across the auditorium. When I'd done the whole series in three separate programmes, we decided to do them all on one day as the final proving of the theory. I wondered whether I'd be up to it – not so much physically as emotionally. The second programme, in particular, was always in danger of breaking down completely. Every time, the pain hit me with new force. Why is it that happiness makes one so much more aware of pain? Relief at having left it behind? Certainly that summer was the happiest time I've ever known, work, friendship and love all reaching heights I'd never dreamt of – and yet I've never cried so much in my life. In love, of course, everything reminds one of the beloved, and there didn't seem to be a phrase that didn't apply (I was able to send letters saying simply, 'No. 35'), and in a sense the performances were like a public affirmation of that love. That was a peculiarly liberating feeling. But I'm afraid that in the end, all the emotion proved to be my undoing.

The separate programmes rolled on, gaining ever greater momentum, both in performance and in publicity. Godfrey Smith of the *Sunday Times* had chanced upon the first performance, and began to write about it, culminating in a full-page spread in the Review. Attendances doubled, then trebled. The Lyttleton and once the Olivier were sometimes as much as half full, not common for six o'clock Platform Performances. My exposition of the theory became more and more lucid; my readings of the sonnets less and less so. My passion for them was taking on a life of its own. Before the scheduled afternoon marathon in the Olivier at which I would perform 148 sonnets, we scheduled a dress rehearsal at the Guildhall Drama School. I think I peaked there. The next day, the day of the marathon, I was somewhat tired, my voice a little hoarse, and my nerves in shreds. All 1,200 seats had been sold long ago, all the critics had been invited, and amongst other people with firm views about the performance of Sonnets, the audience included Bernard Levin and Sir John Gielgud: the latter, the more worrying presence.

I staggered on to the stage, my heart beating even faster than it might have done on account of the ten cups of black coffee which I'd drunk in my dressing room. I plunged into the first sonnet – and immediately fouled up a line. Eventually, I calmed down, but the combination of adrenalin, exhaustion and excessive emotion conspired to reduce the afternoon from an exposition of a newly discovered map of Shakespeare's soul to a technicolour, panavision, Todd-AO projection of my emotional response to that map. As it happens, my response was enormous and vivid and possibly quite moving in itself, and of course, phrase upon glorious phrase welled up over the stalls and into the dress circle, but I'm ashamed to say I did not do Shakespeare's sonnets justice. I was applauded to the echo at the end; and god knows, I deserved it for stamina alone (more verse than the roles of Hamlet, Lear and Othello put together). It was a heady moment. People were standing, now, and cheering. I was delighted, but I knew that I'd failed.

The critics were quite keen to point that out the next morning. Personally, I would have thought that reviews of the order of: 'a brave experiment, with some rewards, though basically, alas, a failure' would have been suitable, but no, I was told that the poor reviewer had left the theatre not enlightened but battered, that it was an absurd undertaking, that though the audience cheered, the reviewer was not impressed: had I pulled ferrets from my trouser leg, he might have been. My slips of the tongue were scrupulously recorded, including many that were in fact authentic textual amendments. These were the worst notices of my career; but poor John Padel had an even worse time of it than I: his years of research were dismissed by those towering intellects, the daily critics, as 'nonsense' and 'rubbishy' as well as 'patently false'. On Sunday it was my turn again. James Fenton, describing me as an actor of tiny range (within which I was 'a master', outside of it 'ridiculous'), dismissed the whole venture as 'a monument to Mr Callow's vanity'. It was after these reviews that I got a daily fan mail which exceeded anything I'd ever had before, entirely from people who'd been there and were furious at the misrepresentation. It's not only actors who find The Critics a bit suspect.

A few days after the event I was talking to Peter Hall, and I predicted that Fenton's review would be vicious because he's a poet and poets don't believe in a dramatic approach to poetry. He hesitated and I said, 'I'm not sure you do, either.' He said, 'I think you're a very fine verse speaker. I don't want to boast, but I think if you spent half an hour with me, you could be one of the best verse speakers in the country.' 'That's a half hour we've got to spend, isn't it?' 'Yes!' he laughed, and kept his word. Over the next few weeks, whenever he could slot it in, we spent, not half-hour but hour-long sessions in which he took me through a couple of sonnets, and then 'Oh what a rogue and peasant slave am I'. It was practical, simple – and a revelation. It's the Poël tradition, essentially: spotting antithesis, apposition and alliteration; realizing the metaphor; sensing the pulse of the metre, which is such a clear guide to meaning, too. Finally he told me something surprising but immediately effective: the meaning of the line very often resides in the second half, so go towards that, which has the additional advantage of sustaining the forward movement of the verse. I tried it out on

> Like as the waves make towards the pebbled shore
> So do our minutes hasten to their end.

I had been sweeping into the line: 'Like as the WAVES make towards the pebbled shore/So do our MINUTES hasten to their end' – a false apposition and an energy rundown. The moment one says: 'Like as the waves make TOWARDS THE PEBBLED SHORE, So do our minutes HASTEN TO THEIR END', the meaning becomes clear and the poem starts to move. Giving the metaphor its life is the secret of the whole undertaking. A poem should be like a piece of wood that the microscope reveals to be, not a solid mass, but a kingdom seething with life, swarming multitudes of molecules. 'I think you may have a tendency to fall in love with the wrong word,' Peter gently said. In fact throughout *Amadeus* and during our whole working relationship, Peter never stopped trying to get me to phrase by the line instead of the word, and I am eternally grateful to him for it. It's taken a long time for *that* lesson to sink in, but I think it finally has: I managed to phrase Donleavy's juicy text of *Balthazar B.*, language full of lures for the wordoholic, in whole paragraphs, never mind sentences; and the gain was enormous. Any kind of heightened language, I discovered, has a pulse which compensates for the richness of texture, which would otherwise tend to drive the play into the past, lingering over its beauties. The forward motion of the pulse counterbalances it and brings it where it should be: the present.

Subsequent performances of the Sonnet programmes (in three separate parts again) attempted to incorporate the new insights. It wasn't until I went to Cambridge, Massachusetts, six months later and performed an altogether different selection at Harvard that the lessons completely filtered through. One thing, however, has remained constant: the picture of Shakespeare and his creative self that John Padel's research reveals has been greeted with amazement, fascination and above all *relief* by almost everyone who's heard it. In Santa Fe, I was thanked warmly by my students for making Shakespeare the man approachable, because real. In America, but, to a lesser degree, in England too, the Bard looms like a kind of unsurmountable mountain, an ultimate test of which the rules may never be learnt, only somehow mysteriously inherited or transmitted. The couple of hours that I spent with Peter Hall should be available to all actors in some form. Of course, we're all too frightened to ask, because it's an admission of ignorance. Thus I suppose many actors never fully experience the pleasure of playing Shakespeare. It's important that everyone should, because Shakespeare seems to me to be the most dramatic of dramatists; he *is* drama, in the way that Mozart *is* music: distilled, direct: the intervention of the author's 'personality' kept to the minimum possible.

The Sonnets were the climax of my time at the National. The Marathon occurred in the middle of rehearsals for *Galileo*. Dexter, with entirely typical generosity, had rarely called me to rehearse, and then only lightly flicked through the scene. 'Concentrate on the Sonnets,' he snarled affectionately. When the day arrived, he planned to cancel rehearsals to give everyone, including himself, the opportunity to attend. In the event, he had a relapse of shingles and stayed in bed. When I arrived in my dressing room, there was a bottle of Veuve

Cliquot in a bucket, with a card. 'I can't attend, but I'm not heart-broken, because I know you are going to be forced to do a repeat performance by public demand. You will probably end up doing more farewell tours of it than Dame Nellie Melba in *La Bohème*. Love John.' After that, though, the honeymoon was over. Rehearsals were a joyless business for me; and so was playing. An extracurricular diversion was *The Soldier's Tale* at the Queen Elizabeth Hall, in which I fulfilled my life-long ambition: to dance. '*Le diable danse*', says the score, and I begged Maina Gielgud to make as difficult a dance for me as she could. This was very difficult indeed. We decided that the violin (played, for real, by Pinchas Zuckerman) would turn the devil into a ballerina and accordingly I ran the gamut of the classical repertory – as best I could on point, arabesques, and finally the *Spectre de la Rose* port de bras. This was a highpoint of my career from which I have never altogether recovered.

Galileo opened, to huge acclaim. I was still playing in *Amadeus* and *Sisterly Feelings*, which was like many well-written and well-crafted comedies: they reach perfection on their first nights, and never grow, indeed *mustn't* grow. The result is increasing insanity among the cast. Ayckbourn's plays, which I admire deeply, are so beautifully made and written that an indifferent performance will produce exactly the same laughs as a brilliant one. This too is rather depressing for the actors. The production also contained a death-defying hurtle down the one-in-one slope which Alan Tagg had built on the Olivier stage which got harder and harder to perform every time I did it. Waiting with bicycle on the other side of the hill, I tried to think of something else until I heard my cue, when I would rush up the slope, scream 'Geronimo!' and cycle down at an impossible angle. Physical feats of this kind stimulate many actors (Olivier among them, I presume). For me, acting has never been a substitute for hang-gliding. Stage-fights fill me with particular dread (the one in *As You Like It* was terrifying) mainly because so many actors, once the adrenalin is flowing get the scent of blood in their nostrils and suddenly you're face-to-face with a psychopath. I have lost half a tooth and a bit of a thumb in this way; others have lost eyes, ears, and lives. The whole question of stage violence is a problem for me. I'm simply inept at it, having so little experience of it in life. I've never, as far as I can remember, struck anyone in my life. When I try to do so on stage, I become hopelessly limp-wristed. Fear of the violence in myself, no doubt, or fear of provoking it in others; but it's a closed area to me.

My dissatisfaction at the National increased. I had played no major role for a year, and the two parts that I did play were not ones that I would have even considered had I not been at the National. I became acutely aware of a lack of vision. This was much to do with the building itself, a dinosaur from a previous era of civic aspiration, alienating in itself, and impossibly large for any group to feel themselves a company in. Moreover, the number of stages creates a demand for 'product' which is accordingly supplied, but with minimum reference to the passion of the directors. Rather it's a question of 'It's about time for another Ibsen, I'm afraid.' I had been told by Peter Hall that the next production in the Olivier was 'mine'. It passed through various stages of imminence, until one day there were dates. It was six months later than intended, but never mind, it was on. And then one day Christopher Morahan, Peter's deputy, came to me in my dressing room to tell me that for one reason and another, it was off – but the slot was still 'mine' – what would I like to do? My mind went a complete blank and I could only think of twenty-five plays, which I reeled off. There was a good reason for not doing any of them. The best was for *Woyzeck*: 'We've just commissioned a translation of *Danton's Death*,' Christopher said, 'and we rather think that'll be our Büchner for the decade.'

That, in a nutshell, is what's wrong with the National Theatre. In the circumstances, I hardly see how it can ever be different. 'Olivier's National Theatre' was just that: organized around one man and what he stood for, which was understood rather than articulated. I doubt very much whether he could have galvanized the South Bank into a single body of passionate artists. The company, as such, barely exists. The growth of the individual artist is not attended to in the least. Normally casting is a rather squalid affair, each director trying to get the biggest names for every part, and then working his way down the list after each refusal. A tiny handful of actors always play the leading parts. Most of the company, far from slowly advancing through the ranks, decline in them, until finally they're out on the back doorstep with the rubbish. The involvement of the company in decisions is non-existent. Not a single actor, stage manager, scenic artist, designer or musician sits on any National Theatre committee. It is in these subsidized theatres that the directocracy is at its most unqualified. The waste of actors' intelligence and passion (how can you be passionate about anything in which you have had no involvement? All that's left for you is to concentrate on *your role*: unhealthy and counter-productive) is bad enough; but the undue burden borne by the directors, their isolation and their fear is just as bad. Heads in these situations roll with remarkable regularity. The directors must be saved from the situation just as much as the actors. Will they relinquish control, however? With their complete command of the economic reins it seems unlikely. But it is the only way forward; or rather backward, because, as is well known, the rise of the director is a recent phenomenon which on balance has by no means proved its value. The vogue for 'workers' participation' seems to have been submerged in the swelling waves of recession. For me, it was always an insufficient watchword. 'Workers' democracy', as proposed by Wilhelm Reich, is more radical: those who do the work should be responsible for it. Only that way will we have a society which is not mechanical, in which people don't do things simply because they've been told to.

Nine

They never found me a play to do at the National, so I left. By amazing good luck, I immediately went into a play that I loved deeply and had often tried to persuade various companies to mount. This was *Total Eclipse* by Christopher Hampton. Christopher had long wanted to revive it. Within a week, his agent, my close friend Peggy Ramsay, had set it up, with David Hare (another client) as director. It was an exquisite production, exquisitely set by Hayden Griffin and with an exquisite score by Nick Bicât. Hare, a slightly mellower man than when we'd worked together before – I suppose I was slightly less callow, too – worked with his usual witty perfectionism on play and performances. There we were again in St Gabriel's, Pimlico, scene of many a Joint Stock workshop, meticulously charting the course of the French poets' profane entanglement. Poor old St Gabriel! What he has to put up with: rapes, child-stonings, and now a couple of froggie poofs. It seemed a favourable omen, however, that the book I picked off the top of a tea-chest full of jumble (something to do with the church hall's alter ego, a boys' club) was a volume of essays by Charles Morgan. The first one was on Verlaine, and it remains the best thing I've ever read about him. 'No arrow grazed him. They all went to the heart. Other men distinguish among the arrows, avoiding some, raising a shield against others. Verlaine did not distinguish, because, as an artist, he desired intuitively to be struck again and again.' How had Christopher, at the age of twenty, understood such a man so well? Rimbaud, yes, of course. I often thought of Victor Henry. When I'd known him, he'd been rehearsing the first production of *Total Eclipse*, and his identification with Rimbaud was complete. I remembered the story he'd told me about Kenneth Haigh, who'd been asked to play Verlaine. There was a pause at the other end of the phone. 'They used to ask me to play Rimbaud,' he said wryly. Hilton Macrae was the avenging angel in our production. Hare adjusted the balance between us with a fine tuner. He persuaded me to play the Verlaine of the play rather than some Laughtonesque variant of my imagination and encouraged the steel in Hilton's soul.

The first night was exactly what we wanted it to be. That was the show we had rehearsed; not distorted, as so often. The audience was intelligent and feeling, and there was the unmistakable smell of success in the air. Until the next morning, that is. Mild enthusiasm, carpings at the play, dismissal of the performances. Later reviews were better, and finally Fenton raved in the *Sunday Times*. But it was a bitter experience to play the play one loved above almost all others to houses that were only a quarter or a third full, for three weeks. I am at a loss to explain the critical response. It was not shared by those who saw the play, known and unknown. Eighteen months later, people were still introducing themselves to communicate their enjoyment of the production. I found the play deeply moving every time I performed it. (I cannot say that I enjoyed the run, however, and that for a curious reason. David Hare had insisted on a revolve, to eliminate the lengthy scene changes which had so hampered the original production. It had exactly the effect he desired. A side-effect of a revolve, however, is that after every turn of the wheel, the scene being played is accompanied by the noise of the previous set being removed, and the next one being installed, while the floor itself sways gently as stage-hands walk on and off. The result is that one feels that every scene is simply filling in until the next. The feeling of impermanence was most disturbing.)

Edward Bond's *Restoration* is a brilliant play; Lord Are, the character I played, is one of the wittiest roles of the modern stage. The problem with the production at the Royal Court was, as so often, the director. The fact that this was the same person as the author didn't make it any more agreeable.

It seems to me that Edward Bond is a truly classical author. His plays have an ambitiousness in terms of language and scope that is unrivalled. In general they have received a very poor press, partly because Bond's Marxism is regarded as simplistic, but mainly, I believe, because since Gaskill's inspired production of *Saved*, no one has understood the style in which the plays are written – not Gaskill, not Peter Gill, and now, least of all, it would seem, Bond himself. He's very sound on what his style *isn't*, but that's no help at all in achieving what it is. My relationship with the man was stormily enjoyable. We had one thing in common: enormous admiration for the play. Edward has determined that no one shall direct his plays in future but himself. He has not felt it necessary, however, to add to his writer's craft any apprehension of the crafts of either the director or the actor. I suspect that he regards the director as a mere surrogate writer. The actor, I think, he views with distrust and suspicion. He believes that the actor's job is simple and mechanical (say the lines, do the moves) and that the special treatment that they demand and the enormous acclaim that they receive are equally disproportionate to their contribution to the event. He's alternately stubborn and pixieish in his dealing with actors. Because he has no understanding of the processes of acting, he's unable to understand the difficulties, and therefore, unable to help solve them. He has to have recourse to giving line readings, and to running scenes over and over, in the hope that somehow they'll fall into place. They never do. All this is very frustrating, because he understands his own plays perfectly and is always right in what he says about them. But translating what he says into acting is almost impossible.

The role of Lord Are is an actor's dream; a few weeks into rehearsal, it had become a nightmare. My original intuitive conception was wrong, I could see that. Edward stopped me every two minutes to point out a misinflection or an over-emphasis; again I could see that he was right, but that was no good. Why was it coming out all wrong? I had to get my image of the character clear. Edward decreed late-night rehearsals, which in the circumstances took on the nature of detention. At one of these rehearsals, I took the bull by the horns. I was beginning to hate myself for throwing away one of the great roles of the modern theatre. So I said to him, 'Edward, I refuse to leave this room until I say one line as the character.' I reckoned that if I could get the taste of one line, really indulge in that, what it feels like to be Lord Are, I could predicate the rest of the man from it. 'All right,' said Edward brightly. We started the first monologue. He stopped me. 'No,' I said, 'we won't get it like this. What animal is he like?' If I could find the man's shape, it would be something. 'I don't know.' 'Well, I can tell you how I'm playing him: like a camel.' 'Oh no, quite wrong.' 'A peacock?' 'Do you know what peacocks are like?' said Edward. 'Predatory animals, you know. They'll eat the food off your plate.' Somehow he was missing my point. 'OK, what kind of music is he like?' 'Um. He's like a piano being played with a stiletto knife.' Thanks a bunch, I thought. 'And another thing: he's like an eighteenth-century carriage with a steam engine inside.' How could I explain to Edward that what I needed was something much simpler, something concrete, something which would give me a *sensation*. 'I think I begin to see what you mean,' I lied. 'Let's try the speech again.' After two lines, Edward stopped me. 'It is a little bit better,' he said, 'but you're still making it too complicated. Don't you see, when he talks to the audience, he's talking to his friends. He expects them to agree with him.' 'Aaarrgh,' I cried. I was on to something at last. I winged a couple of lines. Edward laughed – for the first time. I tried a few more – then the whole speech. I'd got it. It all came in a great rush. The essential sunniness of the man's temperament became clear. His whole life is played out in the confidence of his friends' approval; and what else matters to a gentleman? We packed up and went home. We both knew that the penny had dropped. The rest was easy – just *doing* it. The life of the character had been established, however, and it would flourish.

This sense of independent life in the character was not strange to Edward. It was he who had answered, when I asked why the man was called Lord Are (R), 'That's all he would tell me.' And he who had told me the wonderful story of his writing *The Bundle*. One of the characters had begun to take over every scene in which he appeared. The RSC phoned every day to find out how the play was progressing. 'Fine,' said Edward, 'but I have no idea how it'll end, because of this character.' Finally, they said, 'We've got to have the play next week to start casting.' 'All right,' he said, 'I'll kill him.' He did, and the play was ready by the weekend.

What Edward never understood, though, was that in order to play the character the actor must experience the life in him, must let that life fill his consciousness. Writers are often proprietorial about their creations: what in fact has happened is that they've given birth to someone who has an independent existence.

He also refused to accept that the act of embodying another human being is a complex and unnerving business, calling for concentration and a certain amount of consideration. To say that an actor should be thought of as a pregnant woman may be going too far, but a similar process of internal upheaval is taking place. You're breaking down your own thought patterns and trying to reconstruct them into those of the character, pushing into emotional territory which may be strange and difficult for you, seeking the bodily centre of an alien being. A certain amount of spasticity sets in, the coordination collapses. Words of the text appear dimly, at the end of a long tunnel. Your mental feelers reach out desperately, while your emotional system seems to be in permanent short-circuit, a horrible constipation of the impulses, a highly charged but completely inexpressive state, not relieved by your unaccountably having developed six hands and fourteen feet. Moving a chair from one side of the stage to the other, or drinking a cup of tea, present insurmountable problems.

Edward could see none of this. Few directors do. Most of them, however, do acknowledge that the work is difficult and requires certain conditions. Not he. Noise, people walking through the rehearsal room, spectators, it was all fine by him. After all, people in factories worked in far more inconvenient conditions. *Yes*, but . . . finally I exploded. We were working on the stage, precious time. The set was up, which was very useful; but as I was beginning the famous, much worked-on opening monologue, a Black and Decker drill started making holes just behind me. I struggled on for a couple of minutes, then: 'Noise, noise, NOISE.' 'Get on with it,' said Edward. 'I cannot work through that.' 'Nonsense.' 'For Christ's sake,' I screamed, 'you have quiet to *write* in.' The driller stopped at that moment, so I have no idea whether Edward accepted my point.

During the first week of playing there was some royal junket, a wedding or an anniversary, celebrated by a massive display of fireworks on the river. The theatre was predictably empty, and the adrenalin which had somehow enabled the production to get away with it was suddenly absent. Everything that was wrong with the show became crystal clear. It was a wretched evening.

I went home in high dudgeon. It was so humiliating. Did he really think a bad production of a radical play was more radical than a good production? Did he think that directors' and actors' skills were unimportant? Did he have any idea of what actors went through in order to create – or rather to re-create – the character. Was he happy that we should have this rather botched production, only for the RSC to put it on in five years' time with Alan Howard as Lord Are, when it would be acclaimed as a masterpiece – which it surely was. On and on I raved to myself as I stomped home under a Jackson Pollock sky of exploding Roman Candles and sky-rockets. Once indoors, I got hold of a bottle of whisky and went straight to my typewriter. 'Dear Edward,' I started, and stated the whole case as unequivocally as I knew how. An hour or two later, my flat-mate came home to discover me still typing furiously, with an empty whisky bottle at my side. 'Whacherthinkathis,' I slurred, pulling the sheet out of the typewriter. 'It says qsthx hsdrat qwtypnk sfgt,' he said. 'Ah,' I said, sliding slowly off my chair.

The next morning I returned to the fray and wrote it again, more calmly and coherently. I was, however, a little nervous of what I'd written. That day I had lunch with Peggy Ramsay, Edward's agent, and told her of the letter. 'You *must* send it,' she said, 'for your sake and for Edward's. Here's a stamp.' I was still nervous, however, and promised to send it within a day or two, when I'd properly considered the implications. That Saturday, Edward came to see the show. It went with great fizz. He was very happy. In the pub afterwards he came up to me. 'I hear you've written me a letter.'

'Er, yes.' I still hadn't had the courage to post it.

'Will you send it to me?'

'It's rather beastly,' I said.

'All the more reason to send it,' he said. Then: 'Come for a walk. I need some fresh air.' We walked round Sloane Square, while he made some observations about my performance, and I reproached him for not having attended the first night. 'I know, I'm sorry,' he said, 'I just can't bear being in an enclosed area with *those* people' – the critics.

'We have to,' I said.

'Yes,' he replied, 'yes, I know. Look – let me take you for a meal. Are you hungry?' We went to Como Lario. He was in an extraordinarily genial frame of mind. We ate and drank and talked freely. He was warm, gentle and modest. 'One day,' he said 'one day I promise I'll write a good play. I promise that.' It was very touching. 'And I'll give a good performance,' I promised.

We got up and walked unsteadily to Edward's car. As he opened the door he said, 'You'd better give me that letter, hadn't you?'

'Oh no, Edward, I really don't think so. I was very angry when I wrote it, it seems to belong to the past.'

'Give it to me,' he said. 'I can always throw it out of the window.'

'Yes, do that,' I said, handing the dog-eared envelope over (I'd carried it around in my pocket for days), 'just do that.'

The next morning I played back the messages on my answering machine. The first was from Edward. 'It's six o'clock in the morning. I've read your letter. I'm very glad I read it, and I'm glad you wrote it. Of course I agree with you. I'll write to you to try to answer what you say.'

He never did.

So much time was spent in these crossed lines and failures of communication that what I regard as one of the most extraordinary achievements of the modern theatre was an interesting failure. Again.

Me again, I mean. I had within a couple of weeks played two of the most exciting roles of my career, and both, for different reasons, had failed to quite make it. Now followed the third.

I was still at the National when Patrick Ryecart, of whom I knew, but whom I'd never met, phoned to tell me that he'd acquired the rights in J. P. Donleavy's play *The Beastly Beatitudes of Balthazar B.*, the moment he'd read it he knew that I was the right person to play the part of Beefy, would I like to have a copy of the script? Indeed, I said. He did know that in a previous incarnation of the script I'd been going to play the part for John Dexter? No, he'd only ever seen me on the television, in *Instant Enlightenment Plus V.A.T.*, but had known immediately that I must play Beefy. The rights had finally come through today, and now he was phoning to invite me to join him as co-producer. 'We don't want any managers getting their hands on it.

Let's put it on ourselves. It's about time actors took the initiative again, don't you think?' I did think. From then on Patrick, with me in amiable support (first *Total Eclipse* then *Restoration* kept me busy), beavered away. By blind faith and unflagging determination mixed in with a healthy quantity of low cunning, within a couple of months he had unbelievably secured a backer, an executive manager and a theatre. When the theatre and I came free simultaneously, we were ready to go. The original director having fallen out, we – Pat, Howard Panter (the executive manager) and I – rapidly auditioned directors. This was a new and not very pleasing experience. Pat and I had to maintain an extremely low profile so as not to appear to threaten the directors' *amour propre*. It's an unusual experience for them: first of all not to cast the play from scratch, secondly to be asked by the actors what their feelings about the play might be. From our point of view it was essential that the director should be responsive to the peculiar mix represented by the title: the bawdy and the beautiful, lyrical and lecherous and that he would be able to get on with Donleavy. We knew full well that the play as it stood needed much attention. It was a very straight rendition of certain episodes from the book, theatrically conventional, linguistically pre-Lord Chamberlain. The book is altogether richer, funnier, more touching. Happily, in Ron Daniels we met someone who understood that perfectly, and who was confident that he could persuade Donleavy to accept all kinds of changes by the simple expedient of reassuring him that he needn't rewrite a word; everything was in the book. Patrick and I were already deeply in love with the novel and had to fight an impulse not to include passage after passage. Ron came back from Donleavy's home in Mullingar with a vastly improved text, and we went straight into rehearsals, with only two out of the cast of ten. New members of cast arrived every day, new pages of script were stapled in, new decisions about the design. All very exhilarating. Before we knew where we were, the previews were upon us, uproariously received, and then the first night, stiffer but ultimately joyous. The usual sequence ensued. Jolly first night party, much carousing, huggings and slappings. 'We did it!' was the cry heard throughout St Martin's Lane.

'Oh no you didn't,' came the answer from Fleet Street. The notices ranged from the friendly to the vituperative, with Milton Shulman hedging his bets: 'I loved it, but I can see it might not be everybody's cup of tea.' (We understand that, Milt, your review is *your* opinion.) Next morning I went to work with Harold Pinter on a charity gala. 'Marvellous notices,' he said. 'What?' I asked disbelievingly. '*Guardian*,' he said, pointing. 'Compared you to Wolfit.' I didn't like to point out that these days such a comparison was not generally regarded as praise; but I did get a sense of perspective from Harold's account of the original notices for *The Birthday Party*.

We were accused of not being faithful to the novel and of being too faithful to the novel, of coarseness and of pusillanimity. In short, they couldn't find a bracket for us, and there's nothing that annoys a critic more. What I felt more keenly then than on any previous occasion was the disparity between our intentions and the spirit in which the work was received. I thought back to those sun-filled days in the church hall in Maida Vale when we had all been possessed by love of the work and anticipation of how much delight we were going to spread. The reviews for the most part seemed to challenge our right to appear on any stage. Had we appeared in St Martin's Lane pumping poison gas into the auditorium, we couldn't have been worse received. The subtext of the press seemed to be 'We'll stamp this one out quick, before it spreads.' Well, they failed, and we played our nine months, and some, thanks to the passionate faith of Naim Atallah, the sole and unwavering backer.

In a sense, they were right. We hadn't really cracked it. It was an unsatisfactory piece of work (though no more so than much that is acclaimed to the echo). And the problem was time. Everything happened so quickly, decisions were taken so summarily, that one was scarcely aware of the irreversible implications of what had been set in motion. Novices that we were, we were not to know that the fate of a production lies in its preparation. The actual rehearsal period is so short and critical, that there is simply no time for major questions to be broached. Above all in the matter of the text (unless there is a rehearsal period such as only the subsidized companies can afford) if it isn't ninety per cent achieved, improvement will only be marginal.

Ron Daniels was delightfully responsive to my work. I felt relaxed and I believe I did justice to what is on the page, an almost impossible text. Of course, no critic realized that. No more had they on *Restoration*, which had been regarded by many people as unplayable. The secret of both (otherwise radically different) texts was phrasing by paragraph, Peter Hall's lesson by now well learned.

I learned much that was new during the 320 performances of *Balthazar*, the most I have ever done – consecutively, at that. By the end of the run, I had been through many crises, in myself, and in my art. I was obliged to ask myself fundamental questions: whether I was satisfied with acting, whether I had lost touch with whatever it was that drove me, whether I had any theatrical ambitions any more. What theatres did I want to work in? What directors did I want to work for? What roles did I want to play?

The answers were uniformly negative: none. Then came a call to act and teach at Santa Fe, New Mexico. I felt that a god-sent opportunity was being extended to me to reconsider the whole thing.

Clearly some kind of epoch was over. Everything I had done had taught me something. I felt well-equipped now. But for what? To continue the career of a successful West End, metropolitan actor? To go from role to role, doing a solid job? There must be more. I was also convinced that there was something fundamentally missing from the English theatre. It was in the hands of intellectual academic puritans. Within the framework of intellectual academic puritanism, they did fine work. What I became more and more sharply aware of was that what was being offered was More Of The Same. I was not prepared to go on contributing More Of The Same, myself. Perhaps in the desert I would find what I had lost, and maybe what could be done.

PART **TWO**

In the first section I tried to trace the thread of acting running through one actor's life. I'd now like to reverse the telescope and present what I suppose could be called the worm's eye view: an account of the experience of the job: what, day by day, even hour by hour, it feels like to be an actor. It's a consciously subjective account, neither fair nor balanced. It is, I hope, the inside story.

Unemployment

The primeval slime from which actors emerge and to which, inevitably, they return.

As for anyone else, it's castrating; but most actors encounter it more frequently and the periods of work in between are shorter. No sooner have you got used to the money and the sensation of work than it's taken away from you. Most acting work, with the exception of long-running series on the television, or a contract with one of the subsidized companies, is temporary by its nature. Halfway through any engagement, you start worrying about the next. Actors *like* to work; they *need* to work; they don't feel they *are* actors unless they're working. This sort of ontological anxiety haunts actors at every level. Because your instrument is you, because you, when it boils down to it, you, and not your skill, which is indivisible from your face, your body and your personality, is what you sell, it's *you* nobody wants. You constantly examine your face and your life wondering why you're not wanted. Are you too fat? Too thin? Too stupid? Too intelligent? Too weak? Too strong? If only your nose were smaller. If only your conversation were wittier. If only you knew more people. You take steps to remedy the deficiency. You have an inch taken off the nose, you force yourself to make jokes, you write letters to directors, you try to go to as many parties as possible. It's all quite false. It's not you at all. But you must work. The desire to be employed has a terribly corrupting effect on artistic ambition, and on courage with directors. Actors like to think of themselves as being 'useful', 'reliable' and so forth. They dread acquiring a reputation of being 'difficult' – despite the unimaginable *difficulty* of dredging yourself to the very bottom for the living emotions of the character you're playing.

It's humiliating – sitting by the phone, or foolishly going in to see your agent in case anything has shown up, when obviously they'd be on the blower like a shot if it had: they want their commission, don't they? After a while, you dread going to parties, or even into the street, because of the inevitable question: 'Working?' If necessity forces you to take a non-acting job – and who can live on the dole without becoming a recluse? – a job, that is, in the *real* world, it's best not to mention your profession, because everyone will cry in unison: 'Oh, you mean you're RESTING!', this wretched word having somehow slipped its moorings and drifted into the non-theatre's ken to become a cruel stick to beat us with. Moreover, if you do have a job, you're mortified to ask another actor if he's working for fear of appearing smug.

The most humiliating side-effect of unemployment is that finally you're forced into wanting jobs that you don't want: *longing* for a commercial, *craving* a two-line part on the television, or an understudy role at the National Theatre. When you get the job, of course, you realize that you didn't want it. 'So leave the profession,' I hear somebody say. Many do; but more stay because they have no choice. It's in the blood and the bones. They may not even be very good actors – but they're actors none the less. Of course the profession is over-crowded, but every one of those actors can play at least one part better than anyone living; and who shall deny them the chance to do so?

I hear somebody say: 'Self-indulgence. What makes it worse for actors than for anyone else?' No, not worse – but not better either, so let it not be said that actors lead cocooned lives, remote from the rest of the populace. Most actors are closely acquainted with poverty and empty-handedness, through no fault of their own. There is, too, an exquisite refinement to the actor's experience of unemployment – a mere matter of days before he makes his trudge to the dole, he may have been surrounded in glamour and applauded intemperately. The psychological shock takes some weathering.

You think wildly: if there were a war, every one of us would be absorbed into the war effort, providing the essential affirmation and entertainment. Is it any less essential now?

With every further day of unemployment you feel less and less like an actor. If you go to the theatre, you feel remote from the people on the stage. If they're not very good, you rage inside at the injustice; if they are good, you feel hopeless: yes indeed, you have every reason to be unemployed, how can you compete with *that*? Although you comfort yourself that acting is like riding a bike and you don't forget how to do it, you get increasingly anxious about your capacity. Unfortunately, unlike piano-playing or classical ballet, it's not something you can do on your own. You could learn a part, or at least study one; I've heard of it happening; but you feel so foolish. An actor without a job is bad enough – but a performance without a production is too Pirandellian to contemplate. There are skills to be learned, classes to be taken – *à l'américaine*. It remains true, however, that only what is learned in the context of a production sticks; and anything you may need to learn, you learn – in that context – at lightning speed.

Classes or no classes, your actor's creative processes don't stop working just because they've got nothing to work on. The character-creating mechanism, above all, can't be switched off. As you walk down the street you find yourself suddenly talking aloud in strange tongues. Maybe you'll find yourself limping, or will have unaccountably developed a hunchback. Expressions of great animation fly across your face. It's the acting, welling up inside you. There's nothing you can do about it, just let it come out. You'll feel better after. It'll be back tomorrow. The time to start worrying is when it isn't.

'I just seem to have an awful lot of people inside me,' said Edith Evans. The surreal vision of Dame Edith's infinitely respectable exterior somehow concealing a swarming horde of alter-egos, as if they were squatters or she an unscrupulous landlord, gives an exact sense of what it feels like to need to act. When you don't get the opportunity, it often turns sour, into bad energy, a kind of constipation.

Getting the Job 1

The degree to which you go towards your potential employer, or he comes towards you, is determined by your position on the ladder of fame. There's quite an elaborate etiquette governing these matters, and different branches of it for different branches of the profession.

At the top, for example, that is if you're a film star, or a stage star of the most enormous *réclame*, or a television personality of Himalayan standing in the ratings, contact is minimal. You may not so much as meet your director till the first day of rehearsal. Everything is done through your agent. An invitation to read the script is an offer. All that remains to be discussed is the fee – and the perks: billing, caravan, chauffeur-driven car, and so on. Maybe, at this stellar level, there's a question of a percentage.

Just slightly below this, a division occurs. For a stage play it's much the same, but for a film, with its vastly greater budget, there may be an invitation to 'meet with' (these gents are usually transatlantic) the director. This will be a very cordial affair, cocktails in a hotel suite, just you and him, general conversation, art and life, and so on, and then, very gently, an inquiry: 'Did you enjoy the script?' The answer to this question has to be very skilfully given. Outright enthusiasm is not recommended. It suggests over-eagerness to play the part, which is fatal. Acutely analytical replies, and, of course, critical ones, are equally unlikely to get you the job. Best is to seize on some detail and discuss it at length – make sure it's something quite trivial, this is not the time to discover fundamental weakness in the script – finally conceding that the writer had a point, after all. A very good ploy is to have a friend with whom the director has worked, and who sends his love. This creates warmth and familiarity. Have an appointment to which you must go, so as not to overstay your welcome, and so as to create an impression of being constantly in demand.

This is very agreeable. Less delightful, film-wise, is the journey down Wardour Street to the film company's office, where, in a room overflowing with copies of *Spotlight* (the actors' directory), old coffee cups and full ashtrays, you will meet, not the director, but the American casting director in company with the English casting director, who has suggested you in the first place, and who can be assumed to be rooting for you. The American will, of course, never have seen your work, nor have the remotest idea who you might be, and is at this moment, and without much concealment, wondering what on earth her English colleague was thinking of. She will take a Polaroid snap 'for her records' and shake you warmly by the hand, looking you straight in the eyes. You may safely assume that you have not got the job.

Television is much the same, except that they probably have heard of you, and probably know you by name. '*Hello*, Simon. Are you still in whatsit?' What they won't ask you to do, unless you're little known, is to read. *Reading* is a great divide on the ladder of fame. After a certain rung, one just doesn't read for a part. It is assumed to be widely known that you don't suffer from dyslexia and haven't got a stammer. What else can a reading prove? The conversation will doubtless be very friendly, and general, and once again there will be the gradual drift to the question 'What do you think of the play?' and then 'How d'you feel about playing Charlie?' You outline a possible approach to Charlie, hoping that it's more or less along the lines of what he has in mind. Be prepared at a moment's notice to change tack completely. 'Ye-e-es, I *think* I see what you mean, sort of more (here you name the opposite quality to the one you believe to be the essence of the character), yes, that's very good, I like that.' You have thus proved that you are amenable to direction, and easy to work with. Of course he may harbour doubts as to how sincere your conversion is. You can never know. Actors try to develop telepathic gifts, reading the mind of the employer, but it's a hopeless task. You end up in knots, trying to allow for every possibility. It's like trying to hit on the combination of a lock, knowing that if you hit the wrong number, the whole thing may blow up in your face.

There is also the question of physical appearance. Here the actor who may not be so well known has an advantage. Having seen from the script that the character he's being interviewed for is upper-class and a bit of a cad, he can shave his beard off, hire a suit, buy a tie and assume cut-glass vowels. This last is a bit risky, because they could so easily slip, thus writing him off as an actor.

None of it is advisable. It's a mysterious fact that one discovers as one goes on that *not to want* the job is the best way to get it. The tables are immediately turned. A television director cannot endure the idea that he can't command whom he wants. There's a very good account of Josef von Sternberg's *Fun in a Chinese Laundry*. Dietrich gave every impression of total indifference to the prospect of playing one of the most sought-after roles in the whole of Germany. Sternberg there and then determined to get her. My own experience, slightly less exalted, is similar. I went for an interview with a television company for one of those costume series. We had the usual desultory chat, and desultorily they asked whether the dates were all right. 'No,' I said, 'I'm afraid not, I'm opening in a one-man show the day of the first readthrough, and playing it for a fortnight after that.' 'Your agent should have told us,' they said crossly. 'Yes, I'm sorry,' I replied. Whereupon, I went to see my agent. As I walked through the door, the phone rang. It was the television company. 'We must have him,' they said. It was a five-line part. 'But you're in Manchester.' 'We'll pay his fare there and back every day.' Which is what they did. The fare added up to one and a half times my fee.

Easy to say: don't want it – harder to do, because acting is based on wanting. (Vakhtangov said: 'Acting is to want, to want, and to want again.')

Theatre auditions are possibly worse. They generally take place in the auditorium of a theatre other than the one in which the play will go on. The director, the assistant director, the casting agent, possibly the theatre's artistic director, probably the producer, are all lounging in the stalls with their feet on the back of the seat in front. There are twenty or thirty plastic cups with cigarette butts lying in an inch of coffee littering the aisles. The air is thick with smoke and raucous laughter. The director has been telling a joke. About the previous actor, you think darkly, and they'll have a little joke about you too when you've gone. People leap up to greet you, the casting director introduces you to everyone, you shake the director as firmly by the hand as you can without betraying your tension. Your voice is trembling oddly. You long for a cigarette, even though you don't smoke, but you don't take the one offered to you because it might seem unprofessional and your mouth is already so dry that it's painful to swallow. Nevertheless you engage rather inadequately in banter for as long as possible, in the hope that they might forget to ask you to read. But no, eventually they stop laughing at each other's jokes, which you can't understand but laugh at louder than anyone, even gurgling for a few minutes after the main body of the laugh, as if the joke were repeating on you like breakfast, and you clamber up on to the stage (there are never steps). You survey the ludicrously unsuitable set that you're now on (though if you've been out of work for a while, it's nice to be on *any* set) and make for the nearest chair. A table is paradise: 'In your own time!' they cry. That's *awful*. You feel some kind of 'method' moody silence is called for, to prove that you're a serious artist. This you therefore give, though in fact it just depresses and frightens you. You give a little nod to the other person on the stage, and you're off, gabbling the lines for every one of which you found a rich and interesting colour last night. Your partner will be either the assistant director, who won't be able to act to save her life, and so gives you nothing, or the star, who has already been cast, has read the lines fifty times with fifty different actors, has nothing to prove – he's *got* the job, for Chrissakes – and gives you all too much. Worse than either of these two is if the director should take it into his head to read with you. Eheu, eheu. He will show off abominably, preparing for his next line while he should be listening to you. During your long speeches he will look up your nostril, embarrassed by the proximity.

When this is over, the director (if, please god, he's not on stage with you but in the stalls) will shout out: 'Very interesting, thank you.' Dread word, 'interesting'. Isn't that what they call plain girls? He'll then clamber up on to the stage, put his arms round your shoulder and say, 'Mmm. I'd like to try that again, if you don't mind, like to have another little go at it.' 'Yes, yes,' you interject, passionately, 'it was *ter*rible.' 'No, it wasn't terrible at all – I'd just like to see a little more vulnerability. [Or majesty, or fun, but it's usually vulnerability. Hilarious that in this firing-squad situation, that's the one thing you can't produce at any cost.] OK?' And off you go again, and it's always better, and it's always worse. So, baffled, you shake hands amid unreal checkings of your agent's phone number, and your immediate where-abouts. As you leave the auditorium, action-replaying the whole episode, examining the director's every inflection, you pass an actor on his way in, and you know immediately that he's going to get the job.

This kind of audition, though full of built-in frustrations is bearable. You get a chance to show some of what you can do, and quite often you get a cup of coffee, too. (If John Osborne's holding the audition, and it's the afternoon, you'll get a cigar and a glass of champagne.) The next rung down the audition ladder has no such perks.

This is the rep audition. Here the hapless directors are required to see the thirty or so actors a day who've written to them enclosing a photograph and a curriculum vitae. The actors, at a certain season of the year, sit down and write letters to every repertory company in the country, every manager, and every agent. A surprisingly large number never reply at all, but those who do require you to perform two speeches, one classical and one modern. You find your way to the Irish Club or the Europa Hotel or whatever acoustically catastrophic venue has been chosen, you sit, as if you were in the clap clinic, avoiding the eyes of the twenty or so other actors waiting to be called in, relentlessly repeating your speeches, suddenly forgetting one in the middle, and panickily resorting to the tattered piece of paper on which it's written. It's more than likely from a part you've never played (it'll be a leading part, a good juicy speech, but one which you probably only partially understand because you haven't had time to read the play) and so its commitment to memory has been purely mechanical. There's much consultation as to what's a good speech for auditions – there are of course compilations of them – but directors report a horrible monotony in the average choice. Jimmy Porter, Saint Joan, and so on. Nevertheless, they do actually contain the best opportunities.

Your name's called, embarrassingly loudly (*just* like the clinic), and you enter a room at the end of which is a trestle table. 'Come and join us,' one of the three or four people behind it shouts. You haven't the slightest idea which is who, because, like you, they don't have familiar faces. To you, however, all hope reposes in them, because a season in rep would give you the chance to spread your wings, to actually get up on the stage and take a part by the neck. A year, or perhaps two, in rep would give you the confidence that you've lacked. They're busy men, however, and the questions are quite brisk. Sooner than you expect they say, 'Well, now what have you got for us?' 'Jimmy Porter, and Launce to his dog.' 'Ah, [disappointed] good.' You go to the other end of the room, filled with sudden horrors. Words swirl around in your brain. The very first line simply won't come into your head. 'I'd just like to check a word' you lie, going over to the stage manager to whom you've given your script. Of course! And then back to that dreaded spot. 'In your own time!' That terrible silence, and you start. You have no partner of course, so somewhere in the middle-air you fix your eye on an imaginary interlocutor. The effect from the other side of the room is rather funny, because the eye-line tends to get lower and lower, and everyone's speeches seem to end being addressed to Toulouse-Lautrec. You're oblivious, however, so it doesn't matter to you. What you are aware of is waves of restlessness coming from behind the trestle table, and no, absolutely no, laughs. 'Liverpool laughed at that one,' you think bitterly, then, suddenly, unexpectedly, a laugh! You expand, milk it a bit, and then – bof! Your mind's a complete blank. 'YES,' you bark at the stage manager, who can barely read the tatters, 'YE-ES,' you cry again. Her tiny little voice calls the line out. 'Oh, yes,' you say, 'of course,' and the speech continues, a shadow of its former self. You announce the next speech, but after a minute and a half the director calls out, 'Thank you very much, very good, I'd like you to try that again as if you were Frankie Howerd.' 'I'm sorry, I'm no good at imitations, I –' 'Well, anyone you like.' 'Erm.' 'OK, let's just kick it around a bit. Let's have a bit of fun with it. You're an Arsenal supporter and Spurs have just scored a goal and you're remonstrating with the ref.' You laugh sycophantically at the wit of his invention, and then make a complete fool of yourself. 'I'm sorry, that wasn't very good, I'm not very good at improvising.' 'No, no, it was interesting.' Interesting. Uh-huh.

There is even worse, though. This is the general audition, now rarely practised, but, times being what they are, I should not be amazed to see its return. A large London theatre would be hired for the purpose, and hundreds, literally hundreds, of actors would walk across its stage until a disembodied voice would scream 'Stop.' One of those who stopped would then be extracted from the ranks, and the ghastly procession would continue.

I have never got a job from an audition, and only rarely from an interview. The audition system is one in which I can never give anything like my best, the falseness of the set-up striking me so forcibly that I'm unable to commit myself to it in the least. It seems to me that auditions, like examinations, only prove that you can audition. It reveals little about your acting capacity. It does prove that you have neither a cleft palate nor a club-foot, which can be useful information. As for interviews, the one-to-one format has its own pitfalls. A personal relationship has to be established in a very short time. My nervousness in the situation (and an element of bloody-mindedness) produces apparent arrogance. I'm also over-free with my opinions, which can cause a director to ask, 'Who does this man think he is?' I have a great fondness for asking a director what *he's* been doing, and what *he* thinks about the play. These questions are usually regarded as his prerogative, though heaven knows why. In the case of the latter question, particularly, it seems to me that a great deal of wasted rehearsal time and confused productions could be nipped in the bud.

The Agent

What an agent is and what an actor would like an agent to be may be two very different things. It's understandable that actors, being for the most part powerless and passive in relation to their careers, should look for a bigger brother to look out for their interests. It is, practically speaking, impossible to negotiate your own wages – certainly it would be highly embarrassing; and moreover few of us know what the market rate is, what it's reasonable to ask, and quite how far you can push your luck without putting yourself out of the running. It is in this financial area that agents are indispensable, and where one agent can be infinitely superior to another. An agent skilled in 'doing the deal', the actual negotiation of fees, and the odds and ends which accompany it – billing (your credit in the programme, on the screen, or on the poster), dressing rooms and so on – can make all the difference to your bank balance and to your position on the ladder. Without exception, every producer, every company and every administrator is trying to get your services as cheaply as possible. They're all playing a game of brinkmanship, and it's important to have an agent who is better at this game than they are. It's also important that all the rancour which can accompany this exercise falls on your agent's head and not yours. Of course they represent *you*, and you must be kept informed at every stage of the game but it's a highly specialized skill, and you will lose your nerve long before they lose theirs. Moreover, the rancour – which may worry you sick: first of all you think you'll lose the job; then you think they'll never employ you again – is all stage-managed, and like lawyers and MPs, after they've fought the good fight, they shake hands and have a drink in the bar to celebrate. There is, it must be admitted, a danger built in to the structure of the job that an agent will get so high on the exercise of his skill, that he ceases to count the cost in human terms, i.e. you. In this case, change your agent.

The financial area is the agent's playground. It is often necessary to point out to an agent that there are more important considerations to a job than money or prestige. In the area of ART (which can seem to be very distant from the world of deals and 'I've got you in a box on the poster in a bigger typeface than anyone else, even the star') you may find your agent sympathetic and intelligent – or not. It's not indispensable. You have to develop a strong sense of your own counsel as early as possible. Advice is liberally and not always disinterestedly bestowed from every quarter. Your agent can be unduly influential in such matters. You have to decide whether his advice is good or not – and then not mind if it isn't. Good advice from an agent on your work is a bonus.

The personal relationship is often extremely close. Agencies vary greatly in their size, and agents vary greatly in the degree to which they wish to involve themselves in their clients' lives. In a sense, it's one of the most intimate relationships of one's life, but the most impersonal too. It deals with one aspect of you in close-up. On any subject related to this aspect, your agent is totally at your disposal. You can talk about your CAREER without apology. Many actors choose to use their agents as independent confidants on all kinds of matters. It is not rare for agent and client to be friends, but the best relationship is fraternal, maternal or paternal: trust and confidence, without the need to prove oneself.

Many actors have not attained this with their agents. They stalk around town, brooding darkly. The word 'agent' brings a curl to their lips. They plot, day and night, to change agents, believing that the present incumbent is the only thing holding them back from Broadway, Hollywood and international renown. They believe that an agent can 'get you work'. It is true that an agent with his ear sufficiently to the ground can propose you – 'put you up' – for a part which he's read about in the breakdown of a forthcoming series/play/film. In one case out of twenty, this will pay off. In general, however, the directors and casting directors are perfectly well apprised of the available talent, and quite clear on the type of actor they want. On or near the top of the ladder, again, it may be a different matter. Your agent can then suggest a production or play. In general, however, agents do not, cannot, get work for their clients. It is a dangerous illusion for an actor to think that they can.

This fact brings with it a concomitant resentment: the agent is creaming off ten per cent of your income from work which 'I got myself'. Bitterness is understandable in the face of whittled-away pay slips, but unreasonable. The agent secures the highest possible fee for you, and should be paying for himself, as it were. If he isn't, CHANGE AGENTS. It's true that for many jobs these days, especially in the theatre, there is a fixed salary for everyone, and the agent's contribution to the deal is therefore nil, but swings and roundabouts must form part of any business relationship. Most agents don't take commission below a certain salary: a hundred pounds, now, I think. For my part, I'm content to pay commission to my agent on all work because of the years in which, in the furtherance of my art, I earned breadline wages and she took no commission.

It is felt that to belong to certain agencies brings clout. I doubt it. On the other hand, it is the most defenceless thing in the world to be without an agent. You feel that prospective employers don't know where to get hold of you, that jobs are slipping through your fingers and that people think you're dead. (Frankie Howerd says his *agent* thinks he's dead, but that's another matter.)

And there is nothing nicer, when you're working, to drop in on your agent with a bottle of wine and sit and talk shop, while the telephones ring merrily in the background. On the other hand, when you're not working, there's no pain on earth like clutching a cup of tea sitting on the edge of your seat, mutely begging for news of work, while the telephones jangle away, bringing offers to people who have too much work as it is. Everyone, it seems, is too busy to talk to you, and if they do, you're interrupted by a long-distance call from Los Angeles with a query about X's availability for twelve weeks' work in Honolulu. You wash your cup and creep out, unnoticed, while the phones ring on dementedly and your agent laughs hysterically. Ask not for whom the phone rings, it rings not for thee.

Getting the Job 2

Between the audition and being told whether you've got the job falls an interregnum, during which it is best not to think about it at all. This is almost impossible, however. Your mind races ahead to what you will do with the part, or how you will spend your days in Sheffield and so on. Some of us are feverishly imaginative to the point that we compose the reviews we can expect. It's also unwise to read the play that you're up for during this period, because the pain of desire can be physically unbearable, as the acting juices start to work, and have to be crushed. This brutal form of 'artus interruptus' has the same aftermath as its sexual counterpart: deep sulking frustration. Many actors refuse to talk about jobs they're waiting to hear about. It's bad luck. But they can't resist saying that there's 'something in the pipeline', and then become gnomic. One always feels it must be something enormous, the lead in a movie or Hamlet at the National, but it's just as likely to be a walk-on part or a week in *Crossroads*.

Your mind keeps wandering back to the possible job. (Not all jobs are equally desired, of course, and the intensity of feeling is in direct proportion to the number of previous weeks of unemployment.) A day has normally been fixed to tell you: 'We'll let you know by Thursday.' You structure your life around this day; everything becomes either before Thursday or after Thursday, with the mental proviso that *after* Thursday, if you get the job (which of course, in your inner, inner imaginings, you always do), all plans will change so as you can prepare for it.

Well, Thursday comes, and Thursday goes, and you hear nothing. This is an invariable rule. Why does it always come as a surprise? You phone your agent. Has he heard anything? No. Never. He'll get 'on to' them. Of course he never does. What's the point? They'll let you know in their own good time, there's no point in chivvying them, it'll only antagonize.

There are variations in this routine, depending again on your position on the ladder of fame. It *is* possible, after a certain rung, to use, or at any rate, to *hint* at the use, of *force majeure*. If the agent feels that his client is sufficiently 'big', or if there are indications that the director is really keen, but some other factor is holding things up,

153

then another pressing offer can be invented, which requires an immediate answer. Still there may be no reply. This game can go on for days, even weeks.

It may be that you are not offered the job, but asked to come back: the recall. This is of course a good sign, they must be interested, but it is agony. What did I do right the first time, and will I be able to do it again? You're always much more nervous on this second meeting. The director will explain that he's worried about the 'chemistry' (Nobel prize winners, some of these directors) or point out some area of the character or the play in which you were not quite convincing the first time around. The mood of the meeting is much more intimate, because you know each other now, but for you, much more tense, especially if you badly want the part.

These recalls may go on. Sometimes you return three, four times, by which time, you've become one of the family, get a cup of tea the moment you come in, sit down, have a natter. The dread moment always comes round, though, and up you get to say (probably) the same lines again, with a diminishing sense of their reality.

It is rare to be told on the spot whether you have the job or not. The joyful occasions are when the call comes through while you're at your agent's. Then you go out and get drunk. That's the tradition. Wherever you are, joy is unconfined, because, for however long the job lasts, limbo is suspended, and you have a future.

Preparation

The job's yours.

The period that follows is delicious, a honeymoon: all future. There's so much to look forward to, and a wonderful sense of security, without any of the difficulties and despair that the work, however exhilarating it may be, will bring with it. It's tempting not to look at the play at all. In fact, though, the work has already begun.

You read the play again and again, resisting the urge to think about your own part. Now is the time to form an image of the play, the whole play, which must be the reference point of all your subsequent labours. You need to get an impression of its character – its personality. When an image has crystallized, you lob it into the pool of your unconscious, and watch the ripples. Wherever they go, you follow. Everything and anything that they suggest is worth pursuing. This haphazard research is one of the crowning joys of the whole business. It gives you the opportunity to spend huge sums of money on anything that might provoke thought: books, records, journeys. Often enough the books remain only glanced through, of symbolic rather than practical inspiration, like Muslim prayer rolls; the records listened to with half an ear; the journeys taken with someone far too distracting; but your mind opens up in a certain direction, and the least fragment – a picture in a book, a particular sound in a piece of music – will remain as a sensation. Finally, that's all that matters. Until ideas become translated into sensations, they're of no use whatever to acting.

What you're aiming to evoke at this stage is the world of the play, its aura, almost its force-field. The work of the rehearsal will be to give tangible organic life to the ciphers on the page: to *restore* them to life, that is; to defrost them, to rehydrate them. To do this, you need to enter into the same creative state the author experienced when he first gave birth to them, so the richer your input the better.

When you're reading your own part, you do it with your inner ear wide open. Eventually, a certain voice will insist. Who is this? You strain to hear (it's like sitting round a ouija board). Oh god, yes! It's X! Well, is the character anything like X? In what way? Like Debussy's sunken cathedral, the part begins to emerge. That's the ideal state in which you should arrive at the first readthrough: imminent.

These are some notes I scribbled down in March 1978 after a first reading of *Titus Andronicus*, a part I agreed to play without having previously read or seen it:

* A ravaged Rome, the Goths at the gates, but Rome itself is almost Barbarian. Social behaviour has sunk to a basic, tribal level. Death, rape. Unqualified self-interest rules. A punk scenario, almost.
* Titus brings his misfortunes on himself by insisting on the death of Alarbus.
* A young man's play. What S. writes about he has not lived through:

it's in the head: an established genre that he tries his hand at.
Hence the relative formality, coolness.
* Why was the play so popular with the Elizabethans? What was
  their attitude to violence?
* During the play's run, the heads of ten rebels were stuck on pikes
  along the length of Westminster Bridge.
* *Revenge.* No confidence in ability of law to settle righteous grudges:
  revenge regarded as legitimate (Cf. vigilantes).
* *Honour.* Cf. Punk boy who killed a man who smiled at him. '' 'E
  was bringing me down in front of me mates.'
* *Dismemberment.* Cf. young Getty's ear from his kidnappers.
* The play evokes and to some extent celebrates a recent past in
  which the fittest survived – the strong slugged it out, blow for
  blow. (Sam Peckinpah) *Exuberant.*
* Written during Plague Years 93–4. 'When will this fearful slumber
  have an end?' Who are the Goths: the play's final resolution embodies
  a compromise with the Goths. Has Lucius/Rome sold out?
* *Not* ritual.
* Why did the play stop being popular? – because it stopped
  answering to people's conception of psychological reality
  introduced by S. himself.

Should you learn your lines?, you anxiously ask. Everything depends on the size of the part. It would, for example, be fatal to learn a
small part whose interest you have to eke out over an eight-week
rehearsal. Equally, it would be fatal, I have come increasingly to
believe, not to learn a large or even a medium part. The amount of
work needed on such a role requires every second of the rehearsal
period, and time spent clutching the book – I believe, contrary to the
Edith Evans and Stanislavsky schools – is time wasted. It merely
delays the moment at which the thought patterns of the part become
your thought patterns, at which the impulses of the character become
your impulses. Moreover, as it is the words which will provide the
clue to your entire conception, the sooner they are passing through
your brain and flowing across your lips, the sooner they will yield
their secrets and their sensations. I've never been able to go beyond
the surface when I'm reading from a page. It's only when I *have* to
rack my brains and ask what word comes next – what word *must*
come next? – that I start to work seriously.

The age-old question asked of actors is: how do you remember the lines? (The other question is: what do you do during the day? To which there can only be one reply: mind your own business.) Micheál MacLiammóir used to say: 'By forgetting everything else,' which is in fact a reply to the question, how do you *recall* your lines? How you memorize them in the first place is a more urgent question. My reply to that is, because you have to. The undertaking is of the order of grocers knowing how much a pound of carrots is just by looking at them. It's a part of the brain which comes into play when you need it. That's all. Of course, we vary wildly in our proficiency. Learning lines is known as *study*, and an actor is either a quick study or a slow one. There are those among us, whom it is hard to love, who have photographic memories. In some obscure way one feels this is cheating, and that such actors will come to no good: a false proposition. I *think* I'm glad, however, that I'm not a human xerox, because the laborious process by which I learn has certain advantages. The method is as above: learn the first line, and from then on simply ask what is the next line, and why? Obviously this involves discovering the character's thought processes, and how he's relating to the other characters. The revelations of character are immense – and the physical sensation of his words on your tongue immediately passes into the rest of your body.

The next day, you will think you've forgotten every word, but the brain is smarter than that. A glance at the page will bring *most* of it flooding back. It's unrealistic to expect to be word perfect on the first day of rehearsal. The reality of being on the floor with the other actors will throw you completely – and quite rightly. By an equation quite difficult to balance, you must be wholly responsive to whatever surprising impulses they may direct towards you, while at the same time being wholly positive in what you offer them. This chicken-egg interplay should ideally go on until the last day of the run.

Some darling friend must perform the intimate task of 'hearing your lines'. This requires tact, patience and modesty. You're not interested in their creative interpretations. Flat simple utterance, cutting the long speeches when they occur, and the discretion to know to correct when you've gone seriously wrong and not to pull you up over every misplaced syllable: these are what is required of this nonpareil. Greater love hath no man, woman or child.

Bill Gaskill has said that his definition of a great actor is 'one who comes to the first readthrough with his lines learned'. On the other hand, I have never been able to follow Laurence Olivier's example (and Gaskill was talking about him) and come to a readthrough with my *entire performance*. For me, the whole point of learning the lines is to be as free to offer alternative possibilities as can be. If you're struggling with lines, your mind is only half-creating – it's mostly sending desperate fishing lines down into murky ponds of words.

Sadly in our theatre, the first readthrough is followed by immediate rehearsal – very occasionally by another readthrough, *then* rehearsal. How immensely valuable it would be if the readthrough took place two or three weeks before rehearsals began, so that the image of the play and the particular colour of the other actors were slowly filtering through your brain as you worked on it in isolation. Work, in the sense of labour, isn't quite the word: the preparation period is more like dreaming, *relevant* dreaming.

First Readthrough

Except at the National Theatre, rehearsals take place in church halls or boys' clubs, the type of building being chosen presumably to remind us either of the ritual origins of drama, or the fact that actors are children. Whichever, they share the same basic character: worn parquet floors, iron bars at the windows, primitive plumbing, no air in the summer, no heat in the winter and no light at any time. On the wall are sidesmen's rotas or football teams for next Sunday. There may be a cyclo-styled newsletter. Everywhere there are tea-chests full of books, bric-à-brac, and plastic handbags: jumble. There are also tables and chairs. Somewhere there is, there *must* be, a kitchen. At all times, but above all on the first day of rehearsals, this is the hub of the operation. Rehearsals are fuelled by tea; but the first day is positively awash with it. The stage managers will have got in half-an-hour before anyone else and ensured that kettles are boiling. They've probably bought a few packets of biscuits, bless them.

Stage management are wonderful at all times, but never more so than on the first day of rehearsal. They're the only relatively relaxed people in the room. They have nothing to prove. They're always very jolly, which is a great comfort. For the rest of us, it's like the worst party we've ever been to in our lives. One by one the actors sneak in, making straight for the tea. They then drift into the main body of the room, desperately sipping at cups which are far too hot to drink and going 'Aah!' after each gulp, as if it were nectar or the first cup of tea they'd had for months, whereas in fact they've been swilling the stuff like lunatics in the local greasy spoon having turned up an hour early. Bit by bit, the actor begins to recognize other actors: if they're famous, but he's never met them, a lot of rather Asiatic half-smiling nodding and bobbing goes on. Eventually, he's sure to meet someone that he knows, slightly, and they'll stand in a group together, making jokes, drinking tea, eating biscuits, smoking cigarettes and trembling. From the outside, it looks as if they're wonderfully relaxed, have known each other for twenty years and are perfectly confident of their abilities. Inside, it's hell.

In general the atmosphere at a first readthrough suggests a group of people who have been called-up, or press-ganged. When actors catch each other's eyes on these occasions, the message that passes between them is of grim sympathy, as who should say: 'Tough luck, old man. We'll get through it somehow, don't worry.' Nowhere, at any time on this day, is there any sense of exhilaration or excitement. If there's a leading actor, his or her laughter will be heard cutting through the air. Poor creature, you think, must be desperate.

Finally, the director, who is clearly in a worse state than anyone else, calls everyone to sit round in a circle, declines to say anything about the play, and suggests 'a gentle readthrough'. That's the phrase. 'Enjoy it,' he says. That's the other phrase. Epidemic of bronchitis. Throats are cleared. Chairs thrust around. Then silence. 'OK, Tony?' he says to the actor who will speak first. 'OK. In your own time.' We're away.

Nobody hears the first few pages. They're trying to work out how long it will be before *they* have to speak. Some may surreptitiously turn forward to their first entrance. Some actors even mumble their lines under their breath while other actors are reading. After a while, though, the play begins to focus attention. The first laugh normally comes about ten minutes in: a waggish actor or a waggish character breaks the ice. A surprisingly large number of very good actors find sight-reading difficult, and there can be tracts of the play which pass in fog. Other actors read brilliantly and you will be amazed at the possibilities of a part which had struck you as dull or elusive.

For yourself, you're always surprised at the effectiveness of certain lines or sections, and disgusted at your inability to bring off the high points of the script, especially long and brilliant speeches. There is also always the lurking conviction that half the cast are thinking: 'How did *he* get the part?' Simply to *hear* it though, to hear the balance of voices and to begin to sense the shape of the whole thing, is exhilarating. It begins to assume tangibility. When the last page has been turned, there's general relief, admiration for the play is expressed – and more tea is called for. The stage management, in fact, will have already put the kettle on, having judged the approaching end of the play. (The great stage-management skill is anticipation.) Cigarettes are lit, conversation is joined and for the first time something like pleasure is expressed. Tea arrives. The director speaks. He doesn't want to say anything about the play, except that we've got a marvellous cast, it's going to be splendid if only we can stop Simon Callow talking (for S.C. substitute any other actor of known thickness of skin), X – the author – is here to answer any questions you may have (author simpers), and now I think we should have a look at the set and all have a word with Rowena (the costume lady).

The viewing of the designer's model is essentially a courtesy, a kind of social ritual, because most actors simply don't know how to read a model, and on this first day are anyway not sufficiently familiar with the play and its problems to know how the set might affect them. The designer always explains the set in considerable detail, the actors ask polite questions, and then everyone agrees it's marvellous.

The costume discussions are quite different. Every actor has bitter experience of costumes which have betrayed his conception of the part, and actresses in particular are very much aware of what suits them, what material or what cut produces which effect. These discussions are from the very beginning close and tough, with passionate bartering on both sides, the designer fighting for her vision, the actors for theirs: a very healthy relationship.

It's unusual for serious work to be done on this first day. The director has meetings with the production staff and so on, so we part, perhaps to have a drink or lunch with chums, or, in my case, to go home and have a nervous breakdown.

Rehearsal 1

For a long time, my mother couldn't work out what rehearsals were for. 'Once you've learned the lines and the director has told you where to stand, what do you do?' And it has always been very difficult to explain the halting, spermy business of rehearsal. What actually goes on?

The pace, level of intensity and daily pattern of the rehearsal are entirely in the hands of the director, and there are as many kinds of rehearsal as there are directors. Many directors, for example, like to set the play as soon as possible, and then work on details of the scene, running it and the play as often as possible. Others are loath to set anything, preferring to allow the actor his freedom to find a natural resting place, only correcting it if sight-lines are obscured or if for some other reason it creates a problem – exits or entrances, for example. Yet other directors have pet approaches: this director will sit round a table discussing the play for the whole of the first week, for instance, while that one will play games with a ball before working on the scenes.

The day generally runs from ten till six, and ten till one on Saturday. The exactness of these hours varies too. There are directors who crack into action on the dot of ten. Others prefer to ease gently into the work with a little chat about last night's television. One gifted director has perfected a method of what he calls Work Evasion, putting off to the last moment the beginning of work, extending the coffee breaks as long as he dare, taking lunch early and coming back late. Happily, the few minutes of actual work that he does are of the highest quality.

The director's conduct of the rehearsal is highly personal. Some favour intense concentration and seriousness. Others relish anarchic high spirits, laughter and improvisation. Unquestionably rehearsing must be an emotional business. For me contained anarchy is the most fruitful. Play should be at the heart of rehearsal as it should be at the heart of performance. So many of the best inventions and the truest impulses have grown out of mad horseplay.

It would, I daresay, gravely upset a taxpayer if he were to walk into a rehearsal room to find grown men and women – including the one who's supposed to be in charge of them – romping around, tears of laughter rolling down their cheeks. The truth is that that's often (I wouldn't pretend always) a very creative state. The playfulness can be of many different kinds – physical or intellectual. Some directors create a very witty atmosphere which becomes highly infectious. However it's done, the temperature in the rehearsal room must be higher than it is outside it. It's a furnace, of whatever kind. John Dexter's rehearsal atmosphere is like the boiler-room of an ocean-going liner – it blasts out at you as you open the door. It's entirely created by him, by his will.

Ideas of what rehearsals are for have of course changed over the years. Most actors of my generation like to do the main work there, in the rehearsal room. Actors of an older generation regard rehearsal as fitting together the pieces of a puzzle: the pieces themselves having been worked on and polished at home. Such a division is in fact quite artificial: whatever sort of an actor you are, the play and the part will invade you twenty-four hours a day. You will hardly be able to say where or when the work is done. The really crucial work, the assimilation of the taste of both character and play, can come at any moment – in the white heat of rehearsal, or over a cup of coffee, or sitting on the lavatory in the middle of the night. These are the thrilling moments, when you cry 'Eureka!'; this is the glorious 5 per cent of inspiration, after which the 95 per cent of perspiration is mere journeyman work.

To begin with, the rehearsal period, whether it's three weeks, or eight, will seem to be a vast impenetrable Amazon forest, to which there are no maps and in the depths of which there is precious little light. For the coming few weeks, you will be feeling your way through a thicket of new relationships – with the director, the actors, the stage management – immersing yourself in an alien imaginative world, exposing yourself to ridicule, shining a light on places in yourself which you don't like to look at in your most private moments, challenging your body and your brain to virtuoso achievements that, frankly, you have never been trained to accomplish.

It's all a bit daunting. Understanding and realization are the two great tasks of the rehearsal, and between them, they can put you on the rack till you scream for mercy. Being both instrument and interpreter, you must proceed always on two fronts. You may grasp the role profoundly in its every element; can you reach it, though? Or perhaps you're a Stradivarius, supple and expressive, both physically and vocally, but you haven't an idea what the part's about.

There are innumerable theories and techniques designed to introduce some order and clarity into this murky task: essentially, your work will be on four interdependent aspects of the play: your character, the narrative, the play's meaning, and its style.

Character 1

A play is an arrangement of the words of characters to tell a story. A play is nothing but characters in action. There is nothing in a play *but* the characters. Every word that is uttered is uttered by a character. I labour this point because it's strikingly different in this respect from any other form of literature. Apart from stage directions, which may be meagre (or, on the other hand, over-helpful, because the physical description is belied by the actor's own physique), and things said about the character by other characters – which must be treated with caution – the character must be construed from his words.

Not the information contained in them, but their taste, their flavour, because, when it comes down to it, the essential question is: what kind of man talks like that?

A failure to answer the question correctly:

Rehearsing Restoration: Edward Bond: June '81
Second Week of Rehearsal

With Are, I have, quite simply, misconceived the part. I saw it in a theatrically based light: a machiavel, a devil, a daemonic, Olivierian figure, bestriding the stage like a colossus, eyes flashing, mouth twisted in a perpetual sneer. I told Edward that I imagined his private life in the Hell-Fire Club to be deeply perverted, concerned with rats and dead babies. He said: 'Very interesting.' In rehearsal however he kept attacking me for being too 'emotional'; too 'sinister'; kept finding fault with my phrasing for being 'speculative' rather than 'certain'; once peevishly stopped me, saying that he couldn't hear what I was saying, couldn't *understand* it, it was just verbalizing. That was tedious of him, but he was right. I wasn't free with it at all; it was rigid, charmless, forced, heavy-handed, isolated. So we had a long talk after which I've been reluctantly ceding my flashing devil, bit by bit, until today I've arrived at my new performance: eighteenth-century man, genial, agreeable, reasonable, rational, with his fixed and highly satisfactory world view. It works.

The character exists on the interface between you and what the author has written. This is not a limitation of the medium; it is its glory; if, that is, the conjunction is the right one. Just as the writer has been slowly brewing the characters he writes, has been musing on certain themes and observations – finally, when they're ripe, committing them to the page – you, an artist in a different medium, have reached a point in your understanding and experience of life and physical development which enables you to play certain kinds of character. Unfortunately for you, *you* have to wait for a character to turn up before you can liberate all that you have to offer.

Character is in a sense a hypothesis: the more of the character and his actions that it covers, the truer the hypothesis will be. If your hypothesis covers every aspect of the role, and brings something more, then you'll give a great performance.

The something more will be a vibration of your personality. The more parts you play, and of course the more you live, the more your personality will vibrate. This is simply a matter of exercise. Few people who are not performers are allowed or willing to vibrate more than a tiny permitted corner of themselves; you have a professional obligation to keep as many dimensions of you alive as you humanly can.

Playing a play then is quite unlike playing a piece of music. The relation of acting to the play is more like that of music to a poem in a song setting. There are poor poems which give rise to great songs; great poems which give rise to poor songs – best of all are great poems which provoke great songs: great as poems and great as songs.

You may know more about the character you're playing than the writer does. Pam Gems was mildly surprised, when she went to see her play *Franz Into April*, that Warren Mitchell (Franz) uttered a number of lines that she couldn't remember having written. At the end of the performance, she mentioned this without rancour – she thought they were rather good lines – to Warren, who replied: 'Look Pam, you only wrote him – I've *been* him.' Of course, actors' literary gifts vary, and plays in general have a form which the writer has slaved to perfect, and is not susceptible of spontaneous improvement

– but it is a sure sign that the character's blood is flowing through your veins and that you have discovered the iceberg of which his words are the tip when you can put him in any situation and speak as him. This fusing of lives – yours, his, and the author's – is the vital anarchic energy without which the play, whatever its superficial energy, will be a dead thing.

To find him where he lives, you must be prodigiously inventive of approaches. No question will fail to yield some fragment of him: what is his job? what does he have for breakfast? what does he get up to in bed? what is his star sign? To begin with you'll probably conventionalize him, see him as a type. You must do this, simply to separate him, stake out the territory. Then day by day, you particularize. Once you've caught the bug, though, it'll start to do the work for you: your conscious brain will sit back, while your motor system – yours and his – takes over. Until you've got hold of the character, you'll be in misery: you'll feel false and laboured; the words will cling to your palette like burrs; your body will drag like lead. You'll blush a lot.

It's not simply a question of seeing the character, knowing who he is. Nor is it a matter of impersonation (though that can help). What it needs is for you to locate him in you. Only then will the energy spring from within, instead of being externally applied; only then will you have renewed the umbilical connection between the character and the author. Then, indeed, you will feel almost irrelevant: a receptacle, a conduit, because the character will start to follow his own instincts and live his own life, just as he did when he first came flowing out of the author's pen.

It's an incomparable feeling. Another person is coursing through your veins, is breathing through your lungs. But of course, it's not. It's only you – another arrangement of you. The French actor Jacques Dufhilo is reported to have stopped rehearsals, saying: '*Ce n'est pas moi qui parle.*' For many years I was dissatisfied *until* I could say '*Ce n'est pas moi qui parle.*' Now I know that unless it's me speaking – some version of me – no one is. When you've defined, by analysis or intuition, those parts of yourself that coincide with the character, you let them rip, while consigning the parts which are irrelevant to temporary oblivion. The sense of expanding into areas of yourself which have been dormant or repressed is exhilarating, even a little frightening: 'Do I have this in me?' Parts of yourself that you've never dared to reveal, as an ordinary inhibited citizen, burst arrogantly forth. It may be your wit, or your romanticism, your sexuality or your homicidal tendencies. Unless it's your own lust, longing, or craving, the audience will only be intellectually aroused: the thing will have been referred to, but not experienced.

And you need to enjoy it. Olivier has made famous a remark of Tyrone Guthrie's: 'If you don't love the character, then you can't play him.' This is surely not true. If you don't love BEING him, you can't play him. You can't love Hitler, but you can revel in experiencing the Hitler-in-you.

In this way, you celebrate the flexibility of human character. You demonstrate the almost limitless possibilities of personality freed from circumstance and environment. We are who we are, you say, because of upbringing and accident – BUT WE NEED NOT BE. In order to survive in the world, we limit ourselves to certain patterns of thought and behaviour, forging an identity which excludes vast areas of potential. On behalf of the audience, you abandon your own identity. Kean in Sartre's play cries: 'Ladies and Gentlemen, I do not exist.' He might better have said: 'I does not exist.'

For a period, the rehearsal needs to be completely indulgent. You wade into the swamp and wallow, indulging, tasting, gorging on the character's sensations. This period of rehearsal is the most intense experience of the character you have. He invades your life. When I played Mozart, I knew that his tempo and emotional volatility were greatly in excess of mine. As the weeks went by I began to work my own inner speed up to fever pitch. It was deeply exhausting for everyone. I ate my food twice as fast as I'd ever done, I spoke at twice the speed, darted mercurially from place to place, and at the end of the day, all but ran across Waterloo Bridge. If I went for a drink, I drank twice as much as I would normally have done. It was necessary to accustom my body to a completely new metabolic rate. Similarly when I played Verlaine, I found myself eating more and more – sometimes in rehearsal, I'd eat three full packets of chocolate biscuits under the influence of the man's greed. I expanded to over fifteen stone during the three-week period.

Rehearsal is a journey to the centre of the character – and back again. It's vital that the director senses when you've reached your destination and are ready to come back again.

We started slowly, but in a way which I have come increasingly to value: Hilton (Macrae: Rimbaud), David (Hare: director) and I round a table, talking through the scenes, trying to find the through-line – what happens? how do they change? etc. – feeling out what the balance between them is. From time to time we restored lines, began to discover that there were good reasons for most of what Chris (Hampton) had written, and that it would be unwise – wrong – to tamper with the style of the piece: a little self-conscious, literary, occasionally facetious and always polished, finished. The speeches are definitely speeches and it's a question of finding that style, the speechifying style.

The day and a half passes agreeably: so much easier than acting, I say. We discover that the Stuttgart scene – when they meet up after Verlaine leaves prison – simply doesn't work. Clearly Chris has tried to put too much into it, while at the same time trying to show that they're now at cross-purposes, miss each other in the dark. The result is that the scene is almost actionless. Indeed, the problem with the play as a whole is just that: so often what reads (in the study) so beautifully and clearly, turns out to be biographical exposition or mood evocation – what Hare calls 'tone'. Both – bio and tone – are unactable as such. The task then is to fill in, to supply: to supply previous circumstances, inner development, subtext, extraneous information (what one knows about them from books, but which Chris has omitted). All in all the *Amadeus* problem. Fancy.

After Day One, the usual slight darkness has set in. Why? Not sure. Perhaps the stiffness of everyone (which one imagines, contrary to all past experience, will go on forever) or the cerebral nature of the enterprise. I've never known a Day One after which I didn't feel lethargic and quietly despairing. Kind of first-day-of-school-ish? Yes; but something else too . . . the first lunch-time, e.g., of Day One always seems interminable, even when one knows everyone. I always long to run away. Ah, perhaps that's it – simple dread of commitment, of there being no way of avoiding it.

Day Two: More reading of script. Then: acting. The play hung rather heavily on our hands. But good work on the first-scene meeting, which we improvised to good effect, proving, as David said, that in the first scene V. is shown handling R. *very well*, *not very badly, that there is a real balance between this* fazing punk and the urbane bourgeois who fascinates him, who even *amuses* him, incredibly, considering his nervousness and hostility, by being indiscreet and casually mocking the establishment. Then SOMETHING HAPPENS. One sees, as I said, not only why V. loves R. but why R. loves V.

And yet there was still at the end of Day Two a lingering feeling of, Is it worth the effort, pushing this great boulder up a mountain? – the juices hadn't really started to flow. I'd forgotten what the experience of working was like.

The next day we worked on very difficult scene, the Dead Rat scene,

Rimbaud telling the Merlin story, Verlaine recounting his foetus-bashing foray. It seemed hopelessly actionless. Then off to the NT to do mat. and eve. *Galileo*, during which I tried to learn the scene. The more I struggled with it, the more redundant it seemed – anecdotal, 'Another Interesting Fact About Verlaine'. Next day, Thursday, Week One Day Four, I said to David: I begin to wonder whether the speech shouldn't be cut. Then we really got down to it. I had to my surprise actually memorized the speech and acted it well. 'You've just talked yourself out of your problem,' said D., and bit by bit, with sustained thinking and work and emotional application, it started to happen – the real thing, the acting sensation – pulse beating faster, brain working quicker, invention and exploration. *Then*, one's appetite for it – for the play, for the part – stirs, one starts slavering, all the preparation and conceptualizing are left behind or snatched up. One becomes like an animal hunting, the scent is in the air, every reflex alerted. Questions of is it worth it? or what for? become absurd, meaningless. It *is*. The act of creation with its irresistible imperatives, is ON. Heady. Like pregnancy. The metabolism seems to change. One's craving for odd foods and little rewards can't be denied. One walks around not as oneself, but as oneself plus another.

It's now too that the facts, the books, the research, the intuitions one had rather coolly considered come into their own, because now one has demands, questions. What did he feel like then? you ask. What did he wear *then*? What was his favourite breakfast? Etc.

Day Five, *Week One*: With all this bubbling around, we do the three scenes at the beginning of the second act . . . The withdrawal. Here's an odd thing about rehearsal. Dealing with emotional scenes, one has a horrible sensation of coitus interruptus. Those three scenes are so painful, so frustrating, so familiar (to *me*, but Hare says: 'Oh my life hasn't been like that at all'), that not working through to the end, to any kind of resolution, leaves me pensive and heavy.

Now that we have the scent in our nostrils, doing anything except the play is unbearable. I know exactly what to do now, how to work. Absurdly, I wish we were opening next week. I love pressure. God help me, I need it. If only, I think, there were some way of switching the temperature up before rehearsals start. I can hardly bring myself to read the play before the first day. Horrible inertia towards the whole project. Once, reckoning I just *had* to, to get through at all, I learnt the play before we started. The gain was immense. *Why* can't I learn from this?

Problem pending: physical contact between Hilton and me. He and Hare think audience will obviously imply . . . etc. Wrong.

My personal project – simplifying my acting, not over-colouring or inflecting – seems to be paying dividends. Simply playing the lines through to the end, phrasing elegantly and economically, does indeed enable one to choose when one really wants to slug 'em. Also the emotional freedom gained in *Amadeus* has not receded. We'll see. This could, paradoxically, be The Big One, by trying to be The Small One.

Don't SELL the word, don't colour it, don't push it down their throats – THINK it. The price of David Hare is eternal vigilance. His essential approach is intellectual, and the concentration needed to fulfil his scheme is quite frightening.

And there the journal, as usual, ends. I have never been able to keep notes beyond the first ten days of a rehearsal period, because the work itself becomes so absorbing; but also because it becomes so complex. It seems to go on at a level that defies verbal analysis. To write about it might anyway be quite rash: like taking a loaf out of the oven to see how it actually rises.

Rehearsal 2

You may spend a great deal of time simply adapting your method of work to your fellow actors', and indeed to the director's. We each have a different approach, deriving from our training and experience, often entirely of our own invention. Hours and hours are spent trying to communicate the simplest observations. It is moreover difficult when two actors of radically different working methods come together – you've learned your lines, for example, but she hasn't; he likes to be told where to move, but you like to leave it open as long as possible.

The two biggest divisions of actors are hares or tortoises, sculptors or bricklayers. The hares tear off, paraphrasing, acting in broad strokes, alarming you by their infidelity to the text and the grossness of their gestures. The tortoises proceed timidly but accurately, not moving on till they've solved each problem, alarming you by their laboriousness and their inability to take the plunge. Sculptors drag messy sprawling piles of raw material into the rehearsal room, flinging themselves at it with their bare hands or a hammer and chisel, giving no impression whatever of a possible end result, while bricklayers come in every morning with a wheelbarrow full of regular well-made bricks which they methodically lay one on top of another.

It is the task of the hapless director to try to balance them off against one another. It can be an alarming business, because each actor's wheel of fortune in rehearsal has brought him to a different level from every other actor. While one is buoyantly flying through the air, the next will be abjectly clinging to the ground. All this is quite as it should be. The wheel is in fact a spiral, and *on recule pour mieux sauter*.

The various approaches are perforce idiosyncratic, because everything you do in the play must be completely grounded in your own personal sensations. For me, music is the most immediately accessible point of reference. Since childhood, I have been immersed in classical music. My first question for myself is what is this character's – and for that matter, this play's – music. I convulsed a theatre composer friend by telling him that I'd tried to play Orlando like Berlioz instead of the way he's usually played: like Puccini. He thought it was the most pretentious thing he'd ever heard (lucky him if *that* was the most pretentious thing he'd ever heard) and it possibly was, but it meant something to me WHICH TRANSLATED INTO ACTING. I could equally have said: I tried to play Orlando nervy, vital, darkly romantic and leapingly lyrical (Berlioz) instead of straight-down-the-line mellifluously passionate, an arrow shot into a blue sky (Puccini). If I'd said that, though, it wouldn't have had the same direct effect on me. Berlioz is a taste I immediately know – even to think of the word does something to my spine, shifts its centre of gravity. The Berlioz-sensation belongs to the head and the hips, the Puccini one to the throat and the chest. Berlioz is on the balls of his feet, Puccini sits back on his heels and opens his arms wide.

It is every director's dream to hit on the words which will translate into acting, and every actor's dream to hear them. As they will be different for everyone, it's a tall order. I remember Yat Malmgren telling a student who'd done a successful exercise concerning his camera (which he loved): 'You can go round the world on your camera.' Freely translated from the Swedish, this meant: You will be able to discover a whole world of emotions and sensations in what you feel for your camera and the depth of your knowledge of it. For example, the sensation of clicking the shutter may be exactly the way in which you tell someone that you don't love them. This is a very different concept to the Strasberg technique of substitution, which seems to me highly dubious: you mask out the other actor, superimposing your camera on him. This is bizarre and surely energy-killing – the real flow between you and your fellow actor is disrupted.

For me it's books, music, pictures – and other actors. I have no hesitation in asking the writer and the director which actor, out of the whole range of acting known to us, dead or alive, film or stage, would be ideally suited to this part. The question is useful in elucidating both style and character. Directors and writers are understandably reluctant to answer the question, because they fear that I'll simply imitate the actor. First, I couldn't, in all probability, secondly, I wouldn't. I'm simply looking for the general framework. So if the director says: Gérard Philipe, from whom I could not conceivably be more different, I'm not going to pathetically try and fail to imitate him in the part: I'll just try him on for size and find out what that frees in me, and what it inhibits, and the degree to which that defines the parameters of the part.

Recently, I did a small play by Michael Frayn in America. We had ten days' rehearsal for a double bill, so decisions as to character were quickly made without discussion. As so often the intuitive leaps seemed to work as well as, if not better than, those agonizingly reached after eight weeks' rehearsal. Half-way through the run, I realized I was playing one of the parts exactly the way a certain actor would have done. Who was it? I couldn't put my finger on it. It wasn't that I was using my body or my voice as this actor would have done – it was the timing technique, my whole attitude on stage. Finally it came to me: my friend Mike Gambon, light comedian of genius (and much else besides). He was as it were, informing the whole performance. I had been dybbuked by him – had so absorbed the sensations of his light-comedy playing that, faced with a light comedy (I don't think I'd ever done one before), out popped Gambon.

Picasso says: 'To imitate others is necessary. To imitate oneself is pathetic.' And of course acting is an art of imitation, of taking on the qualities of another, to find where they match yours, to what extent it would be possible for you to look like/talk like/walk like/feel like that man. The actor, talking to another man, often begins to assume his accent. He is in a state of ontological flux.

Maybe no more than half a dozen people have made an enormous impact on me, to the extent that they've entered my muscles. I know so completely how it feels to be them that I can summon them at will. If you knew who they were, you'd spot bits of them in all my performances. I recycle them unashamedly. Here actors are completely ruthless, with the ruthlessness Shaw claims to be the nature of all artists.

Not many of us are as ruthless as Marlon Brando. There's a well-known story which chillingly illustrates this element of all acting. Making *Mutiny on the Bounty*, Brando befriended an English actor playing a small part. They seemed to have little in common, but during the whole shoot, they were inseparable. On the last day, the English actor went to Brando to take his leave. He was coming back to the States quite soon, would Brando like to give him his address, and they could have a get-together. 'Fuck off,' said Brando, or equally graceless words to that effect. The English actor reeled home, mortally hurt, but above all baffled. He told the story to a friend. The friend roared with laughter. 'Don't you see?' he said. 'The accent!' And sure enough, there, coming out of Fletcher Christian's mouth, is that hapless English actor's accent.

It is clearly, to say the least, an eclectic art. Everything, anything is grist to its mill. Rehearsal is a compost heap, on which finally the lovely flower of art will grow. Or it may be a weed.

Character 2

Can you find the character within you? And having found him, can you believe in yourself as him?

One late night in Belfast in 1968, I sat with Micheál MacLiammóir in the Grand Hotel in Belfast, sipping Bushmills while he as usual sipped gin. We were talking about movies, of which he was an avid devotee, despite his cataracts. We discussed Zeffirelli's *Romeo and Juliet*. He said: 'You see, the boy just wasn't young enough. Oh, to be sure, he *looked* young, delightfully, beautifully young, but he *wasn't* young. Would you *permit* me – now don't be embarrassed, for God's sake – would you permit me to play the tomb scene?' And from memory – had it been forty years? thirty, at least – he spoke the lines, and as he did so, the mask that life had given him dissolved and he became the vision of youthfulness, beside which Leonard Whiting seemed elderly. Micheál believed in it; and it was so.

Often the belief is a matter of summoning precisely the right sensation. Then you simply act under its influence. We've all had regal moments. Re-invoke them, and you're a king.

The pool of sensations into which you so frequently dip your fishing net is memory – muscular memory. The other thing, the ability to remember lines, is a mechanical function, easily accomplished. Muscular memory, though, is at the heart of acting, which is indeed, an Art of Memory. You contain within you a memory bank, comprising thousands and thousands of memories of WHAT IT FEELS LIKE TO BE ... whatever. You never stop observing and trying out for size the behaviour of your fellow human beings. Your eyes are on stalks all day long, prying into people's lives and noting their responses and tics, running them through your own body to find out why. The same applies to yourself, heartlessly scrutinizing every impulse and reaction. MacLiammóir had a story about this: he and Hilton Edwards went to Morocco in the thirties. Hilton went off sightseeing for the day. That afternoon a message reached Micheál that he'd had an accident and was feared dead. He burst into tears and ran downstairs to the reception desk. On the way down, he passed a mirror and caught sight of himself in it. 'Oh,' he thought to himself, '*that's* what one looks like when the person dearest to one in the whole world has just died.'

An actor, like any other artist, is someone who can't forget. A painter's medium is paint, a writer's words. An actor's medium is character.

You need a lot of memory for a role. Every line, every moment, every impulse has to be made particular and grounded in some sensation, because it was so for the character. In finding his life in yourself, you have naturally to discover parallel sensations to his. In rehearsal, you suddenly cry: 'I know what it is! It's what you feel like when you've been caught cribbing in an exam' or, more mysteriously, but equally productively, 'it's neapolitan ice-cream'. It means something to you, and that's what counts.

Rehearsal 3

If character is supremely the actor's responsibility, the other three thrusts of rehearsal work fall into the director's province: narrative, meaning and style. Of course none of the four factors is separable from the others: narrative, after all, is only what the characters do, so if the character is unclear or misconceived, so will the narrative be. And if either of those are in trouble, what chance does the meaning of the play (or its super-objective) have of being articulated? As for style, that being the whole expressive gesture of the piece, it consists almost by definition of the sum of all other elements.

Nevertheless, these things must be insisted on by someone who is not you. It's almost impossible for you, thrashing around in the filthy waters of your subconscious, to maintain an over-view of the play. You must go with the impulses of your character, far exceeding the parameters set by the author. You are, after all, engaged in a slightly spooky biological activity: giving birth in controlled but not completely comprehended circumstances. You're re-inventing yourself. Re-birthing, in fact.

In this sense, actors are indeed children.

You consciously unlearn all you have learned as an adult – how to walk, talk, think; you turn the clock back, and start from scratch. The appalling helplessness of the early stage of rehearsal when you're trying to reform all your impulses exactly parallels a baby's first faltering steps. Slowly, as the work proceeds, childhood and adolescence follow. You begin to gain mastery over yourself. Boisterousness and a growing sense of power come with the first phase; with the second – adolescence – characteristic late rehearsal confusion sets in: doubt in the new body, the new language, and anxiety about the mass of new impulses and energies burgeoning within you. The end of rehearsal sees you finally approaching adulthood, able, as it were, to face the world.

The director's job in all this is parental. In the early stages of rehearsal, he must flood you with amniotic fluid, then, as the performance begins to take shape, he has to guide, nurture, offer himself as a buffer, sometimes disciplining, but always respecting, your individuality. It's as difficult a job as parenthood, and one as little appreciated by the beneficiary.

What is hard for some directors, as for some parents, is that the whole object of the exercise is to give the actor-child his freedom and independence, to phase themselves out and hand over the reins unconditionally. Other directors, more like animal parents than human ones, abandon the actor to his fate the moment the first night is over. That, too, is a betrayal.

How much one asks! Throughout the rehearsal period, the director must ply you with questions. What story are you telling? What emphases are you making, and what effect does that have on the whole play? Why are you destroying the shape of a role with psychological interlardings alien to the style?

Style is the most elusive area of all, and finally the most important. What is the technique, the flavour, the personality of *this* play, as opposed to any other? What is Molière-like about Molière, Feydeau-like about Feydeau? These considerations should be at the fingertips of every actor, but we've lost the habit. Instead we ask: what is this play's relevance? We're virtuosos of that question. With the result that everything we ever touch turns into another Play For Today. So the director must *ask*. He must keep probing, probing, crystallizing, elucidating.

You don't thank him for it; at least, not until after. It's not a pleasant feeling, being on trial all the time. Praise, of which you require large helpings, slithers off you unheeded, but criticism rankles. Not being criticized rankles even more deeply.

The director's comments on the growing performance are called 'notes'. I recall a radio programme where Sir John Gielgud and Sir Ralph Richardson were interviewed. 'Tell me, Sir John and Sir Ralph, do you ever give each other notes?' There was an appalled silence, broken by Richardson. 'Good – God – no!' he cried, while Sir John cooed negatives in the background. 'I can't abide notes,' declared Sir Ralph, 'especially from a director. My idea of a director is a chap who puts me in the middle of the stage, and shines a bright light on me.' Most of us are a little more ambivalent but there's no doubt it's as painful as it's necessary to have an eagle eye trained on your every movement. The director has to develop an acute sense of the graph of your performance. Is what you seem to be playing today merely a phase you're going through, a transition between one stage and another, or a radically new departure, as it appears to be? Because it's going on inside of you, you can be cruelly deceived by what you're feeling as opposed to what you're doing.

The available time has to be carefully divided between form and content. The mechanical aspects of the play must be worked on simultaneously. You have to be utterly fluent in your text, deft in your dances and deathfalls, or they will drag you down. You must find a comparable emotional fluency, for the same reason: to be able to touch the emotion precisely, that emotion and no other, at *that* specific emotional intensity. All these requirements are challenges above all to thought, a technique of emotional impulses. The most important objective of rehearsals is to achieve a clear mind: to have resolved the areas of doubt, cleaned out the mud. It's not easy. The actor's work on himself is a plumbing job, unblocking the pipes which carry the impulses from the inner to the outer world, to express the character-in-him.

Another objective of the rehearsal is to earn yourself the respect to stand on stage and say: 'Here you are! Here's something extra-ordinary!' At no time must you be thinking: 'I hope you're going to like this . . . please like it.' As soon as you start asking the audience for approval, you're done for but you can't avoid it unless you've won your own respect. If you feel you could have done more work, or could have challenged yourself to be a little more daring, your relation-ship to the audience will be craven, depending on their goodwill and indulgence. The work must be proud.

Not that any actor ever reaches this happy state. Some ancient guilt clings to all of us, all the time. Is it because of the unfathomable interpenetration of you and the character? For whatever reason, there is in all of us a lurking fear of being FOUND OUT. Don Henderson used to wander round rehearsals whispering into people's ears: 'They rumbled you yet?' It touched a nerve in everyone.

Rehearsal 4

As the weeks go by, the initially disparate group of people thrown together to put the play on become close. It's a unique closeness. We've seen each other make fools of ourselves, have all perhaps suffered the director's lash, and are all aware of the day when our work will be put to the test. You learn to bite your tongue out rather than offer another actor advice, even though you can *see* exactly what's wrong with his performance. At this stage it's wiser to observe the beam in your own eye, and leave your colleague to sort out his own mote for himself. Bit by bit, you become a sort of family: that is to say, ultimately trusting and therefore free to be rough with each other. It would be sentimental to pretend that you like everyone in every group, but the simple pressure of getting the show on ensures that most animosities are shelved for the purposes of work. To the same end, an extraordinary framework of banter and rough-house develops: each actor is endowed with a couple of characteristics which he may or may not in reality possess. Once these have been established, barriers collapse and we all feel free to put ourselves on the line. In this way, rehearsals assume the nature of a play within a play: the visible rehearsal is the objective correlative of the actual rehearsal, which is going on some inches below the surface.

Here in the rehearsal we can so often seem like children, and this is the other sphere in which the old slur has some truth: a different truth to the one intended, to be sure. In fact, here, to be childish is brave.

The general implication is that actors are immature, irresponsible, promiscuous, out-of-touch with the world, jealous, applause-hungry show-offs. I deny it. There *are* elements in the job – late nights, a degree of transitoriness in working relationships – which produce a certain way of life that is unquestionably different from the rest of the population's. Even so, the whooping-it-up actors are merely the most visible section of the profession, the majority of whom are too poor to do so, or not that way inclined, preferring to take their trains back to Sanderstead – by no means the least interesting type of actor, may it be said.

Ethical behaviour is of a remarkably high standard. I have known nothing but kindness and generosity and respect for each other's work. Political commitment is – now notoriously – intense, and most actors' intellectual curiosity and learning is far above what I've encountered on campuses across England. As for applause, for most actors it is an embarrassment. Of course we are show-offs: we show ourselves off. That's the job. But in the street, at home, in the pub, it's striking how untheatrical most actors are: the ushers and the box office staff are much more flamboyant than any of us.

Within the profession, the 'childish' tag goes deeper and is much more damaging. It ranges from the directorial assumption that actors need to be told what to do – that they have no contribution to make to vital decisions which affect them closely (design, budget, and so on), that box office returns must be kept from them – to the assumption by critics that whatever is good in a production must have come from the director ('Mr X coaxed fine performances from Miss Y and Mr Z' – the day I wake up to read that Miss Y and Mr Z coaxed a fine production from Mr X, I shall know that the millennium has arrived). All these lazy assumptions are a daily affront to actors and what is worse by constant repetition, they become true. You *do* become passive and lazy if no serious thought or responsibility is asked of you.

On the floor, however, what we are engaged in is deeply and seriously childish.

The performance, of course, the very act of acting, is inherently childlike. First of all, we revert to a period of life where personality is undetermined, in a state of flux. Like all children's games, what we do is exploratory: trying out, trying on, investigating, imitating. The child imitates his mother in order to understand her, to be able to deal with her, to take away some of her magic. Play tests things out – the relative strengths of the members of a community, for example, and your own strength. The written or spoken text adds to this the testing out of ideas, the symbolic enactment of philosophies and psychologies. Behind the surface seriousness is the sense of play, assuming roles and ploys and behind that is the seriousness, the danger, of life.

Unless ye become as these little ones, ye shall not enter the kingdom of art. It's neither comfortable nor easy to get hold of your child-self again, but it's behind all great acting and all great theatre.

Rehearsal 5

When the wallowing ends, and you emerge from the swamp of sensation, you go into Action. From now on, every moment of the play must become active: you must always be *doing* something to another character – or yourself, if you're alone – and you must find a million ways of doing it; a million characteristic ways, that is. This is where real virtuosity in acting lies. Having challenged your inner life to the utmost in the swamp-period, you now challenge your physical and mental capacities to the utmost. At first you feel laboured as each variation follows the other with a terrible grinding of gears. You work unceasingly for the ripple of impulses which will finally take over by themselves.

There are a number of distinct phases in the rehearsal which introduce new elements into the work. First is the runthrough. This may occur, depending on directorial inclination, early or late. Either way, it's a shock to the system. What has been slowly assembled is now placed on a kind of moving belt which leaves you gasping for breath. Nine tenths of your painstaking work seems somehow to have evaporated. Your confidence in your capacity to totter across the room is shattered, and it's back to all fours. At the same time, however, you have learned many valuable things: a sense of the overall shape of the play, what variations must be introduced, what areas of the role are opaque and which work. For a long time, runthroughs will be like those early aviators running along the ground with their wings, taking off for a minute and a half and then crashing to the ground in flames. The aviators – if they didn't die, that is – would I'm sure say that it was all worth it for those airborne minutes, that by examining them one would surely find the secret of sustained flight. So it is with the play. Curiously, many things which appear not to work at all fall into place once a degree of speed has been attained. My image for this with *Amadeus* was a spinning top which doesn't hum until it reaches a particular speed.

Another runthrough, which is obligatory, is the one for the technicians – the lighting designer, the sound man, probably the press officer and sundry others. This runthrough has a suicidal effect on all the participants. Experience has taught you to try to ignore it, but the

179

dead silence, the apparently appalled expressions, sometimes the sleep and usually the chain-smoking of the little audience have one reaching for the cyanide before it's over. The general feeling is of being on trial for great crimes against humanity. I call these Nuremberg runthroughs.

Each one though, even the Nuremberg, tells you a great deal. The play is dismantled and put back together again – pipes are unblocked, the energy flow from thought to thought, impulse to impulse, is released. The play is closely examined for narrative clarity, precision of intention and rightness of gesture. If character is at fault, there is grave cause for anxiety. However, the laws of character are mysterious, and it is possible, given a clear enough lead, totally to transform the character you are playing in the twinkling of an eye. It is said that Olivier in *Richard III* and Scofield in *A Man For All Seasons* suddenly produced those famous characterizations the night before their First Nights. It seems to me that character functions rather like hypochondria (I speak from experience). Sense a pain in any part of the anatomy and within minutes it has raced terminally through your entire body. Not stopping at that, you've decided which close friends to break it to, how to alter your will and how best to spend the last few weeks of your life. Some of us compose our obituaries. *Some* of us even decide who to invite to the memorial service. So with acting. A new characterization can race through your body. You will, after all, be familiar with the role. It's simply the emphasis that needs changing, as if, for instance, you were to discover that you'd been playing a 45rpm record at 33⅓.

At this stage – before your arrival in the theatre, when the whole atmosphere changes totally – you begin to distinguish woods from trees. Assuming that your performance is entering its young adult-hood, a few searching questions are in order – because – unlike, or like, life? – there comes a point where the die is cast. A performance or production which is fundamentally flawed by the dress rehearsal will never right itself. A performance or production which is chaotic and unrealized but essentially right has every chance. So you ask yourself some very serious questions to try to assess the quality and direction of your work. The questions are posed by a kind of mental committee, each of which has very different concerns. I always ask myself, for example, what would Christopher Fettes and Yat Malmgren say? (Still. Ten years on and their influence is undiminished.) I have to answer to Christopher for fidelity to the text's world. Is it Spanish? Is it seventeenth century? Or whatever. To Yat I have to answer for the performance's inner coherence. Does it add up? And so on. I have a dear friend who as well as being an exceptional actress and director is a committed feminist. I have to persuade her of the political consciousness of my approach. This is not to say that I change my performance to satisfy any of these demands: it simply means that I know what I'm doing. I also always ask myself what would Laurence Olivier have done; but that only depresses me.

By the time we reach the theatre, I have a fairly clear idea of what the performance is – what it's aiming at and how near its target it is.

The final runthrough in the rehearsal room has its unique character. It's a farewell to the womb. Now comes emergence into the light – literally. Lighting, costumes, make-up, set, auditorium: all these new and alien facts of life will have to be dealt with. Everyone knows that many performances will not survive the new conditions. Exquisite, delicate and witty in the rehearsal room, they may perish once they hit the deck. Others, out of focus and crude, may find their proper environment.

So the mood at the end of the final runthrough, as the coloured tapes which marked out the dimensions of the set are pulled up off the floor, and the token props are crammed into a basket, is mixed, fearful and hopeful in equal measure.

At the same time, there's an excitement in the air. Into the theatre! It is, after all, where we belong.

Into the Theatre

The romantic thrill of that first walk past the stage door, down the corridors and on to the stage, never fails. A theatre is centripetal – everything is sucked into the centre of the building, the stage itself. The division between the auditorium, with its velvet and gilt, or even its mauve and grey concrete, and the functional stage, with its ropes and wires, its steep black brick walls, its little purple lights and tables full of props, wheels and weights, staircases leading down into the bowels of the building, and ladders leading up to the giddy flies, remains a potent phenomenon: the romance of work, the juju of craft – and all secret. Our kingdom.

On the stage will be the set, newly erected. It always comes as a surprise, whether pleasant or not. Its sheer physical reality after weeks of Marcel Marceau doors and walking unthinkingly through walls is quite shocking. Immediately you start modifying your performance, whether shrinking it to accommodate the restrictions the set will impose, or joyfully expanding it in the light of the new possibilities offered. Now too, for the first time, you realize the production is really going to happen, which always sends a tiny shiver down the spine. After throwing a few words into the auditorium, you go to discover your dressing room, pausing to congratulate the stage crew for having got the set up, usually having worked through the night to do so. The stage management are in command now. This is *their* ship, and they're establishing themselves at the wheel, in the engine room, and up the crow's nest.

A little spare, you wander off to the dressing room, to deposit your 'things': make-up, towel, comforting odds and ends. You sniff around, getting the feel of this home from home. Standards of cleanliness and practicability vary widely. Essentially, however, it will be a rectangular room with a wardrobe (or maybe just a clothes rack), a couple of seats, a washbasin, a table set against the wall, and a mirror surrounded in the traditional way by naked light bulbs. The mirror may have a greeting from the previous incumbent scrawled across it in red grease paint. There may be a shower. *Sometimes* – luxury undreamed of! – there may be a lavatory. In some of the older theatres there are odd signs on the wall enjoining you not to drink or use bad language, on penalty of a fine. You may be sharing the dressing room with two or three other actors. If you're playing a leading part, however, you're usually on your own. This is a little unreasonable, in that the leading actors will perforce spend less of their time in the dressing room than others. I suppose the justification is that by the interval they'll be whacked, and need their privacy. More likely is the huge amount of entertaining they'll do after the show. To this end a refrigerator is sometimes provided.

You lay out your make-up in front of the mirror, you hang your towel up and pin a couple of cards to the wall. In these little ways, it begins to be *your* dressing room. By the end of the run, you'll need a pantechnicon van to haul away the accumulated interior decorations. For the time being it's like living in rented furnished accommodation.

In the wardrobe or on the clothes rack, you'll find your costumes. You will have been to the costumier or tailor to have them measured and fitted. The designer will have consulted you closely, and been at pains to please you. (Not always, apparently. One of our leading designers is recently reported to have told an actress who expressed surprise at the texture of her costume: 'Yes, well, darling, we can't always get the best materials – just like we can't always get the best actresses.') There will be few surprises. Yet the moment of first trying the costume on in front of the mirror in the dressing room is powerful and important. What it does to your body is crucial. It can make you taller or shorter, proud or craven. The position and number of pockets, the line of the legs, the weight and degree of elevation of the shoes can all radically alter your performance. A corset, a wig, high-heeled shoes are all transforming. It's very useful to have them in rehearsal – though it's equally valuable to have an injection of something as new and potent as this at such a late stage.

As powerful as the effect of the clothes on your body is the effect of your appearance on your imagination. The moment you see yourself, your brain starts to work differently. In this way costume acts exactly like a mask. The costume, as it were, travels inwards. You start to form the bodily shapes of the man that looks like *that*.

It is said that Nijinsky walked into his dressing room, the squat graceless dancer that he was in life and in class, and walked out utterly transformed as the exquisite golden slave, as the weightless spectre of the rose, as the broken puppet Petrushka. Some voodoo occurred in front of the mirror.

Make-up was one of the older actors' greatest tools. Since the advent of 'white light' it has become almost unknown in modern plays; and much more sparingly used in classic ones. When I was at drama school, I was taught by someone who had not been informed, it appeared, of the demise of footlights. Layer upon layer of Leichner's greasesticks were applied according to their number: 'a little more no. 5, a bit of no. 9.' I always loathed it. I sweat heavily on stage, and within minutes my face was an expressionist nightmare. It was a huge relief to discover that most make-up was redundant.

Older actors sometimes display exquisite skill in their make-ups, creating a perfect mask in front of the mirror; more often than not, alas, when they get on the stage under the lights, the director asks them to reduce it to the point where they might as well not have bothered.

Make-up is, therefore, a dying art. One or two actors of my generation keep it alive. Tony Sher, who is anyway a brilliant painter, comes to mind. For my part in this as in little else, I find myself favouring the Alec Guinness as opposed to the Laurence Olivier approach. Sir Laurence was the genius of the make-up box, covering his face with greasepaint, appending false noses and artificial gums, blocking out his eyebrows and filling in his cheeks. He substituted another face for his. Alec Guinness, on the other hand, by thought alone seems to transform his face from within. He's on record as using a minimum of make-up as such. Similarly I have tried to find the face of the character within my face. I'll grow a beard or stick one on; cut my hair or wear a wig; above all alter the position of my hairline (the single most transforming thing one can do to one's head). I also tend to put on (Verlaine) or lose (Orlando) weight while I'm working on a part, which in itself radically alters one's features. In fact, the real transformation is in the energy revealed in the face. Transformation is not disguise, but the revelation of alternative possibilities in the muscular disposition of the face and the body.

Whichever approach you favour, the assumed or the osmotic, as you stand in front of the mirror, SOMEONE ELSE LOOKS BACK. This is voodoo. The embodiment of another person is black magic, the raising of spirits. Being this person, you will be able to do things you cannot do. You will be able to lift weights that you cannot. You will be able to dance steps that you cannot. You won't mind taking all your clothes off.

It's not you.

But it could have been.

Make-up: Arturo Ui

My suit, shirt, shoes were all three sizes too big. An incipient hump had been built into the jacket. I wore white gloves (clown-like) and the wig, which had been found in the dustbins outside the Royal Opera House, was a lousy fit, quite clearly A WIG. I had a lot of trouble with the face. I tried all the usual stuff – white pancake (without which no self-respecting German Expressionist season could be contemplated), rouged lips, blacked eyebrows, false eyelashes. No good. Firstly, my face isn't sufficiently fine-boned (I just looked like a pudding which had fallen into a pot of white paint), and secondly it seemed to allude to all kinds of theatrical phenomena, MC's, circus, etc. Boring, been done to death. Well, one day, very near the first night, I went to the designer's house to experiment with make-up; we went rather gloomily through the repertoire of my make-up box and then quite by chance my eye lighted on a cheap joke-shop false nose with a Hitler moustache attached. I nearly knocked the poor girl over as I leaped across the room. 'That's *it*,' I said, 'that's it.' I put it over the non-fitting wig so that the elastic string stretched at an angle from left to right of my face, thus splitting it up, like a Kokoschka or Rouault. It was exactly what I wanted but nothing like what I'd intended. It unmistakably said Hitler, but it wasn't human at all. There could have been nothing under that nose and wig, or some peculiar animal. It accentuated my eyes and thickened my lips. It was abstract, neanderthal and robot-like all at once.

The moment I saw myself in the mirror I slumped into an ape posture, head lolling. It teetered on the edge of Groucho Marx, which was all to the good too. All the physical shapes I'd been tentatively exploring crystallized, and I was free. I could do anything now, and I knew it would be all right.

The Dress Rehearsal

There's a charming moment before the first dress rehearsal when the cast comes on to the stage to be addressed by the director. It's the first time they've seen each other in costume and make-up and they come on to the stage shyly – however old and experienced and exalted they may be – like children arriving at a party in fancy dress. The rest of the cast immediately respond with cries of 'Oh that's marvellous – perfect – oh that hat, yes, that's exactly what he'd wear,' and so on, a professional response. Slowly the self-consciousness wears off and you begin to give in to the new and fascinating sensations brought by the costume. It may be that it's the first time you really feel like the character. New gestures begin to appear, the stroking of a beard, perhaps, or thumbs in a waistcoat. For me these moments, not rehearsal at all, just wandering around, picking up a prop, sitting in a chair, pottering about on the set, are as creative as anything that's gone before. It's probably the first time you've had to just *be* the character, instead of having him over the anvil while you beat mercilessly away with the scene or the play. Here, in the dark, or milling casually around with the cast, you can actually feel the slow infusion of the character into your veins and bones. It's quite moving.

The dress rehearsal, with any luck, will be a complete disaster. There's an old saying engraved on all our hearts: 'Bad dress rehearsal, good show.' I can't in fact remember a good dress rehearsal. Hardly surprising in view of the myriad new problems and unexpected materializations of imagined realities. Distances all seem longer or shorter, tables are never quite how you'd seen them, the door sticks, the carpet rucks. Emotional truth goes to pieces; and as for comic timing – forget it. There will be a number of people in the audience, most of whom will have seen it before, when they didn't laugh. Now they won't laugh again. Those who haven't seen it before won't laugh either; or if they do, it'll be in quite the wrong place. The play will seem to last eight and a half hours. You will barely be thinking of your performance because you're haunted by the fact that the lighting plan appears to have been designed by Rembrandt. *You* can't see your fellow actors, so how can the audience? All in all, you just long for the whole thing to be over. It's deeply frustrating being within spitting distance of a paying audience and having to go through this hollow ritual. 'We need an audience now, that's all,' we tell each other. We all know, of course, that the dress rehearsal is essential for the technicians – that lighting plot – and for us too, for sheer familiarity with the set. But these considerations do nothing to take the phoney-war feeling away from the event.

After it's over there are anxious but slightly unreal consultations with those who were in the auditorium. You know that they can't judge anything from what they've just seen, but on the other hand, you're desperate for a first reaction from people who haven't seen it before. If they *were* at one of those early runthroughs, you ask the leading question: 'It's better, isn't it?' 'Oh, YES,' they reply, as if there were no comparison. Sometimes, to show they're not just a pretty face, they'll say: 'Don't like your act two frock (costume) very much.' 'Yes, I *know*, isn't it awful, we're changing it.' 'Oh *good*.' This is, in general, the period of maximum fragility for the actor: the awful period of suspense: not knowing in the least whether his work will pass muster: not believing anyone any more until he's come into contact with the public themselves, the punters. After the first preview, he's up for grabs again, because he has something to hang on to, some reality, that moment of energy flowing or not flowing from us to them.

The First Preview

A terrible shock to the system. It is said that the adrenalin production of an actor at each performance is equivalent to that produced by a major car accident. At the first preview it's a car accident *and* jumping off the top of the Empire State Building. The stress is greater and less than that of the First Night. It's a complete leap into the dark; on the other hand, it's being done for a few perfectly decent good-natured theatregoers out to have a good time, not a couple of hundred friends rigid with anxiety for you to succeed, a couple of hundred voyeurs thinking 'Come on, show us then, smarty pants,' and fifteen vultures composing their copy even before the curtain's gone up.

The novelty of it can hardly be exaggerated. If the set and the costumes were a surprise, how much more is this other missing element, the essential actors without whom we've rehearsed, always imagining their contribution. Rehearsing without the audience is surfing without waves.

The principal revelation is in the area of narrative. It's so easy in rehearsal to forget that what you're telling is being heard by the audience for the first time. Even in a classic, which you may assume a proportion, but only that, of the audience is familiar with, the unfolding of the story is of prime importance. You may well have fallen in love with moments of your performance or the play which fatally subvert the telling of the story. Once the narrative thread has been lost, the audience strays, and the chain of energy has been broken. This first preview tells you unerringly how clearly you're telling the story.

It'll also tell you whether the show is too long – in reality or in effect. Does the play need to be cut, or speeded up? This question of length is directly contingent on the first question, the narrative. If the story's unclear, the play will seem longer. Narrative clarity extends to every department of the production: the staging, the setting (where are we supposed to be? If it takes ten minutes for the audience to work out, that's ten lost minutes which will feel like ten hours to them, anyway), and the character (a development is completely incomprehensible: more bafflement, more time lost, more exhaustion of the audience). The play itself may be at fault narratively – too elliptical, too dense, actually confused. The comments of friends, theatre staff, agents and so on can be indispensable here: sometimes they can say the word that clarifies everything. The degree to which you've lost innocence with the piece, the degree to which it's inside you, is alarming. To such an extent is this true that here again you have to hang on very hard. You can easily get pushed off course at this moment. You have to go back to the play, back to your first thoughts about it. The actors and the director have to renew each other's original vision, and scrupulously assess to what extent they're fulfilling it. If it's the vision itself that people find hard to take, then there is a simple choice.

Ditch it or persevere. The braver choice may be to ditch it. The audience test is quite brutal: either it works or it doesn't. The intensity of work and thought that goes on during this preview period is immense. The play can alter out of all recognition. Sometimes, to be brutally honest, the work of the preview period is the only serious work that has gone on at all. The first night and judgement loom.

Don't expect to sleep during this period. If you do, it will be a sleep infested with demons. The hours of darkness will be filled with the unending and increasingly meaningless recital of your lines on a never-ending loop, interspersed with allegories of impotence.

Dream During the Preview Period of Balthazar:

At the Royal Court, we're trying to do a press show of *Balthazar*. The set has been lost, and we try – Marj (the company manager), Pat Ryecart and I – to fill the audience in on what should be where, the story so far, etc. We keep drying up, not being able to remember the plot. Eventually at the end of the third scene I step forward and tell the audience that this is where the interval would be. 'I hope you're enjoying this experimental art-form we've invented,' I say, hoping for laughter. None. I then say, 'I'm going to take over the scene descriptions completely.' 'No you're not,' says Ron Daniels, the director, finger-clicking and masterful. 'OK, fine,' I say, off-handed. The show stumbles forward. From a sort of (actually non-existent) slips high-up-stage left, a row of devilishly handsome but aggressive men start to abuse us all. Finally one of them drops a glass from a great height. It smashes. Pandemonium. Fire. I remember the exits at the back of the stage, start to climb the ladder with everyone else. But they (the troublemakers) are aiming for the top, where the lighting box is. One of them wants to blowtorch the box. I slip out of a little exit half-way up the ladder . . .

You're haunted throughout the preview period by mingled emotions of expectation of acclaim and intimation of doom. The expectation leaps around in your chest, while the doom hovers over your head. It's a very displeasing state of emotional constipation. You long for the first night – to get it over with, and to hear the verdict. Ken Campbell calls the first night the judging, and that's exactly what it is.

The morning of the first night of *Total Eclipse* I woke from my haunted sleep to boiling anger at the prospect before me. We have laboured passionately for four weeks to bring to life this beautiful and touching and funny play of Christopher Hampton's, I thought. We have read and researched, we have listened to music and gazed at paintings. We have dug up buried and painful emotions. We have challenged our skill to the utmost. We have done all this to share with the public work which will speak to something deep inside them. We may have thought (before we started working) that in some way it might advance our careers, or make a great deal of money for us; once rehearsals began, however, there has been no other thought than giving this play to the public at its most intense and true. And now, I thought bitterly, we are required to offer ourselves up to the judgement of a group of jaded, self-promoting, axe-grinding, non-elected men, who will decide whether the public receives this work of ours. The rage produced by this thought drove me out of the house cursing and pulling my hair out at the roots – what was left of it, that is, because in the pursuit of my craft, I had shaved three inches from my forehead, condemning myself to two months of neanderthal appearance. And indeed, I was not wrong. That night was the best first night I have ever been involved in, we gave exactly what we had worked on, not distorted or changed in any way by the pressure of the event. And they, the critics, greeted it with indifference and confusion. We subsequently played to an average of 40 per cent.

The First Night

Directorial strategy for first nights varies widely. Some directors leave it up to the actors, and simply call everyone together an hour early, say, for a little community chatting. Clearly it's too late for anything to be done. The die is cast. Very occasionally, in a token way, the director will rehearse some detail. There are those directors – John Dexter is one of them – who favour light quick runs of the play in costume, on the set. It seems to me that this can dangerously impair the freshness of the performance, given that one has dreamt the lines all night and will certainly have been compulsively repeating them all day. Dexter's method, however, is all his own, because it has long been his custom to throw a party for the cast at midday of the first night. Smoked salmon sandwiches and champagne are the order of the day, personally served by him. As I have a superstitious dread of drinking on the day of a performance, I become involved in bizarre subterfuges (because, needless to say, there's no resisting him), pouring glasses of perfectly good Perrier Jouet into wastepaper bins.

For myself, a very quick runthrough of the words with the entire company sitting in a circle is a valuable antidote to the gremlins who will be installed along the lines of communication from one's brain to one's lips and tongue: any exercise, in fact, which will counteract the emotional hysteria sweeping through one's body. It's said that Anna Magnani, whose emotional vitality was never in need of stimulation, used to do a crossword puzzle before every performance because it was her mind that needed waking up. I should say that on a first night the same is true for most of us.

The hysteria is not to be explained merely in terms of critics and judgement. It is, for all its disadvantages, a necessary stage in the growth of any production. The temperature is so heightened that certain things can easily boil over, but certain other things can congeal for the first time. Adrenalin, overdrive, and an almost feverish awareness of everything around you can take the performance to hitherto unattainable heights. There has been an unconscious saving of yourself during the previews. Now you let rip. Of recent performances, I well remember how on the first night of *Total Eclipse*, I wept unreservedly at the reminiscence of Rimbaud which closes the play. It simply happened. I wasn't overwrought: they were the cooling tears of emotion recollected in tranquillity. It was exactly what the moment called for; but I had never been able to do it. Thereafter, I was always able to do it. In *Restoration*, Lord Are at the end of the play suddenly identifies himself with the sun. It's an enormous, unprepared leap. On the first night, I made it.

The whole day, from the moment you get up to the moment you hit the sack, almost certainly incapable, is like no other. If anything, it's like some peculiar birthday. Everybody is extremely nice to you. There will be telegrams and cards, possibly presents: booze and flowers. Your dressing room begins to resemble a hospital ward or a funeral parlour, you darkly think. Whether the director has called you in or not, you're unlikely to be able to resist the magnetic pull of the theatre. You'll pick at your lunch. You'll drink many cups of black coffee. When you meet the cast and the director a mood of dangerous hilarity will be in the air. The line runthrough, or play runthrough, or whatever's been planned will almost certainly dissolve into hysterical laughter at some point.

My plan is then to leave the theatre and do my first-night shopping. Most people have planned this for weeks, written the cards over the weekend, and delivered them by lunchtime. Not I. I have found it wonderfully therapeutic to have another problem to deal with; other than the play itself, that is. The giving of presents is a charming tradition which, like Christmas, can become the opposite of what it was supposed to be: an agonizing search for the *cadeau juste*, a skull-scratching quest for the witty phrase which is both personal and funny. In National Theatre companies of forty and more, this can bring you to the brink of nervous breakdown.

For me, it's a godsend. Out into Covent Garden or Soho I go with a blank mind and a blank cheque-book. I allow myself about an hour to do the shopping, half an hour to do the wrapping. This Beat the Clock game is a wonderful preparation. Sometimes I'm still sending my dresser to distant dressing rooms when the curtain has gone up.

The result is that when I reach the stage I am in a highly energized state, but I have barely thought about the play at all. It then requires a strong but simple effort to tune in. All other things being equal I walk on to the stage in a state of focus, instead of the usual dif-fused haze that first nights bring, and with it the risk of complete misjudgement of the energy factor, either inaudibly laid back, or hysterically over-projected, a long-jumper who does a high jump instead. It is into this last trap that I am prone to fall.

One's sense of the length of the performance is the clearest indicator of its success – if it seems over in a second, it was probably very good. If interminable, the chances are that it never hit its proper rhythm. Interestingly enough, the performance which seemed to fly by may possibly have put extra minutes on the playing time, while the interminable one took them off. This curious manifestation of the properties of time is at the heart of any performance, which exists, in the deepest possible sense, in Time.

The first-night audience – as I've indicated – is unlike any other, because all the various sections of it have some ulterior attitude to the performance. No one is there simply to see the play. It's a self-conscious audience: critics disdaining to laugh because it's beneath them – even if they find it funny, friends laughing like lunatics *pour encourager les autres* (and you of course), 'the money', not looking at the stage at all, anxiously scrutinizing the rest of the audience and particularly the critics, First Nighters hoping to be present at the making of history.

Self-conscious as the audience is, so are you, thinking all the time – and this is death to a performance – what did they make of that? or, hell, I fucked that up. It's almost impossible to be in the present with this performance, unless you've reached a high state of Zen and are able to say: The play alone matters. A semi-Zen state, and almost equally useful, is to say, Fuck the lot of you, I don't give a shit what you think, this is GOOD and I'm going to enjoy myself. I'm doing it for (whoever you like: Laurence Olivier, the Queen, the author, God) and the rest of you can go jump in the Thames. This state of mind is not recommended for the rest of the run, but it can cut through the first-night horrors.

If you don't attain it, or something like it, you're condemned to the somewhat nauseous condition of looking in on yourself, observing and commenting. Paradoxically this is also the condition of really extra-ordinary performances, with the difference that the alter ego who's looking in on you on the first night is terribly slow and stupid, and can't understand what's going on at all, whereas the guy who sees you when you're being brilliant has winged feet and an IQ of 150. He's there before you, solving, suggesting, steering. The first-night moron has feet of lead and thoughts to match.

The curtain call on the first night suffers in exactly the same way that everything else has. You're aware that half the audience is rooting for you, so their cheers or heroic applause are touching, but not meaningful. All you're aware of are the three people in the front row sitting on their hands, and the disappearing backs of the critics, scurrying off to seal your fate. You try dimly to discern from their backs what that fate might be, but no Alfred Lunts they.

Back to the dressing room, a hug and a kiss for everyone on your way. You burble. From now on in fact until you wake up tomorrow morning, you will burble, eager to fill in any gaps in conversation which might suggest a lack of enthusiasm. Sometimes, in fact, you carry this horror of silence to such lengths that people come to your dressing room, have a drink, stay for quarter of an hour, and go without your ever once allowing them to express an opinion.

You don't, in any case, believe a word anyone says after a first night. Nobody speaks to you who hasn't got praise: I don't think anyone would be so insensitive as to express reservations about a performance after a first night. The next day, oh yes, and thereafter, people will not scruple to offer the most searching criticisms; and quite rightly so. This night, however, is charmed; the birthday spirit, however strained, is maintained. It's quite unreal, and you long for it to continue forever and to stop immediately. The sword of Fleet Street hangs over everyone's head. Real enthusiasts will wait till three o'clock in the morning for the first editions. There, over a doughnut in Ludgate Circus, you will read in cold print – unbelievably, it seems only minutes since the curtain fell – The Verdict. Then, with traces of make-up still clinging to your face, you'll know whether the last four weeks has been wasted, whether those lumps of bleeding flesh were dragged out of your entrails in vain and whether the public will ever see your offering to them.

The Reviews

The morning after the first night, you will probably wake up with a few damaged brain-cells. Even if you don't, the second night will have a somewhat lobotomized feel to it. Reviews will trickle in through the day but even if they're humdingers, there's no escaping the sense of anticlimax about the performance. The adrenalin obstinately won't flow (stocks depleted since last night) and you feel a bit ashamed about it. The director (if, that is, he didn't fly to Bayreuth on the first plane out this morning) will come round and tell you that it was much better than last night. You always think he's just being encouraging, but he's right: the second night is always a great improvement over the first. The relaxation is a huge gain (the same thing makes matinées frequently better than evening performances) and willy-nilly the lessons of the first night have sunk in.

You can't be said to be into the run proper until the Monday of the week following the first night until, that is, the message of the Sundays has been digested. Up till then, there remains a slightly festive air around the theatre: you're still news (just). If the daily reviews have been bad, you await the Sunday papers in a mood of desperation, analysing the personal characteristics and taste of the reviewer with the kind of interest that he would only normally receive from a parent or a lover. 'Yes, but he likes plays with a historical theme' or 'he can't bear adaptations from novels'. It's depressing to spend so much time in contemplation of people for whom one has so little respect.

There are actors who claim not to read reviews; there are even actors who really don't. Personally I read them all avidly and with rising fury, whether they're good or bad. It's the feeling of being on trial that evokes the bile: that, and their power. There may not be any one critic in London with the *New York Times*'s make-or-break power, but the verdict of four men, those who write for *The Times*, the *Guardian*, the *Sunday Times* and the *Observer*, have been crucial to any play I've ever been in, except on the fringe where *Time Out* is undisputed kingmaker.

It's barely worth rehearsing the tired suggestions yet again, but surely it must be self-evident that it would be so much better for everyone if the critics came on different nights, instead of appearing in their present daunting phalanx. Their presence changes the event. The performance they see is therefore not representative. The report to their readers is therefore inaccurate. Secondly, there is no earthly need for them to practise the impossible art of gathering their thoughts into coherent and truthful shape within two minutes of curtain-fall. Once upon a time, when theatre was front page news, it may have been necessary. Now it's a nonsense. Its principal effect is to encourage the critic to compose his copy as the play goes on. Opinions have crystallized by the interval, and what follows is all too often ignored or bent to accommodate that opinion. Good or bad, every review of my performance in *Amadeus* reviewed the first act – the giggling, the prancing, the dirty-talk. No mention was made of the striking speech in which Mozart spoke of music, in which his deep seriousness was suddenly revealed. There was no reference to his descent into paranoia, alcoholism, penury and agonized death. These were all in the second half. In *Restoration*'s reviews, there was barely a mention of Are's crucial and sensational transformation from man-about-town to Apollonian demiurge. It happened in the last ten minutes of the play. Too late for Fleet Street.

The general tenor of the reviews does of course affect company morale. Particularly if it's a commercial management, anything short of universal acclaim is the signal for many weeks of anxiety. Will the show run or not? Needless to say, the only interest in a review is whether it's a selling review. Good notices *per se* aren't any use at all: do they make it sound exciting? Notices which give the thumbs down in theory can nevertheless be selling notices: 'this disgusting concoction of sex, violence, nudity, anal penetration and mass flagellation' will run and run, whereas 'a tasteful celebration of the civilized values of home-county life' can forget it.

The Run 1

Assume that the notices will sell the play, and a respectable run is in sight. The run will have a distinct graph.

It's well known that long runs are a relatively recent innovation.

The accusing finger is generally pointed at Oscar Asche whose *Chu-Chin-Chow* ran for five years from 1916 to 1921; but of course the phenomenon grew out of social and economic factors: the increased running costs of the new theatres, the growth of the theatre-going public. Certainly before this century, consecutive runs of any length were unheard of. Most of our 'classics' had initial runs of three or four performances and would then, if lucky, be revived as part of some touring company's repertory. Before the copyright laws, of course, it was a matter of financial indifference to the authors how often their plays were revived.

Between the wars, long runs became the norm – though even then, there were often separate casts for the matinée. Since the war, the West End run became modified when Equity negotiated the abolition of the run-of-play contract, indefinite, for the fixed period. The star's luminosity would decree its length. Noël Coward refused to appear for longer than three months. Not many actors have managed to be quite so strict since, though four and a half months is not uncommon.

The last West End run that I did was for nine months. It was hell and I recommend it to everyone.

The Dresser: A Digression to Describe the Most Intimate Relationship that the Run will Afford

When I began acting, there was no question of having a dresser attached to me personally. One of the girls from the wardrobe might come down and help me with a quick change, but that was all. My first experience of a dresser was during my first West End run at the Prince of Wales Theatre. I was sharing a dressing room with a very close friend, who was a militant Trotskyist. I was very much under his sway politically and when he pointed out that the dressers were grossly underpaid because the management expected us, the actors, to subsidize them, I, like him, became indignant and determined not to (we were on quite modest salaries ourselves) as a matter of principle. However, we both felt very guilty about our dresser's poverty and so, absurdly, we avoided using him at all. He would come into the dressing room to find us fully changed. It baffled him, and probably upset him a little too. We'd make our own tea, go to the wardrobe with our own costume repairs and so on. It was A Principle.

The next time I had a dresser was at the National Theatre – four years later. Politically I had moved from Robespierre to Danton and the whole idea no longer seemed quite so obscene. Moreover as Orlando in Dexter's production I had two very quick changes for which an experienced dresser was essential. And so I became one of Sybil's 'gentlemen'. Any thought of not using Sybil's services to the full was absurd. She was so much the complete dresser, so infallibly efficient, so presciently thoughtful, so heroically loyal, that to have denied any of her ministrations would surely have precipitated heart failure or worse. It was a total service. I used to promise her that *this* year she was certain to win the *Evening Standard* Dresser of the Year Award. In truth she would have won it every year. She was in a league of her own.

Sybil had been a soprano at Sadler's Wells before she married a famous singing teacher, Giorgio Coop. Her love of the theatre was overwhelming and when her husband died, she went straight to the Old Vic as a dresser. She had remained to go with the company to the new National. When I introduced her to Peter Hall, the first time he'd met her, she surprised him by saying 'you directed me once'. His first opera – her last – at the Wells. She regarded her job as much more than simply getting the clothes on and off the 'gentlemen'. She was there to offer encouragement. 'Ooh Mr Callow, you do look handsome,' she'd say, as she shoved me on the stage. When I played Stafford T. Wilkins in *Sisterly Feelings* she was hard pressed to think of a compliment but finally assured me that I looked very poetic. 'Really, Sib?' I asked. 'Yes well, they always look scruffy and dirty, don't they?' she replied. I used to say, and mean, that I'd never play Mozart without Sybil in the wings. It's inconceivable that anyone else could have done the twelve or whatever it was changes as quickly as she did; and a minute here or there on the time it took would fatally impede the play's élan – and mine. She very sweetly said she'd refuse to dress anyone but me in the role.

She'd always check to see whether my herbal tea stocks were standing up, and bring in a new box when necessary. If my street clothes were falling to pieces, which they not infrequently were, she'd spirit them away and stitch them up without saying a word. In my dressing room I always play music, cassettes of classical music. I found myself putting on the ones Sybil liked. She'd sing along in her high white voice, before suddenly scuttling off to attend to another gentleman in need, who would then accuse her roundly – as we all did – of hitting the gin (she never touched a drop of anything). 'Oooh Mr Normington!' she'd squeal.

As can be imagined, Sybil is a very special case, and the dressing arrangements at the National where a dresser serves several people, and only sees them on the nights that they come in to play, are quite different from those that obtain in the course of a West End run.

There the relationship is almost like a marriage – a Victorian marriage, needless to say, based on inequality and service, but equally intimate. One's dresser stays in the dressing room throughout the show, so it's his dressing room, almost as much as yours. Nothing is secret from your dresser – your friends, your phone calls, your fears, your hopes, your drinking habits – above all, your body. In that respect, it's like being alone. As you stare at yourself in the mirror, moodily prodding at lumps of fat, or protruding bones, the dresser is there too, and it's only a matter of time before you ask his opinion. You come to know everything about his life too. Together you work out a routine which is inextricably bound up with the show. If the routine slips – if the cup of tea isn't there five minutes before the curtain goes up – it upsets the rhythm of the whole evening. In such a case, you abuse him – a ritual joke-abuse, which parodies the master–servant basis of the relationship, which is never referred to – until another person comes into the dressing room, when the mask is immediately put into place, and he becomes invisible. Even if you introduce him and invite him to have a drink, he'll say little and slip off. It's somehow not right.

Most dressers, unlike Sybil, aren't professional dressers at all and regard the job as transitional. This doesn't affect their efficiency – I've never met an inefficient dresser – but it radically affects the way you relate to them. If, for example, as may very well be the case, your dresser is an out-of-work actor, naturally, in anything to do with that, you will speak as members of the same profession – and there will always be the clear, unspoken understanding that this is not what he does for a living, it's just temporary. On that understanding, dignity returns to the job, and embarrassment goes.

The first couple of weeks are a kind of honeymoon. The excitement and hysteria of the preview and first night washes over them. It's during the first month that the keen theatregoers will come: those who really want to see the show. There will always be a sprinkling of friends and colleagues, who will come backstage. The performances will go with a swing.

Then suddenly – it's generally four or five weeks into the run – the whole thing will turn sour on you. You will attribute it to a poor house (they do exist: nights when the corporate spirit of the audience is hard and cold). The next night, the same thing, and then the same again. You start to panic. You're doing something wrong, not working hard enough, taking it for granted. That's what it is! The following night you go out determined to be brilliant. Worse than ever. This is the end of the first phase of the run.

Restoration June '82:

The pain of acting in a comedy: first of all the despair in rehearsal that it will ever be funny; the forgetting of what is funny about it; the reproach of people sitting around – fellow actors, people just popping in, who don't laugh, etc.

Then the growing sense, as outside people – photographers, theatre staff and so on – do respond in little ways, that maybe there is something there after all, then the previews in which one begins to realize the whole potential of it; the build to the first night, which on a comedy is almost always hard work: then the much more relaxed subsequent performances in which the show actually breathes and lives – the Saturday of the first week blossoming out, the warmth and joy of it. THEN the remembered response of the audience becomes the principal sensation of doing the play, and one starts unconsciously to engineer a repetition of that response – stops, in fact, playing the truth, the character, the situation: starts, in a word, to ACT IN THE PAST, to recreate an effect. Then it stops being funny and one works harder and harder to bludgeon the audience into laughter, to hold them at pistol point – like being determined to have an orgasm for reasons of *amour propre* or sheer obstinacy and slaving away with an insensitive organ until ultimately some joyless and unsatisfactory result ensues: a laugh at last. And the audience, sensing this, gives grudgingly and diminishingly: OK, we'll laugh at *that*, but the next laugh will cost you twice as much effort.

And that's what's been happening in the last couple of performances of *Restoration*; that's what I've been doing – me, the man who only three days ago was regaling the author with my theory that the business of playing comedy was not to make the audience laugh, but to *let* them laugh – to make the audience witty; not to bludgeon them but to awaken them; to tickle and not to rape.

That was written in the fourth week of an eight-week run. The problem by and large righted itself, and so we ended, as it were, during the high noon of the second phase of a run. During the nine months of *Balthazar B.*, there were to be many more phases and many new analyses of what was going on; some of them correct.

Before assessing them, it might be timely to offer a description of a good and a bad performance.

A Good Performance

A feeling of power, but not power *over* anyone or anything: simply energy flowing uninterrupted and unforced through your body and your mind. You are the agent. You are above the performance – *it* is performing, not you. You sense the audience's collective identity and you speak directly to it: Oh you liked that, did you? Well just wait till you hear *this* – not what I will do, but what will happen. You are always forward moving: the thread unbroken, no matter how much laughter or what kind of pauses.

You are the master of time and rhythm, and you play with them like a jazz musician. You create a pleasurable tension and then you relieve it pleasurably. You hear everything as if for the first time. The performance is not so much new as newly revealed, the varnish stripped off, the paint bright again, detail discernible. Such performances always seem very quick, though in actual clock time they're the same or perhaps longer (because of more laughs or more flexible pauses). You feel quite unexhausted by them. The play has played you.

Your relationship to the play is that of rider to horse. *It* is the energy: you are the direction. You must be above it and on top of it. If you are the horse, you lose touch with the audience. The text is sunk into your bones, so that it comes unbidden: it is the inevitable, the only, response to what is said to you. You become nothing but a pair of ears.

No matter how intense or painful the emotions of a part, the more you enter into them in a good performance, the less you are affected by them. It is they and nothing else which are activated. The emotion passes through you.

Above all, there is dazzling mental clarity. The chambers of the brain open up, one by one. The number of levels on which you are thinking is uncountable. One of these levels may be running through tomorrow's shopping. It's a shocking proposition, but it's true.

In a sense, an actor giving a good performance is the human being functioning at its highest level. Not its deepest; simply being exercised in a very demanding way: callisthenics of the psyche. All these things – brain, body, heart in perfect working order, doing somersaults, back-flips and headstands.

It's this that makes it such a dangerous profession for its acolytes: where else will you get the same workout? What other chance do you have to feel the energy pumping through your every faculty, the whole human machine? Life can sometimes seem a sad second.

A Bad Performance

The Opposite. Disjointed, stale; behind the beat all the time; sluggish. Excess external emotion, mental fog. Self-consciousness. Awareness of the audience *out there*, and the lack of communication with them. A sense of being out-of-focus, as if, musically, you were slightly flat or slightly sharp. Uncoordinated. On these performances, you bump into the furniture, trample on other actors' lines, walk through such laughs as there might accidentally be.

Above all, the time is out of joint.

Time is the crucial dimension. The nearest experience in daily life to what an actor feels in performance is the successful timing of a joke: the sense of inevitability about it, the way in which space seems to exist around it, the waves of emotion that it releases in its audience, the sort of halo that descends on its utterer. Having created that kind of effect, for however long, one feels sainted, glowing, somehow bigger. Alas, it fades, and the next person telling a joke inherits the halo. Imagine the halo descending for two and a half hours, and you have the sensation – of a good performance. The sensation of a bad performance is exactly that of a joke falling flat through mis-timing. The humiliation, self-consciousness – those burning cheeks – and desire to be suddenly elsewhere are what consume you during your bad performance.

In fact, of course, most performances consist of a mingling of the elements, or exist on an inglorious plane of competence and craftsmanship.

There is a story of Laurence Olivier which bears on all this. He gave a performance of Othello one night long into the run so brilliant that the cast applauded him at the curtain call. When it was over, he tore back to his dressing room in a towering rage and slammed the door behind him. One of the actors timidly knocked on the door and said: 'What's the matter. Larry – don't you know you were brilliant?' And he said, 'Of course I fuckin' know – but I don't know *why*.'

And you never do: no matter what you do, the performance can go one way or the other and as you rake the embers looking for reasons, the evidence is all contradictory. I didn't have lunch before the show today and I was marvellous; so tomorrow I go without lunch and I'm terrible. I had sex this afternoon and I was wonderful: I have sex tomorrow afternoon and I'm terrible; and so on. The auditorium is too hot; it's too cold. For actors as for farmers, nothing's ever right.

The Run 2

During the run of *Balthazar*, the first crisis was exactly as on *Restoration*. The inexplicable loss of contact with the audience from trying to re-create effects. The remedy is fairly simple – back to the text, back to the rehearsal period. The original impulses need to be renewed. This is relatively easy, and gives the play a new lease of life immediately. The second crisis, eight or ten weeks into the run, has a different cause – complete loss of adrenaline. Familiarity with the play, settled pattern of life, dwindling attendance by friends, all lead to a kind of humdrum quality overtaking one's performance. It becomes mechanical, a job. The solution to this is quite technical, but very difficult. One has to discover the ability to light up an inner bulb which irradiates the performance but which has no immediate cause. One has to locate in oneself a pool of delight, and be able to tap it at will. For comedy especially that luminous dancing spirit is indispensable. It is, when it boils down to it, what people are paying for. The third crisis, four months or so in, is the loss of character. The thought patterns are no longer clear, the character's attributes have become mannerisms, a voice and a walk empty of any impulse. A glance in the mirror has no transforming power. This is a very troubling sensation. A feeling of complete falseness overcomes you from the moment you reach the stage. Something nags away at you all the while you're talking. Your face hangs heavy on your skull as if it were a mask. The remedy for this is to write out your entire part in the first person in character. It compels you to rethink every scene you're in, and restores the eyes and ears of the character to you. The next crisis, which may follow at any time, is the worst. It's the horrors: hallucinations and fainting fits. The lunacy of standing on the same tiny space every night in more or less the same positions, saying the same words in more or less the same inflections, suddenly hits you. It is – during this crisis – impossible to do anything but just get through. You're liable to become morbidly aware of the presence of the audience, imagine enemies among them, suspect mockery or contempt. You see apparitions on the stage. During the run I was trotting across to pick up an actress and throw her over my shoulder as called for in the script, when I stopped stone dead, having seen the moon with a cloud passing over it just behind her head. I thought: Is that a backcloth? Why have I never seen it before? Then I thought: No, it's the moon, there's a hole in the wall. How beautiful. And then I realized it was simply a light. Not for a second during all this did I stop saying my lines, though I did stop moving. Then I stared at the audience and thought: Who are these people? And then – by what automatic pilot device I don't know – I picked Lotte up and threw her over my shoulder. It was over. I was very shaky for the rest of the performance. The whole hallucination had lasted thirty seconds or a minute, but it threw me off course for a week. For these horrors, the only remedy is sleep.

Slowly one's confidence comes back. Confidence is feather-frail. With it you can perform prodigies, but it can be snatched away from you with frightening ease. Miraculously, the simple meaning of the text returns. During this period, words have become more and more bizarre, have taken on their own life. The most unremarkable word can loom up in front of you in lurid shapes, while your mouth continues to emit the rest of the sentence to which it belongs. Like a sixties hippy, you're still thinking: 'Wow, what a crazy word table is. Ta-ble. Tabl. Tuh uh buh luh. Wow.' You're in a trance, a dream. It's as near to going mad as most of us will know.

A lucid but rather embittered phase follows. You determine, obviously, to give up acting. After the narrow escape you've just had, it all seems very clear. It's a nonsensical, a demeaning and an unhealthy job. You will see out the end of your contract and then take up writing/psychotherapy/selling antiques. Your feelings towards the audience during this period are likely to be fairly savage. Why can't they see through it? Why are they laughing like mentally deficient hyenas? Why *aren't* they laughing? It's funny: plenty of better people than them have found it *very* funny. The cure for this phase is to snap out of it, pronto. You have to put yourself on the carpet and talk to yourself very firmly. Have you ever found any other way of earning a living? No. Have you any other *talent*? No. Have you given pleasure? Yes. Then SHUT UP. And so you reach the final phase of the run, the home-stretch. This can last a couple of months, and is often a golden time, in which you finally attain some kind of wisdom.

At the end of *Balthazar*, I discovered the secret of acting. This is it: acting demands the suspension of will. Everything that is will-full in a performance comes between the actor and the performance, because it is inherently future-stressed. The actor must simply be. The character must want, the character must will. But the actor must be, with the totality of his being, in front of the audience *at this moment*. During the last weeks of *Balthazar*, I found the performance bubbling up out of me without the slightest effort. It was lighter, more graceful, wittier than it had ever been. All these qualities have always been difficult for me to achieve on stage, because I have worked at them. This is a paradox: I was absolutely determined to be less wilful. Somehow, after the long and alarming journey, I was able to let it happen. 'Leave yourself alone,' they used to say at the Drama Centre. And now, twelve years later, I see what they meant.

The Audience

At his curtain call, Max Wall says to the audience, 'Thank you very much, ladies and gentlemen, you've been 50 per cent.' And they are. The actor's experience of an audience is very vivid – the undeniable and inexplicable fact that almost all audiences assume a corporate identity within minutes of the curtain going up (some obstinately refuse to integrate: Alabaman audiences) means that you're dealing with a person, not a mass. But it's not enough to respond to them as they walk into the theatre with the state of mind in which *you* walk into the theatre. The question is, what have they come for? And what are you offering them? This is precisely the question on which most theories of the drama devolve. For me, none of them, the Stanislavsky, the Brecht, or the showbiz, answers to the demands of the harsh reality of night by night playing. The Stanislavsky approach, with an almost religious belief in the value of portraying real life, has always seemed to me to require a passivity from the audience which I find unexhilarating. The Brechtian antidote, the constant demand of the audience that they compel their brains to political activity, finds me wanting in the required conviction myself: how can I demand it of them? The showbiz prescription, that you must *love* the audience, is nonsensical and neurotic. Nonsensical because it's impossible to *love* people you don't know; neurotic because it's only the masked demand for the audience to *love* you. What I have come to is this: the essential attitude to the audience is one of compassion. I began to understand this while playing *Restoration*: let the audience laugh, don't make them laugh. Make *them* witty. Into the auditorium they stream, battered, dislocated, alienated, unhuman – feeling the loss of their humanity, the erosion of their human parts. Our job is to restore them, to massage or tease or slap the sleeping parts into life again. Above all we address ourselves to the deadened organ, the imagination. It's like the doctor's art, or the courtesan's. The doctor can't *love* every patient, the courtesan can't love every client. It's common humanity that keeps you going. In this sense, every actor has signed an unwritten hippocratic oath.

I don't think it's merely fear of gaining a reputation for 'unprofessionalism' that stops actors from missing performances. There is behind it an underlying awareness of this hippocratic aspect. A doctor would think hard before cancelling a surgery. I laughed openly when the nurse at Moorfield's Hospital innocently said to me: 'Couldn't you cancel your acting?' 'No more than you could cancel your nursing,' I said. I don't think she followed the comparison.

Without wishing to draw tendentious parallels with the National Health/private practice situation, it is the single greatest abuse of the modern theatre that its trajectory is so circumscribed. The tiny fraction of the population that even considers the possibility of going to the theatre is a bleeding wound in its side, draining it of life. This is a question above all of organization and presentation. Political work of whatever tendency has proved to be as inaccessible to any but its *aficionados* as any other kind of work. What needs to be broken down completely is the concept of the theatre as an exclusive club with rules of behaviour all of its own. It's neither lack of money nor lack of interest that maintains the theatre as a minority art: it is lack of accessibility in every sense. These huge journeys which have to be made! Why is there no theatre in the whole of the South of London, for example? I'm not however pleading for community theatre. The essence of theatre is to be particular and general: it must belong to its community, but it must also belong to the whole community. It must, as it were, bring news of Streatham to the outside world, but it must also bring news of the outside world to Streatham.

Twenty-four Hours in the Life

The moment you wake up, wherever, next to whomever, somewhere at the corner of your mind is a tiny cloud, the size of a man's fist, which says: Show tonight. As the day goes on, it comes to fill the frame completely. It colours and to some extent dictates everything that happens during the day. It won't necessarily stop you from doing anything, but you may do it less, and you will find it hard to give yourself to it completely. You will also have a repertory of antidotes to whatever the outcome of your activities might be. A snooze after a boozy lunch; a run round the block after seeing a movie, just to wake you out of the cinema's darkness and the celluloid's spell. You will be slightly twitchy all day.

First thing in the morning, you will have examined yourself for damage from the night before. You will check that all parts relevant to your performance are in working order. A merest 'mmm' will reveal the state of your voice. The state of your brain may take a little longer to ascertain – halfway through reading the paper, or the first conversation of the day you will realize how many brain cells are at your disposal. Your body's capacity for expressive movement will become quite clear the moment you hit the pavement.

With this information, you plan your day. You never feel that the day is really your own. It's a full eight-hour stretch, most people's working lives, but it's not quite real. A feeling of filling in time hovers persistently.

People vary as to how soon they need to go to the theatre. One has a legal obligation to clock in at 'the half', that is, five minutes before half an hour before the curtain goes up. 'Beginners' – actors in the first scene – are called to the stage five minutes before curtain up, so the show is deemed to start then. The half-hour deadline is theoretically to ensure that the company manager has time to get hold of you if you've forgotten to come to the theatre, or, more likely, get your understudy ready to go on. Personally, I avoid the theatre for as long as possible, all in a desperate bid to preserve the freshness of the show. If the theatre's in the centre of town, however, it's a wonderful *pied-à-terre* for leaving parcels, clothes and so on, even for having a cup of tea.

Once in, it's very pleasant. Your telegrams and cards regale the walls, your kettle will be in one corner, your radio/cassette player in another. After an exchange of convivialities with the stage door man – a critical person in your life, a Cerberus on your side, admitting those who should be admitted, refusing those who should be refused – he's the switchboard operator, too, so ditto phone calls – you greet your dresser, and execute your nightly pre-curtain ritual. It's always the same, though it'll vary from play to play. Mine has to accommodate the drinking of tea at the half-hour, a physical warm-up (drawn from the Drama Centre's work), shaving, a shower, make-up and reading the *Standard* from cover to cover. If any item of this itinerary is not executed, nameless unease sets in.

Down to the stage one goes, not when called, but two minutes later. Stage managers always and rightly call you before you're required. It's up to you to judge the actual requirement. You'd better get it right. Once in the wings, a cuddle with the stage management is *de rigueur*. You stand in front of your entrance and empty yourself. The actual state of an actor in the wings is curious – half in character and half out – like an athlete on the start line, body totally relaxed. The cue and you're on.

Back in the dressing room at the interval: urgent discussion about the way the show's going, whose fault is it, ours or theirs? While I was doing *Balthazar* at the Duke of York's, Rupert Everett was playing in *Another Country* at the Queen's; we used to phone each other during the interval: 'How're yours?' we'd ask, and it was quite statistically improbable how often the tempers of the two audiences were identical. Another cup of tea is drunk during the interval, a change of costume, and then on again, to discover that a gin-and-tonic had altered the audience's mood completely, for better or worse.

Then the curtain call. A number of observers maintain that actors live for applause – recently Professeur Laborit in Resnais's *Mon Oncle d'Amérique*. Whatever vestige of truth there may be in this, the curtain call offers little evidence in its favour. Most actors of my acquaintance find the call embarrassing. One doesn't know what attitude to take. Who is one? Clearly not the character. Is it me, then, bowing in this servile fashion? One smiles (I do now – it took me years to be able to do that. All the freedom from self-consciousness that the role affords is lost the moment it's *me*); some actors can be seen to murmur 'Thank you, thank you'. The Russian habit of clapping back is hopelessly laboured in English hands, and anyway fails to give the necessary release – which can be said twice over, of course, for the now-abandoned but once-fashionable practice of leaving the stage when the play ends and never coming back again at all. It seems to me that in this as so much else in the theatre, we're lost between the death of one tradition and the birth of the next one. Certainly the great bravura curtain calls are no longer possible: Wolfit clinging to the curtain, spent, Olivier's triumphal re-entry. One can still catch something of the grand manner in the opera house: in, for instance, Boris Christoff's magisterial displacement of half a vertebra as he sweeps the auditorium with his eagle eye. The best personal curtain call I ever saw was Eduardo de Filippo's. Having written, directed and starred in the play, at the curtain call he took each member in turn from the line and brought them forward, taking their call with them. When he reached the end of the line, he turned to the audience, touched his chest with his fingers, made a little *moue*, shrugged – and the lights snapped out. It was a gesture typical of his whole cunning art: outrageous delicacy.

For my money, the Guthrie-esque, choreographed call is the best, summing up the play and the characters and leaving the audience on an upbeat. On the other hand, these curtain calls can be very embarrassing, (a) if they're not very clever, or (b) if the show's a flop, and there are ten people in the auditorium who simply *can't* clap any more, or their hands will fall off.

Most actors' attitude to the curtain call is one of calculation. Are they clapping as much as they did last night? Why not? More? Why? It must however be noted that the curtain call is often a bad guide to the audience's whole response. A dead and unresponsive house can cheer at the curtain call (saving it all up, I suppose) and a lovely jolly one will only manage a patter of applause (spent it all). Of the two, the latter is of course much preferable. In fact, you're often a bad judge of the enjoyment level of the audience. People will come round after silent performances, which appear to have been composed entirely of members of the Watch Committee of the Festival of Light, to say what fun they'd had. It would be foolish to pretend that you weren't deeply upset by the lack of response, and that consolations don't affect you very deeply.

The week has its shape. Monday, after a day away, is often agreeably fresh, despite a possibly poorish house. Tuesday is not so fresh and the house is still poor. Wednesday and Thursday hot up. Friday is generally a peach of a performance, and Saturday is always disappointing. Theories as to the quality of the last two days of the week abound. The general feeling is that on Friday people are wide awake, having been using their brains all day at work, but buoyant at the prospect of the weekend. On Saturday, the reality of the weekend has sunk in, they've been shopping all day, and have anyway invested far too much money and expectation in the evening out. We're probably at our peak on Friday, too, whereas by Saturday we're tired and dreaming only of Sunday off.

This is to avoid mention of matinées. Now I and many of my colleagues, contrary to what might be imagined, enjoy matinées a great deal: it's what playing a generally small and often unresponsive though no doubt appreciative house does to the subsequent performance. You're drained before you've begun. However, mysteriously, you do find the energy, and with tiredness comes relaxation, and you're well and truly warmed up, that performance is often rather good, so what am I saying? Nothing more, probably, than that the hour or so between performances feels like playing the lead in *Invasion of the Body Snatchers*. The new scheme of five o'clock and eight o'clock performances on both Friday and Saturday is no doubt more sensible, though it feels as if you're going into a tunnel on Friday teatime, and not emerging till Saturday at midnight.

My own preference is the Broadway model; but every year it's mooted, and every year nothing happens, so there must be something deep in English nature which resists it: a Sunday matinée and Monday night off. It's so beautiful in its simplicity that I marvel at its non-adoption.

There is, you see, no doubt that climaxing at night is not the natural metabolic pattern, and certainly not the natural social one. You long for evenings off, just to have a meal at a normal hour, and not to have to regulate your day as if you were a champion athlete. But *they* don't run every night. No one, in fact, runs every night except actors, who run and run. Opera singers and dancers never perform the same piece on consecutive evenings, never perform at all on consecutive evenings (except for Nureyev). Imagine a pianist playing the 'Emperor' Concerto eight times a week for nine months. Hamlets and Lears do.

After the first few weeks of the run, most of your friends have seen the play. That means that you will return to your dressing room after the curtain call in the expectation of taking off your costume, wiping off your make-up and then going home. It's a little bleak, particularly if the show has been good and the response warm. You drink a glass of wine or two, either alone, or with your dresser, or someone else in the show. Many actors go to the nearest pub, but the noise and the struggle to get to the bar, and very often the rush to get there before closing time rule it out for me. There's a strong chance, too, if the pub's adjacent to the theatre, that you'll be accosted by a member of the audience who wants to chat. This is to be avoided because you have to be on your best behaviour, which is exactly what you don't want to be after an exhausting performance. You mustn't, for example, complain about your leading lady or the set. You cannot, on the other hand, talk about what really interests you, because it's technically esoteric. It is a hazard of eating out in London, if you want to be alone, that members of the public are inclined – with the sweetest of motives – to want to keep you company. On the other hand, it's very charming when people come and thank you for a performance, or ask for your autograph, as several do almost every night during a West End run. The really avid fans, a dwindled but still not negligible band, bring photographs for you to sign which they've ordered from newspapers or sometimes blown up themselves. They're extremely courteous, never sycophantic. In fact, very few of them ever mention having seen a performance. They probably don't have time, with all that filing and framing and standing outside stage doors.

You don't feel famous. Of course, by comparison with Robert Redford or Gordon Jackson, you aren't. But people do notice you in the street; and it doesn't make a bit of difference. You feel neither flattered nor pestered. It is a little tiresome when people know that they know you, but they don't know how. They demand that you identify yourself, which is excruciatingly embarrassing. 'You may have seen me in . . .' 'No,' they reply. And then you drag your way through your curriculum vitae, only to discover that they've mixed you up with Nigel Hawthorne. One woman became very aggressive with me. 'Help me,' she said, 'don't just stand there.'

When I was playing Beefy in *Balthazar*, it was common for people to shout 'Beefy!' at me, across the road, or in shops. Once a woman shyly passed a note to me on a tube-train. 'Are you Beefy?' it said. I smiled yes at her across the carriage. She blushed to the roots and got out at the next stop. At first, it was all very pleasant and very good publicity. As the run wore on, however, and I began to lose my mind – after the two hundredth performance, this would be – I started to resent the character very deeply. His bonhomie and undentable confidence made a mocking contrast with the confusion and despair that I was going through. Sometimes what I felt to be the falseness of my performance, the schizophrenic gap between how I was appearing and how I was feeling, became almost unbearable, and the cries of 'Hullo Beefy!' merely rubbed salt into the wound. 'I'm *not* Beefy, not, not, NOT,' I would madly mumble to myself. 'I'm a complicated, unhappy person. OK?' Often people would come up to me, and engage in conversation, obviously baffled that this rather melancholy young man wasn't anything like the ebullient fantasist of the Duke of York's stage.

Only on one other occasion have the character's lines crossed with mine in that way: after the first night of *Amadeus* when at a party the largely upper-class guests, charming and hospitable though they were, addressed me throughout the evening as 'Mozart'. It was deeply humiliating. I felt like a puppet, a buffoon, and a servant. If it's like this for me, what on earth can it be like for the stars of situation comedies?

Increasingly as the run goes on you receive visitors in the dressing room that haven't been to see the show that night. Not during the show – that's forbidden – but afterwards, on their way to supper having seen some other play. Friends resign themselves to your unsocial hours and adjust their day to them. After a drink, we all go off to one of the three or four restaurants which take orders after eleven o'clock, and there the pent-up high-spirits and the lack of release at the end of the show discharge themselves. Within minutes it seems to be 2.30, your stomach's full, and your brain is slowly melting. In this – medically speaking – worst of all states, you tumble into a taxi, tumbling from there into bed.

And that's it.

The End of the Run

Everything depends, of course, on how enjoyable the show was; or how enjoyable your fellow actors were, which may be a quite different matter. It's safe to say though that any show which has lasted beyond a few weeks creates a web of relationships the ending of which brings nostalgia.

The last performance itself is as unnatural in its way as the first. You desperately want to get it right, to go out on a high; therefore, something comes between you and your character which is not entirely healthy. There's a striving and a straining far from congenial to the living breathing performance. As on the first night, the Olympian indifference to effect is impossible. Unless, that is, you've been unhappy in the production, when a combination of joy at your forthcoming release and liberation from the straitjacket of your performance results in an unprecedented freedom – and a very good, enjoyable performance. This is maddening. You think: why have I wasted the last six months? I've experienced this on several shows but never so vividly as on *Flying Blind* at the Royal Court. I had been extremely unhappy and unsatisfactory in the part of Boyd – a good, haunted man, inside whose skin I had, as usual with good men, failed to get. The graph of the part was classically awkward: a few lines half an hour into the play: a long gap: a few more lines followed by a long and emotional speech: a gap: and then a return to be shot. It's as often as not the graph of the part which makes it difficult to play, not the emotions called for. Moreover, a small part is always harder to play than a large one. You have so much less time to make your points, and every moment has to count, while a leading role can be – must be

– arranged into valleys and peaks. Your instrument, too, has to be warmed up the moment you hit the stage, whereas any leading role contains its own warming up. Actors who have made a career from playing supporting roles have the enormous disadvantage that they have generally been called upon to play the same note again and again, to play it and then depart. Small wonder that they seem not to vibrate in the way that leading actors do! Thus, good or bad, a leading actor who plays a small part often seems to bring more on to the stage with him: he seems to have a life before and a life after. It's simply the concomitant of frequent exposure for long periods of time.

So for me Boyd had been joyless, the last night a long anticipated release. I tripped blithely down the stairs to the stage, gambolled across the understage passage, frisked up the stairs on the other side – and cracked my head on a beam. I walked on to the stage in a dazed state, some automatic pilot conducting the scene on my behalf. Well, he should have been playing the part from the beginning, because it had point, wit, was well phrased, and above all there was no sense of THE SPEECH looming and then being discharged in between inverted commas. For the first time in six weeks, I enjoyed it.

The lesson is simple: not so much that all actors could do with a good crack on the skull (though that may well be true) but that self-consciousness is death to a performance. I had convinced myself that no one could believe in me as a decent person – had convinced myself that it was outside my range. The production had compounded the self-consciousness. The director, an anxious man, sensing my doubts, had imposed a sequence of movements and inflections which had no connection with any impulse of mine. So the last thing I was capable of, as an actor, was simply BEING THERE – until my accident. The sadness is that it came on the last night, and not the first.

The curtain call on the last night may be emotional. During the evening you've been stripping the dressing room walls of posters and telegrams, gathering up cards (it seems unlucky to throw them away – yet), cramming the incomprehensibly large quantity of bric-à-brac you've gathered over the run into bags and boxes. It's no different to moving house, but on a thankfully smaller scale. And the denuded dressing room has the forlorn look of an about-to-be-vacated house; a husk, a *tabula rasa*, a mere box which the next inhabitant will transform again. These images flicker around during the show itself, informing it with some valedictory air. The curtain call siphons all the emotion into itself. The simple routine that you've performed mindlessly at the end of every performance really becomes good-bye, and the ghost of all those other performances, and the spirit of all those other audiences, throng the auditorium. The front-of-house staff, too, who may have seen fragments of every single performance in the run, often stand at the back of the stalls and cheer. It's as if all of us, on the stage, behind it, in the auditorium and running the theatre, had for a brief moment, held hands. The last night of *Amadeus* at the National Theatre was overwhelmingly of this order. God knows, gratitude is a detestable emotion, but then, that night, and on several last nights, there has been a sense from all the participants that they were glad to be there at that moment, would not wish to be anywhere else in the world.

Such emotion is rare in the theatre. It is, after all a job, a highly technical, very demanding job, which can very easily go wrong and demands perpetual vigilance. Emotion other than that required for playing the part is not lightly indulged in. It's especially unwise to dwell on the nature of what passes between us and the audience, their hopes of us, and, sometimes, our fulfilment of them. There is at its best a two-way exchange of such simple generosity that it is easy to become sentimental about it.

The actual leavetaking of the company on the last night fiercely eschews sentimentality. The formula is that we'll meet again soon – as we very likely will, at Joe Allen's, or in the street, or at the dole. 'Have you got anything to go to?' we ask each other, quickly passing on if the answer's no. All the little jokes which have grown up around various members of the company are reiterated. Despite the pressing business of shoving boxes and bags into taxis there's a reluctance, à la Chekhov, to actually go. You feel the company should have got together more often, should have seen more of each other, and now it's all over . . . In fact, the whole thing's quite unreal. How can you conceive, there, inside the building that has been your focus for all these weeks or months, that on Monday life will be quite different. You can't; and it isn't till weeks later that you're aware of any loss.

Longer, perhaps, if you have 'something to go to'. This is of course ideal, however tired you might be. It gives a sense of continuity, of a future. Otherwise, you're consigned to limbo.

Unemployment Again

'You deserve a rest.' No. The only thing I *deserve*, I hope, is a job. If you have a job a few weeks hence, then a gap of a few weeks will be most welcome. But any time, any day not working and without the prospect of work, is dead time, grey time, anxious and haunted time. You could learn German, take driving lessons, night classes in the History of Art. No, you couldn't. Even if you've got any money, which is unlikely, it's impossible to settle to anything. There's something wrong, something missing. When you're working, any of those things would be possible. When you have a job, the day seems infinitely extensible. Doing the show at night, you can then easily find time and energy for a television play by day, and possibly a radio play as well, and there'll be plenty of time to meet chums, and somehow catch the odd matinée, the occasional late-night movie. You manage to read, to write, to go to art galleries, to meet new people and to cherish the old ones.

Out of work, your resources of time and energy, theoretically unlimited, seem frozen. Perhaps the body, in secret league with your talent, has determined to husband them for such time as they're really needed; i.e. for acting. Perhaps unemployment, after all, is essential, a hibernation in which exhausted organs of the imagination and the heart repair themselves. If it is medicine, it's very bitter medicine. And the body itself seems uncomfortable. It has been used to a certain flow of adrenaline, to containable and beneficial shocks to the nervous system and to a generally heightened operation. The mind too misses its exercise. Worse than that is the sense of having been dropped. It's not rational: the job's ended, that's all. There's nothing that you're right for, nothing you'd illuminate, nothing somebody else wouldn't do better than you. You see that clearly. But you still feel dropped. Forgotten, unwanted, unfashionable. You begin – after a week – to doubt whether you'll ever work again. You review possible alternative employments. More hopefully, you try to set up projects. There must, you feel, be a way out of this endlessly repeating cycle. In passionate conversation with other actors, you plot the downfall of the present system, while planning the millennial alternative. At the back of your mind, however, is the knowledge that if anything turns up . . .

You have to believe there's a reason for your unemployment, that it's all for the best. Perhaps you were over-exposed (ha!). Perhaps you were over-worked. Were you becoming a mere acting machine? In danger of vanishing up your own art? Perhaps . . . On the other hand, you feel yourself to be at your prime. These are the good acting years. How awful to waste even a week, let alone a month. Your brain is bursting with new insights which must be put to the test or they'll evaporate. You suddenly know how to play Hamlet. You were walking down the street and you saw a man muttering to himself, and – that was it, you got hold of the sensation, now you must do it! But alas no, you won't do it and the impulse will die.

The week can quickly turn into a month, the month into six. The very best, the most famous, actors at one time or another find themselves out of work for six, nine and even twelve months at a stretch. In order to live at all, they damp down their expectations, learn to live with disappointment and rejection. Their natural ebullience and stage-struck fervour modulates into wryness and a grim sense of fatalism about any job which finally arrives. 'Great – but how long will it last, and what comes after?'

In this sense the conditions of the profession border on the tragic.

Manifesto

Starting at the end of the last century and increasingly during the course of our own, the theatre has become colonized by a determined group: the directors. During the fifties and sixties, a few survivors of an earlier breed, the actor-manager, were to be found in commanding positions, but now in the early eighties, directors hold the economic, artistic and administrative reins firmly in their hands. It is they who run the theatres, they who determine policy, they who engage the artists who actually execute the work, and they who put the stamp of their personality on the production itself, the end result of all our labours.

There are a number of consequences of this unchallenged hegemony which devolve most strikingly on the actors and the writers. Actors, quite clearly, have been stripped of initiative and responsibility. They wait to be hired; having been hired, they wait to be told how to play their roles (how, that is, to fit into the director's 'concept'); and in the execution of the role and their conduct during its realization, they strive to please the director in order to be allowed to exercise their craft again. All important decisions about the production have been taken before their involvement, and they are as much as possible kept ignorant of the factors which govern the fate of the production in which they're involved.

Writers, on the other hand, have been made to believe that the closest collaboration with a director is the only way in which their work will be properly realized – indeed, realized at all, because writers quite as much as actors, are beholden to directors for the opportunity to exercise their craft. In the last twenty years, moreover, a subtle shift in directors' self-definition has occurred which has made the situation even graver.

Before the war, during the first wave of star directors, it was common for the director to be, as it were, an actor manqué: to manipulate the actor into giving the performance that he couldn't or didn't want to give. Since the war, however, perhaps because of the rise of the university director, the director-as-writer has become more common: the director who has manipulated the writer into writing the play that he either can't or doesn't want to write. These directors have realized that their greatest power is over the text, through which they can control all other aspects of the theatre. As the ultimate interpreter of 'the text' they have claimed the right to arbitrate on all matters.

A distressing consequence of this development for actors is that the director has interposed himself between actor and writer, claiming that they cannot speak each other's language. Actors and writers are both warned against the other, as potentially misleading. Moreover, the assertion of the supremacy of 'the text' (as plays have reductively become) has provided a stick with which to beat actors. 'Acting' has become a pejorative term, used to delineate something impure, an accretion and a product of the actor's egomania. The crucial element in the act of theatre, the actor's delight in the opportunities afforded him by the writer, has been abolished, outlawed by a breed of directors who have little experience and no comprehension of the rich and vital processes of acting. The alien notion that a play (as often as not half written by the director himself) is in effect a score, needing no more than accurate performance, has become an article of faith. This notion undercuts everything that writers and actors have understood about the theatre, which was in their hands until so very recently.

The pre-eminence of directors has its roots in the vastly increased technology of the theatre, but also in the increased historical consciousness which burgeoned in the late nineteenth century and which led the Duke of Saxe-Meiningen, for example, to research and re-create the archaeological background to Shakespeare's plays. It is indeed a feature of this century's theatre that the largest part of the repertory consists of revivals, for the realization of which a director's insights and historical sense may be thought to be indispensable. The contrary has proved to be the case. Instead of using their position to uncover the limitless spectrum of other worlds, other visions of the human experience embedded in the range of world drama, they have plundered the past for works on which they can impose their personalities, or exemplify the playing styles of their companies.

The idea of a director's style or indeed a company's style seems inherently to threaten the individuality of the work itself. It is also easier and less interesting to impose such a style than to undertake the enormous task of entering the mind and hearts of people of another time – and as far as plays are concerned, any time before yesterday is another time. All plays are written in cuneiform; they are, as it were, the fragment of a cup found in the rubble of Herculaneum from which an entire civilization can be reconstructed. *That* should be the director's task; the work of rehearsal should be the quest for style, because that is the embodiment of the world and the art of the author. It represents the conjunction between his personality, the times in which he wrote, and the theatrical form in which he expressed himself. Clearly, here the notion of 'the text' as a musical score is quite misleading. A more plausible musical analogy would be with the kind of score sometimes found in a composer's bottom drawer after his death – the melody line merely, unharmonized and unorchestrated. There could be a further analogy with the enormous revival of original instruments, which has transformed the performance of classical music. For centuries scores have been performed on instruments for which they were never intended. It has come increasingly to be accepted that we have not been hearing what the composer meant us to. Handel and Bach have been revealed to be quite different composers to the ones we grew up with, and more interesting too. New sound worlds have been discovered which evoke different worlds of human experience. Progress has been slow, because the old skills have had to be re-learned. Only now are performers able to play their instruments with the ease and expressiveness which enables them to liberate the music in its true colours. The rediscovery of performing conventions and skills has in turn rediscovered the music, and hugely augmented the range of artistic experience available to us.

The fundamental principle that Telemann is not played like Tchaikovsky is one that has gained slow acceptance in the musical world. It has hardly been acknowledged in the theatre. Shakespeare is played like Chekhov or Feydeau, Büchner is played like Brecht, and so on. The effect is an ironing-out of the individual features of individual authors. The style of the eighties is a playing style, not the style of the plays. The result is MORE OF THE SAME. Thus there is a diminution not only of the works themselves, but of the palette of the theatre at large. The error is twofold, and pincer-like. Firstly, the theatre seems to claim the right to use existing material to reflect modern life and needs; secondly, it seems to say: plays are about people, people's psychology doesn't change, therefore, we interpret the plays in the light of psychology as we understand it.

The first claim is a gross violation of the individual nature of the work in hand; the second is false. People, their psychology and perception of the world change radically from year to year, let alone century to century. What is valuable about dramatic literature is that it constitutes a living record of other lives and other worlds. It is live history; and by failing to take the pains to discover the Atlantis that it represents, we turn our back on history, on the richness of culture and on the lessons of the past.

The theatre is one of the archetypal Arts of Memory, on many levels. If we turn it instead into a mere living newspaper we conspire in the processes by which modern man has come to feel adrift in history, without roots and without branches – galactic flotsam and jetsam. Kundera has described this phenomenon most vividly: without a past, we are children. To be grown up is to have a memory. The theatre, relentlessly trying to live in the today, this minute, has become childish.

The questions that should be asked are: What was the author's world? What made it tick? In what ways was it different to our world? What was seventeenth century about a seventeenth-century play? German about a German one? In what ways is a Shakespeare play different to one by Kyd? And then, above all, how do those particulars find expression in the play itself? And how is the play expressed by its playing style? These questions and their answers are habitually confined to the Programme Notes. If they were the whole quest of the rehearsal, our stages would be filled with the most extraordinary, surprising and disturbing visions. Moreover, the actors, instead of enslaving themselves to a directorial conceit with which they may or may not agree, would be immersed in the very source of the work in question, not engaged in decorating its surface.

It is the life in the play that we must go after like a pig hunting for truffles. Too often plays have been brought forward like corpses, rouged and bewigged, their dead limbs manipulated from behind to give the illusion of life. But good plays *are* alive, if only we have the wit to see it.

The role of the director in this work is crucial and indispensable. However instead of being the *fons et origo* of the entire enterprise, he would have been chosen – employed, to be blunt – by the actors specifically for his knowledge of the world of the play and its performing traditions. The actors would use him or her to challenge themselves to the utmost flexibility in reaching the play's world and style.

This simple idea, which in the context of the present directocratic structure may seem boldly radical, is nothing but a reversion to an earlier practice; it has its precise modern counterpart in the organization of all existing symphony orchestras, who are self-governing, who hire conductors according to what they feel to be their needs and whose members participate in every important decision.

Of course, it will be difficult for the actors to begin with. The first thing that colonized peoples lose is their initiative. The post-colonial period will be difficult – there will be terrible failures – it'll be hard to re-discover the ways of independence: but it must be done.

220

The important thing is to restore the writer – whether dead or alive – and the actor to each other, without the self-elected intervention of the director, claiming a unique position interpreting the one to the other. We don't need an interpreter – we speak the same language: or at least we used to.

Gloomy Postscript: A Short View of the English Stage

Of course I have changed in ten years; nothing like as much as the theatre, however. Root and branch, it is almost unrecognizable. The young actor who wrote *Being an Actor* was full of criticism, but fuller still of hope and excitement; infused with a sense of the importance, the life-affirming possibilities, the indispensability of the theatre; aware of certain disturbing developments, but convinced that they could be caught in time.

The repertory companies seemed to be shrinking; the big subsidized theatres appeared to be retreating somewhat from the ideal of the ensemble; the drama schools were passing through a troubled phase; directors seemed to have usurped the creative rights of everyone else in the theatre. It was all very worrying. Little did we know what was to follow. As with so many other aspects of British life, what then seemed to be a period of crisis appears in retrospect to have been a golden age. How immeasurably secure and rich the theatre of the early eighties seems from this distance! And how wretched, a mere ten years after the publication of *Being an Actor*, the prospects of a young actor starting out.

Despite breakthroughs in some areas – to be a woman is no longer a disadvantage for a director; to be gay is not something you need to conceal – the British theatre has during the past decade been undermined at pretty well every level. Critics and press departments insist that everything is lovely in the garden: but those prize-winning blooms are cut flowers. The beds are empty, the bulbs rotting, the soil no longer nourishes. The blooms will soon go off, and there will be nothing with which to replace them. The British theatre's glories, so suavely vaunted by ministers of National Heritage and boards of tourism, were built on a threefold foundation: training; experience; tradition. Each of these is rapidly being eroded. Without each one the theatre will, in every important sense, die.

Training is first in the line of fire. Do we need a training? Only if we want the theatre to deliver all that it is capable of; only if we want our actors to have the opportunity of exploring their possibilities, making themselves vulnerable within a contained structure, away from the exigencies of paying audiences; only if we want those same actors to lay foundations for themselves that will enable them to avoid the temptation of settling for the easiest, most ingratiating options. The purpose of a training is not to acquire polish and skill; those things come all too easily and quickly of their own accord. Its purpose is to inculcate habits of mind which will equip you to work in depth and with the fullness of your imagination whatever the circumstances. It will teach you something about yourself and a great deal about how to think as an artist in character; it will mean that your contribution to the theatre – and to society – will be infinitely richer and more valuable. So yes, we do need a training.

Britain's drama schools, built up in all their diversity over the previous three-quarters of a century, offered a comprehensive education in the craft of acting that was unique in the world; my school, the Drama Centre, though highly individual, is typical of the seriousness and depth of the work. Simultaneously inculcating technique and self-knowledge, they provided a disciplined approach to the curious demands of a unique profession, a practical training in a job requiring very particular skills, both mental and physical. Nor was the spiritual dimension ignored: the aim, after all, was to produce craftsmen and women who aspired to be artists.

And it worked. The general level of excellence of British acting was the proof of it. Sustained by a delicately balanced combination of local authority grants and privately paid fees, the schools managed to survive. Then with rising inflation and changed economic imperatives, they were suddenly undermined. The local authorities, having lost much of their autonomy and now desperately short of money themselves, refused to continue underwriting the training of actors; few would now give grants to students. The result was that only the rich or those few able to get scholarships or private sponsorship could afford to train. Drama colleges were in danger of reverting to the condition of finishing schools.

The effect on standards has been depressing. Twenty years ago, the competition for places at drama school was enormous, and only the cream of applicants was admitted. Because they desperately need the income from fees, the schools now have to think very hard before turning anyone away, and even harder about dropping someone from the course once they have started – an essential feature of the process. This natural wastage identifies those with the stamina, the self-discipline and the will for a gruelling business; talent is only a beginning. It is only a matter of time before the impact is felt on the intake into the profession. As the economic recession worsened, no longer able to survive on their income from fees alone, the schools looked to the State for support to continue their work. If the State was as proud of the British Theatre as it constantly claimed to be, then surely it must be willing to fund the processes which had created the much-trumpeted excellence? This suggestion was naturally anathema to the powers-that-be. Simply allow the drama schools to carry on in the way that they had shown to work? Who did they think they were? The only way in which the State could extend help to the drama colleges would be to integrate them into the existing structure of Higher Education. Why should they be different from any other branch of academic life? This option meant squeezing the training of actors into an academic bureaucratic mould to conform to the latest modish whim of the *educationalists* who have now supplanted mere teachers in running the colleges and universities. The experience and understanding of those who have spent their lives evolving the specific disciplines appropriate to actors (and to no one else) would be overruled.

The result of this must be to turn the drama schools into a branch of the liberal arts. The rigorous trainings hitherto offered will be broadened to become equivalent to the teaching dispensed in Drama departments on American campuses – admirable teaching in itself, but incidental to the pressing needs of professional actors. The purpose of a training in acting is not general cultural enrichment, though that may also happen. Acting is not a liberal art. It is a craft; it prepares you for a job.

Say, though, that despite all the obstacles, you have successfully completed your training. What experience can you expect once you have graduated? The story here is even gloomier. Twenty years ago, it was every actor's dream to join a permanent repertory company, of which there were still something like twenty across the country. You hoped to stay with a company for at least a year, maybe two, gaining confidence and experience, playing a wide range of parts, some suitable, some impossible, discovering your limitations, extending your skills, building stamina, learning how to handle an audience. Away from London, you ate, drank, smoked and slept the theatre; there was nothing else. You learned to know and trust your colleagues (whether you liked them or not); with them you discovered the exhilaration of company playing. Bit by bit you found out who you were and what kind of an actor you might be.

'Technique' was something you learned as practical necessity; it was not an instrument of virtuosity, designed to impress (or conceal); it was a means of expression, a channel to reveal what you had to say about the character and his life. Your work was judged by your fellow actors, by your directors and above all, of course, by your audience; reviews scarcely mattered, written as for the most part they were by the snooker correspondent or the astrologer. The audience was solid and committed; the company was *their* company, and you were part of it. Your progress was watched carefully, your development gauged not only by how well you had played the part but how well you rose to the challenge, and what that said about your future as an artist. For all the frustrations of the life, the technical imperfections, the dank rehearsal rooms, the impossible hours, the dippy landladies and the chintzy digs, the soggy late-night chapatis and the desperate drinks lined up at the bar in defiance of last orders, there was no sense of being isolated: you felt organically connected to the theatre as a whole. You would inevitably progress to bigger parts, other theatres: you would show them what you had learned and who you were. You would then give London a shot; when you advanced further in the metropolitan theatre, you would return to the reps to play leading parts. Finally you would come back to London, in triumph.

And that is what happened. Not to everyone, of course; some fell by the wayside. But every famous actor today who is middle-aged or older took that path; that was how each one mastered the practical craft that was the application of the lessons learned at drama school. Where can you apply those lessons today? The repertories – those few that are left – are now only able to afford *ad hoc* productions in which the group assembles for the duration of the play and then drifts apart again. There can be no sustained growth, no testing of the actors; partial failure as the price of growth is no longer acceptable: in a one-off production, it's now or never. Everyone must be cast precisely to type and be able to deliver the goods to order.

The young actor who wants to work in a company has to start at the top: either the Royal Shakespeare Company or the Royal National Theatre. Inevitably inexperienced, he arrives at these major theatres with little in the way of history, scarcely knowing who he is and what he might be capable of, equipped only with what he has learned at drama school plus his native wit, talent and charm – in other words, as mere raw material. He is ready to be nurtured and shaped. Alas, he will find that no one at either of those two hard-pressed institutions has the time. The great companies too have undergone radical change. Struggling with budgets and schedules, the best they can hope for is to get the plays on as handsomely as possible. The original ideals on which they were based have been knocked out of them by the same pressures which are destroying the drama schools.

Long ago, in what now seems a sort of mythic past, each of the major companies was founded (within a few years of each other) with the express purpose of creating in Britain that form of theatrical life then regarded as ideal: the ensemble. This was something which had never previously existed in England. Where the rep instilled the basic notions of development and group endeavour within the practical framework of getting a new show on the boards every couple of weeks, the ensemble aspired to a state of permanent growth among its members. They would commit themselves to it for long periods, perhaps even for the rest of their lives, constantly striving for closer and deeper rapport with each other, devoted to extending their knowledge of the characters they played and the meaning of the plays in which they appeared; studying, acquiring new skills, broadening their understanding of the world, inner and outer.

It was a sort of utopian dream, but there was no shortage of successful examples – the Berliner Ensemble, the Moscow Art

225

Theatre, the Schaubuhne. These companies had come to England and shown what could be done if the circumstances were right. Beyond the brilliance and authority of the women and men who ran them – and they were pretty formidable characters – the European ensembles revealed the satisfaction of concerted and sustained work in depth. A further revelation was the absence of hierarchy within the companies: in a constant repertory, everyone was developed to the maximum. Tonight's party guest in *The Cherry Orchard* was tomorrow's Coriolanus. The lesson was that an ensemble only means something if it is an ensemble of stars. Young actors were attached to the companies as apprentices; slowly they would begin to discover themselves and be discovered.

This was the inspiration, both for Anthony Quayle and Peter Hall when they gave birth to the Royal Shakespeare Company, and for Laurence Olivier and Kenneth Tynan at the National Theatre. Both enterprises were adventures in creating ensembles, and for a brief – terribly brief – period it seemed that the seeds so bravely sown had taken, and that growth was sustained and fruitful. Then, after a mere ten years, and for a multitude of reasons, social, economic and personal, the dream faded, and the growth stopped. Filling the vacuum left by the faltering West End, both companies adopted the simple objective of producing work of the highest possible quality with a loosely associated group of artists: H. M. Tennent plus subsidy. Increasingly, actors whose ultimate dream had been to belong to one or other of the great companies now announced that they would join them, if at all, for no more than one play, or maybe – at a pinch – a couple; some actors succeeded in playing only two parts in an entire eighteen-month season. The big question was: what can I get out of this? The question: what can I put into it? was hopelessly old-fashioned, quite against the spirit of the age. It was acknowledged that it was useful to have played leading parts in a major company; but only up to a point.

Perhaps the idea of an ensemble was just one of the many lost dreams of the sixties. As political realities dictated ever more pragmatic expectations and the fervent visions of the decade were unceremoniously dumped, so the theatre lost its utopian programme; the influence of Michel Saint-Denis's ideas died with him, the manifestos of Artaud and Kott and Grotowski were no longer cited, Encore faded away, Joan Littlewood stomped off, taking her bloody-minded insistence on the essential nakedness and bowel-wrenching reality of acting with her, 7:84 no longer stalked the land, protesting injustice. Most of this had already disappeared by the time I was writing. It is now ancient history. A new, younger theatrical establishment came into existence, sensible and practical. The most politically passionate playwrights found homes at the major subsidized theatres where they pursued their themes with new-found mellowness; some simply retired. The fringe evolved into a sort of off-Broadway, increasing production values and faithfully serving new writing; its trajectory was inevitably limited by the size of its auditoria. The West End finally ceased producing new work at all.

As the economy faltered and doctrinaire imperatives began to hold sway, the struggle for mere survival became increasingly tough. This was no time for dreams or ideals. Just keeping going was a full-time job. Theatres became ever-more dependent on marketing, which ushered in the age of the theatre as a branch of the advertising industry. Novelty, as in all salesmanship, was the key; the question was no longer how can we realize this play, but how can we make it seem new? The image of a production became as important as the production itself, a process that resulted in what Ken Campbell dubbed 'brochure theatre'. Directors were increasingly judged less by their gift for working with actors or plays than for their ability to engender *concepts*.

The physical aspect of the production became all-important. If the director had no concept, the designer was always on hand to supply one. Very often, the design was the concept, and vice versa. Productions became more and more handsome, more and more ambitious – physically, that is. Audiences delightedly applauded hydraulics, groaning with pleasure as the scenery copulated with itself: the pornography of design. Its language became ever more sophisticated and allusive, spelling out the play's purport to the point where the play itself seemed redundant. On those wittily decorated constructions – or rather, deconstructions – the human figure was inclined to look rather small and uninteresting, the spoken word to echo somewhat tinnily. Interactions were less important than gestures; expressive speech made way for rhetorical effects. In this as in the increasing predominance of spectacle, we seemed in some extraordinary way to be returning – *mutatis mutandis* – to the Victorian theatre.

Actors are great survivors. In response to the changed conditions of the present theatre, denied intensive or exploratory rehearsal periods, they have developed lightness of touch and fluidity; if richness, many-layered complexity, engagement with the basic archetypes of the human condition cannot, in the circumstances, be achieved, then there is always irony, humour, and rhetoric: shape-making. Inverted commas seem frequently to be placed around the work of the modern actor; characters are held up for inspection, rather than inhabited. Characteristics are diligently assembled, but transformation, inner and outer – submitting to another's life, being open to possession – is not attempted; all the ingredients are present, but there is no heat under the saucepan. Thus the experience of the modern theatre-goer is rather cool.

This might appear to be the triumph of Brecht's acting theories: actors and audiences alike distanced from both characters and story, inviting clear judgements on them. In reality, though, this is not the case, since the essential position of Brecht's dramaturgy is a political one, desiring and demanding change. The theatre of the nineties is more in the nature of a leader column in a liberal newspaper, commenting wryly and shrewdly on human life, neither celebrating nor condemning it. The theatre has chosen to forgo its capacity for refreshing the common humanity of the audience, preferring instead to appeal to its intelligence – when, that is, it is not simply stimulating its senses. In these circumstances, the actor ceases to be the very embodiment of the play and its world; he becomes instead simply a part of the author/director's *statement about the play*.

This is not acting as it was understood. It seems that there has been a break in the transmission of the tradition. 'They were actors then!' is a common cry of the misty-eyed romantic. The departure from the stage, however, of the last generation that was truly extraordinary is still well within living memory, and to say that Edith Evans, Peggy Ashcroft, Donald Wolfit, Anew MacMaster, Michael Redgrave, Ralph Richardson, Laurence Olivier and John Gielgud purveyed an experience that is not available to present-day play-goers is no nostalgic fantasy, merely a banal truth. Perhaps the explanation lies in Bill Gaskill's view (quoted in this book) that the social conditions which gave rise to that sort of great acting have disappeared; the *debourgeoisification* of society and the dismantlement of the hierarchies has demanded a different sort of acting. It is equally true, however, that the theatrical structures that enabled those actors to develop their extraordinary talents have also disappeared – the repertory system (including Lilian Baylis's Old Vic and the Stratford Memorial Theatre) and a financially booming West End run by a number of enlightened and aesthetically ambitious producers. But there is something even more important which has changed: the way in which these actors saw themselves.

This brings me full circle to the passions which gave rise to *Being an Actor*. When the book first appeared, it was seen above all as an attack on directors. This was deplored by some (critics, mostly), and hailed by others (actors and writers; even some directors). Certainly the final Manifesto was intended to provoke. I was keen to get on to the agenda the idea of the directocracy – the way in which directors had triumphed in the struggle for power in the theatre. Elsewhere in the book, I had written at length about the complex nature of the director's job, and the almost impossible expectations it provoked. But the argument against directorial tyranny was secondary: the argument for the actor's contribution was the important one, the all-important one, in fact.

The warning I was delivering was not so much about power (though that was inevitably part of what I had to say) as about actors' own sense of the importance, the difficulty, the almost limitless potential, of their calling. I was not saying ACTORS ROOL OK? What I was saying was DON'T LET THEM STOP YOU FROM BEING THE ACTOR YOU COULD BE. Don't let them marginalize your work. I was saying that ours is a great and ancient and mysterious craft which, if practised diligently and passionately, can become an art to rank with any other. I spelt this message out even more explicitly in the next book I wrote, a study of Charles Laughton as a hero of acting. I was staking a claim, in both of these books, for the seriousness and complexity of the job. In so far as directors believed that, and were willing to work towards increasing the depth and beauty of the actors' work, then they were fine by me. In so far as they were more interested in subordinating the actor to schematic notions or staging conceits that killed the human life which must be at the centre of the play – any play, of whatever period, in whatever style – then they were anathema.

When I wrote those sections of the book, I knew that I was

speaking with the voice of the tribe. The conch had passed to me, and I simply articulated what many of my colleagues had long thought but had never expected to hear spoken out loud – such was the stranglehold of the directocrats. It was exhilarating when various enterprising individuals, flatteringly citing my Manifesto as a rallying cry, declared war on the whole system and founded groups of their own: a return to the honourable tradition of actor-management.

It was less exhilarating to discover that some of them thought that simply to assemble a group of gifted and agreeable colleagues and let them loose on a great play was enough. It was positively depressing to see young actors who had waxed lyrical about what I had written arriving on stage, swollen with their own confidence, only to give performances of generalized mediocrity. I wondered whether I had given off the wrong signals. The last thing that I was saying was that actors are simply wonderful people who should be allowed to get on with it. Merely being an actor is not enough. It is a vocation which demands unceasing work on the body, the mind and the imagination. To interpret human life requires unending observation, profound sympathy, wide reading, the ability to open yourself to strange and unexplored areas of your personality and to penetrate deep into the lives of others.

It requires, above all, work on one's own self. That, in the end, is one's medium. In a striking passage in his memoirs, the Irish actor Micheál MacLiammóir summed up the view of that vanished generation of great actors, and many generations before them; his prose is characteristically perfumed, but it goes some way to explaining what made those actors what they were.

Far from being a copyist of life's surface tricks or a facile repeater of traditional antics, the actor should live with such delicacy, with such intensity, that he brings manner and style to all the unimportant trifles of gesture and speech, so that the eating of a fruit, the folding of a letter, the raising of the arm, the donning of a cap, all become in his hands images of significance, profound mirrors of character . . . he works with himself as surely as a philosopher does with his brain, or a prostitute with her body.

Though written only fifty years ago, its sentiments are as remote from present-day actors as the great medieval textbooks of Noh acting. Stark Young had said the same thing a few years earlier: 'If you amount to nothing, your art in the end amounts to nothing; that is a fact almost biological in its brutal certainty.'

These valuable ideas were swept away, along with a great deal of genuinely dead wood, during the egalitarian revolution of the fifties. Actors fell over themselves to become men and women in the street. 'Actorliness' was despised, and those guilty of it – many on that venerable list above – were suddenly stranded, not knowing what to do with their beautifully honed, wonderfully expressive, instruments. Olivier, as always, rapidly adapted, as did Peggy Ashcroft; it was some years before Gielgud and Richardson found their place again, welcomed back like prodigals. Where had they been? everyone wanted to know. They were cherished and honoured; their example, however, was not followed.

A strange thing happened to the succeeding generation of actors. For many reasons – personal and financial – they declined the succession. They went away – some to Hollywood, some just away. The great roles continued to be played, and played well, but there was a strong sense that something had gone out of the theatre. The performances of these crucial roles ceased to be events in the collective life of society. They were intelligent and accomplished and often brilliant performances, but they failed to stir the souls of the audience. The mythic, the archetypal dimension had disappeared. These great characters were being portrayed as individuals instead of forces of nature; the approach was sometimes naturalistic, sometimes stylized, but either way it failed to project a full human life on an epic scale. The acting had become anecdotal.

The same thing has been noted in all the performing arts. Dancing, singing, instrumental performance are all practised with greater technical skill, accuracy and intelligence than ever; and yet they lack the human expressiveness, the resonance and vibrancy of past performances. Linearity has been purchased at expense of depth, and there is a consequent diminution in power. In a word, these performances *mean* less than performances seen and remembered by any of us over forty years of age. The performers offer less of themselves; perhaps there is less to give.

Of course, no society can live without feeling that there are peaks of achievement. These latter-day performances are acclaimed to the echo, many times louder than those of the past, in increasingly hyperbolic terms. Indeed, most criticism consists of nothing – in one direction or another – but hyperbole. Things are either sublime or they are ridiculous. The critics themselves are given less and less space for their reviews while their photographs get larger and larger; the critics too are now being sold. Mere reviews shift no newspapers, which are increasingly written, not by reporters, but by featured columnists – 'personalities'. Criticism itself has become anything but: it is gossip, it is interval chatter, it is homily, it is puff, it is demolition.

The extension of this hurrah/boo axis – the critic as football yob, bawling his acclaim or lashing out with the bovver boots – is the growth of the culture of Awards. These preposterous things – purporting to compare what cannot be compared, deciding whether Dame X's Lady Macbeth was better than Miss Y's Eliza Doolittle, whether Mr A directed the latest David Hare better than Sir B directed *King Lear* – have become orgies of elitist self-congratulation, emphasizing the gap between those at the top and the rest in a way that had not been the case in the older theatre. The continuum that existed – the perception that there was throughline from the actors playing the smallest parts to those playing the largest, and that each depended on the other's excellence – was fast disappearing.

It is a curious paradox that in a time of recession, in which actors' unemployment has soared even above the general obscene level, it is increasingly difficult to cast plays. One of the critical causes of the blandness of the West End is the refusal of many leading actors to commit themselves to runs of any length; actors are equally reluctant to play smaller roles, partly because there are better paid jobs in other media, but principally because it no longer seems a very exciting thing to do. Audiences sense this and cease looking to the dramatic stage for profound experiences. Sensory stimulation and spectacle are the order of the day; escape, the objective. To satisfy these demands, producers have increasingly resorted to the musical in which performance (an essential ingredient of acting, though the reverse is not true) becomes ever more polished and ebullient, exploring ever wider shallows. Here, there is no problem in casting. Actors are delighted to administer the syrup, happy to help audiences feel good. Well, and why not?

Indeed. But there is a terrible danger that audiences will forget that the theatre can be more than that, more even than the civilized evenings on offer on the South Bank and at the Barbican, more than the splendid panoplies of machinery and decor without which no show is now complete, more than the experiments in performance art, inventive and poetic, more than the adaptations of novels, more than the beautiful things done in small spaces. That there is something else, something hugely nourishing, soul-shakingly profound and indelibly memorable, does not need to be taken on trust as long as theatres like the Maly Theatre of St Petersburg exist. Touring the Western World (forced to tour: since the collapse of the Soviet Union, Russia can no longer support its long painstaking working methods; it's a good wind that blows no ill) the Maly demonstrates the results of ensemble work: the play realized in a million expressive details held together by a profound sense of its organic structure, neither demonstrated nor commented on – simply existing before our eyes. The company, each actor a star, creates through its trust and belief a world whose people are both particular and universal. We see not only who they are, but *what* they are; thus the author's story is told. Characterization is not garnish, not a matter of arbitrary choices based on the actor's personal whim or inclination, but an identification of the significance of the character within the scheme of the play. Character is narrative; get it wrong, and you are telling the wrong story.

This ability to plug the specific reality of the play into the general experience of humankind is what is missing from the stage today. Any play, whether set in a bed-sitting room in Stoke Newington or on Prospero's island, is – if it is any good – a myth. Its story, and its people, have been digested and pondered and chewed over by the author to surrender their essential significance. The same is no doubt true of any successful work of art, literary or plastic; painting, sculpture, epic poem, ballet, novel, all aspire to the condition of models by which to understand the world, our outer and inner lives. Truly to be useful, these models, these images, must be indelible; they must lodge in the memories of the audience like shrapnel. For an image of humanity to engage at the deepest levels, it must have been crystallized and intensified by its creator, in the way of a portrait by Rembrandt: the realistic picture of the old lady becomes both a celebration and an analysis of age, womanliness, motherhood.

There is no reason why acting should not aspire to the same qualities. As specialists in character and fellow creators in the performed play, actors too engage in the task of crystallization and intensification; searching ourselves and our world to identify the essence of the character and express it in a selection of representative detail, we aim to create images of lived life that bear the same relation to what passes for character acting, as Rembrandt's portrait does to a snapshot. But we will never do this if we dilute our training, if we are unable to practise what we have learned, above all unless we are prepared to delve deeper and deeper into ourselves, finding ever more expressive means of showing what we know. Self-congratulation will get us nowhere.

WARNING:
THE TREE WILL STAND FOR SOME TIME AFTER THE ROOTS HAVE DIED. THEN IT WILL FALL.

PART **THREE**
Thirty Years On

One

It was a curious thing to do, to sum up one's career when one had only been acting for nine years, and for a while, having written the book, I felt that I was acting, so to speak, on borrowed time. No doubt an astrologer could advance good celestial reasons for the upheavals in my life which occurred in 1982, the year when I wrote the book; a new door seemed to swing open every five minutes. The commission to write the book seemed particularly momentous to me, since it was writing that had always been my first ambition, long before I ever dreamed of being an actor; then I was invited by Mike Ockrent to go with him to Santa Fe to teach, which turned out to involve directing as well; when I returned to England I started shooting a sitcom, *A Chance in a Million*, in which I appeared with Brenda Blethyn; then I was asked to play Emmanuel Schikaneder in Milos Forman's film of *Amadeus*. By the time *Being an Actor* appeared, in 1984, I had directed my first play, Snoo Wilson's *Loving Reno*, at the Bush Theatre (and been nominated as most promising new director for it). So where did that leave acting on stage?

The first thing to note was a loss of continuity. The career documented in the first edition of *Being an Actor* had been an almost uninterrupted series of projects, including a few for television, but my experience of myself was entirely as a stage actor. The theatre was where I felt at home, where I belonged. The auditorium, the wings, the green room, the dressing room—these were my natural habitat and I felt both excited and calm in them, excited by the prospect of what was to happen, calm in my conviction that I knew what I was doing. I was a citizen of the stage.

The long, frustrating run of *The Beastly Beatitudes of Balthasar B* had left me feeling that perhaps it was time to reconsider my allegiances. I had, I felt, acted myself out. The arc which began when I stood on the stage of the Old Vic and blurted out Hamlet's words into the empty darkened auditorium, which had curved on through DramSoc at Queen's University, on through the three life-changing years at the Drama Centre, which had risen on and on through the fervent years on the fringe and reached a kind of apogee with *Amadeus* and levelled out with the three plays in which I acted after leaving the National

Theatre, now seemed finally to have hit the ground. I had in the nine years' span of my professional career acted in pretty well every available arena—both physically and metaphorically—and in the whole available span of dramatic literature: classical, modern, comic, tragic, political, personal. I had worked with some of the most remarkable directors in the world and some of the most inspired and inspiring actors. I had in the process become as well-known as a theatre actor can be (largely thanks to *Amadeus*, which had been seen by everyone of the slightest importance in—well, in the world, it sometimes seemed, as presidents, cabinet ministers, archbishops, generals, opera singers, movie directors and sundry superstars made their way to the Olivier Theatre for the two years during which we played it).

Despite all this, I felt somehow that things weren't working out as I had hoped. It was not a question of feeling failure, or even disappoint-ment. Nor, though I was certainly exhausted and emotionally flat at the end of the run of *Balthasar B*, was it simply fatigue. It was a sense that there was no structure in my development. I was deeply imbued with the ideals of the National Theatre as created by Laurence Olivier, which had been powerfully reinforced by my experience at the Drama Centre; I utterly embraced the concept of an ever-developing ensemble of actors who would grow by working together closely over a long period of time, creating levels of confidence and courage which would enable them to take on the greatest challenges of the repertory with an unprecedented level of depth across the board: every player a star, one day carrying the play, the next day a spear. The actors would be in perpetual training, spurred on by voice and movement teachers; by exploratory workshop sessions requiring a degree of openness and commitment only available to people who have learned to trust each other and risk making fools of themselves without embarrassment; by directors who monitored the actors closely, noting their strengths and weaknesses, shaping the repertory and the distribution of roles accord-ing to a graph of personal development. My two years at the National had been deeply rewarding—nothing more so than the opportunity to work on Shakespeare's sonnets—though it bore little resemblance to the Olivier ideal, despite the maintenance of a permanent company. In the end, they simply hadn't got anything suitable for me, so they 'let me go,' and I found myself free-lancing, going from project to project. Clearly there was something about the dream of an ensemble that spoke to a deep need in me—for a sort of theatre family, I suppose, but equally something that imposed a discipline on me, that provided a systematic challenge. The Drama Centre had instilled in me the notion of an unending training, a concept deeply inimical to most British actors, who feel that three years at drama school is quite enough of a good thing, thank you very much.

These ideals were closely bound up with the notion of being a Great Actor, a very important additional part of my mental baggage. I had a more than slightly Teutonic vision of a sort of Superactor, a supreme warrior of the theatre. The concept owed something to Edward Gordon Craig and everything to Laurence Olivier, who was that *Überspieler* incarnate; it was fed by the legends of actors like Donald Wolfit and Anew MacMaster, the last of the barnstormers. Unlikely as it may seem, in my heart I saw myself as a potential Great Actor in this almost primitive mould and wanted to take all the necessary steps to become one. I perhaps need to explain that this romantic idea had nothing to do with a quest for fame, or power, nor did it really have anything to do with wanting to join the establishment of famous and distinguished actors, many of whom I admired—people like Alec Guinness, John Gielgud and Ralph Richardson—but none of whom I wanted to be like. My ambition was, on the contrary, inspired by a distinctly Wagnerian idea of the theatre as a cleansing, healing, revitalising place, and steeled by a desire to push myself to the very limit of my possibilities. If this was the sort of actor I wanted to be, I asked myself, what was I doing cavorting naked except for some chains and goggles in *The Beastly Beatitudes of Balthasar B* in the West End of London eight times a week?

My dual nature saw no conflict between this position and my wayward and somewhat promiscuous curiosity, which led me to dabble in every conceivable kind of theatrical activity. It was kind of infantile greed, I now see, the desire to do everything, be every kind of actor, storm the heights and wallow in the gutter.

My post-*Balthasar* slump was specifically provoked by the conviction that I had somehow taken a wrong turning and had missed the experience indispensable to achieving Greatness. That meant the classics. In the nine years of my professional career, I had played two Shakespearean roles, only one of which could be considered formative (Titus Andronicus); no Marlowe, no Webster, no Tourneur, no Otway. Nor had there been any classical comedy: no Jonson, no Wycherly, no Farquhar. Nor indeed had there been any nineteenth-century classics—

no Ibsen, no Chekhov. But how could I hope to play these parts outside of the context of a company? The RSC had not shown the slightest interest in me. Indeed, one of their casting directors had confided in my agent that I would join the company only over her dead body; this was later effected—professionally speaking—but still no offer came; and I was unlikely to be asked back to the National. I made a conscious decision to diversify my activities and to follow all the new opportunities which were opening up. In effect, I was turning my back on the theatre.

And it was now that my career lost all semblance of coherence—which is only to say that in doing so it now resembled 90 percent of all other careers. Up until that point there had been some sort of a game plan, an admittedly varied but still thorough preparation for—for what? That was the question that was never to find an entirely satisfactory answer. Once I might have said, to become the Laurence Olivier of our times, to create as he did a series of overwhelming images of mankind, transforming himself physically, facially, vocally, on the grandest possible scale, to haunt our imaginations. I had been encouraged in this by various people, by no means poor judges. The veteran agent Ronnie Walters had told me that he had written to Patrick White, the great Australian novelist (and former actor) to say that he had just seen a young man who was going to play 'all the great parts, one after another.' And Peter Shaffer, inquiring after my circumstances, had said: 'We must look after you. You are one of the Successors.' Now I had to acknowledge that nobody else saw me this way. That had not stopped the young Olivier, slight, lightweight, often rather silly, and with no instinctive poetry. He had by unrelenting hard work on every aspect of himself fashioned an acting instrument unlike any the twentieth century, or perhaps any other century, had seen, and had come to dominate the theatre of his time. But he had a clear context in which to work: rep, Old Vic, West End. I had none.

Or so I said to myself. At the same time, my exact contemporary and archrival Antony Sher had set out at the RSC on the very path that I claimed did not exist. Indeed, with his Richard III, he challenged Olivier on his own territory, and at the very least achieved a draw. At the same time—our careers having proceeded in ghostly parallel—I was playing the part on the World Service of the BBC, reaching a considerably larger audience, but to considerably less effect. I did in the process discover something important: that I had nothing whatever to say about deformed psychopathic regicides. The character is admittedly something of a challenge on radio (a hump acoustic?) but the point was that the sort of virtuosity involved in the part, the sheer thespian relish which is such a large part of Richard's appeal to the audience, was no longer exciting to me. Privately I decided that Tony had inherited the mantle of Great Acting, and that I was no longer a contender, just as I had decided at school to abandon Art when I realised that my best friend was better at it than I was. I declared myself *hors concours*, removing myself from the arena. I would triumph in other ways, away from the competition. The moment had passed for me. No doubt if some director had come to me just then and asked me to play a series of great roles, I should have said yes, and then my subsequent life might have been very different. I had come close. One day during rehearsals at the National, John Dexter, confiding in me that he had been asked to take over the Royal Court Theatre, told me that I was going to open his first season by playing Richard III. The following day he had called me over again and said, 'Richard's too easy. Lear.' I was thirty-one at the time. Dexter had, as so often, jumped the gun, taking an expression of interest as an offer, and he never did take over the Court. So the world lost my juvenile Lear. Again, a year or two earlier there had been some talk at the National that when John Wood left the cast of Christopher Morahan's production of *Richard III*, I should take over, but business fell off before Wood left the show, and they pulled it from the repertory. So that didn't happen either. The last of these Golden Chances concerned John Dexter again. He had, he believed, persuaded John Gielgud to reprise his King Lear at the Cottesloe in a chamber production. Plotting furiously against Peter Hall, he was trying to establish *his* company within the National as a stepping-stone to taking over the whole organisation, and he started to cast the play: Michaels Bryant and Gambon, Sarah Kestelman, John Normington and I were to be the leaders of the group. I was to play Edgar. Edgar to John Gielgud's Lear; I could hardly sleep for thinking about it. Then Dexter leaked his plan to the press, Gielgud felt under pressure, and publicly dissociated himself from the whole venture. Foiled again. And John went back to terrorise the staff and board of the Metropolitan Opera House in New York.

What I lacked, it seemed to me, was a director who had faith in me, or a company which wanted me to be a permanent member of it. They would have to take me on my own valuation, of course, as a leading actor. I was not a star, nor did I want to be one, but I had proved conclusively that I had the energy, the intelligence and the authority to carry a play and anything less, I knew, would leave me frustrated. Again, I felt the absence of a structure within which I would have been rising; in which everything I had done would feed in to my work. I was still wildly ambitious for acting: longing to explore, push the boundaries of what was possible, reach for new forms of expression. I absolutely did not want to become a West End actor. I started to dream urgently of creating a company, thespocentric rather than directorcentric; as I had stated in the 'Manifesto' of *Being an Actor*, the model was the symphony orchestra, run by the musicians themselves. Over the years I made various attempts to create this company; finally I understood that I am not a natural leader. I am sometimes able to articulate in a forceful way what is commonly felt but not expressed, to speak, as it were, with the voice of the tribe. But leadership is something else, and younger men, Kenneth Branagh and Mark Rylance, emerged with that blazing look in their eyes and absolute confidence in their capacities which would forever elude me. I am the man to write a manifesto, but not one to enact it. So I wrestled over the years with the twin problems of what sort of actor I thought I was and the context in which I could work in the theatre. As time went on, I became very comfortable with the medium of film in which I was to work with some regularity; but my heart never failed to beat faster when I entered a stage door, or stood on a stage. I think what I felt, as I confessed in my book *Shooting the Actor*, was that I had loved the theatre more than the theatre loved me.

So off I went, film-acting, writing and directing, becoming dangerously well-known as an ever-present media figure, opining, introducing, compèring. I was often described in the press as a Renaissance man, to which my response was that though I had several talents, they were all rather small ones, so perhaps the phrase Renaissance dwarf might be more appropriate. As for theatre, I felt myself no longer a resident of it, but a visitor.

Two

In 1983 (*Being an Actor* having been written, but not yet having appeared) I made one of my visits when Bill Gaskill asked me to play Lord Foppington in *The Relapse* at the Lyric Hammersmith. We had last worked together when I was a member of Joint Stock some six years earlier; the working relationship had not always been comfortable, insofar as I felt that he basically disapproved of my approach to character. Neo-Brechtian that he was, he considered that in no sense should the actor become taken over by the principle of the character, insisting that the actor should always be visible controlling the character, drawing our attention to what was important. I of course believed the precise opposite. Where exactly this difference of opinion would leave us in working on a piece of theatrical extravagance like Vanbrugh's play I had no idea, but Bill's productions of Farquhar's two masterpieces at the National Theatre, both starring Maggie Smith, had brilliantly combined uproarious comedy with trenchant social comment, so perhaps our difference would be more apparent than real. I was cheered to hear from Bill that he had decided to do the play after directing it with students in America and discovering 'what fun' it was.

Well, of course, one man's fun is another man's funeral, and so it proved on this occasion. Not that I was in the least interested in a *Carry on Up the Restoration* production. Both Bill and I had rather frowned on Donald Sinden's famous performance of the role in Trevor Nunn's wonderfully cast but rompish production for the RSC some ten years before (I had sold tickets for it at the Aldwych when I worked in the box office there). It seemed that Vanbrugh, architect of Castle Howard, had a much more solid universe in mind than the purely theatrical landscape created by Nunn and his designer, Christopher Morley. Presumably Bill would strive to create the real world of Sir Tunbelly Clumsy and his daughter Hoyden, Squire Bull, Loveless and the newly ennobled Foppington, and the rest of Vanbrugh's gallery of Hogarthian types, giving due weight to the twin plots of Foppington's younger brother's quest for a rich marriage and the newly rusticated Loveless's amorous escapades. First, however, we had a read-through of the text, at the end of which he had pronounced himself depressed; no one knew how to speak the language. He kindly exempted me from

243

this stricture; as he had specifically cast me because, he told me, he had been impressed by my use of Edward Bond's seventeenth-century text in *Restoration*, I had hoped as much, though he did tell me that he thought I might be overdoing it somewhat.

He was not wrong, of course, about the read-through: the mostly young actors he had cast had no conception whatever of how to deal with the highly-wrought language. Vanburgh's text is not difficult, as such, unlike, say, Congreve's, from a slightly later date, but it requires a particular attack to realise the sturdy buoyancy which it shares with baroque architecture, long soaring lines exploding in ornament and fantasy. Well, who better to impart this knowledge than Bill, master of the genre, noted teacher and theorist of language (his chapter on phrasing in his autobiography, *A Sense of Direction*, is a classically succinct account of the subject)? Except that he didn't seem to wish to. 'Find out,' he would say when a young actress asked him how to deal with some tricky phrase. 'Upwardly inflect,' he would command some eager lad, and when the lad to whom the remark was addressed would inquire as to what that might mean, Bill would roll his eyes heavenward and sigh 'Tell him, someone.'

Any grappling with the underlying social themes, or indeed the varied styles within the piece, gave way to the desperate struggle to master the text; it was if the play were in German and only a couple of us could speak the language. Oliver Cotton, who certainly could, was left to his own devices in the part of Loveless, which he rechristened Thankless; in the end he gave up the struggle, which is a shame because the whole opening of the play, in which Loveless declares his ache to return to the filthy city, is a superb evocation of a frustrated sensualist, but it requires careful handling both scenically and in staging; this never happened. Bill's general attitude was that we were all hopeless incompetents incapable of doing justice to the play. He would accuse me alternately of being vulgar and Sindenish, or simply heavy-handed. 'You've become so coarse and strangulated,' he said. I challenged him on this: why did he feel the need to be rude? What did he hope to gain from it? There was a pause. 'I used to be much worse,' he said. That superb designer, Sally Jacobs, having had two designs rejected, finally came up with a more or less serviceable alternative which had no visual distinction, and which did nothing to help the actors or the play. I struggled to give Foppington the sort of airy massiveness which I felt appropriate. This dandy is very butch, his anxieties about correct form and his determination to outshine all his rivals in fashion having nothing camp or epicene about them. I had learned the lesson from playing Lord Are in *Restoration* that his asides to the audience presume complicity with them: he expects and indeed basks in their approval, as he negotiates his way round the various barbarians with whom the plot throws him into contact. The part is a very short one—it is in fact an apotheosised cameo—and I suspect that I was trying single-handedly to create the world of the play. But that is impossible; Foppington is quite unlike anyone else in the piece. He should be a wonderful diversion from the serious comic business of the rest of the action, but he must never dominate. It is not a concerto for actor, it is a partita for several soloists, and it needs careful orchestration. The end result, however, in this case was under-imagined, under-rehearsed, under-designed, under-acted—under almost everything except under three hours.

My point is not to re-rehearse the chapter on Joint Stock in the first edition of the book, nor even to restate my anti-directoratic argument in the 'Manifesto.' The important point is the absurdity of trying to do a text like *The Relapse* except with a group of actors who are used to working together and who are either familiar with the style of the play or have a method for acquiring the knowledge they need. There is nothing more exciting and profitable than a working period in which the actors and director set out to master a new style, but for this you need a conscious programme of exercises, classes, explorations, and you need a great deal more time than is generally available. Gaskill, a teacher much in demand in universities and drama schools all over the world, in this instance clearly regarded his teaching as quite separate from his directing. I believe that he was somewhat out of sympathy with the play itself, much preferring the realistic social comedy of Farquhar to Vanbrugh's almost Dickensian exuberance, and quite early on in rehearsals he lost heart, as he so often does. It was dispiriting to watch the group of young, highly gifted actors eager to learn at a loss to know what to do with their energy and their willingness to work, while stalwarts like Cotton and Nicky Henson and Lorna Heilbron, while trying to help their younger colleagues, were equally stranded, in need of guidance themselves; we all were. This stuff is not easy for anyone (except perhaps Maggie Smith).

My next visit to the theatre, a year later, was one of those self-inflicted follies that have characterised my career over the years, but it marked a very significant professional development. Having failed to make a relationship with a company or with a director, I formed one with a commercial producer, Howard Panter. This relationship (based on a very long friendship) has lasted till the present day, not without its troughs as well as its peaks, but it is uncommon enough to warrant a little comment. What it means is that if I have an idea for a project (either as actor or director) I can submit it to Howard, who will either reject it or embrace it; but it means that the terrible passivity of the actor, waiting, hoping for that call, is somewhat mitigated. I had approached him with Edgar Wallace's *On the Spot*, our first play together, during the run of *Balthasar B*, for which he and his then business partner Bill Freedman were acting as managers. We had known each other socially for some time, from the time when he was production manager; before that he had been a stage manager, a lighting designer, a director, a company manager, and he was, soon after I met him, to become a partner in a production company. Having come through the ranks in this way, and having attempted so many of the tasks of the theatre, he is unusually involved in the whole process, which to me is nothing but an advantage. In the case of *On the Spot*, he fell in love with the play immediately, seeing limitless possibilities for it, artistically and commercially.

I had come across the play in the pages of a biography of Charles Laughton; Laughton had had a hair-raising success in 1930 playing the central character, Tony Perelli, a barely masked portrayal of Al Capone, who was at loose in Chicago even as the play was being performed on the West End stage. The frisson for the original audience must have been like that of the Jacobean audience attending a play of Webster's, and thrilling to the bloodthirsty exploits of those filthy Italians. Laughton had disturbed everyone with the psychopathic intensity of his acting and by his androgynous sensuality. I was slowly falling more and more under the spell of Laughton, as I began to lose my absolute admiration for Olivier. In my attempt to understand the sort of actor that I was, I was looking for other models. Laughton had always been a hero of mine, but I hadn't grasped what he was up to as an actor. Olivier's approach was so clear: absolute domination of audiences, drawing a clear line around the character and imposing it unforgettably on the audience's imagination, offering an epic simplification of the part, a dramatisation of its elements. But Laughton seemed to operate more by stealth; there was an extraordinary complexity in his work, and the image that he created, even when it was a startling physical transformation like his Quasimodo in *The Hunchback of Notre Dame*, seemed to create an inner life which overflowed the boundaries of the character's outline and which took you into his soul. Above all, watching Laughton's work was an emotional experience; watching Olivier's, a sensuous one. Olivier introduced you to a thrilling and remarkable human being; Laughton took you into his heart, his mind, his soul. With Olivier, you knew exactly what he wanted you to feel about the character, but with Laughton you were in a much more ambiguous place, fascinated as you watched a creature with transparent skin, through which every impulse was clearly visible, every contradictory impulse revealed. Laughton's began to seem to me a more interesting acting enterprise than Olivier's, and the childish identification I had had with Quasimodo began to formulate itself into a conscious attempt to follow a Laughtonian path in my work: where better to start than with one of his great roles?

Howard was very taken by the play's account of deeply corrupt power and we started to plan a production. I proposed that Robert Walker should direct, my theatre soulmate, with whom I had not worked since the old Half Moon days, when we had our great triumph with *Arturo Ui*. I was nostalgic for the creative freedom we had had in the old synagogue down dingy old Alie Street in the East End, the wild experimentalism, the physical recklessness, the stylistic eclecticism. Howard had seen *Arturo* and readily agreed to ask Rob to direct. However, he said, this was the West End and obviously there were certain standards that must be reached, particularly in the realm of design; the show would sit in a gorgeously refurbished Matcham theatre, not a rat-infested dump, and we should approach it accordingly. He believed that the show's success would be contingent on its being perceived as very classy indeed: an evening of sumptuous settings and gorgeous gowns and richly upholstered performances.

I was very much of Howard's mind. Two years at the National and two years' free-lancing in posh venues had changed my view. If we had the money, we should spend it, visibly. I wanted the experimentalism, linked to swish production values. I could see no contradiction. Rob wanted to work with the Half Moon designer Ana Jebens, then his partner, but Howard and I were eager to link him up with a serious and experienced designer who had worked on a large scale in major venues. In the end, we chose Rosemary Vercoe and Patrick Robertson, a husband-and-wife team responsible for many superb designs at the National and at the English National Opera, often in conjunction with Jonathan Miller, most notably on the mafia *Rigoletto* (which is still the most successful production in the ENO repertory). It seemed a perfect match, and we imposed the golden team on Rob. He took it sulkily, but he took it. Shortly after, rehearsals commenced in Watford, where we would be opening the play; I had been present at all casting meetings, a curiously uncomfortable sensation, but a logical decision, because I could read with the actors. I found myself, however, a part of the management, something which would have not altogether pleasant consequences.

We found it difficult to get the people we wanted because, essentially, all the parts (apart from Perelli) were thinly written. The West End actors from whom Wallace had cast the original production had a lifetime of experience in playing the stock types; the young actors we approached lacked those skills, and were flummoxed by the corny writing. But rehearsals were crazy and reckless in the way of Robert Walker rehearsals. He had a strong sense of gangster culture, derived from movies; he had indeed written a play called *B Movie*, which I had done years ago in the old Soho Poly basement, playing a character based on Peter Lorre. He was also a devotee of Robert Warshow's brilliant essay on gangsters in *The Immediate Experience*. But beyond any sense of genre, this sympathy with gangster culture of his was imbued with his own essential anarchism, a feeling that anyone who was against the establishment, from whatever perspective, could not be all bad. He loved the sleazy glamour of this alternative universe, its sexiness and its drama. This was why he was so unenthusiastic about the extraordinary movie palace of a set which the Robertsons had designed. Dominated by its great many-piped organ at which Perelli is discovered, idly improvising lurid fantasias, to me, it perfectly created the Borgialike world of the court of Capone, the tyrannical society within (or without), a society so characteristic, in my view, of organisations which pit themselves against the rule of law, whether it be the IRA or al-Qaeda or the Krays. Denying the laws of the country, they create their own, equally inflexible, ruthlessly enforced rules—a far cry from Rob's libertarian, Nietzschean vision of a freedom beyond the law. He bridled whenever I described Perelli as a psychopath. Sociopath, he insisted, and even that was a grudging concession. At heart, there was admiration for these self-made monarchs who reinvented the world to suit their own needs.

Meanwhile, I was trying in my performance for exactly the degree of insensate destructiveness which the life of Capone so perfectly exemplified: what kind of a man is it that gathers his rivals together for a conciliatory supper, then removes a baseball bat from a drawer and smashes all of their brains in? What degree of cold rage against his fellow-beings did that betoken? The exterior life of the man was clear enough: subconsciously I appropriated Brando's underhanging jaw from *The Godfather*, and dyed my hair black; I wore false eyelashes and corsets. I invented some kind of an Italian-American accent. I aimed for a kind of dynamic lassitude in the performance, panther-like, glossy, perfectly without tension but ready to spring. I decided that he didn't get high on his own supply (thus teetotal, sharp as a razor, full of undiffused energy). Everyone around me should feel at any moment that I could break their necks between my thumb and my index finger. All this was, I think, skilfully enough done. What was more elusive was the inner blackness, the negation of a negation, which had obviously simply streamed out of Laughton like an inky emanation. Oddly enough, this is what I had thought to be at the heart of Arturo Ui/ Hitler and successfully realised, but because there was no attempt on Brecht's part to create any kind of psychological coherence in the character—indeed, his whole point was that there was none, no centre at all—it had seemed to come easily; I was, too, wearing a mask which was very liberating. Here, the mask that I was wearing as Perelli—the makeup, the physical life—was one of extreme constriction and control. Somehow it was harder to access the darkness. It felt as if I was sending a bucket a very long way down into a well and coming up with a thimbleful of what I needed. My personal anger—of which I have a great deal—is a violent, explosive and quite alarming thing, but as in a summer storm, the sunshine generally follows shortly after. This other emotion was of a very different order, and the sensation as I engaged with it was disturbing and far from pleasurable. It literally produced a bilious taste in my mouth. I was convinced, however, that the play would only work if the audience believed that they were in the presence of fathomless destructiveness—as they had with Laughton.

Curiously, the events of my own life were bringing me very close to darkness. I have written about that terrible time in *Love Is Where It Falls*. My partner Aziz Yehia was falling ever more despairingly into the manic-depressive condition that dogged and finally claimed his life; my best friend Peggy Ramsay had discovered a cancerous lump on her breast. Friends—contemporaries—were dying, sometimes by their own hands, sometimes by others'. When Aziz came to see the show, he fell into a dark silence afterwards. My performance disturbed him; he had not known that I had that blackness within me. He had hated and feared the character, so different either from the man he knew and loved, or from the other parts he had seen me play, bursting with extrovert energy, full of human warmth, and this troubled him deeply. Did he really know me at all? Who was I? These were the last questions he needed to be asking himself at a time of such abject self-doubt; what he needed was a confirmation of goodness and positiveness, available to him at all times. 'I'm an actor,' I told him, airily, 'we're unknowable.' I suppose Aziz's response to my work was something of a compliment, though in truth the performance was not a successful one, or if so it only served the character, not the play. The cost of my nightly attempt to locate this tiny vein of pure negativity in myself was a loss of dynamism: my Perelli was withdrawn, self-involved, and demanded a level of compensatory energy from the cast which they were not able or willing to give. Why should they? they may well have asked. Rob embraced the murky depths of the performance, and orchestrated accordingly, but it was a struggle. The play itself was a struggle, and though the notices at the Watford Palace Theatre were good, audiences were sparse and those who came were uncomfortable. We kept working, but things were not improving; Rob's relationship with the management was not good, because he was absolutely convinced that the set killed the evening. 'I'd like to take a fucking blowtorch to it,' he said.

Halfway through the run, Aziz killed himself. I continued with the play, partly because of the curiously deeply ingrained sense that the show must go on, but also because it was the only way I could keep my sanity. Everybody was admirably tactful and discreet; we carried on working on it, but the blight was on the show by now. I remember one evening, after the show, two friends of Aziz having come to see it and dissolving into tears the moment they entered the room, followed by Robert in a black rage with Howard, Howard in some despair because of the box office failure, and Kenny Baker, R2D2 from *Star Wars* with whom I had worked in *Amadeus*, throwing the door open with characteristic gusto and breaking into a riff of ribald high spirits. I felt like a sad old clown.

The run ended; we had a little party. As often with troubled productions, there was a great closeness between the actors. The West End transfer, despite the poor business at Watford, had been agreed, and we all parted with a promise to see each other in two weeks. Except that I, as part of the management, knew that a decision had been taken to recast three of the parts. And here I was, like Perelli himself, hugging and kissing the very actors I knew would not be transferring with us. One of those actors subsequently left a series of menacing, abusive messages on my answering machine; the same machine on which I had so recently received the news of Aziz's death. I didn't blame him; it was a vile thing to have happened, and it no doubt hadn't been done very well; there is no good way in which to do that to someone. I went away for a fortnight to Capri, on someone's recommendation, and grieved in solitude for Aziz; when we reassembled—plus the new actors—I decided to change my performance radically. The new thinking was simple—that Perelli *did* get high on his own supply, that he was in a permanent, dangerous state of intoxication. I thought that might release some of the darkness, rather than constipate it. And so it did, which resulted in a much more florid, operatic sort of a performance. This was good for the play, good for me, good for the other actors. Its first manifestation was, however, somewhat alarming: at the first rehearsal of the new version, I asked for carafes of water (in place of wine) to be placed on the set, and plotted the places at which I would swig from them. Naturally we went over and over the scenes, and I started to get very very drunk. I was hardly able to say the words without slurring, and found myself staggering. None of this was intentional; my view was that regardless of his intake, such a hardened drinker would only betray it by increasing emotional volatility. I suppose that a version of the placebo effect is at work here: my imagination had convinced my brain that I was indeed drinking alcohol and reproduced all the effects.

Rehearsals were a little strange because Robert was shooting a film and so unavailable during the time allotted. A distinguished actor with some experience as a director came in and tried to tighten the whole thing up; some of what he did was good, some not. Only very occasionally is it a good idea for a production doctor, so to speak, to come in and edit the show: generally only when that person is the head of the company and knows the actors very well. It is true that sometimes a director runs out of energy, emotional and mental, by the end of the rehearsal period, and an infusion of fresh vigour is needed, but that is better done by giving the director a day off or massive reassurance. Sometimes, it is true, a company is so disenchanted with a director that only his absence will change things. This was not the case here; just a general nervousness in the face of a West End opening. As it happens, we had a tremendous first night at the Albery and a uniformly good press: one critic said that my performance 'finally' confirmed that I was 'a great actor' (I had still only been acting professionally for ten years) and the play was hailed as a discovery. But the audience didn't believe the reviews, and failed to form queues at the box office as instructed. And on the whole, I think they were right. We had made the basic error of treating the play with excessive respect. This one, though not without a certain interest, fell comically short of the claims that I had made for it in the programme—Jacobean, I kept calling it. It is true that the plot could read like the synopsis of a Jacobean play— what with Perelli's onstage murder of one of his lieutenants, his cold-blooded despatch of the henchman for whom he professes the greatest love on a setup mission, his sadistic relationship with his Japanese girl-friend. But the language had no quality to it at all, being the formulaic gangsterese of the day.

The only thing that would have saved it was if we'd devised a way of staging it that was raw, surprising, sexy rather than stately, imposing, elegant. A way that broke down the dreary conventions of the well-made play of 1930. As it happens, that way was staring us in the face: it was the way Rob had wanted to do it all along. The very first few minutes of the production was all that remained of the way he had hoped to do it—in front of the Perelli mansion set, which glittered mysteriously in the background—the opening sequence, a mob killing followed by the arrival of an ambulance and paramedics, was played out in shadows with handheld lights strafing the faces of the actors. It was impressionistic, dangerous, and it evoked a world of dark deeds. Who knows whether Rob would have pulled it off, but his principle was the right one. It took me a couple of years to realise this, in con-versation with somebody one day, and when I did I wrote him a card apologising and telling him that if we'd done it his way, the play would have still been running. His approach anticipated by some years that of Stephen Daldry, who returned abstraction and expressionism to the mainstream with his startling production of *An Inspector Calls*. Howard and I had got it wrong. Nobody has a monopoly on getting it right; you ponder, you dream, you experiment, and you come to a conclusion. At a certain point, you have to commit to that conclusion and everything else follows. Sets are built, costumes made, actors cast. Sometimes you can change horses halfway through a production period, but generally, you're stuck with the logical consequences of your conceptual choices. Fortunately, Howard and I got it right on many of our subsequent ventures; but *On the Spot* was not the most auspicious start. We closed after three weeks.

During the brief run of the play, I had a curious encounter with the director Terry Hands, then co-Artistic Director of the RSC with Trevor Nunn. He had seen the show in Watford and pleasantly explained to me afterwards how technically inadequate—though not without interest—my performance was. I regarded this opinion as simply batty, and did not take it to heart. But given the agreeableness of his manner, I wondered whether there might not be an opening for me in the RSC. Perhaps my delayed dream of classical glory might after all be realised. My agent called him and made an arrangement and we duly met at the restaurant Jo Allen. Hands is an extraordinary-looking man, still boyish, but like a boy who has known things no boy should ever know. He has the appearance and manner of a debauched head prefect: perfect casting for Angelo in *Measure for Measure*, the face that of a severe sensualist, full-lipped, with glazed grey eyes that seem to have looked on midnight horrors. He greeted me charmingly, telling me how delighted he was that I had got in touch. 'Why have you never worked for us before?' he asked. I thought that was a question he might be able to answer better than I, but I simply smiled as if to say, 'Oh, life, you know, funny old thing, what?' 'Yes,' he continued, 'you're such obvious RSC material. When Trevor and I started the company'—Peter Hall might have found this an interesting statement; I wondered how long Trevor Nunn was going to stay in the sentence—'we looked across to Larry at the NT, and his actors were so glamorous, so brilliant, so skilful, we wondered how we could compete. And we thought there was only one way to go: we would hire *rough* actors. Now,' he continued, puckishly, 'you're one of the roughest actors around, so *why* haven't you joined us?' Uncertain as to whether I was being praised or damned, I simpered and waved a noncommittal hand. 'Let me ask you some questions,' he said, and proceeded to list his fellow-RSC directors. One after another he quizzed me as to what I thought of them. Surprisingly, he offered his own views, which were without exception uncomplimentary; finally we arrived at Trevor Nunn. Before I could even express an opinion, Terry said: 'The finest director in the world, without exception, of Jacobean tragedy.' A somewhat arcane compliment, this, I thought. 'Less certain when it comes to Shakespeare,' Terry continued, a fascinating verdict on the man who had been running the RSC for the last fifteen years. I had no idea whether my views on Terry's colleagues had been the right ones, but I was under no doubt that I was undergoing a test.

'A few more questions,' he suddenly said, pulling out a large chart on which were written the titles and *dramatis personae* of all thirty-seven of Shakespeare's plays. 'Which part,' he said, 'would you want to play in *All's Well That Ends Well*?' And so on through the canon. I was acutely aware that in almost every case I gave the wrong answer. When we got to *The Merchant of Venice*, for example, I said 'Antonio.' In *Coriolanus*, I had plumped for Menenius. I realised that what I was being tested on was the scale of my ambition; my appetite for glory. And I was failing. I saw the disappointment in Terry's eyes, and I did not think it was because he feared that I had a low self-image. Rather it was because if I had expressed a desire to play Macbeth, Henry V, King Lear, he would have had me in a vicelike grip: my longing for these parts would have given him a Mephistophelean hold over me. One starts thinking that way in Terry's company; it is in the air, part of the natural oxygen which the man breathes. A perfectly ordinary restaurant becomes a corner of some Borgia palace; shadows seem longer, eyes more hollow as one is transported into the second part of *Ivan the Terrible*. As he put away the chart, he said 'I'm sure we can find something that would satisfy and interest you. But if we do, and if you join us in Stratford, I'm afraid we would have to lay down a condition. We should have to ask you to lay down your pen for the time you're with us. You are an observer and a commentator on the scene, and we would be asking you to lose that objectivity and be one of us.' This was like Beria's table talk. I wondered how they would impose this condition: midnight raids of my Waterside cottage, seizing notebooks, smashing typewriters? Earlier he had spoken of an actor with whom he had worked, a gay man, whose performances had always been given, Hands said, to please his mother. Then she died, and he had been liberated to play altogether nastier, more dangerous types. At some other stage of the conversation, he had told me how another actor (one of his associates) had become a better actor since he had had a baby. As we parted, he mentioned an extraordinary improvement in the work of one of his directorial colleagues, and he wondered why. 'Lost a mother? Had a baby?' I volunteered, airily. The faint sardonic smile which always lingers about his lips disappeared and a flash of real anger replaced it. 'Cunt,' he said, and then rearranged his mouth.

I never heard from him, of course. I was moved to reflect on this examination which I had so badly failed. Why was I not consumed with desire to play all the parts that every actor worth his Equity Card is supposed to yearn after? It seemed to me that the factor which united most of them was power: almost all of the so-called tragic roles in Shakespeare, and the heroic ones, are centrally concerned with power. Now power, in the political, or even in the personal sense, has never engaged me. It is not a drive of mine. I do not wish to have power over anyone, and feel acutely uncomfortable when I do. It is true that I am exhilarated by the power that acting—acting well, that is—can confer, but it is not specifically power over an audience that I experience. It is rather a sense of liberation from the inadequacy and mess of my life; I described this in the first edition of *Being an Actor*. I suppose, to use some early twenty-first century jargon, I feel *empowered* when I'm acting well. The chimera of Great Acting is essentially bound up with portrayals of power, very often of soldiers. Interestingly, Ralph Richardson seemed unable to engage with this drive, too, and so failed as a classical actor, for the most part, and even Gielgud—by common consent the greatest classical actor of his generation—was not noted for his Macbeth, his Othello, his Shylock (who, though no soldier, is dominated by his drive to acquire the power of life and death over another human being). His great achievements were Hamlet, Lear and Prospero, all three, of course, conditioned by the absence of power, failing to attain it, renouncing it, being stripped of it. Olivier, on the other hand, was profoundly interested in power, and it was his genius to explore that drive in role after role. It did not stir my juices at all. The small list of parts that I longed for included Captain Boyle in *Juno and the Paycock*, Falstaff, Peer Gynt: human, all too human, all of them. And beyond even that ambition, deep, deep in my desires, was the dream of creating a clown. If I had created Chaplin's Tramp, I should have felt that I had really made a contribution to humankind's understanding of itself. Meanwhile, I remained as baffled as ever as to what sort of an actor I really was.

One answer to the question was offered, but never tested. Between the Watford and London runs of *On the Spot*, I had been offered the leading part in a Feydeau farce that the National was to do. In my gut and my groin I knew that I was the right actor to play Feydeau; I had had a breakthrough with his work when I was at drama school. It seemed to me that if I was anything, I was a natural farceur. The energy, the high definition, the speed of thought and physical flexibility required are all attributes I possess in spades, much more so than, say, the qualities called for in social realism. Instinctively, I want to make big shapes and follow through powerful drives. But there was no question of my not doing the West End transfer of *On the Spot*. I pleaded with my management, arguing that I was sure I would have a big success with the Feydeau, and that my sitcom was about to come out and would certainly be a triumph, and then—in six months' time, or a year—we could revive the Edgar Wallace, when I would be a huge box-office star. They were unimpressed by these arguments. Well, let the dice fall where they may. But it is still a source of sadness to me that I have never played in a farce; soon arthritis will have set in and I shall no longer be able to rush about from side to side of the stage with the requisite driven energy (though the great Henry McGee not so long ago did marvellously well in a wheelchair in a Ray Cooney farce), to say nothing of the steel mental control needed to deliver the lines with machine-like precision.

Later that year I did, for a very short season in London and an even shorter one at the Edinburgh Festival, a play which was as far from *On the Spot* or indeed Feydeau as any play could possibly be: *Melancholy Jacques* by Jean Jourdheuil, a one-man meditation on aspects of the life and work of Jean-Jacques Rousseau. It was an exquisite creation, designed by the great Lucio Fanti, the painter who has designed so many of Peter Stein's productions, and lit by the equally great André Diot, and it is everything that we mean by arthouse theatre. Witty, allusive and deconstructive, it presented Rousseau on an island of books, upon which he has erected a tent, and from which he boils water on a Camping Gaz, to brew himself reflective cups of Nescafé. He is haunted by his love of Julie—'ah, Julie!'—and shaken by his loathing of Molière. From time to time he opens the cover of one of the books that form the island; a light concealed in the book exquisitely isolates him as he reads from the work of one of his detested writers. Fiction itself comes into his sights and he denounces it, spinning out fragments of his own autobiography—the night he had a giddy spell in Menil-montant, for example—savouring the towering phenomenon of his own personality. The action is punctuated by the same lilting phrase from his opera, *Le Devin du village*, a work he wrote shortly after denouncing opera as immoral and subversive. The play ends with a starcloth coming wonderfully to light as he dreams of his lost love. Designed to be played in very small spaces, it was an opportunity to achieve a kind of intimacy, an interiority, which I had never before attempted onstage, and never felt able to attempt. The text need not so much to be performed as to be sighed; the challenge is to avoid monotony, to keep the audience absolutely engaged. The trick proved to be total involvement with the physical world—the coffee, the tent, the books, so that I never played the text, the text simply arrived on the back of the actions. It was perhaps like playing Chopin in a very small room. Irving Wardle in *The Times* very generously said that it was the most perfect instance of Stanislavsky's 'small circle of concentration' that he had ever seen onstage; that was exactly what I was trying for. It was deeply satisfying to perform, and strangely calming. One night, on account of a light which had fallen onto the cloth, the tent burst into flames rather spectacularly. Without interrupting the flow of words, I sauntered over and picked up the saucepan, sprinkling its contents over the flaming tent, and then sauntered back to where I had been before. It was like za-zen, and the—not numerous—audiences who came to see it felt the same. A very cleansing evening of theatre, and a useful insight into the mind of a man whose influence on the development of modern consciousness can scarcely be overstated.

As it happens, while I was playing it, I was going through another period of emotional turmoil (again documented in *Love Is Where It Falls*) during which I came as close to insanity as I have ever done; it was the only occasion in my career when I nearly missed a performance, paralysed by an image of my own mind as a hinge out of which the nail was slowly being drawn. And one night during the show I simply had no idea where I was or what was coming out of my mouth. As in a trance, I went through all the motions of the show, was warmly applauded and sat in my dressing room and wept.

*

The year was 1984; not everything was as grim as Orwell had feared. This was the time, for me, of *A Room with a View*; shortly after, I appeared in *The Good Father*, a film which performed disappointingly despite starring Anthony Hopkins, being directed by Mike Newell and being written by Christopher Hampton. I had started writing my book about Laughton, which forced me again to consider what I thought acting was, what is was for, and where I fitted in. Laughton had a fitful relationship with the stage after leaving England to go to Hollywood for the first time; having had an uncomfortable time as a performer of classical plays, he discovered that movies offered him an opportunity for a certain kind of creativity that perfectly suited his gifts. Perhaps I would find the same? I also found myself closely considering the question of the personal cost of extraordinary work, when you demand everything of yourself emotionally and mentally, and of the relationship of happiness in one's private life to one's work. Pleasure, said Proust, is good for the body, but it is pain which develops the mind. Was that true? I also noted that Laughton derived huge satisfaction (and rather large number of dollars) from the reading tours that he made, mostly around campuses, spreading first the Good News in his Bible readings, and then the Even Better News, from his point of view, of the power of art. In his programme entitled *Charles Laughton: The Story-teller* he brought all his genius to bear on performing extracts from the world's greatest literature—Plato, the Bible, Shakespeare—bringing the story up to date with Jack Kerouac (which was very daring of him in 1955), interspersing the extracts with anecdotes, some from his own life, designed to show that, as he said with one his great rising cadences, 'The Spirit. Goes. *On!*' Perhaps, I wondered, there were other ways of reaching audiences than just appearing in plays.

In 1985, again at the Bush (where I had performed *Melancholy Jacques* and so many other plays over the years), I acted in *The Kiss of the Spider Woman*. A friend, Alan Baker, the translator, had called me to ask if I'd like to perform extracts from Manuel Puig's novel for a television documentary about the Argentinian writer. (Hector Babenco's film had been shot but not yet released; I knew nothing of Puig or his writing). When I read a page or two of dialogue he sent me, I was fascinated by what seemed to be a remarkable and original relationship between two convicts, Molina, a flamingly camp window-dresser in prison for molesting a minor, and Valentin, a battle-hardened guerrilla, intellectual and unsmiling, aching for his girlfriend. After initial violent hostility, largely thanks to the web Molina's story-telling spins, they become lovers. I asked if I could read the novel, and then Alan revealed that Puig had written a play from the novel (which is, in fact, in dialogue form throughout). As soon as I read this I knew I must do it, and took it immediately to my friends Jenny Topper and Simon Stokes at the Bush, who read it overnight, and agreed to programme it immediately; without hesitation, Simon (with whom I had worked on *Juvenalia* some ten years before) offered to direct it. Such a sequence of events could never happen now, even on the fringe. The whole thing took about a week, from Alan showing me the play to it being announced for production. At the end of his life, Orson Welles used to lament that movies were no fun anymore because of the delay between getting the impulse to make a film and actually making it. What used above all to characterise the fringe when I was part of it was spontaneity. In a sense, that was lost as a result of its success. Jenny and Simon and their associate Nicky Pallot had transformed a rough-and-ready, if often very exciting, little black box of a room above a pub into a highly efficient organisation maintaining the highest standards in every department, both in playwriting and in production values. The best actors, the best designers, the best directors and the best writers vied to work at the Bush, and no allowance ever had to be made for quality. Accordingly, planning became longer- and longer-term, ever greater care was taken with scripts, directors and casts were chosen after long and exhaustive consideration.

On this occasion it was, in fact, nothing more than a happy accident that the Bush had a free slot when I came to them with *The Kiss of the Spider Woman*, the cast (or at least half of it) came with the play and the director was on the spot, but boy, was it exhilarating. Robin Don, absolute master of the curious space that is the Bush, agreed to design it the moment he read it. We then swiftly met a number of actors for the part of Valentin and had no hesitation whatever in casting Mark Rylance, who, though not necessarily everyone's idea of a guerrilla— he had just come from playing Peter Pan as well as the part has ever been or will ever be played—had an inner strength, a poetry and an emotional freedom, combined with a stubborn intellectual tenacity which have made him one of the most original and searching actors in England today. (To say nothing of his qualities as an actor-manager of positively Elizabethan flair and commercial instinct, which has made of the now world-famous Globe Theatre on the South Bank—of which he was the first director—a vital theatrical force, not the Disneyland it might so easily have been.) So with everything thus auspiciously disposed, I went off on holiday with the new love of my life to a Greek island, where, every morning on the harbour, I would learn the lines until the sun was too high in the sky to do anything other than plunge into the Aegean.

This learning of lines in advance had by now become a matter of policy with me. What it does is to instil a shape of the play into one's mind, a chamber of the brain which belongs exclusively to its actions and its emotions. To resort to the inevitable technological metaphor, it sets up a drive in the hard disk of one's skull which is dedicated to the play in hand and nothing else. The fact that one knows the lines is a huge advantage in rehearsal, of course, and the act of committing the words to memory demands constant questioning—Why does he say this after that? What is he trying to achieve? And so on. But more important than that, I have come to believe, is this other thing: this creation of a kind of cathedral of thought, the mental space, the pegged-out territory of the play, which is filled with the thousands of pictures evoked by the text and the web of relationships predicated by the story and the character. It is a kind of cosmos, with the paths of the thoughts criss-crossing like the paths of the planets. It is inside of that space that you must live during the play, of that space that you must become a citizen. And it is having created it that kills nerves, because it is a kind of homeland that you carry with you onto the stage. If I know what I'm thinking, I can have no fear, no anxiety. Otherwise you are dependent on a mere mechanical recall of words, or an unreliable succession of emotions. This concept has a great deal in common, I discovered later, with the Elizabethan Memory Theatre so vividly described by Frances A. Yates; her book *The Art of Memory* makes clear how much more than mere recollection is involved.

So by the time I returned, bronzed, blissful, from Mykonos, I had installed the play into my brain. Only one thing was missing: I had no idea how Molina should speak. I believed I knew him, as a man, his speed of thought, his camp vivacity, his neatness and would-be daintiness; I saw, too, the emotional openness, the sexual need, the instinct for subservience, for service; and I had a most vivid sense of his dream life, filled with the myths he had drawn from his obsession with the screen, and especially its love goddesses. I saw, too, that his own submission to the stories with which his head was filled, and which he was so expert at re-telling, gave him a haunted quality, a real poetic intensity. Sitting spellbound in the dark, eyes wide-open, staring up at the screen, other dramas playing out in the back of his mind. I saw all this, and felt it in my bones and in my muscles. I could become Molina at a moment's notice. Except for one thing: how the hell did he talk? The voice is almost invariably the starting point for me: until I hear the right sound coming out of my mouth, everything sounds false, out of tune, and my body ceases to behave as it should. I feel awkward, blocked. The problem with Molina was an entirely conceptual one, but it nagged at me. He was an Argentinian. I knew his English counterpart very well, those girly boys whom one used so often to find in the wardrobe department of theatres, and quite often still found in the choruses of musicals: limp of wrist, with pouty lips and eyebrows, often plucked, permanently raised to the point where they seemed about to leave the brow altogether and join the hair, for whom every man was 'she' and every word contained *doubles* and sometimes *quadruples entendres*. So often these boys were brilliantly witty, and often fiercely intelligent, and then one would suddenly come upon them sobbing, mascara running. I had talked to Puig himself when he came to England before rehearsals and he had confirmed my view as well as in his own person, inadvertently giving me a perfect example of the sort of creature Molina was. 'She is a shopgirl, dear,' he told me. 'Whatever happens, don't play Molina like William Hurt. Oh! She is such a boring woman, that Hurt! Molina must be funny, silly, she must shriek and scream and cry. What was Hurt thinking of?' Whenever I spoke the lines aloud, or in my head, I immediately fell into the characteristic arch, lisping voice of the queen. But it seemed to me ineffably English, while the situation of the play—the regime, the revolution, the kind of prison they were in—was deeply foreign. How to convey this, though? It is the perennial problem of doing a foreign play in English: our accents, speech patterns somehow reduce the characters to specific British types—Cockneys, Northerners, Home Counties dwellers. And yet if we avoid any of these choices, the characters cease to be people, become simply stage figures, since no one is devoid of accent, and in England accent is always significant. Sometimes directors—Zeffirelli has done this more than once—have had their actors speak in the accents of the author; in de Filippo it worked very well, but there have been nightmarish productions of Chekhov with all the actors affecting tenth-rate Rrrrrrussian accents; and that begs a question, too—how well are these people supposed to be able to speak English in their foreign accents? Do they from time to time grope for words, as almost anyone who is not wholly bilingual will do? But if the character is highly articulate, what then? I knew that I was opening a particularly troublesome can of worms, but the question would not go away.

So much so that on the first day of rehearsals, at the read-through, which, in common Bush practice, was held in front of the staff of the theatre, I turned to them, with their eager and expectant faces, and said: 'Ladies and gentlemen, I would like to apologise in advance. What you are about to hear from me is totally unprepared. I have no idea whatever how to play the character. I hope it may serve some purpose as a sort of talking book for the blind, but not much more.' Then I proceeded to give the best performance of anything I have ever given in my life, a total account of the part, in the camp lisping accent I had so resisted, which proved to be a perfect vehicle for the emotions of the character. It was not me, it was Molina. Now this was rather extraordinary. I am not, as far as I know, an effeminate queen. Camp, I daresay I am, but in a rather fruity, actorly sort of way. But here at the first read-through I slipped unhesitatingly and completely into the hotpants and knotted shirt of Molina. It was as if I had been waiting all my life to behave like this. I knew every emotion, every impulse, every change of thought, every gesture from deep personal knowledge. I had known a few queens of this sort, but not well. Somehow they had entered deep into my subconscious and were now ready to take me over completely. This has happened so rarely in my career that it is worth drawing special attention to it. It is a real mystery. Had I managed to play a theatrical stereotype with great brilliance, that would have been impressive, but not surprising. But I was doing something more than that, something quite different. I had been taken over by the soul of another. The question of the accent suddenly seemed quite unimportant: this was Molina speaking, that was all there was to it.

It seems deeply immodest of me to speak like this, but it is the opposite, because I can claim no credit for it. I made no special study of Molina-like people, I had not read the book over and over again. I made no effort to explore the emotions of the part. It all leaped out of me, fully formed, like Herakles out of the thigh of Jove. And this very completeness brought some difficulties with it. It did not help Mark, for example, in much the harder part, the anguished revolutionary, aching for his mistress, terrified that he will give away secrets under torture. Filled with my character and able to do no wrong in the eyes of the director and—to be candid—myself, I was a little impatient as Mark struggled up the mountainside, trying this, rejecting that, digging deeper and deeper into himself. I liked and admired him so much, enchanted by his physical beauty and the radiant warmth of his nature, but was somewhat bemused, like someone who has perfect pitch baffled as to why someone else can't sing a simple tune straight off. Simon Stokes had to play a very careful game, praising me, but not at Mark's expense, while containing Mark's wide exploration of the part so that it would not overrun the boundaries of the play.

The journey of the two characters is a long and intense one. The play is a perfectly-fashioned account of an impossible love. It starts with curiosity on Molina's part and disgust on Valentin's, moves on through Valentin's illness from malnutrition and Molina's nursing of him, to growing tenderness, sexual consummation and finally separation when Molina is released. I had persuaded Manuel to let us include a scene that he had believed theatrically impossible, a painful and unsparing morning-after conversation, the day after their first lovemaking, which contains some of the most profound writing in the novel. The story, psychologically precise and dramatically satisfying, is taken onto another level by Molina's recounting of the plot of his favourite films, especially Val Lewton's *Cat People*. Molina uses the telling of the story as a source of power, bringing Valentin to a point of deep frustration by withholding the next turn of the plot. But as the relationship develops, the story becomes a projection of their own story, and the strange imagery of Lewton's masterpiece permeates the whole play with mythic power. The play possesses real poetry, a quality I was seeking more and more in my work in the theatre.

As we rehearsed, I was often overcome by emotion. At the heart of Molina's actions in the play was a nurturing instinct, and his acts of kindness overwhelmed me sometimes—cleaning Valentin's bottom, for example, when he was racked with diahorrea, or cooling his brow. The lovemaking scene, played in the dark, is an unsensational (but perfectly accurate) account of anal penetration but also the most tenderly imaginable realisation of what happens between two people when a sexual act becomes an act of love. 'I wanted to touch the mole on your brow,' says Molina, 'and then I realised that you don't have a mole. I have a mole, not you.' Robin's set was a remarkable rendition from canvas and wood of the stone of the gaol, turning the Bush into that prison, and Simon's choice of Gluck's *'Che faro senza Euridice'* from *Orfeo* as scene punctuation music was inspired. Each element made its unerring contribution. It was a perfect work of theatre. And it ran for three weeks, which made it even more perfect for me. Every performance was packed to the point where we were in breach of the fire regulations; every performance was a journey for the audience which was deeply cathartic. The auditorium was awash with tears to such an extent that it almost became dangerous for the actors; we had to control it very carefully or it would have dissolved into some terrible sort of collective wail. That was not what Manuel meant; not what art means. The spectre of AIDS was already beginning to haunt every play about gay sex; here the possibility of a perfect encounter between two people whose orientation is neither here nor there but whose humanity is everything was deeply hopeful.

I can say with absolute conviction, as I doubt whether I can say about any other play I have done in my life, that nobody who saw it will ever forget it. And the beauty of it was that it had more or less sold out before it opened. The first night, despite 70 percent of the audience consisting of reviewers, was incandescent. I called Manuel in Rio where he now lived and told him 'London has taken Molina to her heart.' He never saw the production; two years later he was dead. The notices on the whole were favourable. The *Sunday Times* said it was one of the most perfect plays about love ever written, and that our performances were unimprovably good (though he did not name us). Nicholas de Jong, gracious as ever, observed in his opening sentence that I had for once eschewed my usual over-the-top, Donald Wolfit-like hamminess, and was giving a credible performance. He praised Mark, too, but ended the review by suggesting that watching the love scene—the tender, overwhelming love scene, played in the dark—was 'like watching a hippopotamus being mounted by a gnat.' None of it mattered in the least: every seat could have been sold twice over, and those who came needed no guidance from critics to understand what they saw. I changed the message on my answering machine to say 'Wolfgang Amadeus Mozart meets Peter Pan: The Kiss of the Spider Woman. Book Now,' but it was unnecessary. Bush regulars got their tickets, and after that it was a scrum. One day Robert de Niro's chauffeur appeared at the box office to ask for a ticket for the great man, but he was turned away. 'If Mr de Niro wants to queue for returns, he's most welcome,' the box office assistant called after him with pardonable *Schadenfreude*. The bond between Mark and me grew powerfully with every performance. There is a curious kind of a public intimacy in performing a two-hander, especially one as emotionally charged as this one. It is a kind of love affair, so exposed, so dependent, so liberating. With Martin Sherman's *Passing By*, it had been the same, but on that occasion I *was* having an affair with my fellow actor, which gave a particular extra frisson; here, where I was not, the combination of mutual loving support and a kind of creative tension as we each developed our roles and our understanding of the play produced a very intense interaction. The intensity was increased by the limited nature of the run. There was talk of a transfer, but we both had other commitments (I was about to direct Maggie Smith in *The Infernal Machine* by Cocteau, he was doing a film) and so it remained this extraordinary perfect event, during which there could be no decline into routine, no falling off of audience numbers or audience response, no adjustment to a larger auditorium, no concern about sightlines. It was what it was from beginning to end. About ten years later, we did a reading of the play at the Bush to celebrate the theatre's twentieth anniversary; it worked in exactly the same way as it had the first time, though in the interim Mark, on his own admission, had become less of a Stanislavskian fourth-waller and more interested in his relationship with the audience. Far from lessening the emotional power of his performance, this only made it fuller and freer.

Three

Was it a subconscious dread of disappointment that kept me away from acting on stage for three years after that? I had gone off full-tilt in pursuit of other challenges, other worlds. In particular, my directing career had become very well established: there were two small plays at the Offstage Theatre (*The Passport* and the one-man play *Nicolson Fights Croydon*, which I had devised for my old friend Angus Mackay), *Amadeus* at Clwyd, Cocteau's *The Infernal Machine* with Maggie Smith at the Lyric Hammersmith, *Così fan Tutte* at the Lucerne Opera House, Milan Kundera's *Jacques and His Master* at the Los Angeles Theater Center and *Shirley Valentine* with Pauline Collins at the Vaudeville; I had written my second book, a biography of Charles Laughton, translated the Cocteau and the Kundera and had acted in a number of films, notably *A Room with a View*, *The Good Father*, *Maurice* and *Manifesto*, about which I would subsequently write another book. On television, I had made three series of the sitcom *A Chance in a Million*, played Handel, Mr Micawber in *David Copperfield* and the erotic engraver Marcantonio Raimondi in Leslie Megahey's exquisite short film *Cariani and the Courtesans*. Inevitably, I had been thinking a great deal about acting, partly in the course of writing about Laughton, but mostly as a result of directing. It had been lost on no one how droll it was that having penned a rousing denunciation of directors, I had immediately become one. Patiently I had pointed out that it was the institution of directocracy, as I dubbed it, which I had denounced, not the very existence of directors, for many of whom I had warm admiration, and had said so. Clearly, however, I was in some sense setting myself up as the better sort of director. This was easier said than done. I had some very hard learning to do very quickly. I had been obliged, for a start, to separate my own practise as an actor from that of the actors I was directing, and to focus intensely on what it was that would help them to realise their roles in the most imaginative way possible. Although I was very interested in interpretation, and concept, in design, space, light and sound—the *Gesamstkunstwerk*—I was doing the job above all to create the best circumstances for the acting. I can put up with anything in the theatre as long as the acting is compelling. And acting and actors fascinate me: their different approaches, their complex temperaments, their brains. I'm not talking about cerebration; I'm talking about the acting mind, the mental processes involved in acting.

As well as the question of what I could do for the actors, I was also very interested in what they could do for me, and it was in that area that I learned perhaps the most. Seeing actors from the side of the director's table, I saw how pointlessly obstreperous I had often been in the past, how frequently I had come to rehearsals ill-prepared, how lazy I sometimes was. Some of this, of course, was the legacy of the directocracy—the very thing I had been at pains to point out in the first edition of *Being an Actor*—the erosion of individual responsibility in a structure where the director believes that everything must come from him, the sulky resentment of the colonised, the petulance of the disempowered. But I was struck by how often actors simply didn't seem to think that it was up to them to open their imaginations, to lose themselves in their characters, to volunteer alternatives. I was also increasingly conscious of technical deficiencies—vocal, physical, verbal—as if the actor felt that he needed to do no work on his instrument as such, and that the discovery of 'the truth' would solve all technical problems.

I believe that I only became fully aware of the degree to which technique is liberating when I directed Maggie Smith in *The Infernal Machine*. It was an unhappy rehearsal period, to put it mildly—with many of the problems brought on my own head by overconfidence in my ability to draw performances from people who were simply not ready for the challenges both Cocteau and I had set them—and I floundered about with this profoundly difficult play, knowing what was required but having only the vaguest idea of how to achieve it. It was not perhaps the ideal play on which to teach oneself how to direct. The mix of temperaments in the cast, moreover, was horribly misjudged and a mood of despair prevailed at most times; I was unable at that early stage in my directing career to create the mood of basic optimism without which any production period becomes hell. My problems were nothing to do with actually directing Maggie, though: she is the Rolls-Royce of actors, and the only challenge is to understand the power and brilliance that you have at your disposal. The merest turn of the steering wheel, the lightest touch of the accelerator, and you're off, hurtling round that bend, speeding down the motorway. Gear changes are effortlessly accomplished, and she has certain special features, such as an ability to take a note in such a way that not only does she change the line in question, she instantly adjusts the whole of the rest of her performance to accommodate it. She is the supreme mistress of tone, able to modulate within a paragraph from high comedy to emotional verisimilitude to stark tragedy; her thought processes are so highly articulated that a moment's mental connection will take her to places undreamt of by most actors, and her ability to conjure up pictures for the audience as she speaks is the glorious source of her comedy. All this I saw, as I struggled with my own problems and those of the production, and greedily tried to assimilate them for my own future use. Everything Maggie Smith is as an actor, I should wish to be; but of course that derives from what she is as a woman, and I have no temperamental affinities with her. So all I could hope to acquire from her (apart from the sublime performance that she soon delivered in *The Infernal Machine*) was in the area of vocal technique.

I studied her phrasing minutely, imitating it to get the feel of what she was doing. Imitation is a widely underrated technique of learning (Maggie herself has always been candid about what she learned in this way from, among others, Kenneth Williams and Alistair Sim): it activates certain muscles, vocal and mental, which you might never deploy. I discovered from her phrasing how, by certain musical choices—rallentandos, a touch of rubato, slight rhythmic hesitations—she created a constant sense of surprise, leading the audience's ears to expect one thing and get another; to shock by suddenly impaling a word as with a harpoon; to create space by odd false starts and then an unexpected fullness of tone. All of this cleverness, it must be stressed, is in the interests of the thought being expressed. There are other aspects of her technique which are quite specifically to do with engendering laughter for its own sake, and that, too, can be glorious. But it is her genius for releasing thought with precision and matchless freshness that I wanted to steal, and have been trying ever since to do. No performance I have given since working with her has been uninfluenced by that aspect of her art. But more important for me even than that has been her diction, which is a marvel, unparalleled in the modern theatre; and it is here that she is the real heir of Edith Evans, who similarly engaged with consonants as a creative act. Our tongues and our lips are what fingers are to pianists, and we need to practise, and to be acutely aware of the impact of the different sounds. Apart from anything else, the only way that we will really be heard—rather than idly listened to—is by biting on those consonants, caressing those vowels. At close quarters, Maggie's final consonants may sound exaggerated—she hits her *d's* and *t's* with a heavy hammer—but from the front row of the stalls, there is nothing but relief: the audience really get what is being said. If punctuality is the politeness of kings, properly placed plosives are the politeness of actors. One of the most moving sights in my career was catching Maggie, in occasional spare moments during rehearsals, sitting in a corner of the room, chanting her diction exercises: this great actress, at the peak of her fame and her powers, saying over and over again at speed 'what a to-do to die today' and 'red lorry, yellow lorry, red lorry, yellow lorry.' Something called 'Voice' is widely taught (to rather dismal effect, if what one hears is anything to go by) but diction is rarely named. No doubt it is one of those discredited skills, like arithmetic, that we have jettisoned as somehow incorrect, oppressive. Serious attention to it would transform the theatre-going experience, not only for clarity of speaking, but also for energy: the consonants so often drive the sentence, give it buoyancy, stop it from dribbling to a halt or crawling along evenly like cold porridge.

I speak from no position of smugness. Having been told from an early age that I had a good voice, I never really applied myself to work on it. What people meant was that I had a pleasing tone and talked posh. I was also versatile vocally, always able to slip into accents; and I was loud. But I knew nothing of breathing and less of diction. My old school, the Drama Centre, had let me down in this area (they were experimenting with some oddball theory or other at the time I was there), but this failure was compounded by my secret conviction that all the lessons were directed at the others, not at me. I scarcely grasped that unless you can breathe, you can't phrase—that is, you can't shape your text, easing it into vivid meaning. I knew that Olivier had prodigious reserves of breath, but I put that down to his general exhibitionistic virtuosity: one didn't need to be able to breathe like that to do what I wanted to do as an actor. In fact, the opposite was true. I had high ambitions for what I wanted to do with my voice, and I attempted all sorts of daring things, without having the slightest idea how to make my voice respond. I made grand vocal gestures, but they were all splash and no substance. Instead of diving in, I simply fell off the diving-board, very often hitting myself on the bottom of the pool. The result was a lot of botched vocal virtuosity, verbal pratfalls, gasped ends of sentences and constant complaints that I was inaudible. I privately concluded that all these complainants were in denial about their incipient deafness, and carried on blaring incomprehensibly away. I had my first glimmer that this might not after all be quite as good as I thought it was when I worked on radio and actually heard the results of my fabulous vocal technique: drooping lines, breathlessness, monotony. It was working with Maggie Smith that really made me understand what was involved. There is no better way of observing an actor than directing them; simply acting with them (as I had done with Maggie on *A Room with a View*) is too close an experience. Directing lends distance, and with distance comes enchantment.

My reflections on the art of directing—and more usefully, perhaps, on the experience of directing—what it's *like* being a director—belong elsewhere (although I believe every actor should attempt to direct, if only in order to understand why this meddlesome figure is behaving as he does), but when I returned to acting onstage after what seemed an enormous gap, I believe I had somewhat changed in my attitude to the process, aware that we all have problems, and that we should share them. I found that directors were a little nervous of directing me now that I was one of them, too, but they need not have worried. When I was acting, it was a huge relief to be thinking only about my role, rather than being required to have an opinion about everything, which is the director's lot. (As it happens, I do have an opinion about everything, but it is a deep liberation not to have to be the one making the decisions.) I had also changed as a result of having acted so much in film. After a somewhat unnerving start with *Amadeus*, I had, under the calm eyes of James Ivory and Mike Newell, begun to get the hang of it, realising very rapidly that the essential difference between film acting and stage acting—and there is a difference, *pace* Alec Guinness, who claimed there was none—is one of projection. In a theatre, however small, the performance must always be projected out to the audience; that is the essential experience, however much it may be concealed. On film, however small or large the performance, it must never be projected at the camera. The camera simply observes it. Orson Welles used to note with some relish that Olivier was not a good film actor because he tried to dictate to the camera, just as he dictated to the audience in the theatre. The experience for the actor, as I've said elsewhere, is as if one had swallowed the camera: it is not *out there* at all. It is shy, it prefers not to be acknowledged. It is deeply interested in everything you do, but it doesn't want any fuss made of it. The people whom the camera loves, those famous, blessed people, are those who will allow it to come right up close without becoming self-conscious. Once this relationship is right, it becomes the essence of the experience of filming: you are doing something for the camera, but not at it. It can be a deeply satisfying experience, very intimate, very liberating.

But in the theatre, the audience is everything. Their comprehension, their satisfaction, their diversion, their instruction, their transcendence is the whole purpose of our work, and if something doesn't reach the audience, then scrap it.

Four

My return to the stage could scarcely have been more ambitious: all of Goethe's *Faust*. I had played the part of Faust on radio for David Spenser: one BBC radio's grand projects, seven hours of broadcasting. Ronnie Pickup was Mephistopheles and I struggled through the title role, awed by the capaciousness of Goethe's spirit, although never exactly comfortable with the character of the man I was playing—not, frankly, convinced that there was a character. Ronnie was having a wonderful time spitting and growling satanically, ironising and womanising and generally running rings around the very unamusing Dr Faust; one understood why Gustav Gründgens (Klaus Mann's Mephisto) had become a great actor playing the part, and why no one could remember who'd played Faust. But any such niggles were swept away by the grandeur of the vision and by the sublimity of the thought, or at least the impression of sublimity in the thought. Something was no doubt lost in translation, but it was curiously difficult to pin down what it actually meant—what one was actually saying. The overall sense of restlessness, of striving, of dissatisfaction was recognisable enough, however, and the final apotheosis in heaven was deeply moving (with memories of Mahler's setting of it in his Eighth Symphony hovering in the ether), Fathers ecstatic and profound, sinners and virgins, all aspiring towards the Great Upward and Onward, led on by the Eternal Womanly. I read *Lives of Goethe*, and as much of his vast output as I could lay my hands on in English—plays, poems, novels, tracts on colour, botanical theses, travel books—and rather fell in love with this man seething with such inner turbulence that he felt the need to create an external life for himself of the utmost calm, as Minister for Roads in Weimar, and to apply himself to pursuits (like cataloguing plants) which required him to be absolutely methodical. I felt that we had scratched the surface of his *Meisterwerk* with the radio presentation— splendid as it was—and that it was a great story which had to be dealt with properly, on stage; no major company had ever attempted it in Britain, which was hardly surprising given its vast length, though surely, one felt, Part One, which is a relatively well-made play, should have had an outing. It is scarcely more difficult than Marlowe's play on the same theme (from which, ultimately, via the English puppet

271

theatres which toured Germany with it, Goethe's play is derived). But nobody seemed in the least interested.

So when I met David Freeman, the young Australian opera director, at the first night of his astonishing production of Glass's *Akhenaten* for the ENO, and we fell into conversation, the discovery of a mutual fascination with *Faust* led to a very quick decision to try to mount it somewhere. This was worth taking to the boards again for. Only this time round, I would play Mephistopheles. Sorry, Ronnie. I knew Freeman's beautiful, complex, radical work on *Cosí fan Tutte* and *La Calisto* as well as Harrison Birtwistle's *Yan Tan Tethera*; Goethe's play is essentially operatic. It seemed to me a brilliantly right idea, and I immediately took it to my friend Peter James at the Lyric Hammersmith, for whom I had now directed two plays, and for whom I had acted in one (*Total Eclipse*). He was at the height of his innovative programming for the theatre, having established the idea of staging the international repertory with international artists of the brilliance of Nuria Espert, and he scarcely blinked at the notion of giving his theatre over to a company of twenty actors who required three months' rehearsal, a group of percussionists and a composer (Nigel Osborne) in order to stage Part One and Part Two on alternating evenings, except for the days when we staged the whole thing, all seven hours, in one go. Not only did he not baulk at it, he revelled in it. This was exactly what his theatre existed to do.

Meanwhile, the Glasgow Citizens Theatre had stolen a march on us; David MacDonald had translated the play and adapted it to a containable four hours in one sitting. When I first heard that this was their plan, I called MacDonald, an old friend, and suggested myself and Roy Mardsen for Faust and Mephistopheles. 'I don't think so, my dear,' he replied, 'it'd be like having Laurel and Hardy, don't you think?' Nonetheless I went up to Glasgow to see the play and discovered that MacDonald had produced a wonderfully free, allusive and speakable text, which I recommended to David Freeman. David, though a man of extremely strong views and a horror of what he calls 'a certain kind of theatre'—which he cannot even bring himself to name—is a great collaborator and sought my participation at every level. We set about casting the play. Great physical dexterity was a key requirement for the actors, plus specialist skills in mime; the Freeman approach is to render every dramatic impulse in physical terms, especially game-based ones. His practise is to create an analogue of the world of the play, not to reproduce it literally. He seeks his models in the playground and in tribal cultures. This was what had distinguished his opera productions, taking them a world away from not only Royal Opera House conventions, but also from the attempts of directors like Jonathan Miller to instil the rudiments of acting, character and psychology, actions and objectives, into the singers. David is not interested in acting, as such, only in interacting. He sees the play not as a text but—as in Cocteau's definition—a pretext, something to be borne along by the physical interactions created by the game being played. Thus Ahkenaten's kingdom in Glass's opera was made of sandcastles, and its destruction a particularly disturbing event comparable in intensity to the child's experience of having his sandcastle kicked over. I was intrigued by this concept; intrigued but a little uneasy. I myself, as may by now be clear, am very fond of acting, and I have little or no connection with my own childhood. David's concept of a ludic underpinning to the action rang no bells of delight for me. Whenever anyone says to me 'Let's play a game,' my heart sinks. Whenever someone says 'Let's do some work,' I light up. However, I was very keen to submit myself to a new approach, to be asked new questions, to have all my old answers subjected to scrutiny.

We quickly assembled our company of athletes, acrobats, dancers, mimes and actors. Meanwhile there was the small matter of casting Faust. We needed an actor who was able to make the journey from 120 to 25 and then slowly age back up again to incomputable ancientness over the course of the seven hours; one who was interested in conveying intellectual passion; one, above all, who wanted to go on the rehearsal journey that David was outlining. After another interminable and inconclusive casting meeting, I heard myself say, 'Well, I suppose I could play Faust.' The joyful cacophony which greeted this remark temporarily blinded me to the fact that I had just given up one of the great parts in world dramatic literature in favour of one of the most unplayable, as I knew from personal experience. All the months of squeezing myself into the devil's cloven shoes wasted, as I faced the prospect of trying again to embody Goethe's questing inner spirit and give it a human face. Put like that, of course, it wasn't such a depressing prospect, and we started to trawl Spotlight for Mephistopheleses. Many of the same requirements as had applied to the quest for a Faust applied here equally—stamina, openness, interest in conveying brilliant thought. We found a technically masterful young actor called Peter

Lindford, who was strikingly handsome in a slightly foxlike way—almost diabolical, you might say, in some lights—and we were on.

Rehearsals took place in one of the most dispiriting parts of London, Acton Central—the very name places a cold hand on hope—and were as thorough and inventive a pursuit of David's method as could be imagined. We started the day with movement sessions designed to unlock our sense of space and to find the trust and the familiarity upon which this sort of production utterly depends. We improvised, we played games, we experimented with fabrics, we dressed up, we undressed; we learned how to climb ropes up to the arched metal frame which was the central element in the set designed by David Roger; we sat in a circle with Nigel Osborne and hummed till, like Buddhist monks, we created harmonics. I took part in all of this with a sort of rictus on my face which I remembered from games at school, when I had likewise tried to pretend that I really cared who won, and that I found success on my part thrilling and failure on others' risible and damnable. And all the while, I was wondering when we would actually start staging the seven hours of Goethe's *Faust*. Eventually, a little tensely, I wondered out loud to the group, pointing out that Part One starts with what is essentially an interrupted forty-five-minute monologue for Faust. David immediately saw the point of this, and I was given leave to go off into corners with the stage manager and run lines while the games continued without me. But it wasn't just my text that I was worried about. Everyone had long swathes of the stuff to speak. Memorising it was not the problem; they were all young and eager. But many of them had very little experience of using words on stage, and these words were especially elusive. I had dimly felt on the radio that the problem was simply that *Faust* is not a play; it is a poem. Now I knew it. Had not Goethe murmured, as almost his last words on earth, "Never do *Faust* onstage"? And he meant Part One. If the idea of staging *that* troubled the Sage of Weimar, what would he have felt about attempting Part Two, where he appears to have swallowed a tablet of lysergic acid, his wild fantasies spinning across history and human possibilities, absorbing centaurs and homunculi, crazy Holy Roman Emperors, the reclamation of the shore, and then spiralling up into the farther reaches of the human spirit? Wonderful, exhilarating stuff, but thousands and thousands of words, assembled over a lifetime. *Faust*, he said, was his profession; he added to it as if it were a kind of commonplace book. He never planned to give it a dramatic shape;

that was not his purpose. If it was to be staged, dramatic life had to be imposed on it, discovered for it.

David maintained the extraordinary optimism which is his birthright. He believed, he said, as he started to work on the actual piece, that if the basic game of each scene were established, it would play itself: it would never be necessary to stage it at all. I could just about see how this might be the case if he had a company of actors who had trained together, and worked together, and were in absolute accord with his philosophy. But we were a singularly disparate group, from very different backgrounds, of different ages and life experience. I was as bereft of the skills of some of these charming young people as they were of mine. My skills made them look foolish, their skills made me look inept. Again, I could see very clearly how, in an operatic context, what David proposed might be true, because the music was there to bind everything together; the music, in fact, created the drama. Nigel Osborne's music, drawing on Tibetan models, was of its nature incidental rather than fundamental, fine though it was. Bit by bit we started to assemble the great woolly mammoth of a play. Peter Lindford was developing a strong sardonic presence as Mephistopheles; Alison Spiro was a passionate, forthright Gretchen. The other actors, too many of them to list, each seized a moment, creating characters as best they could. But the trouble with David's method, which might have worked with *King Lear*, was that it depended on the existence of a great play. His deconstruction and reinvention of Mozart and Cavalli, even of Philip Glass, worked brilliantly as a counterpoint to highly structured, densely dramatised originals—here there was no form to deconstruct.

I, meanwhile, laboured on with the vast text, knowing that for all David MacDonald's brilliance, I, too, was making bricks without straw, striving to endow what was meditative and wayward with thrust and at least incipient conflict. Of course, in German everything is different. I read it daily in the original, in a dual-language version, and spoke it out loud. It is clear, somehow, even to someone with my rudimentary grasp of the German language, that something profound has been given definitive expression, something, moreover, which is finding its form for the first time; the language is being made, this poet its inventor and supreme master. He is Shakespeare. Not in our version, although MacDonald cunningly creates a series of echoes across other poets which is both witty and suggestive but . . . Goethe is Goethe, the mastersinger, the man of a thousand voices, all equally compelling, whether pellucid and classical or romantically tormented or bitterly ironic. And the song is all. Character is not his strong suit. They *are* their words, his people, and we cannot express them in English. From an actor's point of view, the great technical problem of playing Faust is that he can never be satisfied, so with the brief exception of a moment's delight in the young Gretchen, it is a question of finding a thousand different ways of saying one is unhappy. Moreover, for the first third of the play he is a hundred years old, with a corresponding limit to the range of expression; then he's rather younger than I was at the time (forty), so I tended to present him as a blithering idiot (as all twenty-five-year-olds, of course, are). By the time of the death of Gretchen, I had allowed myself to age up a bit—without the slightest justification in the play—so that by the beginning of Part Two I was my own age. And then starts the great journey through history—the chemical wedding with Helen of Troy—the battles fought, the elderly couple dispossessed—as Faust sinks into decrepitude, until finally he says to the passing minute—in Louis MacNeice's version—'Stop, you're exquisite.' Satisfied for one second, he is able to slough off his mortality and is swept on high (via a terrifying rope journey to the flies, in our production).

David's production had a number of moments of genius—staging the Holy Roman Emperor's battles as children's flour fights was masterly, and much of the finale, with its ring of candles and Nigel's weird harmonics made by running fingers round the edge of glasses, created a properly ecstatic and mystical conclusion. Elsewhere there were unexpected intrusions of literalism which worked jarringly; the costuming was curiously unimagined. I spent quite a large portion of Part Two looking like a mediaeval sofa. But there was no mistaking the scale of the enterprise. On the whole, we were very well reviewed, and business was exceptional, especially for the occasions when we did the whole play on one day. Peter James increasingly programmed this marathon, which became for me—onstage for five and a half of the seven hours—a mighty mountain to climb. Peter Lindford, wiry, focussed, powerful, gave a performance astonishing for someone who had been acting for no more than a handful of years, though when we had run Part Two immediately after opening Part One, he had wept from beginning to end of the show, without ever once missing a line or a cue. Nerves, exhaustion, frustration hit him over the head; the following day he was fine. What doesn't kill you, as I murmured to him, makes you stronger.

My personal reviews got it about right—admiration for stamina, but not much note of creativity. There was very little of that. I was getting through it. The one great source of satisfaction was that I learned more and more about how to speak the text—about how to speak, indeed. Although I was hoarse by the end of the evening, having used every note in my voice as I made my way across the seven ages of man, I now knew how to phrase through to the end of a line, I knew where to breathe and where to place my voice. I had a letter from Bill Gaskill, no less, telling me what pleasure my phrasing had given him—how well I had orchestrated the part. And certainly I had proved, if that was required, that I could carry a whole evening, both in terms of stamina and variety. I don't think people were bored. They may not have been excited, or even greatly moved, by my performance, but they were held. That is something. Not negligible. It had of course been a veiled bid for inclusion in the ranks of the Great Actors, and I believe that I thought I was in with a better chance for having avoided the well-trodden path of the English Classical repertory. The result hardly justified that, though in some ways it proved that I was at least a contender. Somehow, it seems that I was destined to be *sui generis* to forge some idiosyncratic category of my own. Not necessarily a Great Actor, but at least a Greatly Interesting one. In some sort of way, I felt as though I was growing up as an actor, becoming my own man.

Many people came to see the play out of curiosity, having known of it without knowing it; among them was Arthur Miller, who came backstage and said that he was glad he had seen the play—once. Indulgently, I lamented the thanklessness of playing the title role. 'Yes,' he said, 'Faust is what we in the American theatre call the second banana role.' It was, I think, a noble venture. Again and again, I felt that we could have spent the whole three months on realising just one scene, in releasing all the contents of Goethe's exceptionally complex and subtle brain. In rehearsals we touched on the alchemical theory which permeates the play, and we could have spent a month on that alone, teasing it into some sort of dramatic life. But we just touched on such things, passing swiftly on in a blur of slightly suggestive ideas. I suspect that even in the German theatre, *Faust* is something of an *ignis fatuus*, though an extraordinary Mephistopheles is still able to justify an entire production. Needless to say, it is a supreme example of the sort of play that an ensemble company could devote some years to, showing its work in fragments perhaps, until finally ascending the summit. And I should be very happy to be part of that effort. (The RSC did stage the whole play later, though I fear they had little more success than we did.)

Nor do I dismiss David Freeman's approach, which has been triumphantly successful in many different contexts. I suspect, however, that I should never be able to work with him in that way. It doesn't release me, and my commitment to it becomes simply dutiful, which I take it is the opposite of what it is meant to be. You have to be frank about these things. There is no approach which automatically releases every actor. For some, learning the lines and getting the moves may be the only channel for their creativity, while others cannot start to function until they have given the old bean bags a toss or two. I started work with Peter Hall on his workshop for what turned onto a trail-blazing production of *The Oresteia*, but a sort of claustrophobic horror of masks and their denial of the most expressive part of my anatomy sent me fleeing. Speaking of expressive parts of one's anatomy, the production of *Faust* warrants a footnote in my own personal history. It was the last time I ever appeared naked onstage. I had acquired something of a reputation for stripping—publicly confirmed by my appearance as a skinny-dipping vicar in *A Room with a View*: two gazelles pursued by a hippopotamus—and a British critic, the late Jack Tinker, once rather sadly observed that he was more familiar with my private parts than with his own. As described elsewhere, it had been rather liberating for someone who had once been rather uncomfortable with his own body (although of course I *never* stripped unless it was *strictly* necessary from An Artistic Point of View), but now enough was enough. I was beyond the point of no return as far as avoirdupois was concerned and felt I could inflict my flesh on the public no longer. So now, with my rebirth in the witches' cauldron in *Faust*, the hazards of nudity—the sudden shrinkage, or worse, the unstoppable tumescence—were, so to speak, behind me.

What was ahead of me was entirely unexpected and the result, I suspect, of my having (just before *Faust*) directed Pauline Collins in the West End production of *Shirley Valentine*. David Aukin, then administrator of the National Theatre, invited me to appear in and co-direct a new play by Alan Bennett, then called *Spy Games*. It was a double-bill consisting of a stage version of the television play, *An Englishman Abroad*, about the actress Coral Browne and the defector Guy

278

Burgess, broadcast with huge success some years earlier, and a new play, *A Question of Attribution*, about the art historian and spy Anthony Blunt. I was to play Burgess, with Alan directing; he would play Blunt, directed by me, and we would both appear in small roles in the other's play, as it were. Reading *A Question of Attribution* and knowing that it was being offered to me was one of the happier moments of my career. The wittiest, most elegant of plays, it was also a teasing meditation on the meaning of loyalty, culminating in an encounter between Her Majesty and Blunt in a corridor of Buckingham Palace, a scene which is one of the jewels of post-war comedy—perhaps, as George Steiner suggested, of all classic British comedy. In *An Englishman Abroad* I was more than happy to be playing the role so exquisitely rendered by Alan Bates on television, with its potent distillation of whimsy and melancholy and loucheness, and enchanted to have the task of conveying the Blunt play to the stage, though it was so clearly a screenplay (the words FADE OUT after each scene were a bit of a giveaway). Bruno Santini, my then partner (we had worked together on *Shirley Valentine* and *Infernal Machine* and indeed everything I'd directed so far), and I found a way of dissolving from scene to scene with the use of slides—managing one change out of the interrogation room into the palace with some panache by unfurling a red carpet from left to right across the whole width of the stage without the aid of human hand, to the sound of ceremonial music specially composed by Dominic Muldowney, as an entire painting-laden wall of the palace flew in. Alan and I cast the play to our entire satisfaction, with that superb actress and master-comedienne Prunella Scales as if by divine right taking the star double-role of Coral Browne in *An Englishman Abroad* and HMQ in the other play.

There remained only the question of the title, which nobody liked. I offered to think about it, and the next day was idly working my way through famous lines from Shakespeare (the essential recourse for play titles, as everybody knows) when I landed on Gertrude's great line, 'Sorrows come not single spies / But in battalions.' Alan was underwhelmed by it, but I've scarcely been prouder of anything in my life: it was, quite by chance, of positively Stoppardian—sorry, Alan—Chinese box–like ingenuity. Both men were spies, they were both single (being gay), the two plays were single-act plays, and spies did come in battalions. The National were rather keen on it, too, and prevailed only because Alan hated his own title even more than he hated the new one.

Posterity owes me another debt, too. While we were preparing the production, Alan pointed to one of HMQ's lines: 'One Minister of the Arts wanted to loose Francis Bacon on me . . . He did the screaming Pope, didn't he? I suppose I would have been the screaming Queen.' 'I'm going to cut the line,' Alan said. 'It's too cheap, isn't it?' With difficulty I persuaded him to leave it in; needless to report, it was the biggest laugh of the evening, or of pretty well any evening I've ever been involved in.

Rehearsals were very curious. In *An Englishman Abroad* Alan was absolutely permissive as a director, only disturbed that because I didn't know any Anglican hymns, I substituted Catholic ones while being coached in Rock of Ages, and that I was completely ignorant of the works of Gilbert and Sullivan. Otherwise the play worked perfectly, as we always knew it would. The exquisite sequences when Browne and Burgess listen to Jack Buchanan singing 'You stole my heart away' were of an ineffable sadness and tenderness, uniquely English, and quintessential Bennett. In the role, I was trying for an effortlessness that is not entirely natural to me; to achieve it requires, in fact, a great deal of effort on my part. I had in mind a glancing, airy quality with a sort of honeyed vocal delivery, like that of the great Michael Redgrave; when, eventually, I found this quality, I discovered that I was often in tears. I'm not sure why; perhaps wonderful writing may have something to do with it? Superbly crafted though it is, it is nonetheless definitely a television play and not a stage one, whose particular effect to a large extent depended on a kind of intimacy and a large number of close-ups. The challenge Pru and I faced in the cheerless Lyttleton was to lift the piece without coarsening it. Alan played the tiny part of the tailor with hilarious economy. With *A Question of Attribution*, I was in a surreal situation, directing the author in his own play while acting with him. The word *hubris* comes to mind; as does the word *folly*, particularly since there was precious little hilarious economy about my performance as Chubb, the interrogator whom I had endowed with a heavy-handed London accent (on the dubious basis that he mentions having a wife in Croydon). The all-knowing director found himself in the curious position of trying out a different performance every day—now Irish, now Mancunian, now stupid, now cunning—while the actor he was directing (who happened also to have written the stuff) serenely proceeded to give a master-class in the art of comic acting. I was rather more at ease directing the scene in Buckingham Palace, in which I did not appear, and was actually able to help a bit by blocking the scene quite efficiently (something of a challenge, since it's set, by its very nature, in a corridor, and thus flat on to the audience). Pru was a little uncertain at first about some of my insights about where the laughs would be—she having been one of the leading British comediennes for some thirty years—but we all soon trusted each other very well; the younger actors making a great deal of their small roles. I was a touch worried that in the two lectures that are part of the play, Alan was perhaps a little dry. The character of Blunt slightly puzzled me: he was described by everyone who met him as overwhelmingly charming, but I found photographs of him cold and almost repulsive, with his skull-like features, and his lank, clammy presence—interesting, but not attractive. That was not what we wanted for the play; that was another play. Then someone loaned me a videotape of the opening of the Queen's Gallery, of which he was the first director. In it he is interviewed by Richard Dimbleby, who proclaims himself, very convincingly, an absolute dud about art. Blunt charms him instantly, praising the broadcaster, flattering his comments on the pictures and generally seducing him. Dimbleby positively glows. The single most remarkable thing about the seduction, however, is his voice, pure velvet, which he wraps round Dimbleby to wonderful effect.

The next day I burst into the rehearsal room with my *aperçu*. 'I've got it, Alan, I've got it: Blunt was *sexy*. You have to be sexy. It's all in the voice.' 'We'll have to get another actor, then,' said Alan, not entirely humorously, 'we'll have to re-cast.' We didn't, and everything went remarkably well, after a somewhat nerve-racking preview period in which the slide machine broke down, carpets failed to roll, sets got stuck, paintings on the wall seemed to have been done on the painting by numbers method. The *Daily Mail* managed to smuggle a photographer into the Lyttleton Theatre at an early preview, and to the play's inherent merits was added—as with *Amadeus*—the welcome element of scandal; it had until very recently been forbidden to represent a member of the royal family in the theatre at all, and here Her Majesty was, bold as brass, on the stage at the recently ennobled Royal National Theatre. The first night was a sensation. Unbeknown to us, Alan Bates and Coral Browne were there—how strange it must have been for her—and she was wonderfully true to her reputation. 'That fucking coat has to go,' she said of Pru's costume in *An Englishman Abroad*, 'and I never wore a hat like that.' But in every other way she was very generous about the evening, as was more or less everyone. It was as big a hit as I had been connected with since *Amadeus*, and the reviews were of unmixed enthusiasm. My personal reviews, as an actor, were somewhat muted, most of them penetratingly pointing out that I was not Alan Bates, and that my performance was less delicate than his had been. It seemed not to strike them at all that it would have been impossible even for Bates to give onstage the performance he had given on television. I continued to derive great pleasure from doing the play. How could I not? I chain-smoked throughout (I was still smoking like a beagle in those days), chomped real cloves of garlic (a shared passion of mine and Burgess's) and lingered over the touching moments of contact between him and his boyfriend.

Doing the show was nonetheless a curious experience because of my directorial responsibilities. In *A Question of Attribution*, I was in scenes on either side of the great Buckingham Palace scene, and would watch it most nights from the wings to take notes. One night, I thought I'd better give it more than a sideways look, so I slipped round to the front of the house to watch it from the director's booth at the back of the stalls. Having duly observed, and made my notes, I pushed the pass door through which I had come, only to find it locked. I was in costume as Chubb, with my false moustache and my cardigan, and members of the audience for the show in the Olivier Theatre were passing by, interested at what appeared to be an unscheduled foyer event as I first tapped then hammered at the door, crying out with increasing desperation to be allowed to get back onstage. Someone passing on the other side opened out of curiosity and I stumbled onstage with seconds to spare to continue the cross-examination of Sir Anthony Blunt. In truth, I was never entirely comfortable with the character of Chubb, and was always conscious of the absurdity of the situation of my directing the author in his own play while acting with him. In fact what developed was a very healthy situation in which we all three, Pru, Alan and I, gave each other notes on our work. I was deeply envious of the absolute security of Alan's performance, which scarcely deviated by a hair's breadth from night to night, and by his command of the audience. He has in the intervening forty years gone so far beyond the fringe that one sometimes forgets that he is, after all, apart from everything else, one of the supreme revue artists of the twentieth century, and revue technique was exactly what was called for in the play. I tried to learn from him (and Pru, who is similarly a mistress of the contained comic style), but I was always wanting to burst out somehow. While thrashing around in the shallows of my character, and trying to refine my comic skills, I fear that I gave Alan more than a couple of duff cues, but he rode them without complaint, and indeed without sacrificing the laugh.

Under the management of my friend Howard Panter, we transferred to the West End, as had been the plan from the beginning, very fittingly ending up at the Queen's Theatre, and we played there happily and successfully. Well, successfully, anyway. My happiness was impaired by a most curious incident. The play opens with a speech of Coral Browne's direct to the audience, followed by one by Burgess. This was always slightly unnerving because it was a prologue, appended to the television script, and one never had time to accommodate to the convention. That's what I felt, anyway; I don't think Pru saw it as a problem at all. One afternoon, I walked out, after Pru had spoken her speech, and I began the urbanely witty text: 'Hearing that Stalin had died, one cheered up no end. It was not simply that one was glad to see the back of the old bugger, though I was, but for the first time since I'd come to Moscow in nineteen fifty-one—' At that point, I caught sight of my understudy sitting in one of the boxes. It seemed to me that he had a peculiarly malevolent glint in his eyes. I instantly knew that he hated my performance, thought he could do the part—and in particular this speech—much better, and wanted me dead. Filled with the awful realisation of this, I started to falter in the speech. At this point my eye, desperate to avoid the box and its vengeful inhabitant, turned towards the auditorium, only to come to rest on the radiant features of Dame Peggy Ashcroft, looking up at the stage seraphically, as was her wont. I then started to burble. Absolute drivel poured out of my mouth, neither grammatical not meaningful in any way. I was speaking with tongues. 'And yet despite beyond twelve never gurg breeeeeell go. And still they have neither yes nor hat. Goobyot.' At this, I turned decisively, even triumphantly, and left the stage.

It would be only a slight exaggeration of the truth to say that I never entirely enjoyed a performance of *An Englishman Abroad* again. I had to calm myself down at the five-minute call, find someone to chat with about this and that, resist the temptation to go over and over the speech again, and learn to appear to stroll onstage, though my palms were clammy and my brow burning. Bit by bit, I regained my confidence, but for the first time in my life, I understood what Stanislavsky meant when he described 'the terrifying black hole of the auditorium.' I had always thought of it as a friendly space, but now, with the twin spirits of Dame Peggy, seraphic, and my understudy, diabolic, hovering around somewhere in the ether, winged, like *putti*, waiting to swoop in at any time and unnerve me, I was not so sure. No one else noticed, of course; even the spectacular collapse of meaning occasioned only the mildest comment, and my understudy continued to be as cordial as ever.

Another curious episode occurred about a month after we had opened in the West End. There had been a number of explosions that year, 1989, and one afternoon we received a bomb threat just as the curtain was about to go up after the interval. We were all instructed to leave the theatre and foregather on the pavement outside the theatre, which we did. This meant that, to all intents and purposes, Her Majesty the Queen (Pru's resemblance was quite striking), Sir Anthony Blunt and sundry footmen were to be found lounging about Shaftsbury Avenue on a sunny April afternoon, to the surprise and pleasure of passing tourists, who snapped merrily away. Presently the all-clear was given, and we took to the stage again, feeling strangely authentic. Then there was the occasion a little later when, for reasons too complex and technical to go into, I had to be re-circumcised, an operation requiring a local anaesthetic and a lot of bandage. This bandage resulted in a spectacular bulge in my pants that was certainly justified by Burgess's legendary endowments, and may have slightly increased my fan club, but which caused Pru as Coral Browne to perform a rather spectacular double-take on entering the stage. I know I should have showed her beforehand, but I was too shy. (Actually, I quite deliberately hoped to provoke the double-take, but it exceeded my wildest hopes.)

Despite the bombs (and the bulge), audiences continued numerous and appreciative, though perhaps never quite as appreciative as at the National; it was, like *Amadeus*, a perfect play for that theatre, witty, elegant, intellectually stimulating, not simply a good night out in the theatre. Alan has a morbid dread of being visited by celebrities in his dressing room, preferring to cycle off into the night with his Marks and Spencer's television supper in his basket, leaving me to deal with Liza Minelli, Shirley MacLaine, Richard Dreyfuss and the rest of the gang. It was very agreeable, as I received compliments on the play on behalf of the author, and sipped the champagne he was regularly given but which he detested ('You might as well have it,' he'd say, moodily). One day the phone rang in my dressing room. It was Mike Nichols. In all the prevailing euphoria, this didn't surprise me at all. 'I saw you in the play last night,' he said, 'and I have taken a vow that I will never make another film without you in it.' This, too, seemed perfectly in order. He asked me to be in a film in which I would be playing opposite Meryl Streep and with Shirley MacLaine and Gene Hackman. Fine, I said, fine. And the film actually happened (*Postcards from the Edge*). It was, in fact, West End stardom, though I wasn't quite sure that it felt like it. It was entirely enjoyable, but it didn't seem to be me, somehow. Perhaps this is because stardom of any sort was never something I had sought. It seemed like a wonderful bonus for something, a sort of working holiday. But it had nothing to do with my dreams, my visions, my ideals. My Catholic conscience may be responsible for this inability simply to be pleased when things are going well. What about Art, I would ask myself, constantly. Not that Alan's work was artless. On the contrary, it was a highly sophisticated, theatrically ingenious, intellectually provocative piece of work (the second part specifically concerned, indeed, with Art). It was not titanic, however, and some significant part of my nature is drawn to the huge, the grand, the epic, the life-changing. It's the Donald Wolfit in me.

Meanwhile, I was living the good life. My name and indeed face hovered thirty feet above Shaftesbury Avenue; I was earning, in my terms, fabled sums of money—my salary as an actor, my fee as a director and royalties as both. After three months I left the cast, to be replaced by the admirable Clive Francis, whom I then had to direct in the role I had just been playing without in any way suggesting that he should play it the way I did, another tricky little assignment. I was leaving because I was about to transfer *Shirley Valentine* with Pauline Collins to New York. I remember saying to Richard Eyre (then head of the National Theatre), 'My God, in three weeks' time I shall have productions on in the West End and on Broadway!' 'Remember this moment,' he said, quietly.

Five

This *annus mirabilis* was 1989. *Being an Actor* and *Charles Laughton: A Difficult Actor* came out in America simultaneously; and at the same time I was asked by Ismail Merchant to direct a film from Carson

McCullers's *The Ballad of the Sad Cafe* with Vanessa Redgrave and Rod Steiger. *Shirley Valentine* opened triumphantly; Pauline won the Tony. And my domestic circumstances changed completely. I bought a magnificent new house, and moved there with a new partner.

It was to be four years before I acted onstage again. I spent those years directing *The Ballad of the Sad Cafe* and acting in a few films directed by others, directing a number of shows and writing a couple of books. The splendour which seemed presaged in 1989 did not materialise. *Carmen Jones* at the Old Vic was, admittedly, a triumph, winning every award that year; by contrast, *My Fair Lady* the following year did not come into town despite a long and successful tour. *Shades* by Sharman Macdonald, again starring Pauline Collins in the West End, did not entirely work. *The Ballad of the Sad Cafe*, when it appeared, was that unhappiest of creatures, an arthouse flop. Despite a few important influential good reviews, the general response was one of impatient dismissal, with an undercurrent of 'Who does he think he is?' At a critics' preview in London for *Ballad*, I overheard the man from the *Mail* say, 'Isn't he a sitcom actor? He should stick to that.' The movies that I acted in either failed to appear or were disappointing. No theatre parts were offered. I was yesterday's ham. By 1993, I had had to sell my house. My relationship with my partner was teetering. My secretary sacked me. One of the books I had written (*Shooting the Actor*) was scuppered when the publisher was pushed out of the firm by his demented boss on the very week of publication, with the result that it was not reviewed at all except by the lunatic fringe of the embittered unpublished, who joyfully rubbished it. I had completed two pieces of work for which I had some hopes, but they were not due to appear until the following year. One was *Four Weddings and a Funeral*; the other was Volume One of a life of Orson Welles, *The Road to Xanadu*.

At this point, the American producer Frank Gero sent me Larry Kramer's play *The Destiny of Me*, the sequel to *The Normal Heart*, to see whether I'd like to direct it. I knew Larry of old—that impossible, indispensable man—and had very nearly played the central character of Ned Weeks in the London production of *The Normal Heart* when the Bush Theatre was intending to produce it. Alas, Larry proved so demanding and rude that they washed their hands of it and of him. It was one of those plays that is more important than good, a searing and terrifying report from the frontline of the AIDS battlefield, offering a wholly credible self-portrait of an unbelievably tiresome man who does something no one else is able or willing to do, goading and riling everyone, including—*particularly*—those on his own side, till things finally start to happen. The full terror of AIDS, the seeming impotence of science in the face of it, the vicious disruption of lives were all the more remarkably conveyed because of the dramaturgical clumsiness. No ingenuity was involved in this, no attempt to polish, hone, refine, crystallise. There was no time for that. The facts needed to be known, and no theory of the drama was going to come between the author and the audience. If it mingled Brechtian *Lehrstuck* with agitprop and threw in a good dose of soap opera to tear at the heart, what the hell? The important thing was that people needed to *know*. And it did its work. Just occasionally, the theatre can express more vividly, more responsively than any other medium the mood of the time; John Osborne's famous dictum about theatre being a minority art with a majority influence was never more apposite than in this play.

The Destiny of Me, its sequel, is an altogether more ambitious piece of theatrical art, mingling the theatre of information with classic Millerian American family drama, adding an element of Tennessee Williams in the sweet poetry of the relationship between the young Ned (Larry again, of course) and his older self, touchingly singing show tunes together. The older Ned spends half of the play in a bed, dying, until in a desperate and heroic final gesture he rips out all his tubes and spurns the medical establishment with which he has done battle from the beginning. Ned remains the same opposing man we met in *The Normal Heart*, and once again I was fascinated by the tension between the admirable thing done and the tiresome doer. The play was by no means perfect, but it was big and passionate and opened out the fight against AIDS in a powerful way. We offered the part to a number of leading actors, but they were all daunted by the piece on one level or another, either finding the form of the play hopelessly sprawling, or finding the character of Ned objectionable and irredeemably unsympathetic, or worrying about the ugly darkness of so much of it.

You can see what is coming. At the end of another of those casting sessions, just as it had in *Faust*, my voice emerged from my throat saying something which my brain had not authorised. 'I suppose I could play Ned and direct.' 'Could you? Would you?' And I found myself arguing that as he was in bed for a great deal of the play, I would be well placed to keep an eye on the production. Done. Everyone was delighted. We swiftly cast the other parts with some strength, and Frank secured a slot for it at the Haymarket Theatre in Leicester. Larry sent a message to say how delighted he was, and we all assembled in London to rehearse. We had a read-through which was very moving; Larry said it was already better than the off-Broadway performance. He talked to us at length about his life as an activist, about his messianic warnings to the gay community to contain its promiscuity, about what it is like to have been HIV-positive for nearly eight years. At my urging, we sat around the table for many days, getting to know the play and each other, pooling our experience of sickness, love, family. Jason Durr, James Kennedy, Patti Boulaye, Peter Woodward, Gary Waldhorn, Ann Mitchell: I name them all because when the director is also performing in the play, everyone else becomes part of the directorial effort, and because they were all so exceptionally free with their own emotions and life histories. When we hit the deck, we began to understand the swift-moving, kaleidoscopic form of the piece, a memory play, like so much American theatre. I had made a more or less successful attempt to learn the great rambling role before we started rehearsals, but for the first couple of weeks, my understudy would play the part, and I would slot myself into the scenes.

We began to run the play, and it began to work; better, I must confess, than I had thought it might. Larry meanwhile had buggered off without a word. One day he was there, the next day, gone. He sent a message from New York a week or so later to say that it was going so well he had nothing further to contribute; we never saw him again. We had seen very little of the producer, either. We were beginning to feel a little neglected. We moved down to Leicester and started the technical rehearsals, which were immensely complex; Christopher Woods (my then-partner) had designed a remarkable setting in varieties of transparent materials, able to evoke a high-tech hospital and then plunge us into the sitting room of Larry's family in Washington or create a rainstorm outside his Manhattan apartment. It took a lot of clever lighting and some ingenious blocking. All this was in progress when Paul Kerryson, the artistic director of the theatre, approached me during the break. Drawing me discreetly to one side, he said, 'I hope you and your actors won't mind too much if nobody comes to see the play.' 'I think we might,' I said, 'just a little. Why do you say this?' 'Because,' he replied, 'they never do.' 'What, never?' 'No, never,' he said cheerfully. 'Not plays.' 'What if the reviews are very good?' 'Doesn't make any difference.' 'Why do you do them, then?' I asked. 'The Arts Council likes it,' he replied. I returned to the technical rehearsal, thoughtful, and continued to try to fix the lighting while my understudy stood in for me.

In the fullness of time, I climbed into Ned's bed myself, and we ran the play, with me occasionally shouting out instructions from my recumbent position. Occasionally I would attempt a bit of acting, but then I'd spot something out of the corner of my eye which needed to be different—sometimes this was a performance, more often a prop—and would make a mental note to adjust it. The producers had meanwhile finally showed up and looked ashen; there was no advance in the box office, and we didn't seem ready to open. I reassured them that we would be ready to open; as for the box office, there was nothing that I could do about that. Tonight was the first preview; I now had to go off to give technical notes and then notes to the cast; after that I had to give a radio interview, then I had to apply a little makeup, then strap myself into the elaborate device which would enable me to bleed from many wounds at the end of the play. For one brief moment as I sat at the dressing-room window, I caught my own eye, and I realised what an idiot I had been. I had failed myself as both director and actor. As director, I had denied myself the all-important experience of sitting in the auditorium when most of the technical problems are solved and simply watching the show, half fiercely focussed, half dreaming the potential production within what was onstage. I had failed myself as an actor by denying myself the necessary selfishness with which an actor must pursue his quarry, the character. I had spent no quality time with Ned Weeks, just walking around with him, thinking his thoughts, sensing his muscular disposition, looking with his eyes. I had not spent time in rehearsal fighting his corner, discovering his strength relative to that of the other characters, creating the space in which he feels absolutely at home. Some of the most precious time in the development of an actor's work on a character is spent simply staring at himself in the dressing-room mirror, subtly shifting shape according to impulses that he doesn't quite understand, rolling the taste of the person he is playing around his tongue. This quick moment of eye contact with myself on the day of the first preview was the only moment of any of this I had had.

I snapped out of my reverie as quickly as I had fallen into it. And then we were off, off on the three-and-a-half-hour roller coaster of

Larry's public therapy. Of course the production got better, tighter, more communicative. That great actress, Ann Mitchell, as Ned's mother gave one of the most extraordinary performances I've ever been around, fearless and original, creating an enormous journey for the eighty-year-old woman, crystallising every moment of the way in startling and perfectly realised choices that etched themselves on the memory of the audience. This was the art of acting as I understood it, a primary creative act which went far beyond the expectations of what Larry had written, but which completely fulfilled it. Her final manifestation, as a sort of elderly hippie wise woman, gave the play an epic quality that the whole production should have had, might have done if I hadn't been playing Ned Weeks or if someone else had been directing it. The reviews were poor for play and production: of me, *The Independent* simply said 'Ned Weeks (Simon Callow, unimpressive).' So much for more than three hours on stage, painfully following Larry's Stations of the Cross. The producers disappeared. Audiences, as predicted, were pitifully small. But something remarkable came out of the poor attendances. Instead of them leading us to despair, we collectively and unspokenly decided that we would do the play as if for ourselves, striving to improve it night after night. And we did this. I have never before to this degree quite experienced, with a relatively large group of actors, the sense of chamber music, of each actor listening acutely to the others, maintaining ensemble, expanding here, refining there. And of course this communicated itself to the audience, who were drawn into the intensity of our work, to the sense of work in progress, of nothing having been locked off. Everything came into focus: the performances, the set, Kevin Malpass's beautiful title song which Jimmy Somerville had recorded for us, gratis.

Our leavetaking of each other was rather emotional. Stupid, stupid waste, I felt to myself, to have gone so far, to have learned so much together, and then to part. How will we ever move forward if not together?

Six

After *The Destiny of Me*, there was another hiatus. *The Road to Xanadu* came out and did very well for itself; *Four Weddings and a Funeral* did even better. There were more films, more opera, more books. Then, in 1996, Bill Alexander asked me to do *The Alchemist* as a co-production between the Birmingham Rep and the National Theatre. I had seen a lot of Bill's work and greatly admired it (he had directed Tony Sher in *Richard III* amongst many, many other productions for the RSC); once he told me a tantalising thing that is worth repeating here in view of what is evidently a theme of this extended theatrical history, my failure to become a classical actor. In 1982, he said, Adrian Noble had come to the RSC, was given *Henry V* to direct, and the brief of the artistic director had been to attempt to break the mould of the part, to reinvent Henry for the eighties. And a shortlist had been drawn up which finally consisted of two names: mine and Kenneth Branagh's. For whatever reason, Ken, of course, was chosen, and had a huge and merited triumph with the part, but when Bill told me this, some years later, I idly speculated on how different theatre and indeed film history—to say nothing of my own life—might have been had Ken been unavailable or unwilling. Whatever happened, he would have gone on to glory of one sort or another, because it is in his nature (and his stars) to have done so; perhaps my life would have been radically changed. Or perhaps the production would have been a disaster. Adrian had, of course, directed me in *Titus Andronicus*. On the last night of that for both of us very successful production, he had said, 'What next?' and I had replied, without hesitation, '*Timon*,' and he had said 'Done,' but in the event it wasn't me that played the part for him when he did it the following year in Bristol. By then I was doing *Arturo Ui* and *Mary Barnes* and shortly to play Orlando for John Dexter. My nature (and my stars) were carving out a very different route for me.

When Bill asked me to do *The Alchemist* all those years later, my familiarity with Ben Jonson's work was not extensive. I had had one of those small drama school triumphs playing Justice Overdo in *Bartholomew Fair* in a rehearsed reading in my second year; I had seen Guthrie's unhappy production of *Volpone* for the National Theatre at the Old Vic, where the actors impersonated the animals after which their characters are named, and Trevor Nunn's very funny production of *The Alchemist* with Ian McKellen and John Woodvine at the Aldwych. At one point, I had been about to play Sir Epicure Mammon for the Young Lyceum Company in Edinburgh. But I had not thought much about Jonson or about his plays. My friend Peter Barnes (whose version of the play Nunn had used) passionately believed Jonson to be a much greater playwright than the—to Barnes—preposterously overrated Shakespeare; this bizarre view baffled but intrigued me. Of course I said yes; it was now four years since I had been onstage, and whatever else it would be, it could scarcely fail to be challenging. I asked Bill which of the two central parts he wanted me to play, Face or Subtle, but he was happy for me to play either. Both McKellen and Woodvine had had a whale of a time with their roles; but I was particularly haunted by a moment at the end of the play when Face is finally revealed as Jeremy the butler, and McKellen had seemed frighteningly cold and empty, the face behind the many faces of Face pallid, clammy, like something you might find under a stone, or a snail out of its shell. Subtle was the actor-manager of the operation, the Grand Panjandrum of their show. With him the comedy was theatrical; with Face it was ontological, the archetypal actor. Who was he? I plumped for Face.

Then I went away and directed Cavalli's *La Calisto* in Glimmerglass, in upstate New York, and it proved rather difficult; at the same time I was writing an introduction to Lord Snowdon's collection of his theatre photographs, and that proved very difficult ('Oh, it's simple,' he said, 'you just have to write everything that's happened since Suez.'). The result of this was that I was not as well prepared for *The Alchemist* as I should liked to have been. I had planned, as per my now invariable rule, to have learned the part, but I failed to—failed to because it was curiously resistant. Or was it I that was curiously resistant? I had read the play eagerly, but rather slowly because it is stupendously obscure, having as its central element the rubrics of alchemy, with which I had had some truck during rehearsals of *Faust*, but which Jonson of course wilfully renders even more obscure than it is, since he regards it as claptrap with which Face and Subtle are pulling the wool over their victims' eyes. The London slang of the period is another obstacle; but worse than that, as I read on I began to feel that the spirit of the author was not a generous one. We are presented with a universe unredeemed by kindness, humanity or warmth. Mankind is paraded as without exception gullible, lying, cheating, deceitful, risible, crude. This is satire at its most savage. It reminded me of another author whose plays I had recoiled from for their cold, airless, loveless atmosphere: Joe Orton. I had positively disliked acting in *The Erpingham Camp* in Lincoln at the very beginning of my career because I felt that the author had only contempt for his creatures and indeed for his audience. The archness of Orton's style never made me laugh; it seemed entirely manufactured and mechanical, a formula. With Ben Jonson, there was another element. It seemed to me that he was writing not for his audience at all, but for other writers. He was showing off not only his vaunted classical learning, but also his dramaturgical audacity. The play starts in the middle of a furious row between two con men and their moll. It is almost impossible for an audience to follow, which means that the play gets off to a very bad start and requires huge energy and ingenuity to claw back the relationship with the audience. Everything that I read about Jonson confirmed his extraordinary arrogance: the conversations which his host, Lord Drummond of Hawthornden, recorded during a rather uncomfortable visit of his to Scotland, are particularly hair-raising in his utter contempt for all his contemporaries, above all Shakespeare, whom he regards as pitifully crude and ignorant. It didn't surprise me in the least to discover that he had once killed an actor; the only surprise was that he had needed a knife to do it: rehearsing one of his plays would surely have sufficed. (He had good reason to be fond of the classics: it was his knowledge of Latin that got him off the hook when he was condemned to death; because of it, he was judged under canon law, and pardoned.)

How to explain the disparity between the enjoyable production of the play I had seen at the Aldwych and the leaden text that I was now reading? The answer was simple: the RSC had used Barnes's version, which was in effect a translation. By ingenious substitution, obscurity was made transparent; by simplification, the plot was made comprehensible. I presume something of the same must have been done when John Burrell produced the play at the Old Vic in the 1940s, and when Guthrie did it in the early sixties. But Bill Alexander had decided against making a version before we started, preferring to cut the play as we went along in rehearsals, finding out what worked and what didn't, which was reasonable, but which meant that a series of amateur dramaturges—the actors and the director—were forever fiddling about with the text, depriving it of any sense of structure. Almost all the actors were novices in Ben Jonson; quite a few of them were novices, full stop. The situation was not unlike that of *The Relapse*, though this Bill was a very different one from Bill Gaskill—kindly, gentle, democratic. Subtle was played by the immensely experienced and powerful Tim Piggot-Smith, himself an actor-manager, head for some years of the Compass Theatre Company; Doll by the inspired comedienne (and demon improviser) Josie Lawrence, Abel Drugger by the wonderfully wide-eyed Jamie Newall and Sir Epicure by Geoffrey Freshwater, a stalwart of the RSC, huge in his appetite for acting and his carnal delight in text. The younger actors threw themselves with delirious abandon into the excesses of their characters, gladly leaping through the hoops Jonson holds up for them, joyfully crashing to the ground as the characters inevitably do. But we were all frankly somewhat at sea.

It was quite a large group, with many small parts which had little contact with each other. By no stretch of the imagination were we an ensemble. A Tyrone Guthrie or a Trevor Nunn might have galvanised the company, imposing a style on the production. But this was not Bill's way. Bill liked a play slowly to reveal its truth as a result of gentle inquiry. That would never happen here, in this alien world of Jonson. British actors are so deeply grounded in Shakespeare that they have to remake themselves when they approach the works of his contemporaries. One feels rather stranded, only realising in their absence quite how many and various are the ways in which Shakespeare helps the actor, by innumerable human touches, by the melodiousness and expressiveness of his verse, by the emotional freedom of his characters, by sheer knowing stagecraft. Above all there is a palpable sense of the author behind the work, not on the surface, as is so strongly the case with Jonson, whose personal presence is unavoidable: Look at me! Listen to this! Isn't this clever! And isn't everyone else stupid? Shakespeare's permeating presence is profoundly compassionate, one who has opened himself to the whole of human experience, rejecting none of it, submitting to its joys and sorrows, enduring its agony and its ecstasy, laughing and weeping with humankind, not at it.

These thoughts are of course terribly old-fashioned, and probably politically incorrect, but I suspect that most actors who have appeared in Shakespeare's plays, and indeed most people who have read them closely without seeking to deconstruct them, or semiotise them, or otherwise make themselves feel superior to them, will have felt something similar. And for God's sake, there must be some reason why Shakespeare's plays have travelled the world and have maintained an unbroken hold on the affection of audiences. This is scarcely the place to address the well-rehearsed arguments of the scholars of the Shakespeare industry, the analysts of cultural hegemony. My point is simply that contact with the works of Shakespeare is life-enhancing; contact with that of Ben Jonson, an indubitably brilliant writer and an acute critic of human folly, is not.

Scarcely the ideal mood in which to rehearse, you well think: active dislike of the author. Alas, these things happen. Often you fall in love with a play, as with a person, but closer acquaintance reveals a serious incompatibility. I flung myself into the play with everything I had at my disposal, and God knows the part of Face is a shape-shifter's dream: between dentures, moustaches, wigs, humps, limps, accents, I seemed to be giving the character actor's audition from hell—or perhaps for hell. During rehearsals people watched with respect and even possibly admiration; they never laughed. This is not always such a bad sign: one must beware becoming one's colleagues' court jester. The generous laughter that invariably greets the sallies of the court jester unaccountably dries up outside the friendly walls of the rehearsal room. But the reaction to my Face was somewhere between the slightly appalled, as if an acting machine had gone berserk, and the positively repelled. This was partly due to my conception of Face as Hitler. Certainly, there is no denying the sinister aspect to the character, as McKellen had so memorably shown all those years ago. What was so striking, I now realise, about his performance until that moment was that there had simply been a series of perfectly taken assumptions, as of masks effortlessly changed; one had no sense of who was underneath them. Rejecting a purely theatrical approach to the character, I was determined to find the man behind the faces who was so controlling, so vicious, so dangerous. Thrashing about, I came upon *Hitler: Psychopathic God* by Robert G. L. Waite, which advanced the striking thesis that Hitler's entire horrifying career had its origin in the absence of a testicle. 'Hitler has only got one ball,' the army used to sing during World War II, and Waite had discovered, he believed, telling evidence that this was no mere propaganda, but nothing less than the truth. Monorchidism, it transpires, is a well-documented medical condition, with many psychological consequences, in compensation for which the subject develops delusions of omnipotence, psychopathic rages, and a need for domination. In addition, there can be a chameleonic quality.

I had my man, I thought. So I attempted to plunge into the same murky waters whose depths I had so signally failed to plumb in *On the Spot*. I had in mind a dark angel of a young man, perhaps a little like Damon Albarn of Blur, and owing something to the Malcolm McDowell of *A Clockwork Orange*. I still believe that there was something to this line of investigation, but there were two questions: could I bring it off? And did it serve the play (as opposed to the character, a critical distinction)? On the first matter, it was perhaps a little difficult to imagine a stocky, nearly fifty-year-old greybeard like myself as the psychopathic cherub of my imagination, though I was, it must be said, losing weight very rapidly. Whatever else he is or isn't, Ben Jonson is very good for the waistline. Something about the speed of thought required, as well as the sheer physical activity, means that he is that unusual thing, an aerobic author (Shakespeare, being essentially compounded of emotion and sensuality, is the opposite); I toyed with marketing the Ben Jonson diet, but it would only, of course, be available to Equity members. I believe that I was beginning to achieve something of the strange and dangerous flux that I felt was at the heart of Face/Jeremy. But did it serve the play? Here I was less certain. The real problem was that I was never quite sure what the play was, mostly because of the language. No matter how vividly I presented the character, or how dynamically I played the actions, I could never do so through the language. I could do some lively things, physically; I could make all sorts of vocal shapes. But it was never through the medium of the text. It was above it, around, underneath it, but never through it.

I recognised a familiar problem from Shakespeare's plays: the playing of the clowns. I thank my stars that I have never been asked to play one of these, because I might perhaps have been tempted to accept it. Watching the joyless routines devised by wonderful actors to try to make these elusive personages deliver their goods is among the most excruciating experiences that theatre has to offer. At their best, the hapless actors create an alternative comedy to that presented by the text—physical gags, brutalisation of the text to create spurious humour; at their worst, the actors simply make that noise we all know, that strained facetiousness that makes you want to reach for a meat-axe. Even more dreaded is the directorial concept that turns the Shakespearean clown into the emcee from *Cabaret* or a skinhead. But then, to confound all this, an actor will suddenly appear to whom the text in question is the most natural thing in the world, and the audience roars with joyful laughter. I saw Tony Haygarth wreak this miracle on Touchstone, and, later, my friend Hilton Macrae, in broadest Dundonian do the same thing for—this will be hard to believe—Young Gobbo in *The Merchant of Venice*. I went backstage and accused Hilton of improvising the text. He hotly denied my accusation, producing the text to prove it. There is a manner of utterance, a stance in relation to the material, that releases it, bringing it up as fresh as paint. No doubt Morecambe and Wise's routines, to someone who had never seen or heard them, would be bewilderingly unfunny. For some reasons, certain actors have access to the Elizabethan sense of humour. I do not know whether it can be taught; but if it can someone should give Messrs Haygarth and Macrae a school of their own; I would enrol in it tomorrow, because there's a lot of good work there. And the clowns are at the heart, not only of the comedies, but of *King Lear*. Ben Jonson's text was for me like a Shakespearean clown text: it made all the noises that were clearly designed to provoke laughter, but remained absolutely unfunny, and, worse, incomprehensible. Now, for me, this is a catastrophe. The text is the starting point and the ending point of any performance of mine. My physical life derives from the text's rhythms, colour, music. I never heard the music of Ben Jonson, partly because, though I understood it, I could not convey its meaning. And because of this, I would, in performance, uncharacteristically, forget my lines. I was always in the past, thinking 'What did that mean? Did they understand it?' And the answer was generally no.

It was my first time back onstage after four years, and I was appalled. I had feared that I might be nervous. Not at all. As we stood backstage on the first night, Tim, Josie Lawrence and I, waiting to go on for that first very difficult scene, I was relieved and rather moved to experience again the uniquely satisfying feeling of contained adrenalin, of the engine ticking over very nicely, poised for the brake to be eased off, the foot hovering over the accelerator. But once I hit the deck, running (literally), talking twenty to the dozen, I had the feeling that I was playing in front of a foreign audience, to whom what I was saying meant nothing at all, and was, indeed, somewhat offensive. I would slip up, paraphrase, cut. Thank God for Tim's absolute stability. He is one of those rare actors who is able to keep an eye on everyone else's performances as well as give his own, and was always ready with a bridging phrase, a helping hand, lest one should need it. I needed it more often than I would like to admit. I was possessed with an almost irresistible temptation to stop the show, hold up a hand and say to the audience, 'Ladies and gentlemen, may I just ask if anyone knows what is going on here, or what is being said? It's a rather interesting scene, in fact, ladies and gentlemen.' And then we'd wind back, so to speak, and then perhaps we might feel that something was happening between us and them, to which occasionally they could have a response, rather than some arcane ritual of a forgotten tribe unfolding before them.

The design, by the brilliant and award-winning designer Bill Dudley, was part—a small part, but a part nonetheless—of the problem. Bill had an idea that it might be illuminating to set the play in a future where cars and the appurtenances of the motorway had become precious and hoarded; the setting was accordingly made up of these elements. Nobody in the audience could conceivably have understood the notion. What they saw was simply a house made out of a pile of junk. So we were in no-man's-land. Doors, so crucial to farce, were oddly shaped and for the most part unstable; often they stuck. Now, in any other circumstances, one would have lamented this, but it proved the salvation of certain moments of the production. Actors would find themselves unable to enter or to exit, and so one would be forced to improvise. Suddenly, the play came to life, we were doing something comprehensible (rising to the situation) which the audience were part of. On other occasions, my false moustache, due to my lifelong inability to find a spirit-gum which can withstand the copious flow of sweat which gushes forth from my upper lip the moment I step on a stage, would keep falling off, and I'd have to keep devising ever-more elaborate ways of pushing it back on. It was Face's false moustache rather than mine, so this was perfectly legitimate, and the audience adored it; they rose to Face's dilemma (which happened also to be mine) and something real was finally happening.

But such moments were rare, and any attempt to repeat them or fake them would have been unendurable, so we'd revert to the energetic ritual reanimation of the corpse of Ben Jonson. At one performance, I spotted out of the corner of my eye a deaf-and-dumb signer at stage left, vigorously translating the play. 'How come she knows what I'm saying,' I thought to myself, 'and I don't?' At which point, of course, I forgot what I was saying again, and Tim Pigott-Smith had to come to the rescue again, and I felt more than ever that I never wanted to do a play again for the rest of my life. Only at one point in the evening did I feel happy, and that was at the very end. It was not simply because it was the end, though of course one was very grateful for that, but because I had chosen in the final speech, when Jeremy addresses the audience, to speak each line in turn in one of Face's accents, ending with a line in my own voice. It was on that final line that I sensed a change in the energy between the stage and the auditorium. There was communication at last. We were in touch with each other. It was a huge relief; but it took three and a half hours to get there, and it was over in a second. I felt sure that there was a lesson in there somewhere, but what? Not, surely, that character was a barrier between audience and actor? That all actors should simply be themselves? I knew that both of those propositions were false, but there was something important to be gained from what I was experiencing at the moment. I was unable wholly to focus on it because of sheer frustration and exhaustion, but also because of two physical conditions which were perplexing and troubling.

The first was to do with my leg, or rather my foot: I acquired the condition that is known, graphically enough, as dropped foot. One's foot loses the capacity to extend upwards, which results in a droop, which in turn creates a limp. As I was supposedly cantering up and down stairs throughout the evening, this was very disturbing; I trust that audiences assumed that, with this dot-and-carry movement, Face had pulled one other physical trick out of the hat. Doctors looked long-faced when I brought the problem to them: it seemed to suggest a dead nerve, and when a nerve has died, nothing can bring it to life again. Fortunately it turned out that only the melanin of the nerve (located in the knee) had been destroyed—thanks to my habitually pressing my leg against my desk when I wrote—and the droop died, and I was bounding up and down again like a mountain goat. More significant was a constant hoarseness of voice, which, given the seven different voices that I was attempting, was somewhat distressing. Neither the Birmingham Rep nor the Olivier Theatre are particularly voice-friendly. The National, especially, seems to have some version of sick building syndrome; the air conditioning unendingly recycles germs. I bumped into Paul Scofield, appearing in and as *John Gabriel Borkmann*, and he had nearly lost his, a thing which had never happened before in his whole career. But though that might be part of the explanation, I knew that there was something else. My nose and my ears seemed to be permanently bunged up. I lost the top part of my voice almost immediately I started to speak. This upper register had been a real asset in the past; I played almost half of the part of Mozart in its further reaches. It was the excellent Pigott-Smith who put me on the right track: 'Dairy products.' I knew that I was prone to catarrh, had been since childhood, and I knew that there was a connection between dairy foods and its production. But when, at his behest, I gave up milk in my tea, cream with anything and—bitter blow—any kind of cheese, everything improved enormously. Someone else suggested an inhaler for the dressing room—nothing fancy: a ceramic pot with a spout and a glass tube protruding upwards which, filled with boiling water, wonderfully eased the sinuses. I had always regarded my voice as indestructible as long as I used it intelligently; now, as with so many other body parts, middle age meant that I could take nothing for granted. A later medical consultation revealed that I have a slightly crooked septum, and a very narrow Eustachian tube; the former promotes the production of catarrh, the latter means that the vibration of the skull during heightened speech (and that is what one is producing in any auditorium with over seventy seats) will tend to block my ears. So I have had to learn to sense the sound from the physical sensation within the throat rather than from the evidence of my ears. In fact, says A Harley Street Doctor, we all really hear ourselves through the vibration of the resonators; the blockage in my ears means that even that is unreliable.

I'm afraid to say we were counting the days to the end of *The Alchemist*—at least Tim and I were—and parted exhausted and defeated. Tim and I are both theatre warhorses; it's a sad sight to see two such troupers so dispirited. Trevor Nunn, director-elect of the National, came to see one of the last matinees of *The Alchemist* and very kindly said how nice it was to see me up there, dominating the Olivier stage, 'where I belong.' I smiled bleakly; it didn't feel like it. I personally felt that my path through the theatre in recent years, as chronicled here, had been nothing but negative. I seemed to be unable to find a context in which to function happily; I had lost my joy in creation; and I had lost any sense of who I was doing it for, or why. I could think of no reason to bother with the theatre anymore. I daresay I should be able to keep working in films; I would continue directing and writing—writing about the sort of theatre I longed to be part of, even if I couldn't actually find it, or my place in it. But then, dear reader, just when I thought it was all up for me and the theatre, the gloom lifted, the clouds parted, and everything changed.

Seven

Before describing the life-changer in question, I would like to make a small digression to describe another, one whose consequences have been considerable. Over the years, I had read with great pleasure many books about acting, historical, practical and theoretical. I devoured them insatiably, as some people read thrillers or science fiction. All, or most, had thrown light on some aspect of the craft; had clarified, defined, illuminated. But during the doldrums around the time of *The Alchemist*, I came upon a new version of a book which I had read, more or less uncomprehendingly, as a drama student, and I found that it expressed better than anything I had ever read everything that I believed about acting. Since I was at such a low ebb, it could scarcely have arrived at a better time; but it also identified with great precision something that had troubled me for some years. The book was *On the Technique of Acting*, the original version of the book known as *To the Actor*; its author was the great Russian actor and teacher, Michael Chekhov, and it restores the imagination to its central place in the acting process.

Chekhov revered Stanislavsky, as anyone who cares about acting must, both as a man and for his deeply sincere lifelong quest to discover the laws of acting. But Chekhov's conception of acting was as different from the older man's as were their personalities. Stanislavsky's deep seriousness, his doggedness, his sense of personal guilt, his essentially patriarchal nature, his need for control, his suspicion of instinct, all found their expression in his system. At core, Stanislavsky did not trust actors or their impulses, believing that unless they were carefully monitored by themselves and by their teachers and directors, they would lapse into grotesque overacting or mere mechanical repetition. Chekhov believed, on the contrary, that the more actors trusted themselves and were trusted, the more extraordinary the work they would produce. For him, the child playing in front of his nanny, improvising wildly, generating emotions with easy spontaneity, changing shape according to the impulses of his fantasy, was the paradigm of the actor. Stanislavsky was unable to look back on his own childish efforts without embarrassment. Stanislavsky believed that the only acceptable truth in acting was to be found within the actor's own experience, whereas Chekhov was profoundly convinced that the imagination was the key to all art. Acting, he said, should never be autobiographical; constant recourse to one's own experience would lead, he said, to 'degeneration of talent.' The imagination, once engaged, never lost its freshness and power, but the limited pool of individual experience quickly stagnated. The actor's work on himself should focus on encouraging and liberating his imagination, by consciously inventing and fantasising, rather than by dredging the subconscious. For Chekhov, fairy tales were the ideal material for his teaching: all plays, in his view, aspired to the condition of fairy tales.

As far as the text was concerned, Chekhov had an almost mystical relationship to language, crystallised by his exposure to Rudolf Steiner's Eurhythmy. He insisted on the vital importance of sound, of the vibrations which were released within the actor and within the audience by the consonants and vowels themselves. Stanislavsky had a very different approach. Interestingly, the great actor was what we would now describe as severely dyslexic, and always sought the subtext, the emotional life behind the words, rather than engaging with the words themselves, which he was notoriously inclined to paraphrase (to the rage of his partner at the Moscow Art Theatre, Nemirovich-Danchenko, himself a playwright). As for character, Stanislavsky believed it had to be constructed painstakingly, detail by detail. This was anathema to Chekhov. 'They call this work,' he wrote in *The Path of the Actor*. 'It is indeed work, it is tormenting and difficult—but unnecessary. The actor's work is to a significant extent a matter of waiting and being silent "without working." ' To him the all-important prerequisite for acting was 'a sense of the whole.' In a parallel characteristically drawn from the natural world, he believed that character was like a seed which contained the whole future life of the plant within it; if you grasped one phrase, one gesture of the character, you had access to all the rest; everything would fall harmoniously into place. Here was the origin of his famous 'psychological gesture,' the embodied essence of the character, a transforming and liberating principle of being which awakes the character into instant and complete life, and which then proliferates into a thousand details which spontaneously and harmoniously evolve. Stanislavsky believed that the actor must be wholly immersed in his character, who becomes a second 'I.' Chekhov, rather, believed that in a successful performance, the actor was always watching his character, moved by him, but never 'violating his personal emotions.' This *standing apart*, he said, 'enabled me to approach that state whereby the artist purifies and ennobles the character he is playing, keeping him free from irrelevant aspects of his own personality.'

Finally, and most significantly, Chekhov increasingly believed that the core of the theatrical event was to be found in the actor's relationship with his audience. For Stanislavsky, the audience was both intimidating and corrupting; he feared what he called 'the black hole of the auditorium,' but even worse, he feared his own desire to pander to the audience. To solve this problem, he erected the notorious imaginary Fourth Wall. Chekhov saw it differently. It was vital, he said, to engage with what he called 'the will of the auditorium,' to reach out to each member of the audience and share the creative act with him or her. 'I understood that members of the audience have the right to influence the actor during a performance and that the actor should not prevent this.' He spoke, mystically, of the actor *sacrificing* himself to the audience.

As the reader of the first part of this book will be aware, I was trained in strictly Stanislavskian principles, and it is the foundation of my work. But it comes at a price. Stanislavsky's noble work has served its purpose; but it is Michael Chekhov, it seems to me, who speaks to the crisis in our theatres. Audiences feel neglected. They are offered more or less naturalistic work which engages neither their imagination nor that of the actors. Prophetically, Chekhov wrote of naturalism: 'The legacy that naturalism will leave behind it will be a coarsened and nervously disordered audience that has lost its artistic taste; and much time will be needed *to restore it to health*.' He says that it breeds the necessity 'of giving its audiences a series of "powerful sensations" capable of arousing shock through a chain of pathological effects.' Since actors no longer think of themselves as creative artists, they have lost their self-respect. To be mere interpreters of the written word is not enough for them, or for their public, though it may be enough for some writers and directors. This is why the public increasingly turns to what is called 'performance art,' as if the theatre was not by absolute definition a performance art—as if the work of performance artists was expressive and imaginative, but that Marlowe, Ibsen, O'Casey, David Hare required mere photographic realism. It is particularly absurd to attempt to perform the classics with a naturalistic technique, the very idea of which would have been inconceivable to a writer of the Elizabethan period: in the admirable epigram of the Shakespeare scholar

303

Graham Holderness, 'an actor playing naturalistically in an inn-yard is likely to be confused with a waiter.'

Michael Chekhov was a highly individual artist, and it would be wholly inappropriate to hope for a generation of Michael Chekhovs. On the contrary, the central purpose of his teaching is to encourage the actor's respect for his or her own imagination and the freedom to create from it. It opens up the possibility of a full and reciprocal relationship with the audience, who can once again be introduced to the idea that actors provide them not with photographic facsimiles of life, but with works of art in which the actors' voices, their bodies and their souls are the medium for the production of unforgettable, heightened creations. In the past, when ballet dancers originated roles, they would speak of them as 'creations.' 'Every single performance that we give as actors should be of the same order,' in the words of Charles Laughton, an actor much after Michael Chekhov's own heart: 'Great acting is like painting. In the great masters of fine art one can see and recognise the small gesture of a finger, the turn of a head, the vitriolic stare, the glazed eye, the pompous mouth, the back bending under a fearful load. In every swerve and stroke of a painter's brush, there is an abundance of life. Great artists reveal the god in man; and every character an actor plays must be this sort of creation. Not imitation—that is merely caricature—and any fool can be a mimic! But creation is a secret. The better—the truer—the creation, the more it will resemble a great painter's immortal work.' The possibilities are limitless, far beyond the demands of naturalism. Why should the art of the theatre be more restricted in genre than any other?

All our lives in the theatre we have heard this maxim: less is more. Most of the recent great explorations of acting—Brecht, Brook, Grotowski—have been directed towards this *less*: stripping back. But very often less is simply less, and more is actually *more*. We must overcome our fear of the theatre theatrical when it comes to acting. A theatre is where we are. The theatre is the place where extraordinary things happen, where you see people behaving, not as they do on the street, but as they might in your dreams. Or your nightmares. When the shaman does his dance, nobody says: Could you do a little less, please? When the great comedians, the great clowns walk on stage, we know we are in the presence of something else, something well known to us but outside of our experience. At the very least an actor should, as the great Irish actor Micheál MacLiammóir used to say, 'displace air.' But he should also transform the energy in the auditorium; he should invade the collective unconscious of the audience and bring them up short. He should not merely quite interest them or quite amuse them. He should brand himself on their souls, breaking down the prison walls of logic. This used to be the job of actors, and of clowns. As Michael Chekhov might say, it requires a certain openness to the great forces of the universe to attempt it.

This is not an impossible dream. We have seen this sort of work within our own lifetime and on mainstream stages. When Ralph Richardson (another actor of whom Chekhov would warmly have approved) played John Gabriel Borkmann at the National Theatre in the mid-1970s, in the visionary final scene when Borkmann, nearing the end of his life, gazes down upon the docks, surveying the great world of capital to which he has sacrificed his soul, a noise escaped Richardson's lips that was like the hoot of an owl or the klaxon of some tiny tugboat negotiating the waters of Hades: *woo woo woo woo*. Nobody who heard it will ever forget it. It was unmistakably the sound of a soul escaping from the body. After the performance, I rushed home to find out what stage direction of Ibsen's had provoked this unearthly utterance, but there was nothing; nothing at all. I asked Peter Hall, who directed the play, whose idea it had been. 'Ralph's.' 'And what did you say when he first did it in rehearsal?' 'Nothing. We just knew that it was absolutely right.' The supremely rational Hall, directing a play by the great realist, Ibsen, acknowledged that instinctive genius can fulfil the play's potential in a way that logical solutions are unable to supply.

Film and television will perfectly satisfy the demand for realism. It is only when the need for something which goes further is felt that people have recourse to the theatre, an inherently poetic medium. Actor-poets are what the theatre as a unique art form needs. Why else bother to go to the theatre? The profound importance of Chekhov's work—he would have hesitated to call it a system—is that its aim is to breed just such a race of actor-poets. The beauty of his approach is that he offers a direct route to the actor's creativity by the simplest of means. Stanislavsky's anxiety about his own lack of creativity, his insistence that what Chekhov called 'inspired' acting was only available to the very few preternaturally gifted ones (of whom he did not consider himself one) and that only a cautious, logical method will pay dividends, is replaced by Chekhov's faith in the naturalness of the acting instinct, his conviction that, if left untampered-with, it will soar into the zones of human experience to which only the imagination has access. Using his work won't necessarily make you a great actor, but you will be approaching acting as an artist.

Eight

So, filled with all this inspiration, I was looking for something to use it on. It appeared, and it was indeed a life-changer. I had met the producer Brian Brolly during the course of working on a new musical called *The 5,000 Fingers of Dr T*, which Brian eventually agreed to produce. Shortly after we'd met for the first time, he called me about another matter altogether. Would I be interested, he wanted to know, in reviving Micheál MacLiammóir's 'entertainment,' *The Importance of Being Oscar*. He knew that I had briefly been Micheál's dresser, and that I had a passion for Oscar Wilde, had indeed, in my green youth, written a play about him in twelve scenes (the Stations of the Cross, of course. I was eighteen). Characteristically of him, his impulse to revive it was to honour MacLiammóir and his partner Hilton Edwards (who figure earlier in this book, and whose influence on my life had been enormous, out of all proportion to my actual contact with them). Brian had worked with them when Hilton had been head of drama at Telefís Éireann, and like everyone else who encountered them was intoxicated by their arresting mix of outlandish flamboyance and steely hard work, struck by the generosity of their contribution to the arts in Ireland and conscious of a quality in the work that was at once very old-fashioned but also strangely challenging, preserving somewhere within it the colourful audacity of Diaghilev, plus some of the jaggedness of the Expressionists. What it was that suggested to him at that moment that he should contact me, I don't know. I had already turned down a previous offer from the Dublin impresario Noël Pearson, partly because doing it in Dublin seemed simply suicidal, but mostly because I couldn't trust myself to escape the unforgettable cadences and inflections of MacLiammóir's unique voice. But Brian called at the right moment.

I had not so long ago gone to Dublin to make a radio documentary about the great man, and had sought out Pat MacLarnon, who had written to me after publication of the first edition of this book, saying that I was the first person to get Micheál right in print. He would, he said, be leaving me in his will Micheál's first theatre design, but that I was not to get too excited, he was expecting to be living to at least ninety. We corresponded for a while, and then lost touch, and it was with some difficulty that I tracked him down to his house in Bagot's Lane. There was a great clanking of chains, and turning of rusty locks, and the door swung open to reveal an ancient, pebbled-glassed midget of a man supported on sticks. This was the man who had been Dorian to MacLiammóir's Lord Henry Wotton. My initial shock was only increased by what followed. First, he thrust a half-pint mug into my hand and filled it with whisky, crying, 'I've got something for you.' He pulled open a drawer and with eager hands rummaged through a heap of bric-à-brac till he triumphantly produced a golden ring, one I instantly recognised as MacLiammóir's, a striking intertwining Celtic love-motif in gold. 'It's not real,' Pat cackled, 'Micheál was so tight.' Seizing my hand, he slipped it onto my finger; it fitted, effortlessly, which no ring ever does on me. After this Cinderella-like interlude, snatching my tape recorder out of my hand, chucking it onto a sofa, he took me into the garden, crying, 'I've got something to tell you. Micheál MacLiammóir wasn't Irish *at all*.' Shortly after, a book came out confirming this startling allegation—that the most famous Irish actor of the century was English through and through—whereupon everyone in Dublin immediately said that they'd known all along. But they hadn't.

It certainly explained the mysterious accent, which was a sort of essence of Irish rhetoric. In fact, years later I heard a recording of Herbert Beerbohm Tree, to whose Fagin Micheál had given his Oliver Twist in 1912, and the inflections were identical, though Micheál's vowels had been marinaded in Bushmills. But the passing on to me of the ring—the mantle, so to speak—seemed to me immensely significant. I suppose that what MacLiammóir represented to me was the idea that actors were not as others. The discovery that he had invented himself only confirmed this: we have to create ourselves as projected personalities. We come to embody in ourselves a certain aspect of human life, and then we have to find all the variations within that creation that we possibly can. A Maggie Smith or an Alistair Sim or a John Gielgud are rather extraordinary, rather exotic, and that is why we find them so compelling. The theatre is, in a sense, a zoo: we go to look at the animals not because they are identical to us, but because in some profound way we see reflections of ourselves in them; we compare and contrast their behaviour with ours, we see that they have similar dilemmas to ours, and, later, when we have left the zoo, we recall them in looking at ourselves and other humans. The extraordinary actors I have mentioned worked hard on themselves; on their personalities. They are not simply spontaneously original and unusual; they have developed, consciously or unconsciously, into more expressive creatures. In a sense, they forge masks out of their own faces, they loosen up their bodies, they extend their voices in order to reveal more and more. MacLiammóir put it vividly in his autobiography, *All for Hecuba*: 'As an artist works on his canvas and a prostitute on her body, so does an actor work on his personality.' The aspiration to be ordinary is a very peculiar one for an actor. It is, in fact, to aspire to something which is impossible on the stage: to reproduce real life. Why? The media of television and film do this quite brilliantly. In the theatre the attempt will always fail; hence the increasing disappointment of modern audiences with what is called the 'straight' theatre, and why they go more and more towards 'physical' theatre. The attempt to create verisimilitude onstage is always doomed to a poor imitation of life: it is scarcely ever more than *fairly*similitude.

Which brings us to Oscar Wilde, who denounced any form of naturalism, insisting that it is life that imitates art (or should). I had been mesmerised by Wilde from extreme youth: his wit, his anarchic spirit, his generosity and, of course, his homosexuality had all endeared him to me, but it was the coruscating, life-enhancing charm of his personality that I had fallen for so completely; I believed that I actually knew him. It was this quality of personality that MacLiammóir conveyed so brilliantly, but through the medium of his own only slightly less remarkable personality. The form in which he chose to introduce Wilde to the public was, as far as I am aware, of his own devising: in it he, the narrator, the storyteller, the *séanachai*, as Micheál preferred to say, tells the story of Wilde's life, becoming Wilde's characters, occasionally becoming Wilde himself, but never losing the spellbinding power of direct contact with the public. He had devised this form, initially I believe, because he knew himself to be physically unqualified to play Wilde, whose outstanding corporeal characteristic was sheer bulk: six foot two inches he stood in stockinged feet, with broad chest and wide shoulders; he had been quite capable of sending the pugilistic Marquess of Queensberry scuttling when the marquess and attendant thugs bearded him in his own house. I had the same reservations about playing Wilde; I am a little taller than Micheál was, but there could be no question of my dominating by sheer scale. So necessity had bred something much more interesting than mere impersonation. There is something deadening about an actor in a one-man show coming onstage in character; you are condemned to some sort of Ancient Mariner experience, eyeballed and lapel-grabbed, in which the storytelling is inevitably linear, one damn thing after another. Here, it was Wilde filtered through MacLiammóir, a conjuring trick in which Oscar was summoned out of the ether; the whole theatre became a giant Ouija board through the medium of which not only Wilde, but his times, his friends, his lovers, his characters, his mind itself, became manifest.

One might easily hesitate to attempt such a brilliant conjuring trick oneself. The piece requires great virtuosity, particularly in an inspired distillation of *Dorian Gray* in which the narrative voices multiply, first-person and third-person narration is juggled, whole sections of dialogue are kaleidoscopically compressed in a phenomenal evocation of the Victorian melodramatic theatre, and later, in another quite different sense, during a fifteen-minute condensation of Wilde's long prison letter *De Profundis*. A severe technical challenge, no doubt about it, but I thought I was up to it. Despite the unsatisfactory nature of so much of my work onstage, I had been steadily accumulating skills, strengthening muscles, getting ready for—for what, exactly, I knew not, but for something very difficult. What made me deeply nervous, however, was my ability to stand onstage as myself and tell a story: to be sufficiently compelling to hold an audience for over two hours. Micheál had been so arresting, both physically and vocally, but above all in his raconteurial prowess: he stands among the two or three most spellbinding conversationalists I have heard, with a very special gift of instant intimacy, both flattering and irresistible, and an ability to switch from high poetry to piercing observation to downright naughtiness and straight back again to poetry in a single breath. It was a nearly impossible act to follow, not least because his unique voice had never ceased to echo in my head through the thirty years since I had met him; indeed, I had been impersonating him unrelentingly down the intervening decades.

Patrick Garland, whom I knew slightly, was engaged to direct the show, and we immediately forged a great bond, based on our mutual love of Wilde and of the theatre and of poetry and of music and of storytelling and anecdote and practically everything, really. Rehearsal by conversation was our method, as we worked our way through the gorgeous snippets Micheál had assembled for us; being moved to laughter and tears as if we'd never heard them before. *De Profundis* was quite difficult to get through, sometimes: Wilde's emotional nakedness, especially in his lament for the children that he would never see again, is absolute, and his rehearsal of the terrible scene at Clapham Junction when he was transferred from one gaol to another remains, as the passengers on the platform spat and laughed at him, one of the most distressing of all accounts of human insensitivity. We found ourselves changing a few things here and there: Micheál sometimes got a fact, or a date, wrong, and (no doubt because of the time and place in which he wrote: Dublin, 1960) he could sometimes be coy. He refrained, for example, from quoting the Marquess of Queensberry's famously dyslexic card—'To Oscar Wilde, posing as a somdomite'—and it is quite hard to guess from the text why Wilde went to prison at all. Too witty, perhaps? Too successful? We made slight amendments to catch up with contemporary audiences, but otherwise I was astonished at what a good dramatist MacLiammóir proved to be. The piece did not, it seemed in rehearsal, depend on him; it was a piece of theatre in its own right.

So it proved. The first performance, at my suggestion, was a preview without lights or set. Brian, passionately determined to do honour to MacLiammóir and Wilde, proposed that we should start at Oxford University, in Magdalen College, Oscar's British alma mater; the warden, Anthony Smith, arranged it, and a curiously emotional event it proved. Wilde has only slowly been rehabilitated; when he was imprisoned, every organisation and pretty well every person with whom he had been connected instantly denounced him. Amends are only slowly being made. Our venture was beginning to take on the quality of a homecoming: for Oscar, for Micheál (a very nearly forgotten man, certainly in the British theatre) and for me. After playing in Dublin— Trinity; a godforsaken science lecture hall, without lights, but Trinity nonetheless—Belfast (*my* alma mater) and Manchester, where the response in the old Town Hall was unexpectedly passionate, we came to town at the Savoy Theatre, adjunct of the hotel where Oscar's dirty linen had caused such a stir at the Old Bailey. Here in Basil Ionides's astonishing silver-leafed auditorium, Chris Woods's witty set, a picture frame continuing and completing the silver theme, and Nick Richings's endlessly subtle lighting transformed the piece into a dramatic statement. In a one-man play, more than any other, the set and the location provide the geography of the show, carving it up, giving it a spatial context. We all believed that the piece was only worth doing if it was dramatic, not a recitation or a solo turn. There had to be a journey; contrast and conflict. Very often it was the lighting and the set that defined what that was. The Savoy, supposedly a difficult acoustic, proved completely accessible; I compared it favourably to the Olivier Theatre, where I had just been appearing in *The Alchemist*. The Olivier also holds 1,200 seats, but gives the impression of being a vast public place, as opposed to the intimacy of this auditorium, which glowed even in the dark and where one could whisper to the back row of the gods. (Maybe my voice had become overdeveloped in the past few years: Alec Guinness reports in his last book that when he came to see the show one of my fortissimi caused his very expensive new hearing aid to leap out of his ear, falling to the ground, where it shattered irreparably. Characteristically, he said nothing about it when he came round to the dressing room to say hello, though I did notice he wasn't hearing too well.)

For me, doing the show was a revelation, or rather, a rediscovery of something that I had almost lost. From the first preview, I experienced acting again as I had not known it for ten years. Firstly, I was creating characters. From the moment I started acting, that had been my joy and my gift. Transformation was the original thrill of acting for me; to become someone else. Here, as character succeeded character, I had the opportunity to submit completely to another principle of being, to experience myself quite differently. Part of this was a question of accent, of physical posture; but more and more I experienced the characters in terms of the way they held their mouths, and, even more significantly, the way they looked out of their eyes. Eyes and thought are indivisible; and speed of thought was crucial in this curious art form. I realised that it was like playing a musical instrument: the fiddler hits the string at exactly the right place, knowing exactly the note he will strike. At the same time, he is living through the emotional journey of the piece, which coincides exactly with the note he has struck. The note had been so elusive for me recently, and the emotional journey seemed to be unconnected to it. Equally, the orchestration of the whole piece—the dynamics, the colour, the rhythm, even, if lucky, the harmonics—were completely in my control. I was able to shape the evening from beginning to end. *Had* to: it would have been intolerable otherwise. This was something I always loved to do; but with other actors it is always a delicate matter. It's no good creating a rhythm if your fellow actor goes against it completely; it's no good trying to create a dynamic build if your partner is either unaware of its existence or bent on random shouting at the point where a delicate fortepiano is called for. My musical sense—so advanced, though I am unable to sing in tune—was given free rein at last. I was able, too, to explore physical and vocal gesture—the extended shape, whether of vowel or of arm, consciously creating an image packed with meaning, just as a painter might. 'Great acting is like painting,' as Charles Laughton had said in the passage quoted above. The art of acting, until the mid-twentieth century, has always been the art of gesture; it was for Brecht. In the past, the very recent past, the job of theatre critics was above all to report and evaluate the gestures invented by actors, not analyse them: to report them, to preserve them, to record their power (or feebleness). In *The Importance of Being Oscar*, thanks to what Mac-Liammóir had brought to it—a very nineteenth-century sense of theatre, learned with Tree—was a sensual, physical insight into another world of expression, another way of being, and it brought back to me my first impulses towards acting.

As a concomitant of all that, but more important than any of it, I was in direct contact with the audience, and I was speaking in my own voice, not Micheál's. There was, from the first moment of the performance, an unmistakable sound in the auditorium: silence. People were listening. The piece had been so constructed that they immediately knew they were going to hear a good story, well and wittily told (" 'There goes that bloody fool Oscar Wilde,' a gentleman in the street had audibly remarked as he had passed the poet by, and the poet turned to his companion and said: 'It is quite extraordinary how quickly one becomes known in London.' "), and they relaxed in a beautifully alert way: open to what they were about to hear, and expecting to be delighted. Of course they adored Oscar's jokes, and Micheál's jokes, but the important thing was that they wanted to know what was coming next and what it all meant. There was a surprise for me, though. I had thought that the poetry would prove an obstacle, especially the slightly wistful fin-de-siècle rhyming couplets favoured by the young Wilde (I never doubted that *The Ballad of Reading Gaol* would knock them sideways). But, to my amazement, the moment I start to speak verse, the silence deepened. I came to the conclusion that regular rhythms reproduce the sound of the mother's heart in the womb; certainly a most extraordinary contentment spread over the house as the lights went down and I started with those strangely prescient lines penned by the young Oscar: 'To drift with every passion till my soul / Is a stringed lute on which all winds can play, / Is it for this that I have given away / Mine ancient wisdom and austere control?'

I must confess that, beyond all that, the most remarkable experience for me was that I had a wholly new sense of warmth from the public. They seemed genuinely pleased to see me up there. I remember Olivier saying of his Richard III that it was in that role that for the first time he had really felt liked by his audience, and he was so happy about this that he forgot to limp. I, too, was taken aback; just as I was taken aback by the warmth of the reviews. It seemed that Wilde + MacLiammóir + Callow was a combination that made sense to the public. Even the press suggested as much. 'He returns to the stage like a king returning from exile,' said the Sunday Times reviewer—forgetting that he had given a rather sniffy review to my Face only about six weeks before. (Nicholas de Jongh, however, ever-generous and ever-perceptive, remarked that this was the kind of acting that had thankfully disappeared from our stages.) The first night was a celebration, not a judgement; it was given a frisson by my drinking glass suddenly rolling from the middle of a perfectly stable table and smashing itself on the floor, halfway through the first act, a reminder from MacLiammóir that he was still in charge. Among the guests that night was Oscar Wilde's grandson, Merlin Holland; another sort of a frisson. It was an immensely emotional, immensely enjoyable time that I had of it; the run only lasted nine weeks, but it was in constant development, communicating more and more directly with the audience. I found that I could use a huge dynamic range: when the audience had been caught, I could pare my tone down almost to a whisper.

Brian Brolly, I believe, had achieved what he set out to do: he had honoured both MacLiammóir and Oscar Wilde. This extraordinarily emotional man, with his strangely soft skin, like a baby's, and his fine white hair swept back to give him a profile strangely similar to that of the conductor Stokowski, and his curious vowels (bred in Belfast and complicated in South London), and his chuckling, grave, confiding manner, like a papal nuncio's, did everything in great style; not for nothing was he the man who had created Apple for the Beatles and the RUC for Andrew Lloyd-Webber. There was no way in which he could have made money from the venture, but he and his equally el-egant assistant, Peta Boreham, with her lynx eyes and wittily puckered lips, ensured that nothing was stinted; the first night party would have done honour to a troupe of a hundred, let alone the single stocky chap who wandered blinking into the great dining room at Simpson's in the Strand.

On the last night of the run, I made a curtain speech, urging every-one to come to Reading Gaol the following day, where I would speak the *Ballad* in its entirety; it was the centenary of Wilde's release from prison. Despite having made all the arrangements in advance, when we got there we were not allowed inside the jail (now a remand home for young offenders), though we were given a copy of Wilde's poem and a little pamphlet explaining how conditions had improved since Wilde's day. In an adjacent ruined chapel, I read the great ballad to a handful of onlookers, we shed a tear and then repaired with a few close friends to Reading Station in all its tawdriness to drink a bottle of champagne in honour of this intensely lovable, hugely flawed man. The confusion and the shabbiness of it all was wholly in keeping with Os-car's last days, somehow evoking the feeling of the famous remark Oscar made to Robbie Ross on his deathbed, with which Mac-Liammóir so brilliantly chose to end the piece: 'When we are lying in our porphyry tombs, Robbie, and the last trump sounds, let us pretend, dear Robbie, that we do not hear it.'

The run of *The Importance of Being Oscar* brought me full circle many times over. It celebrated the actor who made such an overwhelming impact on me when I was nineteen years old. It allowed me to honour the writer and man who had dominated my adolescence, a great glo-rious gay man of irresistible charm and fascination. It had restored me to the audience with whom I had lost contact. And it started my acting juices flowing vigorously again. In a sense, the show was the quintes-sential acting experience: telling a story, and transforming. Moreover, it gave absolutely free rein to my passion for words. Language was always the starting point for me, from my word-drunk childhood and adolescence, and my curious teenage resolve somehow to acquire A Voice with which to stir people. The ability to speak words in such a way that an audience was moved to profound thought and to deep emotion (and there was no mistaking those times in the theatre), to be remembered long afterwards, was really to have done something, in my view. Audiences have been discouraged from thinking and listening: it is said that they are no longer capable of these things, but in fact nothing thrills them more. I recollected what I still think to be one of the most theatrical experiences of my life: hearing the historian A. J. P. Taylor standing in a spotlight and speaking, without notes, for forty-five minutes on the origins of the Second World war was an incomparably exciting drama, and I believe that we plugged into something of that in *The Importance of Being Oscar*. More to the point even than that, the audience were called upon to use their imaginations. Here after all was one small bearded man in a velvet suit standing on a stage in a picture frame, with a table, a chaise longue and a glass of water beside him. Everything about the physical setting and my person contradicted the things and people I was evoking: Lady Bracknell, Reading Gaol, Salomé, the Old Bailey, Berneval, the boulevards of Paris. But the audience leaped to these images like salmon out of a stream. The theatre is precisely the place where you go to exercise that slack muscle, the imagination. It is the imagination's gymnasium.

My sense of having been embraced by the public, of them having affection for me (this sounds dangerously like an Oscar acceptance speech, I know) was somehow, it seemed to me, connected with them being able to place me. This is a very significant moment in an actor's life. Sometimes it comes about with a particular role; sometimes it is a more general impression of image. Hitherto, I had not been entirely clear in the public's mind: lively, energetic, ambitious, intelligent—but who *was* I really? To the press, I was the archetypal *luvvie*, that phrase coined to denote the fathomless contempt of British journalists for any actor who has the audacity to try to say anything about his profession which suggest there might be more to it than remembering one's lines and not bumping into the furniture; not an actor, but an *act-or*. As long ago as the eighties, I suppose this must have been a general perception; once, I was asked by a cab driver where I wanted to go, and I replied 'The National Theatre,' and he said, 'Where else?' Even earlier than that, in my very first digs in Edinburgh, the landlady had asked me what my job was; when I told her that I was an actor, she said 'I kent that. Ye mind me of the late Sir Donald Wolfit.' I was twenty-three at the time. I suppose I give the impression of being someone not quite of the present. My immersion in the past, from earliest childhood, seems to have given me a capacity to play the great dead with conviction (Mozart, Schikaneder, Verlaine, Handel; the list is endless). Micheál MacLiammóir, of course, seemed not entirely to belong to the present either, though it would have been hard to state exactly to which past he belonged: the theatre past, perhaps. And, to this extent, I identified with him. When Jessye Norman came backstage after *The Importance of Being Oscar*, I told her that I had been nervous of doing the show; Micheál had been such an exotic personality. 'And you're *not?*' she had asked in her most thrilling mezzo-profundo. The public, too, seemed finally to know what I was about, to know what they could come to me for. It was to do with words, with a certain flamboyance, a relish: guilty pleasures. They would not accept me in everything; they had no desire, it seemed to me, no need to see me play all the classical roles—but when I found the right part, I would be one of their favourites.

This sense of coming full circle had been underlined by my having written *Love Is Where It Falls*, a book in which I finally came to terms with the loss of two of the great loves of my life, my partner Aziz Yehia and my most intimate friend, Peggy Ramsay. In rereading all the letters we had exchanged, I had been obliged literally to relive the emotions of a decade of turbulence; and in publishing them, I felt both stronger and more vulnerable. As an actor, I felt more known as a person, which may or may not be a good thing. I read the book on the radio, and later recorded it on cassette tape. I read the letters of Oscar Wilde in the same formats, too, as well as *The Ballad of Reading Gaol*. I was aware that I had become a conduit for certain kinds of sensibility. So what next as an actor in the theatre? I had an idea, but before I had time to do anything about it, Patrick Garland had another, which threw me into a state of high excitement.

Nine

Patrick had read the first volume of my life of Orson Welles, *The Road to Xanadu*, and had been fascinated by Welles's relationship to the character of Falstaff, which he played three times: once in *Five Kings*, in the late 1930s (a sort of prototype of *The Wars of the Roses*); later, he trimmed it down to one evening, *Chimes at Midnight*, which played unsuccessfully in Belfast and Dublin in 1960; and finally (using his theatre work on it as a basis) in the film of the same name, which many, myself included, regard as his greatest, most personal achievement. Could we not, Patrick asked me one day, do the stage version of *Chimes at Midnight* at the Chichester Festival Theatre? Was it not the ideal show for such an organisation? Patrick had twice been the artistic director of that strange but stimulating space. Olivier had been the first director, and he continued to run it for a couple of years after he'd taken on the directorship of the National Theatre at the Old Vic, spreading the repertory over the two theatres; thus the world-famous productions of *The Royal Hunt of the Sun*, *Othello*, and *Uncle Vanya* had made their debuts there. The theatre had passed through the usual vicissitudes, constantly trying to redefine its relationship to the local community (a potentially large group comprising the inhabitants of several counties) while maintaining a high profile within the theatre at large. There had been a tendency in recent years for well-loved stars to use it as a platform on which to give performances which might or might not transfer to London; the standing companies which Olivier and his successor John Clements had maintained to such rich effect had long since been abandoned.

What Patrick was suggesting was a return to the feel of those days, if not to the actual structure. *Chimes at Midnight* would be a big, bold statement of vigorous epic theatre with a large, eager company; at the centre of it would be three actors, Keith Baxter (Hal to Welles's Falstaff both onstage and in the film, now to play the king); Tam Williams, young, dashing and passionate, as Hal; and myself as Falstaff. Welles of course had framed the play around himself as Falstaff, so Falstaff was inevitably the focal point of the action. I don't know why it had never occurred to me that one day I might play Falstaff. I suspect that subconsciously I believed myself to be physically unsuitable: Falstaff must be massive. His grossness is described by virtually everyone in the play who ever encounters him. But, on reflection, this seemed to me an absurd objection. Of course I would be grossly fat—Paddy Dickie, who had built the excellent padding for Gareth in *Four Weddings and a Funeral*, would see to that—and I was perfectly capable of producing the size of the man's personality. What fascinated me was to create the grandeur of Falstaff as well as the squalor. I had seen Falstaffs grand and Falstaffs squalid, but a Falstaff who united the two would triumph, in my view. I withdrew to a small town outside Amalfi

317

to lose myself in the man; with me I took Welles's script, the usual twenty or so books on the subject, and various editions of *Henry IV* Parts One and Two.

As I studied the plays, I began to have certain doubts about Welles's version. It was ingenious, yes, but Shakespeare's succession of scenes was so masterfully organised, alternating genres to depict the several worlds of the court, the highway, the battlefield, the tavern; the density of the relationships was so skilfully created, and his weaving together of the two great journeys in the play, England's towards a renewed destiny and Hal's towards manhood and kingship, so majestically achieved, that Welles's reduction of the plays seemed just that. In essence, he had arranged the material to tell the story of the twin pulls on Hal's affections between the king his father and the Fat Knight, alternative father and Lord of Misrule. The effect was Brechtian rather than Shakespearean, a sequence of more or less contrasting scenes with occasional interventions by an actor impersonating the chronicler Holinshed (Shakespeare's main source) to recapitulate the historical situation. I knew this already, of course; I had provided the script from which we were working. But actually working on a text, and in particular preparing to play a part in one, demands that you ask very different questions from those required by a mere study of it. Well, there was no point in dwelling on what was lost, so, apart from requesting a reprieve for the reinclusion of certain lines, one just got on with it. What was in the play was enormously rich, and a phenomenal opportunity for Falstaff; Welles ends *Chimes at Midnight* with the scene from *Henry V* in which Bardolph, Pistol, Mistress Quickly and Falstaff's page recollect his death. It was the Falstaff story, and no mistake.

Immersion in the text was like jumping into spa water—envigorating and exhilarating, resulting in tingling sensations all over. I roared the lines across the Amalfitano hills: the language, an occasional obscurity apart, is as natural and as organic as if it had just been transcribed from the mouth of the sort of sottish old party that I would sometimes run into on the hills: peasant bosses, cunning, drunken, randy, lordly, the centre of whatever group they were in. There were Falstaffs aplenty on the piazza at night, too, when I'd go to get my supper. The fascination of Falstaff, of course, is that though he chooses to spend most of his life in stews and taverns, he is perfectly capable of bantering with courtiers, and thinks nothing of being the partner in crime of the heir to the throne. The deeper I went into Falstaff, both from his text and from the books I had brought with me, the more extraordinary a figure he seemed, almost unprecedented.

He is widely described as Shakespeare's greatest creation and his best-loved character, which in the circumstances is no mean claim. The adjective *Falstaffian* has long passed into the language. We all know what it means: fat and frolicsome, gloriously drunk, bawdy, boastful, mendacious; disgraceful but irresistible; above all, fun. Not only, as he says in *Henry IV* Part Two, witty in himself, 'but the cause that wit is in other men,' Falstaff provokes cascades of comparisons both from critics and from his fellow characters in the play; to see him is to be irresistibly impelled to describe him. Because of all this, we feel we are very familiar with the character, comfortable with him; we know, we feel, who he is. It is easy to overlook quite how spectacularly original a creation Falstaff is. There is no other character in Shakespeare to match him; no other character in the whole of Western literature, as far as I am aware, quite like him. There are, of course, plenty of braggarts, innumerable sots, and reprobates galore. In the theatre alone there is the *miles gloriosus*, the bragging soldier of the Roman comedy of Terence and Plautus; mischievous rogues are a staple of the city comedies of Jonson and his contemporaries; and comedy through the ages, from Aristophanes to Terry Johnson, could scarcely survive without the figure of the drunkard. There are even somewhat similar characters in Shakespeare: Parolles in *All's Well that Ends Well*, Sir Toby Belch in *Twelfth Night*, elements of the Thersites of *Troilus and Cressida*. But even to mention these other characters is to affirm the uniqueness of Falstaff. In his never-failing wit, the abundance of his appetite and the bigness of his spirit, he contains—embodies, indeed—a life force which is so overwhelming as to be beyond type, certainly beyond morality and even beyond psychology.

Above all, he is extraordinary, in the two parts of *Henry IV*, because of the relationship he has with the young Prince of Wales, soon to be the great warrior-king, Henry V. Here is the seventeen-year-old heir apparent choosing to spend a large part of his life with a debauched, besotted, monstrously fat old reprobate in an East End brothel. It is as if the young Prince Charles had slipped away from Buckingham Palace to hang out with Francis Bacon—except that Falstaff is not only debauched, he is positively criminal: he and his dubious cronies beat people up in dark alleys and take purses from innocent travellers. Moreover, the young Prince Henry is no constitutional monarch's son;

he is the heir of the divinely anointed and all-powerful absolute monarch, who in his very person *is* England. What is going on, then? Is
this mere truancy? Is the boy simply getting it out of his system, sowing
his wild oats? Or is there something deeper going on? It seems
there is.

It would be one thing if Hal were to have taken up the company of
tarts and pimps, or to be slumming around with chums of his own age
and class, in the manner of Darius Guppy and the young Earl Spencer.
But it is quite another for the prince to have adopted this old scoundrel
not merely as a friend but as a mentor, and to have extended to him
every appearance of love and tenderness. What do they want from each
other, this odd couple? What Falstaff gets is, in a sense, obvious: the
excitement of being so close to the heir to the throne, and the opportunity to practise his habitual *lèse-majesté* at the very closest quarters;
and the delight of being connected to youth, the most gilded youth of
all, clearly has a tonic effect on the old rascal. But what does Hal want
from him? Alienated from his cold, anxious, controlling and guilt-
ridden father, he has clearly chosen Falstaff as a surrogate father, an
antidote to the sterilised atmosphere of the court, as commentators
have understood from as early as Maurice Morgann in the eighteenth
century. He is liberated, relieved, made to think by this fallible, permissive, funny creature of animal warmth, who inverts all the pieties
and the truisms he has had dinned into him. It is with Falstaff that he
discovers his humanity, the common touch which enables him to do
what his father has never been able to do, to unify the kingdom and
to reach out to his subjects in a way which they can understand.

But clearly Falstaff is just a phase that he's going through, the su-
pervisor of his rites of passage. To have this absurd, impudent figure
at his side after he has ascended his throne would be out of the question, an embarrassment and a dreadful example. He has to go, as Hal
understands from the beginning of the play; it is not a question of
whether, but of when. The scene at the coronation in which Falstaff
is rejected is both devastatingly upsetting and profoundly necessary;
Old Hal makes way for New Hal. There is a sense of elation at the
establishment of a new order, but also a tremendous sense of the price
that has to be paid. 'Banish plump Jack,' Falstaff says in Part One,
'and banish all the world.' Not all the world, perhaps, but some rich,
natural, flawed, human part of it without which we are all poorer. It
is this theme that Welles stresses in *Chimes at Midnight*; the title itself

has a consciously elegiac intent. For Welles the rejection of Falstaff was the death of Merrie England, with its natural harmony, and the birth of the modern world, willed and coldly realistic.

But as so often with Shakespeare, there is a sense of something else, deeper, stranger, behind the simple narrative, an impression of buried rituals, ancient lore, vanished conceptions, which account for the profundity of our response. With the Reformation, England had undergone a profound change just before Shakespeare's lifetime. It becomes more and more clear that the old faith, and the even older faith that it had absorbed, were still present in the dramatist's consciousness and that of his audience. The glorious, abundant, anarchic life in Falstaff, wholly credible within the world of the play, has an additional energy which is also somehow pagan, primitive, even primal. Shakespeare's sources for the character are, as always, diverse; first named Sir John Oldcastle, after the real-life rebel of that name, he was rechristened when Oldcastle's surviving family, the powerful Cobhams, vigorously objected to the scurrilous portrait Shakespeare presented. Sir John Fastolfe, whose name Shakespeare borrowed more or less at random, also really existed, but bore no resemblance, not even a faint one, to the character in the play. But behind these shadowy historical personages lay another figure, one often referred to in the course of the plays: the Vice of the medieval morality plays, with whom Falstaff is specifically identified again and again, corrupting the youthful hero and finally overcome himself. Dover Wilson's great monograph, *The Fortunes of Falstaff*, makes a very good and clear case for Shakespeare's reworking of this relationship.

Something in Wilson's thesis does not quite ring true, however. It neither explains the loving warmth of Hal's feelings, nor does justice to the magnificence, the positively regal expansiveness, of Falstaff's spirit. It was a little-known American anthropologist, the late Roderick Marshall, who pointed to the existence of another tradition which is more likely to be the fundamental underlying matrix of the character and the relationship. He identified Falstaff with a figure common to many cultures, known variously as the Substitute King, or the inter-rex. When the Divine King in these cultures becomes ill or incapable, a Substitute King is sought from among the banished descendants of the Divine King of the previously conquered peoples; once captured, 'this King for a day, a week or an indefinite period of atmospheric danger, has to perform rites of over-eating, over-drinking and excessive coupling . . . to reinvigorate the reproductive powers of nature.' His job is to initiate the heir of the Divine King into the rituals necessary to make the conquered soil flourish—secrets unknown to the conqueror. The parallels with Falstaff, Hal and the ailing Henry IV are evident. Marshall identifies various figures in different cultures who correspond to the inter-rex. Some are familiar and obviously Falstaffian. Silenos, grossly fat, drunken, debauched, followed, like Falstaff, by a dubious rout, was the tutor of Dionysos, and was one of the pre-Athenian gods, the children of Kronos, whose task was to shriek, dance and copulate as noisily as possible after midnight to waken the sun, which might otherwise slumber on indefinitely. Bes, the Egyptian god, tutor to Horus, is the god of life's pleasures, who presides over parties and children; he is described, in perfectly Falstaffian terms, as 'the old man who renews his youth, the aged one who maketh himself again a boy.' Janus, the Roman god, lord of the Saturnalia, is identified with the ancient god of sowing and husbandry, and presides over 'the golden age of eternal summer'—Merrie England by another name. It is at the Saturnalia that the declining powers of the sun are encouraged by sympathetic magic: roles are reversed, the Mock King is appointed, and perhaps at some point killed. 'The whole state becomes child-like to encourage the sun to do the same.' And thus, at the court of King Falstaff, Hal is able to become the child that his father's court refuses to indulge; and having been truly a child, he can then become truly a man.

These figures (and many more with striking similarities to Falstaff, always including great girth, bibulousness, hairiness, great age and seeming agelessness, profanity, sedition and endless wit) suggest the profundity of the archetype: but how did they filter through to Shakespeare? Marshall suggests a link. Researching the seventeenth-century mummer plays, which almost certainly derive from earlier folk plays which Shakespeare may very well have known, Marshall was struck by the familiar pattern of the characters: the leading character simply called the Presenter, but also known as the Recruiting Sergeant, Fool, Clown and Father Christmas; his wife Mother Christmas, also known as Dolly; the subsidiary characters Little Devil Don't and Old Tossip, the red-nosed drunk, his followers; and Saint George, also known as King George or any other English king, including Henry. Father Christmas is hugely fat, red-faced, wears bullock's horns and has a bladder. He is 'in many ways a bearded child who . . . though just turned into his 99 years of age . . . can hop skip and jump like a black-bird in a cage.' Father Christmas helps the king to fight two battles, but, like Falstaff, he is dismissed and dies.

Falstaff is part of the great culture of fertility which underlies our entire civilisation. We may control fertility, chemically and socially, but the grand patterns of human nature will not be so easily manipulated. Hal's initiation and growth to responsible manhood can only be achieved as a result of a negotiation with nature, a negotiation which we have largely abandoned. It is salutary to think that as recently as four hundred years ago, the greatest genius of the language placed a primitive figure right at the centre of his great saga of English life. C. L. Barber links him with what he describes as the holiday tradition of Festive Comedy, a tradition out of which arose the popular rituals and pageants licensed by the authorities at certain times of the year. These rituals, filled with mockery and raillery, inverting all society's values and hierarchies, are inverted, this inversion being embodied and per-sonified in the riotous, expansive figure of the Mock King, whom Bar-ber dubs 'the festival celebrant.' When the holiday is at its end, the temporary reign of the Mock King (or Substitute King or inter-rex) is over and he is dethroned, banished, even put to death symbolically.

The parallels with Falstaff are evident, and enlightening. Moving him into the realm of the mythic begins to make sense of him. His manner is nothing if not regal; whence comes this extraordinary aura of splendour? To say that he has deep roots, this Falstaff, is not to say that his branches and his foliage are of no significance: on the contrary. Falstaff as written by Shakespeare transcends the Mock King almost as completely as he transcends the Vice. Barber sums this up with an incomparable insight: 'It is as if Shakespeare asked himself what would it feel like to be a man who played the role of festival celebrant his whole life long? How would the belly of Shrove Tuesday feel from the inside? He moves, so far, in a realistic direction. But the man he creates is not merely a man. He is an incarnation.' The carnival aspect of Falstaff—for all these holidays at which the Mock King reigns are spe-cies of carnival—reveals itself in the flesh. Barber notes certain other parallels with the popular theatre, seeing Falstaff's anarchic counter-point to the main action of Shakespeare's plays as having a possible model in late medieval plays—the *Second Shepherd's Play* in the York Mystery Cycle, for example, with its satirical running commentary on the sublime events of the Nativity. Neither Barber nor other critics writing in the same vein are suggesting that, though Shakespeare was alluding to these early manifestations or prefigurations of Falstaff, he was doing so directly or consciously (though he may well have had opportunities as a young man to encounter these performances); the influence was working at a deeper level. 'So perfect an expression and understanding of folk cult was only possible in the moment when it was still in the blood but no longer in the brain.'

'The carnivalising imagination,' says Graham Holderness, citing the work of the Russian anthropologist Mikhail Bakhtin, 'creates gargantuan images of huge bodies, enormous appetites, surrealistic fantasies of absurdly inflated physical properties.' The body in question is not simply one man's body, but the collective body, 'undifferentiated into "isolated bourgeois egos."'[5] And the dominant style of carnival discourse is the grotesque. 'All that is bodily becomes grandiose, exaggerated, immeasurable.' This is the language of Falstaff, glorying in his enormity: 'I do here walk before thee like a sow that hath overwhelm'd all of her litter but one,' and more often than not, allying himself, as carnival figures invariably do, with the animal kingdom.

Now, what on earth is the heir to the throne of England doing consorting with an archaic, monstrous, majestic creature like this? We are no longer talking about befriending some fat funny chap you might meet in the pub one day, good for a laugh and getting pissed with and picking up a couple of tarts and shagging them. If that was what young Prince Henry wanted—and there's no accounting for taste—he or his minders from the palace could certainly have arranged it. But we're clearly far beyond a simple notion of wild oats being spent. To begin with, Prince Henry—rechristened Hal by Falstaff, and referred to as such by Falstaff alone—is not just a laddish toff, nor is he the mealy-mouthed scion of constitutional monarchy: he is *the Prince*, England's son, soon enough to be England himself. Driven away from the court, where sickness and anxiety reign, he is in need of wisdom and energy and liberation before he can assume his proper responsibilities; he needs to complete his education, and it is to this mighty pagan creature that he has been drawn for the necessary extracurricular tuition. It has been well said that Hal is on holiday when he is at the Boar's Head. Falstaff is the living embodiment of holiday; this is Hal's gap year, spent exploring not interesting Third World countries, but the further reaches of his own psyche.

All this meant that I came back to England ready for rehearsals in

324

what you might think was a slightly overwrought state. But I was well and properly prepared; I knew the text intimately. I had prepared myself physically. I cannot pretend that I knew how to bring the Carnival world onstage with me, but it was never far from my thoughts. In the same way that Shakespeare's kings have to stir some atavistic sense of the divinity of the monarchy, some deep and dark tribal sense of the leader as hero, Falstaff had to echo back through the millennia to the very birthplace of human life. This is what my teachers at the Drama Centre had taught me: the capacity of a great text to embody the core of human experience, to take us into the haunted back room of history, the place at the base of the cortex where all of our dreams live, Jung's collective unconscious. And yet the richness of Shakespeare is not that his characters are simply archetypes, but they are also recognisable human beings. They have surface psychology as well as the larger underlying pattern; they have an identifiable social status as well as a purely theatrical existence. In particular, I had become completely fascinated by the fact that what scholars call 'the Shakespeare moment,' the historical crossroads at which he started to write, was Janus-faced, a culture striding forward to the Renaissance but still deeply steeped in a nearly pagan, largely rural world. Only in Shakespeare, of all his contemporaries, do we have the phenomenon of fairies and half-human characters coexisting happily—in dramatic terms at least—with kings and boatswains, lovers and soldiers.

To let Falstaff live on this level was my ambition. To do this as a solo effort is not a promising possibility. Patrick was sympathetic to my task, but he had a quite sufficient job of his own in trying to weld together a group of disparate individuals, yet again, into some semblance of a team, given the now absolutely standard inability of over half of the company to speak verse at all, alongside some who had been speaking it for over six decades. Keith gave a sterling lead, speaking the king's great text impeccably (why is this part not considered one of the major roles?); others gamely contributed. Then there was the problem of how to help some of the younger actors to inhabit the low-life characters without going off into the world of Monty Python. But the play was a great help: its juices are so rich, its range of emotions so immense, that we all became caught up in its truths. Rebecca Egan as Doll Tearsheet and Sarah Badel as Mistress Quickly became supreme in that area where Shakespeare seems to diverge into a kind of surrealism of imagery; while Tam and I went as deep into the relationship between Hal and Falstaff as we knew how. Tam has a most uncommon quality on stage (and in life): a sort of chivalry, an inherent decency which we may assume to be a crucial part of Hal and the ideal he comes to serve. The aspect of Hal's nature that demands he must wallow in the mud of human life came less naturally to Tam, but he found a most original way of being drawn to Falstaff, as if the old git were like some fat, permissive old sow, warm and succouring; our scenes together were full of this need for the comfort of the sty. We had improvised for hours on end with a friendly barmaid drawn from the company; much wine was consumed, much licence taken. I had not improvised in that way for many years, and it was richly instructive. Tam was brilliant, too, in showing Hal's reckless determination to prove himself on the battlefield; his verse-speaking was not yet what it has become, but the triple tension between himself, Keith and me was powerfully present, while Timothy Bateson and the late Johnny Warner as Shallow and Silence stopped the show at every rehearsal.

Indeed, run-throughs became very powerful and very moving. I felt utterly secure, vocally—for some reason, despite my almost continuous immersion in Shakespeare's sonnets for over ten years, Elizabethan prose seemed to suit me better than verse; the same, oddly, was true for Charles Laughton. Though a great poet as an actor, prose was his natural form of verbal expression. It allows you, of course, greater latitude in phrasing; I suspect that that is what released me, too. The metronome is not always ticking. I was also in good shape physically; I had rehearsed in my padding from the first day (for orthopaedic reasons as much as anything else) and began to believe of myself some of the things that the other characters say of Falstaff. Once or twice during rehearsals we would go on the huge, daunting, wide-open Chichester stage to try out a scene or two. I quickly realised something troubling: I had pitched my voice in the very lowest end of my register; this was fine in the rehearsal room, but on the larger stage it rendered me inaudible from anything further back than the front few rows of the stalls. I increased volume, but the strain on my voice was immediately evident. I started to think of ways in which I could unpick the vocal patterns I had created, but all too soon we were into technical rehearsals, with a fierce performance load. It was evident, too, that the vast stage required more people than we had to give it a semblance of life—whole armies were reduced to two or three people, the court a tiny handful; and technical deficiencies which had seemed easy to ignore in the rehearsal room were blown up horribly. Christopher's epic setting, too, due to compromises in the workshop, was not quite what one had imagined it might be, though his costumes remained superb. The play (or rather, the version of it which we were doing) itself seemed excessively episodic; it was also too long, and large chunks, including some particular ripe Falstaffian passages, had to go; but I could scarcely complain, with my text outweighing anyone else's by two to one. In fact I was beginning to wonder whether there was not altogether too much Falstaff, for my own and for the play's good. Shakespeare rations his appearances very carefully, but Orson had not been so frugal.

We worked on during previews, and everything got better (which of course is by no means always the case with *improvements*), though I was conscious that I was pushing my voice, and thus my performance. No matter how many Fisherman's Friends I might consume, no matter how many hours I spent bent over the inhaler, there was a roughness to the voice which would not go away, and I seemed to be producing catarrh by the bucket. This is not to say that everything was lost; and something was gained on the day in the dressing room when I was playing with the various pieces of false hair that I'd asked for. Having grown my own beard to bushy length, I didn't need them, but on impulse I stuck my beard into my hair, and accidentally produced horns of hair identical to the ones on the famous Barberini faun at the Villa Medici in Florence. The archaic, pagan, mythic element in my appearance for which I had been groping was suddenly there; I ran down the corridor dragging people in to look at it, and they all obediently agreed that it was remarkable. For me it was the transforming element which unlocked something inside me, some prancing, feral quality that was quintessential Falstaffian.

The first night (how often you have had to read this) was triumphant; friends were astonished; fellow actors came and gave unmistakably sincere plaudits; the management hugged themselves with delight; old Chichester hands thanked us for bringing back the days of glory; and the press was simply dreadful. For production, set, cast, version, but above all for me, the hatchets were out. Frequently I was attacked for not playing the part the way the ailing Robert Stephens had played it for the RSC: a jester at his last gasp. The graph that I tried to trace in the play, from the riotous Falstaff of most of Part One to the figure in relative decline in Part Two, went unnoticed. I had made the fatal mistake of writing a long, slightly academic piece in *The Independent* containing some of the ideas above, and many critics felt obliged to point out the disparity between what I was describing and what they saw, or simply to deride my having written at all. 'It's not an essay, Simon,' began the *Daily Mail*'s reviewer, my old friend Michael Coveney, relentlessly dismissing the performance as heartless and superficial. This came as something of a surprise to my fellow actors, with whom I had stood onstage, performance after performance, sobbing. The theatre management was somewhat in shock, too; they had thought that this was the harbinger of a new golden age for Chichester. As will by now be clear, I am not my own greatest fan, but I know that as Falstaff I achieved something of weight and power and comic force, something which went beyond mere portraiture and helped to evoke the amazing landscape of Shakespeare's imagination, where, as Graham Holderness so memorably puts it, 'a chivalric medieval prince could meet a band of 16th century soldiers led by a figure from immemorial carnival.'

Audiences who came enjoyed it, regardless. The show was by no means without flaws, but there was something there to chew on, something not wholly unworthy of the great plays Welles had conflated. Towards the end, there was a gentle tapping at the door and Alec Guinness stood before me. I was in the dressing room he had occupied when he played Shylock. Nobody had much liked that, either, though I thought it overwhelming. I had stood with him on the last night of the production as he took off the tiny amount of makeup with which he transformed himself from the solid citizen that was now standing in the doorway before me into the embodiment of a Wailing Wall that he created in the role. Now he was there, with his huge, grave Cheshire Cat smile, mirthless but kindly. 'I enjoyed. Some of it. Very much. You were very good. The honour speech is the best I have ever heard it. Really marvellous. Penetrating.' And that was it. He declined any offer of drink or refreshment and disappeared.

I had by now become obsessed by the plays, and a year or so later I wrote a small book on each part for Faber and Faber. They express everything that now excites me more than anything about Shakespeare's plays: the possibility of catching 'the Shakespeare moment' in all its complexity, containing within the whole spectrum of pagan, Catholic and Renaissance. I shall play Falstaff again, and next time I shall win.

Ten

After *The Importance of Being Oscar* closed, such was my taste for the genre that I immediately started to think of another subject suitable for the same treatment. The field was limited to writers whose lives were as interesting as their works (or vice versa); they had better write in English, too. An evening in translation was ridiculous, which swiftly ruled out Balzac, to whom I had been strongly drawn. So I plumped for the obvious: Charles Dickens, whose public readings I had reconstructed on television some years earlier. It was only then that I had learned about his history as a performer of his own (and other people's) work, and it seemed to me that the theatrical theme would lend itself very well to the sort of presentation I had in mind. The thing that pulses through his work like an electric current is his almost carnal need to communicate with his readers. His relationship with them far exceeds in intensity any other relationship in his life: those with his children (devoted but formal), his wife (initially affectionate, ultimately disgusted), his friends (passionate but erratic), or even his hidden mistress, Ellen Ternan, thirty years his junior; we can only conjecture at the nature of his feelings for her, though it is safe to say that an element of play-acting—he adopted the persona of 'Mr Tringham' to throw the curious off the trail—must have formed a large part of them.

His relationship with his public was something quite different, altogether more real. Simply put, he needed their love in order to exist. Like a lover, he responded instantly to their moods and to their wants; they for their part expected him to speak for them, to express their joys and their miseries, to create for them their monsters and their comic heroes. Almost shamanically, he was possessed by their spirit, the great popular Carnival spirit. His playful, metamorphosing language—distorting, personifying, now engorging, now withering, transforming a city into a single breathing organism or an individual into a swarming mass of grotesque features—is the vernacular mode at its most extended and its most exuberant. He embodies appetite, glories in extremes. This is where he can most be compared to Shakespeare, his immediate superior in the pantheon of English literature—in this, and in his matchless creation of character. Only in the matter of sex is he oddly reticent, almost blank. In every other area, his inventiveness is

329

almost surreal, which is why adaptations of his books, attempting to treat him as a social realist, or a psychological realist, are so rarely successful. The screen and even the stage have a confining effect on the psychedelic fantasias of Dickens's pen.

In true Carnival spirit, Dickens's work is a performance, generous and unstinting, for his audience of readers. We never forget that it is him that is doing it, nor that he is doing it for us. And, on cue, we laugh, we cry, we moan, we applaud. Dickens is the writer as actor. In life, of course, he acted whenever he had the opportunity, finally, triumphantly, taking to the boards with great tours of England and America in which he 'read' his own work. In fact, his readings were memorised and meticulously rehearsed and performed with a degree of histrionic energy that drew the stunned admiration of the theatrical profession. His audiences (who also knew his books by heart and who were more or less chanting the words in unison with him) were in ecstasy: they thronged to him in their thousands and the performances became cathartic experiences, both comic and tragic, on a grand scale. They were unprecedented events, only to be compared today in their emotional fervour to rock concerts; but they were implicit in the novels themselves: the literal performance was the logical extension of the literary one.

I proposed the idea to Brian Brolly, but he was dubious, perhaps imagining that he would lose money on the show, and having no personal memory to honour in this particular case; moreover, he wanted to concentrate on *The 5,000 Fingers of Dr T.* So I went to my old colleague and chum Howard Panter, who immediately agreed to commission a play from the author I had identified as being self-choosing, Peter Ackroyd, writer of the definitive modern biography of Dickens and a man strongly fascinated by the stage, as his novels will testify. I called Ackroyd, who expressed enthusiasm, I sent him a copy of *The Importance of Being Oscar*, and within ten days he'd written the play. Or *a* play. We then sat down with several bottles of wine and tore it apart, then in a week's time he wrote another, then after a few more bottles, and another two days, a third. The last version came overnight, and we were ready to rehearse. Patrick Garland had agreed to direct; Christopher Woods would design; Nick Richings would light it. It was always intended as *Son of Oscar*.

Patrick, Peter and I then sat down for a week, rooting out passages that were too long or too literary, seeking the illuminating detail, the theatrically apposite phrase or gesture. Peter, who had never written a play before, showed an amazing theatrical audacity: a passage in the second half where he has Dickens mesmerise the audience ('Keep your eyes on me. Look at me. Now my eyes are on you. I need to be connected to you, and you to me. Then I can come alive. Then I can transform. I am Quilp. I am Pecksniff. I am the Artful Dodger. I am Vincent Crummles.') is almost pure theatre—nothing happens, nothing is said except to create a spell. He had, too, written a text for me— the narrator's text, that is—which was like my voice, but not quite my voice. It was 'Simon Callow' rather than Simon Callow. Could I reach it? Yes; I relished the slightly archaic locutions he put into my mouth: 'please to note here that . . .' and the constant questioning of the audience: 'How did Dickens, at this triumphant moment in his career, how did he see himself? Think of himself?' There was no equivalent to this in MacLiammóir's text. We engineered a conscious *hommage* to *The Importance of Being Oscar* in the Sikes and Nancy sequence (invariably, of course, known as Sid and Nancy), where, building on the melodramatics of the *Dorian Gray* sequence, we would try to convey something of the impact of how Dickens performed the piece through the medium of the Victorian theatre. Dickens of course simply stood at a lectern; I would never do that. My great predecessor Emlyn Williams had, as I did on television, bearded himself and donned Victorian evening dress during his recreation of the readings; that was of course dead against the principle so ingeniously formulated by MacLiammóir.

Our work went with astonishing speed; after that first week spent around the table, Peter more or less withdrew and Patrick and I and our gallant and indispensable stage manager, Matthew Darby, rehearsed the first half in one week. That weekend I learned it. The following week we rehearsed the second half, and I learned that. It is an interesting fact that learning a one-man play (or a very long speech, come to that) is much easier than learning dialogue. One only has to ask oneself what comes next, and why, in a one-man show, whereas in a scene with others, one has to know what it is that they say in order to supply the bridge to what one says next, and why one says it, without actually having it in one's brain. There are actors, it is said, who learn the whole script, but the danger there (apart from the difficulty of motivating oneself to learn something that one will never say) is the death of spontaneity: it is a very healthy thing to hear what another actor says to one as if one didn't know it, while knowing the rhythm.

On the Tuesday of the next week we took it for its very first outing to Campbell College in Belfast, where my old Queen's University chum Neill Morton was head of English (he's now headmaster of Portora Royal, Oscar Wilde's old school; is this some kind of stalking?). It went down a storm; similarly in Wilton's Music Hall, where we did it once for local residents, free, and then again for a gala audience. And then we took it on the road. At first, all was not well when we hit the paying customers. In the rather antiseptic surroundings of the Victoria Theatre Woking, it seemed rather like a lecture with funny voices. Howard, the producer, was worried: where was the theatrical excitement? Why would anybody want to spend an evening at the theatre seeing a show like this? Did we think this was the Open University? Or what? Thus goaded, Patrick and I took thought. The problem, I quickly realised, was that I was telling the audience the facts of Dickens's life, not sharing them with them. In fact, the question Howard was raising was, who was I? If I was someone who knew it all, that was boring. But if I was someone who had found out some rather astonishing facts about this famous but in his private life little-known man, then it might be something else—a discovery, a revelation. I also needed, I realised, to allow the characters to manifest themselves through me, rather than labour to produce them. It was a distinct technique—the same, of course, as with *The Importance of Being Oscar*, but different because of Dickens's infinitely broader approach to the creation of character. Wilde wrote pretty well within one class, and with the exception of Lady Bracknell and Lord Caversham, pretty well within one well-modulated tone of voice. Dickens, in true Carnival manner, creates a series of grotesques, described in the most extreme physical and metaphorical terms: it is indeed the surrealism of Dickens's imagination that excited me most, the wildness at his heart. There is the same wildness in his approach to life, and we saw comic potential in that, as when, for example, he ascends Mt Etna during an eruption, insisting that 'he must look into its smoking mouth,' is rained down on by cinders and ashes, stands triumphantly on the very brink of the volcano 'looking into the flaming bowels of the earth'—and then comes down again 'alight in half a dozen places.' All of this is from a letter of his; we mined every book we could get our hands on for nuggets of that sort.

And very soon we realised that we were on to something very powerful indeed. The combination of Dickens's monstrous and moving

332

characters, his intoxicating language, and Peter Ackroyd's beautifully phrased rhetorical enquiry into his life, seemed to work even more effectively than *The Importance of Being Oscar*; Dickens's scope is simply wider and the range of his sympathies greater. As we toured the country, audiences were loudly and generously vocal in their enthusiasm; they wrote me letters by the dozen, they queued at the stage door, they stopped me in the street. I had never been on tour as an actor, except for those early and deprived days of Joint Stock and the Young Lyceum, where we struck the set the moment we'd finished the show, and where we most often played one-night or two-night stands. Now, the whole joyful business of feeling feted in each new venue was deeply satisfying; it seemed as if I were engaging in one of the historic activities of actors, taking to the road, peddling my wares, creating a bit of a stir, making direct contact with an audience which would only otherwise know me from the screen. It was entirely life-affirming; most of the theatres, being nineteenth-century in construction, were wonderful to play in, and most of the hotels (and, yes, indeed, I was staying in the best hotels) were well appointed and smilingly efficient. I got to see an England much of which I didn't know. As the tour went on we seemed to gain momentum, playing in ever-larger houses. In Glasgow we played in Matcham's magnificent Theatre Royal, 1,500 seats, packed to the ceiling, roaring back its witty appreciation. I have scarcely enjoyed anything as much in my career. And London, first at the Comedy and then at the Albery, simply built on this. I had the best crop of notices of my career; even Nicholas de Jongh, breaking that habit of a lifetime, managed uncomplicated praise. I'll bet he was cross when he saw it printed the next day. We broadcast the show live by Internet; the first (and I believe only) show to be so broadcast. After we finished transmitting, a man e-mailed us from Chicago to say that it had been wonderful, now he'd draw his curtains, light a couple of candles and watch it all over again. Eventually, this version was shown on BBC television, and is now a videotape.

In fact, the show has never stopped evolving during the two and a half years (at time of writing) over which we have been performing it. Every audience teaches us something new. We drop characters, passages, biographical details; very occasionally we add more. The greatest challenge is to speak normally to the audience I'm addressing, to befriend them, not to seek to dominate them; anything that comes between them and me must go. I know a lot about Dickens, but not as much as many other people (Peter Ackroyd, for example). My pleasure is to introduce the audience to this exceptional human being, and they may come to feel, as I do, grateful that such a man existed on our planet. It is the energy of the man, first of all, that I am aware of, in performance. Inhabiting his world, becoming his characters, becoming *him*, I am seized by the suprahuman vitality which so overwhelmed his contemporaries, and which enabled him to perform such prodigies as writer, as editor, as social reformer, as magician and, yes, as actor. His public readings were the rock concerts of his day, high-octane emotional events which sent his audiences into heightened states of consciousness—aware of course that they were in the presence of the most famous man of his time, famous and loved, not an invariable combination—but also mesmerised by the shape-shifting powers and visceral intensity of the slight, rather haggard man with his wispy beard standing at his lectern, so dramatically lit by the encircling gas jets.

It is this sense of being a conduit for energies and powers that I don't entirely understand that is the essential experience for me of doing this show. In fact, I scarcely play *him* at all: I play me, I suppose, or 'Simon Callow' as imagined by Peter Ackroyd, but he's my quarry, the one I set out to catch, to lure his strange genius into the auditorium for a couple of hours. Sometimes it is a little spooky. Sketching him in very lightly at first—a gesture, a facial flicker—as the evening goes on, he insists more and more, and then, almost at the end, at his farewell reading tour—'from these garish lights I vanish for ever more'—the emotion of parting from the audience from whom he drew his whole strength, on whose love (unlike that of individuals in his life) he could utterly rely, takes me over, makes my body sag, my voice crack, my eyes fill. Then, above all, I believe, the force is with us, an absolute blur between me and Dickens, now and then, the theatre and history.

It's impossible for me not to be moved, even as I'm performing, by his trajectory, by the unending giving of a man who was not necessarily generous by nature, by the sheer practical impact of a man who lived above all in his imagination. This secretive creature to whom public life was oxygen and alcohol all in one, a performer through and through, the writer as actor. As an artist he is inexhaustibly various, which means that everyone will take something different from him. In Dublin, they detected levels of wit unsuspected by the people of Chicago, who were above all stirred by his social conscience. In New York, they loved the majesty of his prose, while in London his evocation of the city creates a curious sense of identification and pride. In Belfast, it's the size and the earthiness of the characters that ring bells. Everywhere people are surprised by his life. 'Who knew?' said a not-uneducated friend in New York. 'I thought he was a vicar who sat in a cottage just churning out novels.' And everywhere, in the end, people are moved, not simply by the work, or by the life, but by the fact that such a man existed. That's the most frequent response—a sense that the whole race is enhanced by one of its members having attained such immensity of spirit.

And the jokes, too, the best jokes ever written. Dickens's laughter must be the most titanic since Jove's. It shakes the theatre, as it shook his tiny body, right up to the exhausted end. To have been all that, and done all that, and never to have stopped laughing is quite something. Doing the readings in the end killed Dickens; he couldn't speak for ten minutes afterwards. The effect on me is the opposite. It's a mountain to climb, but the triumph at the top is nothing but exhilarating. Playing *The Importance of Being Oscar*, I was sometimes drained by the languor, and crushed by the sadness of his decline. Dickens blazes from first to last, but instead of burning me up, he fills me with life. I have to watch the voice—thirty-seven characters and one towering genius take their toll. But the spirit soars, and in the end that is what matters. Dickens's embrace of life. He was a dynamo, and anybody who touches him receives the gift of life.

When we took the show to Broadway, we added two elements that I had always wanted to include: conjuring, and a moment of old-fashioned theatre bravura, when the scrim at the beginning of the play, through which I am dimly seen, as in gaslight, suddenly whips away and the light is nearly blinding. The tricks are simple: a flash of gunpowder, and a glass of water that turns to red wine, but they get their gasp and their round of applause, which is what Dickens would have loved, and what turns his life story into a celebration everywhere. Almost everywhere.

The experience of New York was striking and sobering. All my acting life, I have imagined that one day I would play Broadway, and that I would feel deeply comfortable there. The reality proved a little different. For a start, we took a gamble, arriving at the end of the long season which had started with Osama bin Laden's cadres killing themselves and three thousand other people in the wreck of the World Trade Center. By April of the following year, when we arrived, audiences had been through the wringer: shows had folded, others had heroically survived, the city had put money into sustaining the season, but everybody was on their knees, longing for the season to end, for the Tonys to be distributed and for everything to clam down until September. In these circumstances, the arrival in town of an only slightly known British character actor in a one-man show about a dead British novelist was likely to cause only the mildest of stirs ('They don't know he's dead,' the doyen of New York agents, Robbie Lantz, reassured me). Our New York partners told me that I must be seen at every first night party; at the first one I attended, a very nice man who wrote for *Playbill* rushed up and told me that he was thrilled that I was finally appearing on Broadway. 'You have a following, you know,' he swooned. 'It's tiny,' he continued, 'but it's *definitely* a following.' How deeply true his words proved. Meanwhile, he was busy demolishing the performance of the evening's star. Then he launched into a scientific analysis of the show's chances of survival. Clearly this was what interested him much more than the merits of the show. On Broadway, theatre is like horse racing: it's a gamble, and the thrill is in who wins and who fails. Put a little more brutally, it's a blood sport, in which failure, and bloody failure at that, is a cause for deep satisfaction. There are always expressions of profound sympathy, but there is no mistaking the feeling that something necessary and useful has happened; in this Darwinian world, the fit who survive feel their survival the more acutely by contemplating the demise of those who do not.

In this harsh world, image matters a great deal. It is necessary to remind the Tony Award voters of your existence at every possible moment—even before you've opened. My visibility was low: the producers had decided not to waste money on the massive cost of advertising in *The New York Times* on a show which would mean little to anyone, but to concentrate the budget on promoting the wonderful notice we were sure to get from that newspaper. If the notice wasn't wonderful, it was understood, we were dead. The only evidence of our existence was on the marquee of the theatre, but since there was no sign there of our presence on the rest of the outside of the building, it looked rather as if we had just closed rather than being just about to open. I began to feel increasingly like Sydney Carton heading ineluctably towards the guillotine, a sacrificial victim—but for whom or what was I sacrificing myself? And was it a far far better thing, what I was about to do, than I had ever done before? And was I going to a far far better place than

I had ever known? A week before I was due to start previews, the English actor Henry Goodman had been summarily relieved of his starring role in the first cast change of Mel Brooks's *The Producers*. I had by chance seen his performance on the Saturday matinee while the takeover cast was still in previews; nipping into the restaurant next door during the intermission to book a table, I had been addressed from behind by an oddly familiar voice. Turning, I found myself face to face with Mel Brooks. I burbled that I was watching his show, golly, *what* a coincidence, and wasn't Henry doing well? 'Maybe he'll get there,' Brooks growled. 'He's a good kid.' Later that night, in the same restaurant, after having had supper, I bumped into Henry and congratulated him. He was quietly hopeful, feeling that at last he was beginning to make the role his own, despite the producers' desire that he should offer a carbon copy of Nathan Lane's original performance. We embraced. Next in the queue waiting to talk to him was Mel Brooks. 'Henry, I love you,' he said, enveloping him in his arms. The next afternoon, the Sunday after the show had come down, sitting in his dressing room, Henry received the call from his agent in England telling him that his Max Bialystock was history; he was out of the show from that moment. This made front-page news in *The New York Times*. For once, even the Broadway community seemed a little amazed at the savage laws of their own jungle, and there were vague murmurs of some kind of protest, but in the end the only rule is survival, and Henry had failed. The Broadway community, much spoken of, really does exist. It needs to. There is no London equivalent. In London, actors inevitably bump into each other, but they don't huddle together for comfort in quite the same way as New York actors. Life in London seems a little less precarious.

This is partly because of the existence of a dozen newspapers, all of whose critics' views are significant, rather than just one; of equal importance is the staggering cost of putting on a show in New York, which means that nursing something which is not an absolute smash hit is prohibitively expensive. The hire of the theatre is a huge cost, but it's only a beginning. All you hire is the shell of the building, so everything else has to be installed: lights, sound equipment, show relay. Then every theatre comes with its labour force, which you pay for regardless of whether you use them. When our tiny little set, with its rostrum and its one-and-a-half picture frames, was installed into the theatre, it took four times as many people four times as long. When, near the end of the technical rehearsal, there were still many elements of set dressing that had not been installed, I said to the production manager that I would gladly stop working (it was 10 P.M.; we were due to finish in an hour) to allow them to do these small things, he replied, 'Oh, I couldn't possibly call the boys now. I couldn't psych them up to work at this hour.' 'But I thought they were working till eleven?' 'Yeah, but on standby.' 'What does that mean?' 'Well, they're standing by.' 'Standing by for what?' 'Just standing by.' 'But not actually able to work?' 'Yessir.' 'So what are we to do?' The first preview was the following day. 'It's perfectly acceptable,' he said, 'for there to be missing elements at a first preview.' 'To whom?' I said. 'To everybody.' 'Not to me,' I said, and resumed the technical rehearsal, prepared to do bloody battle. Oddly, the things that needed to be done were done by the next morning.

There are other curious aspects of the Broadway experience for a Briton which are for the most part simply different, and thus mildly disorientating. In Britain, calls are given five minutes before real time. Thus the so-called half-hour call is given thirty-five minutes before the curtain goes up, the five-minute call ten minutes before and beginners' is five minutes before curtain up. This sounds complicated, but it is for us the habit of a lifetime, and always ensures that there is a certain leeway. Broadway calls are given in real time, which makes the British actor (me) feel slightly panicked. In our case, we couldn't afford to instal an entire show relay system for the one performer who was after all onstage throughout, so the dressing room was oddly, eerily silent before I sallied forth to do battle, the audience more a rumour than an actual presence; the stage manager, the veteran Frank D. (Franklin Delano) Hartenstein, had to come and deliver the calls himself, which he did with the air of doctor giving particularly bad news as gently as he could. In Britain the company manager is an ever-present figure in the theatre and has been with the company throughout rehearsals, co-ordinating the whole running of the show; he or she is a kind of buffer between management and cast, implementing management policy, but at the same time protecting the actors. In a one-man piece, he or she becomes a sort of floating crisis manager, ensuring the happiness of the enterprise. On Broadway, he or she is more strictly a management representative, who comes to the show at the half-hour (i.e., actually half an hour before the curtain goes up), makes pleasant small talk, then once the show has started goes to the box office, collects the take and returns to the office. I missed my affable, omnipresent British company managers terribly.

This is a mere matter of creature comfort. More disturbing—seriously unnerving, in fact—is the system by which critics do not attend the first night itself, but filter in to the last few previews. The effect is to extend the agony, because one has three or more completely unreal performances to deal with instead of one. Producers are naturally very anxious that the performances that critics attend should be as lively as possible, so they pack them with people on complimentary tickets who know that the press are in; they cease to be theatre-goers and become part of the hanging tribunal. Of course, since there is only one review—it is universally know as The Review—the night that The Reviewer is in is particularly tense, all the lesser *tricoteuses* focussing on Mme. Defarge. I knew all this, of course, from having directed *Shirley Valentine* on Broadway thirteen years before. What I hadn't realised is that while in Britain press night, which is also, of course, the first night, is tempered by the arrival of waves of cards, telegrams, bottles and bouquets, and by a procession of people to the dressing room urging you to break a leg, have a great one and fuck 'em, on Broadway there is nothing and no one. One comes into the theatre on the press nights to deathly silence; it is like checking in to Sing-Sing. Somehow one knows when the press are in, and when The Reviewer himself is in, though no one has officially told you and no one alludes to it. The two press nights for *The Mystery of Charles Dickens* were particularly hellish. Where up till then there had been, in the American fashion, roars of laughter and cheers and unstinting rounds of applause throughout, all this suddenly ceased as if on an order, and I played the jokes and extravagant fantasies of Dickens to solemn and apparently resentful silence.

The first night proper is something else, potentially a different sort of a horror. This is the night when the great and the good are invited, as many famous people as can possibly be packed into an auditorium, celebrity wall-to-wall and up to the rafters. The promise of a party at the end of the evening is no guarantee of good humour on the part of these people, but on this occasion, they proved a kind of dream audience, restoring—again, as if on a command—all the handclaps, laughs, gasps, rounds of applause that had so suddenly stopped on the two previous nights; they topped it off by a very violent and sudden standing ovation which rather took me by surprise (this essentially un-British phenomenon always seems to contain within it the possibility of becoming a lynch mob). It was wonderfully exhilarating, as was the presence of a wildly enthusiastic selection of the G and G backstage in my dressing room, now properly crammed with blooms, bottles, cards, telegrams. Richard Adler, with whom I had a rather sticky time when I directed his show *The Pajama Game* in London a couple of years before, surprised me, not only by being there at all, but by hugging me warmly and proclaiming to the room, 'This man has to be the best actor in the world,' to which proposition no dissenting voice was heard.

It was all enchanting, but it meant absolutely nothing at all. That is to say, our fate had long been sealed. The life-or-death verdict was even now, such are the refined tortures of the twentieth century, speeding electronically into the hands of the publicists and the producers. At least this procedure relieves us of the ordeal which I too well remembered from *Shirley Valentine*, when the general manager had rushed up to me, waving *The New York Times* in his hand, demanding that I read out The Review to the thousand or so people gathered in front of me. As I approached an appropriate vantage point from which to do this, I quickly scanned the notice and realised that though Pauline was enthusiastically reviewed, as was the set and the production, Willy Russell was dismissed as having nothing to say and not saying it very interestingly. Willy was sitting immediately in front of me, his shining face turned pleasantly towards me. Under no circumstances was I going to utter a word of that deeply stupid opinion; on the other hand, it seemed wrong to read out praise of Bruno Santini and myself for our contributions. So I wove my way through these various landmines, blurting out the few absolutely ringing phrases in praise of Pauline, and then sat down abruptly. Everyone was surprised at the brevity of the review, and deprecated Frank Rich's woeful inability to write at proper length, but then carried on happily quaffing and munching. At least we were spared that at Sardi's after *The Mystery of Charles Dickens*, though I did notice Howard exploding with a kind of desperate merriment which my long experience of the man has taught me is a pretty clear indication that something is wrong, and just to prove it, shortly after, this conspicuously party-loving man took his leave, with many apologies about having to get the pregnant wife to bed, etc. I dismissed this clear indicator of doom from my thoughts, drank a great deal and ate what was left (that's the trouble with first-night parties for one-man shows: there is only you to talk to, which everyone wants to do, and food rarely reaches the mouth that has been working so busily for the last two or so hours). I tottered off home to a vinous sleep. My partner Dan was already up when I woke the next morning and he had the paper in his hand. I knew from his face, and from my vivid memory of Howard's the night before, that it was all up for us, and I was half-inclined not to read it, and go out and have some breakfast and let life just go on, but I took pity on Dan and opened the paper.

The first two lines read: '*The Mystery of Charles Dickens* at the Belasco is like an evening in the company of the English teacher of your dreams. Or nightmares.' I couldn't read any more; I didn't need to. We were dead. It was the words *English teacher* that did it: everything we had achieved over the last two years in pushing the show away from being a lecture and into being a piece of theatre—a process which had culminated in the version we staged at the Belasco, to the general agreement of everyone who saw it—was destroyed at a stroke. What was needed, frankly, was a simple rave, like 'You will never be able to face your grandchildren if you tell them that you didn't see this show when you had a chance,' that sort of thing.

What we got, as I later discovered after forcing myself to read the piece from beginning to end, was an ambivalent, occasionally enthusiastic, now and then carping kind of an essay on the show. In London, it would have passed as a good, even a very good, notice, in conjunction with other equally good reviews; here, it was death. I discovered that a *New York Times* review is not read, it is decoded. People are not asking of the review, would I like this show? but: will it sell? Not is it any good, but do I need to see it? Is it one of the shows that one really has to get a ticket for? The answer to all these questions, was, in our case, perhaps. Maybe. Who can tell? And that was our death certificate. The other reviews were, without exception, ecstatic. Clive Barnes in *The New York Post* gave it a review that made me blush, as did the thought that, fifteen years ago, he was the critic of *The New York Times,* and the same review in a different paper would have ensured a thriving black market on the sidewalk outside the theatre, the same sidewalk that would now be sadly unpopulated.

And it was. Houses were small, even tiny. But then a little miracle happened. The people who came were there because they wanted to be. All complimentary tickets stopped instantly, and only those who were interested in Charles Dickens, or in me, or—praise be!—both of us, came to the show. And they were wonderful audiences. They did the very thing I had been assùred no Broadway audience could do: they listened till you could cut the silence—a silence which prevailed even over the roar of the air conditioning in the adjacent building, over the shriek of the police cars and the wail of the fire engines, over the festive sounds of the Puerto Rican Carnival Parade passing by Forty-fourth Street. They laughed and cried, and, at the end, however few of them there may have been, they rose to their feet. They were waiting for me—sometimes it seemed like the whole audience—at the stage door, asking for signatures and promising to truss the critic of *The New York Times* up on a lamppost. 'That man doesn't know what he's talking about. It's a disgrace.' They apologised over and over again. I smiled serenely and said how happy I was that the people who came seemed to like it so much. And I meant it.

Backstage at the Belasco, that fine old theatre, on the wrong side of Times Square, but only just, all Tiffany lamps and square columns, the ceiling covered in Golden Age frescoes, its auditorium like the foyer of a grand hotel, still splendid despite the wanton tearing out of its boxes for the short-lived *Rocky Horror Picture Show* some years earlier, all was calm support. The crew were rather scholarly and literate; my dresser was writing a novel set in the eleventh century; the master carpenter, whose job was to bring out the scrim at the top of Act One and Two, was a world traveller, with complex and subtle views about human life, which he would patiently expound up to the very moment the curtain rose. The two prop men—their task was to replenish the water carafe at the interval—walked to and from the stage with expressions of infinite sadness, as if remembering times when there really were props. Billy, the stage door man from Charleston, South Carolina, with the boisterous air of a true denizen of Catfish Row, carried on as if we were the biggest hit in town. I lived in hopes that the ghost of David Belasco would put in an appearance, as he was rumoured to do; any extra bodies in the auditorium, dead or alive, would have been welcome. His presence, though never actually manifested, was very strong. Above the auditorium was his private apartment, the walls richly decorated in Renaissance style, in which had been drilled a peephole through which he could view the traffic on the stage; it was now in rat-infested ruins, with an air conditioning system brutally smashed through those splendidly ornate walls. Here Belasco would ravish young ladies in the company, later appearing in the foyer dressed in clerical garb, a character from one of his own melodramas, just waiting to be set to music by Puccini. Dickens would have been fascinated by him.

On the street, things were rendered more difficult by people constantly coming up to condole with one. Long faces, hands on shoulders, much sad nodding of heads. 'It's okay,' one would say, 'it's fine, much better this way than a long-drawn-out death.' In fact the notice of termination was not posted till the week before we closed, because, like everyone else on the Great White Way, we had been waiting for a possible Tony nomination. There was some confusion as to which category we should be entered for: Best Performance, Best Play, Best Entertainment. There was really no question of my *winning* a Tony; the only hope was that I might secure a nomination for one, which might prolong the show's life. In the end, it was decided to submit the show for the Best New Play category, which technically, of course, it was; its natural category, Best Entertainment, was, everyone said, out of the question because of course Elaine Stritch would win it. But, I argued, we know we're not going to win anything; a nomination—especially in the face of that competition—would be a great honour. I was overruled. There were excited rumours of friends of friends of the members of the Tony committee who had *loved* the show—we were in with a very good chance—it was almost certain. And so on. In the end we didn't, of course, get nominated, and we immediately announced that we were closing, the first post-Tony show to do so. Others followed soon after. It was hard not to feel disgraced in some way, though the last week of performances took on a festive character; some members of the audience were back for their second or third visit. The whole *Private Lives* company, their collective heads covered in Tony glory, came on the final Wednesday matinee, which was curiously moving. On the last performance, a Sunday afternoon, the crew gathered in my dressing room and we drank from a magnum of champagne that some extravagant well-wisher had sent for the first night, so very very recently, and yet so very very long ago, back in the time of hopes and dreams.

I flew back to London early the next week. A few days later, I received a Best Newcomers Award (New Faces of 2002, my agent joked) at another award ceremony, which Adam Godley, who also received one for his radical and brilliant performance as Victor Prynne in *Private Lives*, picked up for me. It will be the comfort of my old age.

The show goes on. We have since taken it to Melbourne and Sydney, to particular acclaim. Of course, I shall act with other people again one day. Micheál MacLiammóir was often asked whether he preferred doing *The Importance of Being Oscar* to acting. The answer is that *The Importance of Being Oscar*—and *The Mystery of Charles Dickens*—is acting and then some. I am asked whether I don't feel lonely. What, with thirty-seven characters and Charles Dickens in all his multifariousness to keep me company? To say nothing of the stage manager (the incomparable Matthew Darby, except when he was barred from coming to Broadway), the company manager, the crew, and Patrick Garland, the director, who is a most regular visitor. Above all, it is the audience with whom I spend the evening, and who banish any thought of loneliness. 'This is a pretty old arrangement!' Charles Laughton used to say when doing his solo programme, 'an actor and an audience.'

★

I realised only recently that the ritual I have evolved while playing the show—which is not unlike the ritual I perform for every show—is strangely reminiscent of something else: getting ready for a date. I am preparing myself for my encounter with a new audience. The preparations are rather elaborate. I arrive at the theatre about an hour early and eat a snack of pure protein, a few slices of ham or chicken or turkey, enough to line the stomach, giving sufficient fuel for the performance, but none to spare; nothing fatty because of the dreaded mucous. I then go out for a brisk walk to digest what I've eaten and get a double decaffeinated coffee and an evening paper. I come back just as the half-hour call is being made. Then I have a shower, mostly to get the steam into my nostrils and onto my vocal cords, but also symbolically to wash the day out of my hair, to be born again as this actor in this play; a little baptism. I sing loud hymns to existence, mostly in falsetto, again to open up the resonators; only when I have an easy and free upper register will I have my whole voice at my disposal. Back in the dressing room, I play loud, energetic music, preferably highly rhythmic. I roar and moan along with it. Then I play something different, subtle and complex, and imagine myself playing it, partly to bring my emotional and physical temperature to the boil, but also to start thinking musically. All acting, as Oscar Wilde so nearly said, aspires to the condition of music. I am a musician, at a deep level, but one who finds it impossible to submit to an external pitch, an outside rhythm. I have to create my own internal rhythms, my own pitches. Hubermann playing Beethoven, Beecham conducting Chabrier, Jeff Buckley singing Leonard Cohen, anyone who's shaping, phrasing, inhabiting the breathing life of the work, inspires me. Sometimes, absurdly, I dance around the dressing room. Is this not exactly what one does when getting ready for a date? I read the paper in snatches. I never, not once, sit down. I speak a line or two out loud, acting it out, just as one finds oneself before the hot date, saying to oneself 'You look lovely' or 'Where have you been all my life?' I look at myself in the mirror as each stage of dressing changes my appearance; I fix myself a drink (tea). A couple of sucks of the Nelson's inhaler to make sure the nasal passages are perfectly open. Then a spray or two of perfume. A clean handkerchief for the trouser pocket, a starched one for the jacket pocket.

All this can just be achieved—just—before the beginner's call. And then one is ready; ready for a hot date with the audience, in a state of quasisexual excitement. Not arousal; readiness. Ready for the chemical reaction which is the *sine qua non* of the whole event. The word that Radu Penciulescu introduced me to right at the beginning of this strange, eventful journey is the appropriate one: *disponibilité*—openness, availability to impulse. By the time one hits the stage, one must be alive in every fibre, alive as one rarely is in daily life; the brightness of eye, the glowing skin, the physical well-being that you see as a hot couple face each other over the dinner table—that is the state in which one should approach the encounter with the audience. It is not, as you stand in the wings, a question of being in character—and, in the case of *The Mystery of Charles Dickens* with its thirty-seven characters, to attempt to do so would be to invite a nervous breakdown—but being ready for the character to take over. Character is an assumption, not an imposition; it must be doffed as easily as a hat. One's impulse must hit the sensation of the character as unerringly as the violinist hits his note. In the wings, a state of heightened neutrality, like a car ticking over, is the order. Conversation in the wings, scatty, probing, passionate, is not merely acceptable, it is very useful, but the division of the brain vital to a successful performance has already taken place. One half of the brain is chatting, joking; the other half is bubbling with another energy. Any attempt to go through lines is disastrous, robbing them of their freshness, dulling the brain. A state of complicity with one's fellow actors is crucial, the contained excitement of a night on the town. This is as true for *Titus Andronicus* as it is for

Hay Fever. And, of course, one mustn't blow it all at once. The secret of a successful evening—whether opposite someone at a dining table or on stage—is to hold something back, to play a game, to play out the line bit by bit. And then the consummation can be deeply, deeply satisfying.

The other day I was asked, as one is always asked, what are the conditions for good acting, and on this occasion I answered—it will be different next time—but on this occasion I said: first, you must need to act. Wanting to act is not enough. There must be something deep within one which will never be satisfied by anything other than acting. Second, you must have talent. This seems obvious to the point of banality, but it is the vital question every actor must face, and the answer may not be immediately evident. Does one have the capacity for expression on the stage? Is one's work interesting, striking, compelling? Third, I said, on this occasion (and for some reason the answer always seems to come in a list of three), third, and most important, you must have a good character. Now the reputation of actors is not for good character, and needless to say I am not speaking of sexual morals, much less fiscal probity (else who should scape whipping?). What I mean is that, in order to be an actor, you have to show up at the theatre on time, you have to know your lines, you have to know your cues, you have to keep fit, you have to keep your brain alive, you have to be aware of your colleagues' needs, you have to fight against the inherent difficulties of saying the same lines over and over again, you have to want to give the audience something for their money, you have to understand that they have come to the theatre looking for something that they believe no other medium can give them, and you have to care when they are disappointed. You have, moreover, to learn how to keep your difficulties, personal, professional, physical, away from the audience. It's none of their business, they don't want to know. You may hate your fellow actor, but you must act as if he were the person with whom you are happiest to be. You may have stubbed your toe, but must stroll along as if you were walking on air. You may have a throat filled with phlegm, and you must learn the complicated cordal calisthenics necessary to flip the stuff around so that you are never heard to clear your throat. You must give the same commitment to your performance if there's a dying mother at home, or a monstrous tax demand. You must know that while others are scoffing three-course meals or playing cricket in the sun, you will be in the darkened and often dank purlieus of some ancient, disease-ridden building.

And on the whole, you know, actors do have good characters in all, or almost all, of these ways. My frustration with many aspects of the theatre is all too evident in the preceding pages, but for actors— especially, perhaps, actors in the theatre—I have nothing but love and admiration. The theatre remains one of the few areas in which people acknowledge that something more important is at stake than their own personal gratification or reward. We could all, all of us actors, be better, and there are many practical changes which could effect that improvement, but it is still an infinitely touching experience to talk to a group of drama students, their idealism bursting out of every pore, or to sit round with a group of old stagers and talk about the great ones of the past, or to find oneself at a table where all the weariness and cynicism of professional experience is dropped as eyes burn brighter and emotion begins to rise at the thought of what the experience of going to the theatre might be. Scarcely anyone I know became an actor to make money, or to become famous, or to get a damehood. They all started with a realisation that something can happen in a theatre which is ancient and new at the same time, which is potentially life-changing but which also reminds us of who and what we are, which binds a group of human beings together for the duration of the evening or afternoon to remind them of the sense of community otherwise dead or forgotten, which massages the tired imagination back to life and celebrates human possibilities in the living shapes of the actors themselves. It doesn't take very much to remind an actor that that is why he is one. The struggle to prevent the disappearance of audiences who, for many many different reasons, have ceased to believe that all of that—which they deeply want—is in fact still on offer, is a struggle against immense forces commercial, bureaucratic, cultural. But I have no doubt that at the forefront of the struggle will be actors. It's a pretty old arrangement, an actor and an audience, and we're not going to let it die.

Index